TRAFFICKING HARMS

TRAFFICKING HARMS

CRITICAL POLITICS | PERSPECTIVES | EXPERIENCES

Katrin Roots, Ann De Shalit,
and Emily van der Meulen

Fernwood Publishing
Halifax & Winnipeg

Copyright © 2024 Katrin Roots, Ann De Shalit, and Emily van der Meulen

All rights reserved. No part of this book may be reproduced or transmitted in any form by any means without permission in writing from the publisher, except by a reviewer, who may quote brief passages in a review.

Copyediting: Erin Seatter
Cover design: Jess Koroscil
Text design: Brenda Conroy
Printed and bound in the UK

Published by Fernwood Publishing
2970 Oxford Street, Halifax, Nova Scotia, B3L 2W4
Halifax and Winnipeg
www.fernwoodpublishing.ca

This book has been published with the help of a grant from the Federation for the Humanities and Social Sciences, through the Awards to Scholarly Publications Program, using funds provided by the Social Sciences and Humanities Research Council of Canada.

Fernwood Publishing Company Limited gratefully acknowledges the financial support of the Government of Canada through the Canada Book Fund and the Canada Council for the Arts. We acknowledge the Province of Manitoba for support through the Manitoba Publishers Marketing Assistance Program and the Book Publishing Tax Credit. We acknowledge the Nova Scotia Department of Communities, Culture and Heritage for support through the Publishers Assistance Fund.

Library and Archives Canada Cataloguing in Publication
Title: Trafficking harms : critical politics, perspectives and experiences / edited by Katrin Roots, Ann De Shalit and Emily van der Meulen.
Names: Roots, Katrin, editor. | De Shalit, Ann, editor. | Van der Meulen, Emily, 1977- editor.
Description: Includes bibliographical references and index.
Identifiers: Canadiana (print) 20240288173 | Canadiana (ebook) 20240288203 | ISBN 9781773636689
   (softcover) | ISBN 9781773636863 (EPUB) | ISBN 9781773636870 (PDF)
Subjects: LCSH: Human trafficking—Canada. | LCSH: Human trafficking—Political aspects—Canada. |
   LCSH: Human trafficking—Law and legislation—Canada. | LCSH: Human trafficking—Canada—Prevention.
   | LCSH: Migrant labor—Canada.
Classification: LCC HQ281 .T725 2024 | DDC 364.15/510971—dc23

Contents

Acknowledgments ix
Contributors x

1 Understanding Human Trafficking: An Examination of Discourses, Laws, Policing, and Migrant Labour
  Katrin Roots, Ann De Shalit, and Emily van der Meulen 1
  Trafficking Discourses and Representations 4
  Trafficking Laws and Prosecutions 9
  Trafficking Policing and Surveillance 15
  Trafficking and Migrant Labour Exploitation 19
  Conclusion 24
  References 24

Section One
Trafficking Discourses and Representations / 33

2 Beyond Carceral Humanitarianism: Antiblackness as the Structure of Anti-Trafficking Discourse
  Lyndsey P. Beutin 34
  The Many Abolitions: Antiprison, Anti-Trafficking, and Their Feminisms ... 36
  Carceral Humanitarianism 40
  Anti-Trafficking and Solidarity with Black Lives Matter: Three Approaches ... 42
  The Limits of the Critique of Carceral Humanitarianism 45
  Conclusion: How Antiblackness Structures Anti-Trafficking Discourse ... 47
  Note 50
  References 50

3 Emergence and Convergence of the Pimp and Trafficker in Media Discourse: Creating a New Super Folk Devil
  Stacey Hannem and Chris Bruckert 54
  Methodology 55
  The Pimp Discourse 56
  The Trafficking (and Trafficker) Discourse 59
  The Emergence of the Pimp/Trafficker 63
  Conclusion: The New Super Folk Devil 68
  Notes 70
  References 70

4 A Narrative on Anti-Trafficking Discourse and Advocacy
   in Newfoundland
   Laura Winters 74
   Conflating Sex Work and Trafficking... 75
   Anti-Trafficking Funding 76
   Relationships with Police.. 78
   Police Anti-Trafficking Efforts 79
   Conclusion.. 80

Section Two
Trafficking Laws and Prosecutions / 81

5 Prosecuting Trafficking in Persons Offences: Problems
   and Pitfalls in the Post-PCEPA Era
   Tamara O'Doherty and Hayli Millar 82
   Our Study.. 83
   Prosecution Patterns Pre- and Post-PCEPA 84
   Pitfalls in Prosecutions.. 87
   Problematic Dismissal of Fundamental Justice 92
   Conclusion.. 96
   Notes.. 96
   References... 97

6 Human Trafficking Law and Policy: Exacerbating Racial
   and Gendered Violence in Ontario
   Sandra Ka Hon Chu and Robyn Maynard 103
   Ontario's Sociolegal Anti-Trafficking Context..104
   Imprecise Understandings of Trafficking and the Impacts
   of Current Approaches..106
   Conclusion..112
   Notes..114
   References...114

7 Targeting Asian Massage Parlours in the Name of
   Anti-Trafficking: Experiences of Asian Women in Toronto
   Elene Lam...119
   Background 121
   Method of Inquiry 123
   Working in Massage Parlours 124
   Navigating the Licensing Bylaw...125
   Impacts of Law Enforcement 129
   Conclusion..135
   Notes..136
   References...136

8 A Narrative on Defending People Charged with Human Trafficking
   Mash Frouhar 139
   Experience with Human Trafficking Cases 139
   The Case of the Wrongfully Accused 142
   The Case of the Chanel Purses 144
   Specialized Crowns, Victim Services, and Police 145
   Concerns about Anti-Trafficking Efforts 146
   Notes 147

9 A Narrative on Being Charged with Human Trafficking
   Anonymous 148
   Getting Arrested 149
   Being Questioned at the Police Station 150
   Pleading Guilty and Being Sentenced 151
   Being in the Media 152
   Receiving Support from Family and Friends 152

Section Three
Trafficking Policing and Surveillance / 153

10 Anti-Trafficking and Data-Driven Policing:
   A Whole-of-Society Strategy
   Robert Heynen 154
   Intelligence-Led Policing, Surveillance, and the Work of Anti-Trafficking 158
   Data Gathering, Technology, and Intelligence-Led Anti-Trafficking 163
   Trafficking Indicators and the Work of Data-Based Profiling 166
   Conclusion 171
   References 173

11 Anti-Trafficking Policing in Vancouver: The Denial of Crimes
   against Asian Sex Workers
   Alison Clancey and Julie Ham 177
   Hoping for Change 178
   Hoping for Help 180
   Criminalizing Assistance 185
   Conclusion 188
   Notes 189
   References 189

12 Challenging Notions of Benevolence and Protection:
   Settler-Colonial Anti-Trafficking Policing in Manitoba
   Julie Kaye and Cerah Dubé 192
   Canadian Anti-Trafficking and the Reproduction of Conditions of Violence 193
   Settler Colonialism and Indigenous Feminist Decolonial Thought 197

Anti-Trafficking in the Settler-Colonial Prairies:
Unfolding Approaches in Manitoba... 200
The Hospitality Sector Customer Registry Act:
A "Benevolent" Policing Intervention... 205
Conclusion.. 209
Note 210
References.. 210

13 A Narrative on Being an Indigenous and Trans Sex Worker
    in Winnipeg
    Victoria Erin Flett 214
    Clients 214
    Experiences with Police 215
    Community Support and Social Services... 216

Section Four
Trafficking and Migrant Labour Exploitation / 219

14 Discretionary Decisions in Immigration: Accessing a
    Temporary Resident Permit as a Victim of Trafficking
    Jessica Templeman..220
    Temporary Resident Permits for Victims of Trafficking in Persons 222
    Notions of Fraud and Illegality 224
    Notions of Foreignness and Temporariness... 231
    Conclusion... 235
    Notes.. 236
    References.. 237

15 Redefining "Exploitation": Reconciling Human Trafficking
    Provisions with Canada's Migrant Farm Work Program
    Shane Martínez..239
    Defining and Redefining "Exploitation"... 241
    Insulation through Redefinition 244
    Conclusion... 247
    Notes.. 248
    References.. 249

16 A Narrative on Organizing for Migrant Farm Worker Justice
    Chris Ramsaroop...252
    Defining and Mobilizing "Human Trafficking" 253
    The Anti-Trafficking Capitalist Response.. 255
    Beyond the Trafficking Framework.. 258
    References.. 260

Index 261

Acknowledgments

We dedicate this book to the community organizers, legal advocates, and critical scholars who have challenged the normative anti-trafficking framework, and to those who have experienced its harms firsthand. This includes each of the authors of the chapters that follow. We are indebted to them for their willingness to share their thoughts, experiences, and expertise, as they advance much-needed counternarratives.

Thank you also to Fiona Jeffries, Anumeha Gokhale, and Lauren Jeanneau at Fernwood for the endless support and encouragement. They seamlessly and expertly guided us through the publishing process, making all aspects of the experience enjoyable. We also greatly appreciate Erin Seatter and Brenda Conroy for the meticulous and proficient copyedits.

To the two anonymous reviewers, we extend our gratitude for taking time from your schedules to thoroughly engage with the book and its arguments. Your thoughtful and valuable feedback has undoubtedly made it a stronger collection.

And finally, we are grateful to Wilfrid Laurier University, the Office of the Dean of Arts at Toronto Metropolitan University, and the Awards to Scholarly Publications Program for their generous financial support.

Contributors

Lyndsey P. Beutin is an assistant professor of communication studies and media arts at McMaster University and a Visiting Research Scholar in African American Studies at Princeton University. Her book *Trafficking in Antiblackness: Modern-Day Slavery, White Indemnity, and Racial Justice* (2023) explores how campaigns against human trafficking use the memory of transatlantic slavery in ways that reproduce antiblackness. She earned her PhD in Communication from the Annenberg School at the University of Pennsylvania and was a predoctoral fellow at the Carter G. Woodson Institute for African-American and African Studies at the University of Virginia.

Chris Bruckert is a professor of criminology at the University of Ottawa. Over the past twenty-five years, she has devoted much of her energy to examining diverse sectors of the sex industry. To that end, she has undertaken qualitative research into street-based sex work, erotic dance, in-call and out-call sex work, clients, male sex workers, and management in the sex industry. She is the coeditor of *Red Light Labour: Sex Work Regulation, Agency, and Resistance* (2018), *Getting Past 'the Pimp': Management in the Sex Industry* (2018), and *Sex Work: Rethinking the Job, Respecting the Workers* (2013).

Sandra Ka Hon Chu is a lawyer and co–executive director of the HIV Legal Network, where she works with community to uphold the human rights of people living with HIV or AIDS and other populations disproportionately affected by HIV, punitive laws and policies, and criminalization in Canada and internationally. Sandra has worked alongside sex worker rights organizations for more than a decade as a member of the Canadian Alliance for Sex Work Law Reform and supported the HIV Legal Network's interventions in key court challenges to Canada's sex work offences.

CONTRIBUTORS XI

Alison Clancey is the former executive director of SWAN Vancouver Society, an organization that supports im/migrant sex workers in Greater Vancouver. Her public education, advocacy, and policy efforts focus on raising critical awareness of the harms of mainstream anti-trafficking initiatives, policy, and enforcement. With over a decade of working with police on sex work and trafficking-related policy, practice, and investigations, she has developed a deep understanding of the risks and limitations of doing so.

Ann De Shalit is an assistant professor of gender and social justice at Trent University. Her primary research uses labour and migrant justice approaches to expose the broadly defined impacts of anti-trafficking discourse and practice, and to assess harm, vulnerability, and intervention. She has also been involved in community-based research and campaigns advocating for access to services for marginalized communities, improved conditions for precarious workers, and prison health.

Cerah Dubé is a white settler who was born and raised in Win-nipi (Winnipeg) and currently lives and works in Brandon, Manitoba, in Treaty 2 territory and Métis homelands. She is completing a Master of Arts in Sociology at the University of Saskatchewan and is also a community organizer in Manitoba. Drawing on anticolonial and feminist thought, her scholarly and community work interrogate colonial and racialized projects of policing, criminalization, and incarceration.

Victoria Erin Flett is a Sixties Scoop survivor with over twenty-three years of lived experience of homelessness, addictions, and indoor and outdoor sex work. She has overcome all of these barriers and has been sober, for the first in her life, since May 18, 2021. She works in community development for a nonprofit organization running a drop-in safe space for current and former sex workers. She hopes to inspire change through her journey and her life experiences and bring comfort to the people that she passionately serves on a daily basis. She spreads the love.

Mash Frouhar is the founder of Frouhar Law. She was called to the Ontario Bar in 2009 and joined a prominent criminal defence firm in Ottawa in 2010. Before joining the firm, Mash worked as an assistant Crown attorney as well as a defence lawyer with Legal Aid Ontario.

During her many years of practice, she has conducted numerous trials related to human trafficking, murder, attempted murder, driving offences, drugs, sexual assault, and domestic-related offences. She has also taught criminal law at a local community college for numerous years.

Julie Ham is an assistant professor of sociology at Brock University. Her research centres knowledge production with migrant and minority communities and the criminology of mobility (www.mmmk.ca). Her work on the criminology of mobility, gender, and migration has been published in *Anti-Trafficking Review*; *The British Journal of Criminology*; *Criminology and Criminal Justice*; *Critical Social Policy*; *Culture, Health and Sexuality*; *Emotion, Space and Society*; *Gender, Work and Organization*; *International Journal of Qualitative Methods*; *Sexualities*; *Sociology*; *Theoretical Criminology*; and *Work, Employment and Society*.

Stacey Hannem is a professor of criminology at Wilfrid Laurier University. Her research and publications examine how structural and institutional forces, including law and criminal-processing institutions, are implicated in shaping and reinforcing the stigmatization and marginalization of targeted groups. Stacey is a coeditor of *Stigma Revisited: Implications of the Mark* (2012). Her research has appeared in the journals *Deviant Behavior*, *Symbolic Interaction*, *Feminist Criminology*, *Criminologie*, the *International Journal of Offender Therapy and Comparative Criminology*, and *Sexuality and Culture*, among others. Her newest coauthored book, *Defining Sexual Misconduct: Power, Media and #MeToo*, was published in May 2022.

Robert Heynen is an associate professor of communication and media studies at York University. His research interests include historical and contemporary forms of surveillance, especially in relation to biometrics, eugenics, and anti-trafficking. He is the author of *Degeneration and Revolution: Radical Cultural Politics and the Body in Weimar Germany* (2015) and coeditor of *Expanding the Gaze: Gender and the Politics of Surveillance* (2016) and *Making Surveillance States: Transnational Histories* (2019). Relevant journal articles include studies of trafficking, celebrity, and white saviourhood; sex work and surveillance; and trafficking discourses in Canadian news reporting.

CONTRIBUTORS XIII

Julie Kaye is an associate professor of sociology and the academic co-ordinator of the Certificate in Criminology and Addictions Program at the University of Saskatchewan. As an anticolonial scholar, she specializes in the areas of colonial gendered violence, community-engaged and Indigenous-led research, racialized (in)justice, racialized policing, and decolonial community organizing. Her book *Responding to Human Trafficking: Dispossession, Colonial Violence, and Resistance Among Indigenous and Racialized Women* (2017) provides an important intervention through critical anti-trafficking scholarship.

Elene Lam is an activist, community artist, community organizer, educator, and human rights defender. She has advocated for sex worker, migrant, labour, and gender justice for more than twenty years. She is the founder of Butterfly (Asian and Migrant Sex Workers Support Network). She holds a Master of Laws and Master of Social Work. Elene is a PhD candidate in the School of Social Work at McMaster University, where she is studying the harms of the anti-trafficking movement. In 2019, the City of Toronto awarded Elene the Constance E. Hamilton Award for Women's Equality for her work with Butterfly.

Shane Martínez is a Toronto-based lawyer with a practice focused primarily on criminal defence and human rights. He litigated the first successful human rights case of a migrant farm worker in Ontario, as well as a landmark case that found the Ontario Provincial Police had racially discriminated against dozens of migrant farm workers during a DNA sweep. Shane also serves as the legal director at LIUNA Local 3000 and is an adjunct professor at York University's Osgoode Hall Law School.

Robyn Maynard is an author and scholar based in Toronto, where she holds the position of associate professor of Black feminisms in Canada at the University of Toronto-Scarborough in the Department of Historical and Cultural Studies. She is the author of *Policing Black Lives: State Violence in Canada from Slavery to the Present* (2017) and the coauthor of *Rehearsals for Living* (2022). Robyn has also published work in an assortment of peer-reviewed and trade publications on the topics of policing, abolition, sex work criminalization, and Black freedom struggles.

Hayli Millar is an associate professor of criminology and criminal justice at the University of the Fraser Valley who specializes in critical and comparative sociolegal research, as well as human rights–based and evidence-informed criminal justice policy reform. She has worked on domestic and international research projects concerning gender, migration, and human trafficking and published technical reports and peer-reviewed publications on the intersections of human rights with the enforcement of human trafficking laws.

Tamara O'Doherty is a senior lecturer in criminology at Simon Fraser University. Her research expertise includes critical criminology, human rights law, participant-driven action research, and legal research methods. In addition to postsecondary teaching and decolonizing legal pedagogy contributions, and two decades of community-based collaborative knowledge production activities with sex workers and other marginalized groups, Tamara's research and publications have focused on the effects of criminalization, victimization (including state crime), and human trafficking law.

Chris Ramsaroop is an organizer with Justicia for Migrant Workers (J4MW), a grassroots activist collective that has been organizing with migrant workers for nearly twenty years. J4MW's work is based on building long-term trust and relationships with migrant workers. Chris is an assistant professor at New College, University of Toronto, where he is also the coordinator of the Community Engaged Learning program as well as an instructor at the Centre for Caribbean Studies. He is the co-director of the Migrant Worker Clinic at the Faculty of Law, University of Windsor, and is working to complete his PhD at the University of Toronto's Ontario Institute for Studies in Education. His doctoral dissertation examines resistance by migrant farm workers in Canada.

Katrin Roots is an assistant professor in criminology at Wilfrid Laurier University. She has researched Canada's anti-trafficking efforts for over a decade and is the author of *The Domestication of Human Trafficking: Law, Policing, and Prosecution in Canada* (2022). She is also the coauthor of numerous peer-reviewed articles and book chapters on trafficking law, enforcement, and policing technologies and the coeditor of *Violence, Imagination, and Resistance: Socio-legal Interrogations of Power* (2023).

Jessica Templeman is a SSHRC Postdoctoral Fellow at the Peter A. Allard School of Law, University of British Columbia. Her work traces the operations and effects of processes interwoven between the immigration and criminal punishment systems in Canada. Her doctoral research examined how collateral immigration consequences inform decision-making on sentencing in Ontario-based courts. Jessica's postdoctoral work builds from this project, examining criminal materials to consider how removal decisions are made in practice by actors in the immigration system.

Emily van der Meulen is a professor in criminology at Toronto Metropolitan University. She conducts participatory research in the areas of critical and feminist criminology, sex work and human trafficking, prison and community-based harm reduction, and surveillance studies. She has coedited numerous books, the most recent of which are *Disability Injustice: Confronting Criminalization in Canada* (2022), *Making Surveillance States: Transnational Histories* (2019), and *Red Light Labour: Sex Work Regulation, Agency, and Resistance* (2018).

Laura Winters is a sociologist, adjunct professor, research fellow, and community worker. In her academic life, Laura researches stigma resistance, especially in the everyday "talk back" of people who do sex work. She has been working with community organizations in her home city of St. John's for over a decade, currently as CEO of Stella's Circle and most recently before that as the executive director of the St. John's Status of Women Council and Women's Centre. Laura believes in social justice, the power of harm reduction, and the collective responsibility of systems to respond to the needs of those most underserved.

1

Understanding Human Trafficking

An Examination of Discourses, Laws, Policing, and Migrant Labour

*Katrin Roots, Ann De Shalit,
and Emily van der Meulen*

Much has been said and written on the topic of human trafficking, especially regarding its prevalence, the dangerousness of perpetrators, the helplessness and "risky" behaviour of victims, and the urgent need for governments, law enforcement agencies, nongovernmental organizations (NGOs), religious groups, and members of the public to unite in rescue. Though the intention is to end exploitation and violence, anti-trafficking responses in practice have largely extracted a diverse range of experiences and conditions from their complexities and consolidated them as a problem of sex work, irregular migration and border insecurity, inadequate legislation, policing and surveillance, and personal shortcomings. They have fallen short of meaningfully and substantially mitigating the issues they are alleged to address, or, worse, they have intensified them and other harms. Given the valid concerns of sex workers, migrant labourers, and other marginalized peoples, providing clarity on the consequences of anti-trafficking efforts is important. With chapters by scholars, activists, lawyers, and people who are most directly impacted by anti-trafficking activities, this book aims to do just that.

While the book is primarily focused on anti-trafficking in Canada, the same concerns have clear relevance to broader international contexts. Indeed, a number of critical Canadian scholars and organizations have paved the way for global discussions on the anti-trafficking framework and its embeddedness with anti–sex work and anti-migrant sentiments, neoliberal individualization of social issues, and colonial, white supremacist, and carceral rationalities (for a short list, see Beutin, 2023; Durisin, 2023; Hunt, 2013, 2015; Kaye, 2017; Kempadoo & Doezema, 1998, 2015;

Maynard, 2018; Roots, 2022). They have also traced important and harmful impacts of anti-trafficking policy on international, national, provincial, and municipal levels (e.g., see Chu et al., 2019; Fudge et al., 2021; Global Alliance Against Traffic in Women, 2007; Lam, 2018a). Many of the issues at the centre of this book are similarly grounded in the local but point to global patterns and contribute to transnational debates.

Human trafficking is complex and contentious, in part because it is an umbrella term used to capture an array of social conditions and activities while excluding a variety of others. The term embodies gendered, racialized, sexualized, and classed dimensions, and intersects with workers' rights, migration, border control, and much more. It is also applied to circumstances involving child abuse, intimate partner violence, sexual assault, missing and murdered Indigenous women and girls, sex work, and notions of modern-day slavery. Thus, definitions of trafficking tend to vary widely, as seen in government laws and policies, reports from civil society groups, and media coverage, resulting in a lack of a clear consensus on exactly what kinds of activities and experiences constitute human trafficking. Even different levels of courts in Canada have varied in their descriptions and definitions (Sibley & van der Meulen, 2023).

Until relatively recently, human trafficking was understood as a transnational phenomenon whereby organized crime groups forcibly transported women across national and sometimes regional borders, usually to engage in sex work. To a significantly lesser degree, men could also be trafficked, though into other labour sectors. This understanding emphasized the need for a global, collaborative, and criminalizing-securitizing approach and was fuelled by the passage of the United Nations *Protocol to Prevent, Suppress and Punish Trafficking in Persons, Especially Women and Children* (commonly referred to as the *Trafficking Protocol*), which Canada ratified in 2002. Following this, and coinciding with a rise in transnational migration that many nation-states saw as a potential threat to their border security, anti-trafficking measures emerged in the early 2000s as a top priority globally.

The perceived need to manage and control migration and borders has since been used to justify the introduction of new surveillance and biometrics technologies, increased policing, stricter immigration policies, and the movement of borders offshore to prevent the entry of "risky" populations (Miller & Baumeister, 2013; Mountz, 2010; Pratt, 2005). The framing of border control in terms of the need to protect women from human traffickers has enabled Canada and other Western countries to condone these measures while identifying as a rescuer of the "Other" — a white knight of sorts (Jeffrey, 2005; Musto, 2016; Pickering & Ham, 2014). Critical trafficking and migration scholars have condemned such policing and border control practices, arguing that they undermine the human rights of migrants and lead migrants to take greater risks with their health, safety, and lives in order to migrate (Jeffrey, 2005; Kapur, 2005; Kempadoo, 2005; Pickering & Ham, 2014).

While the conceptualization of trafficking as a border security issue continues to inform policy decisions in highly restrictive and criminalizing ways, anti-trafficking efforts in Canada over the past decade have become increasingly concerned with "domestic sex trafficking," which does not require the involvement of deceptive or coercive movement across borders. This approach is not exclusive to Canada and has been documented in other countries, perhaps most notably in the United States (Bernstein, 2010, 2012; Musto, 2016; Weitzer, 2007, 2011). Informing and fuelling the focus on "domestic sex trafficking" are prohibitionist and anti-prostitution assumptions that sex work cannot entail consent and is inherently exploitative and violent due to the lack of real alternatives; thus, anyone providing sexual services may be deemed a victim, while those purchasing or managing such services are deemed criminals. This reductive approach ignores the constraints placed on the decisions of all workers in capitalist societies and, at the same time, denies the agency and right to self-determination of people who sell or trade sex (Durisin et al., 2018; Kempadoo, 2005). Indeed, advocates for sex worker rights soundly "reject the idea that all prostitution is forced and intrinsically degrading" (Anderson & Andrijasevic, 2008, p. 139). They view the state itself, in particular the long arm of the law, as responsible for creating the conditions in which violence, abuse, stigma, and discrimination thrive. Sex workers have found the anti-trafficking framework to be especially incapable of addressing their legitimate concerns; instead, it often (re)produces them. Rather than further criminalization, they emphasize the need for workplace protections and employment standards for people engaged in sexual labour, and appropriate safety measures and supports for all people who sell or exchange sex (Abel et al., 2010; Anderson & Andrijasevic, 2008; Chapkis, 1997; Durisin et al., 2018).

It is precisely these kinds of debates and critical appraisals that the following pages of this introduction and the book as a whole analyze in-depth. With methods and approaches ranging from ethnographic and media analyses to interview-based data collection, personal reflections based on lived experience, and the examination of court cases, parliamentary debates, and government policies, chapter authors provide the book with analytic rigour and a kaleidoscopic view of the issue. Across four thematic sections — trafficking discourses and representations, laws and prosecutions, policing and surveillance, and migrant labour exploitation — the book draws intersectional attention to the impacts on sex workers; migrant workers; Black, Indigenous, and racialized communities; and other marginalized populations. Written from the vantage points of their respective authors, some chapters are scholarly engagements, some are based on empirical research, and some are short personal narratives told from a first-person perspective. These latter chapters are labelled as such and included at the end of each section. The dynamic authors and their areas of expertise — whether academic, activist, legal, experiential, or a combination of these — highlight the harms produced by anti-trafficking measures and the need for critical perspectives to prevail.

Trafficking Discourses and Representations

Concerns over trafficking can be traced at least as far back as the "white slavery panic," which emerged in the United Kingdom in the nineteenth century and focused on the purported kidnapping, luring, and sexual exploitation of white British women and youth across Europe, primarily by racialized men (Doezema, 2010). The importance of their protection stemmed from white women's role in reproducing white British society (Durisin, 2023). Efforts against white slavery targeted the sex trade, driven by what Jo Doezema (2010) describes as powerful and inherently racist discourses that borrowed "the language and the sense of moral outrage generated by anti-slavery activism" (p. 82) and worked to erase the distinction between consensual sex work and so-called sexual slavery (see also Bunting & Quirk, 2017; Kempadoo, 2005).

These discourses have continued to the present, anchored in the United Nations *Trafficking Protocol* (2000), and convey that human trafficking, especially of women and girls for sexual services, urgently requires government intervention, international collaboration, and tough-on-crime mandates (Bales, 2005; Kara, 2009; Perrin, 2010; Shelley, 2010). This new abolitionism, as Julia O'Connell Davidson (2015) calls it, is criticized for its lack of definitional precision and continuous expansion in contemporary notions of modern-day slavery as they relate to sexuality and sexual labour, all in the name of protecting victims of trafficking. Annie Bunting and Joel Quirk (2017) note the diverse and sometimes competing agendas of an array of practices and problems that have been loosely knit together under larger global causes variously termed modern-day slavery, contemporary forms of slavery, and human trafficking. In recent years this equation of modern-day slavery with trafficking has increased, as seen in the shift from "invoking slavery imagery for rhetorical flair to explicitly suggesting that *slavery* should replace *trafficking* because the latter term is a passé, if not inaccurate, descriptor" (Chuang, 2014, p. 624; emphasis in original). This reconceptualization and representation of trafficking as slavery has become a powerful tool for reframing a broad range of practices, particularly in the sex trade but also within intimate relationships (Chuang, 2014). At the same time, the framework has ignored the conditions that manufacture unfree labour in a vast array of workplaces and service sectors (Choudry & Smith, 2016; LeBaron & Phillips, 2019). As Robyn Maynard (2018) and Lyndsey P. Beutin (2023) further demonstrate, the use of the label "modern-day slavery" by the anti-trafficking apparatus has allowed the cause to attach itself to anti-racism movements despite being structured by antiblackness and contributing to and endorsing the carcerality of Black people.

Since the initial concern over the now widely debunked nineteenth-century "white slave trade," there have been numerous waves of panic over sex trafficking. These waves are cyclical and have typically emerged in times of increased migration. The most recent concerns arose in the 1990s following the breakdown of the Soviet Union and the western migration flow from Central and Eastern Europe. Ideological constructs of the victim of sex trafficking were placed on Central and Eastern European women, who were perceived as always-already victims, regardless of how they identified themselves. Shortly after, women from Latin America and Asia were brought into the trafficking discourse as "backward victims" (Hua & Nigorizawa, 2010). While Eastern European women were perceived to hail from failed nation-states and associated with their countries' communist shortcomings (Durisin & Heynen, 2015), their whiteness ensured that they were recognized as only temporarily "backward" or "immoral" (Hua & Nigorizawa,

2010). Women migrating for sex work from Asia and Latin America, on the other hand, were tied to a presumed long-standing "immorality" and "backwardness" due to their cultures (Hua & Nigorizawa, 2010). Together, these discourses and rationalities were used to distance Canada from "Other" cultures and political circumstances with the help of stringent immigration policies, raid-and-rescue missions, and enhanced carceral measures. They also prepared Canada to adopt the *Trafficking Protocol*, which would officially establish it as an anti-trafficking state on a global scale.

Over the last two decades, as noted earlier, a discursive shift has been seen in the construction and representation of the victim of trafficking away from the so-called foreign to the domestic. This has aligned with a broader shift in the depiction of trafficking from a transnational offence to a domestic one, which, as Elya M. Durisin and Emily van der Meulen (2021) observe, brought with it a change in the perceived root causes of the problem. Whereas those initially concerned with transnational trafficking saw structural causes of poverty, lack of employment, significant social issues, and an overall collapsed global economy as push factors, domestic trafficking landed primarily on intimate relationships and was considered largely to be the product of low self-esteem and past personal traumas, with the locus of blame placed on individual women and girls or individual "bad" men. In this interpretation, trafficking is reduced to sexual exploitation; correspondingly, a whole host of activities and relationships in the sex trade, be they problematic or not, are deemed sexually exploitative.

Central to the discursive casting of victims of domestic trafficking is "the girl next door," seen as the innocent and naive young white daughter from a nuclear Canadian family who is vulnerable to being trafficked anywhere and at any time (De Shalit et al., 2023; Roots, 2022). This representation is frequently invoked by politicians, NGOs, religious groups, the media, and police, with her age (unsupported by scholarly evidence) routinely noted as thirteen. The emphasis on the age of trafficking victims is an effective method of garnering support for increased police resources, expanded laws, and harsher punishments, as the image of youth sexual exploitation easily shuts down any critical conversation (Durisin & van der Meulen, 2021).

The girl next door is contrasted with the young Indigenous woman, who is understood as being at an elevated risk for victimization by traffickers due to marginalizing factors resulting from colonization by the very same state that is now representing itself as her saviour. And while the state's attention to the crisis of missing and murdered Indigenous women and girls after years of advocacy by Indigenous groups is a positive step, some scholars argue that the relabelling of colonial injustices as trafficking not only redefines Indigenous experiences through the lens of white feminine subjectivity but also reinforces reliance on a violent colonial legal system and redirects attention from harmful state practices to individual "bad men" (Hunt, 2013, 2015; Kaye, 2017, 2023).

In line with the discursive changes about who constitutes, or who is most likely to be, a victim of trafficking, are parallel shifts in discourse regarding the trafficker. Along with the 1990s concerns over the trafficking of Eastern European, Asian, and Latin American women into Canada came a focus on Russian and Chinese men as transnational traffickers operating or working for international organized crime rings. The threat in that instance stemmed from outside of Canada's boundaries, necessitating stricter border control measures to protect the Canadian citizenry and allowing for the construction of Canada as a "civilized" nation in contrast to the "savagery" of the trafficker (Jeffrey, 2005). More recently, the domestic trafficker, whose victims may not even cross municipal or provincial borders, has taken on numerous discursive forms. He is increasingly conflated with the prototypical image of the sex trade "pimp" (Bruckert, 2018b; Mensah, 2018; Roots, 2022), a deeply racialized, classed, and gendered construct that reinforces stereotypes of Black men in connection with sexuality and crime (Hill-Collins, 2004; Horning & Marcus, 2017; Jeffrey & MacDonald, 2006; Kalunta-Crumpton, 1998; Mensah, 2018).

The image of the homegrown trafficker has been challenged by critical scholars (see Bruckert 2018b; Marcus et al., 2014; Mensah, 2018; Roots, 2022; Williamson & Marcus, 2017), with research finding that it is more accurate to think about the relationship between sex workers and third-party managers on a spectrum when it comes to supervision, facilitation, and control (Bruckert, 2018a). In the context of the United States, Anthony Marcus and colleagues (2014) likewise explain that the stereotypical "pimp" figure is far less common in reality than dominant narratives suggest, and their research highlights sex workers' expressions of agency and control over working conditions and relationships. Nevertheless, anti-trafficking efforts continue to paint sex workers as always-already — that is, before they can themselves speak to their conditions — controlled and exploited by ruthless (and often racialized) men.

The proposed responses to trafficking are inextricably linked to the criminal legal system and broader carceral measures. Elizabeth Bernstein (2010, 2012) calls this "carceral feminism," a term she coined to describe and critique the efforts of a subset of feminists to address human trafficking by turning to punishment-based solutions with heavy buy-in from police, prosecutors, and the prison system. Starting in the late 1990s, secular feminists in the United States collaborated with evangelical Christians and state agents to advocate for the passing of human trafficking laws that equate sex work with human trafficking. As Bernstein (2010, 2012) points out, these initiatives represented a commitment to carceral paradigms and support for law-and-order agendas with harsh punishments for traffickers and the purported rescue of victimized women.

Carceral feminists and certain antiviolence organizations around the world continue to have well documented partnerships with police, calling upon increased criminal legal interventions to reduce violence against women, where sex trafficking is said to be located (Bernstein, 2007, 2012; Bumiller, 2008; Suchland, 2015). Canadian-based research, too, reveals an uncomplicated and rather enthusiastic relationship between social service providers and law enforcement (De Shalit, 2021). Given the majority of anti-trafficking organizations work in the sector of violence against women, it means that a number of such agencies have resorted to individualized punitive measures, including rehabilitation and self-improvement, isolation, and surveillance, to intervene in socioeconomic conditions they are otherwise wholly underfunded and underresourced to address.

Building on and expanding the themes presented above, the first section of the book consists of three chapters that further examine trafficking discourses and representations. In Chapter 2, Lyndsey P. Beutin exposes the antiblackness that informs and is reinforced by anti-trafficking discourses and framework, and examines their role in co-opting and undermining the politics of anticarceral abolitionism. Chapter 3 by Stacey Hannem and Chris Bruckert traces a shift in the "pimp/trafficker" discourse from the 1980s into the mid-2000s, demonstrating the relatively recent emergence of a new super folk devil on whom a host of social ills can be downloaded. Chapter 4 reveals the effects of normative trafficking discourses on sex workers, including the negation of their rights and agency by NGOs, through the first-person narrative of Laura Winters, a sex worker rights advocate in Newfoundland. Together, these chapters illuminate the discursive underpinnings of anti-trafficking efforts, how trafficking comes *to be* through these mechanisms, and their impacts on the people who are harmed, targeted, and, equally, neglected by this framework.

Trafficking Laws and Prosecutions

The legal regulation of human trafficking in Canada began with the 2002 enactment of section 118 of the *Immigration and Refugee Protection Act* and the 2005 inclusion of sections 279.01 to 279.04 of the *Criminal Code*. Both sets of laws were developed in response to Canada's ratification of the United Nations *Trafficking Protocol*. The federal immigration provision governs the cross-border trafficking of migrants and has seen minimal use to date, with only a handful of cases prosecuted since its enactment and no convictions (Ferguson, 2012; Millar & O'Doherty, 2020a; Roots, 2022). The *Criminal Code* trafficking laws, on the other hand, govern both transnational and domestic trafficking and have seen much greater application, particularly since 2014. This timing corresponds with, and must be understood in the context of, changes to the federal anti–sex work laws, which legally and rhetorically aligned sex work with human trafficking and thus facilitated the application of human trafficking criminal charges to sex work cases.

In 2007, three current and former sex workers, Terri-Jean Bedford, Amy Lebovitch, and Valerie Scott, filed a lawsuit against the federal government, claiming that Canada's sex work laws were unconstitutional. Known as *Canada v. Bedford*, this case challenged key sections of the *Criminal Code*, including section 210, prohibiting the operation of a bawdy-house; section 212(I)(j), criminalizing living on the avails of prostitution; and section 213(I)(c), criminalizing communicating for the purpose of prostitution. The plaintiffs argued that these laws violated section 7 of the *Charter of Rights and Freedoms*, which permits everyone the right to life, liberty, and security of the person, and in the case of the communication law, also section 2b, which guarantees freedom of expression. On December 20, 2013, the Supreme Court of Canada struck down all three laws in a unanimous decision, acknowledging that the provisions themselves create dangerous conditions for sex workers and further "prevent people engaged in a risky — but legal — activity from taking steps to protect themselves from the risks" (*Canada (Attorney General) v. Bedford*, 2013, para. 60).

In response, the majority Conservative federal government of the day introduced the *Protection of Communities and Exploited Persons Act*. Enacted on December 6, 2014, it follows an asymmetrical criminalization model that prohibits the purchase of sexual services and targets clients and third-party managers, positioning (some) sex workers as victims (Department of Justice Canada, 2014; Durisin et al., 2018). Notably, however, sex workers tend to be seen as victims only if they embody certain predetermined characteristics of victimhood (Sibley, 2020), and therefore most still experience direct criminalization under this decade-old regime. Together, the shift in focus to domestic human trafficking and the changed federal anti–sex work laws made it easier to categorize sex work as human trafficking, upholding the assumption that the sex industry is inherently exploitative and resulting in enhanced criminalization of those involved in sexual service provision.

Asymmetrical criminalization, sometimes referred to as the Swedish model, has been the subject of ongoing national and global debate. First implemented in Sweden in 1999, it focuses on the perceived vulnerability of those working in the sex trade to abuse, exploitation, and, most importantly, human trafficking, particularly when "foreign" women are concerned. Versions of this approach have since been enacted across various nations including Norway, Finland, Iceland, France, the United Kingdom, and, in 2014, Canada. While the approach may appeal to state governments, many researchers and sex workers have raised serious concerns. Jay Levy and Pye Jakobsson (2014), for example, show that Sweden saw no reduction in sex work following the adoption of asymmetrical criminalization, which was a key goal in the first place. Instead, sex work was pushed further underground and made more dangerous (see also Gould, 2002; Kulick, 2003). Similarly, recent studies by Niina Vuolajärvi (2019, 2022) on the impacts of the model in Sweden, Norway, and Finland found that a majority of the issues and harms faced by sex workers are not related to their trade but rather to the policing and immigration policies enacted to address sex work. Among the consequences of asymmetrical criminalization are harsh working conditions and increased violence.

In addition to contestation of Canada's legislative approach to sex work, the state's federal human trafficking laws are also the subject of critique. And, as scholars have pointed out, the *Criminal Code*'s anti-trafficking laws are eerily similar in intent and wording to laws against procuring (Millar & O'Doherty, 2020b; Roots, 2013, 2022; Sibley & van der Meulen, 2023). For example, the *Criminal Code* defines those guilty of human trafficking as follows: "every person who recruits, transports, transfers, receives, holds, conceals or harbours a person, or exercises control, direction or influence over the movements of a person, for the purpose of exploiting them or facilitating their exploitation" (s. 279.01(1)). By comparison, the procuring section captures "everyone who ... recruits, holds, conceals or harbours a person who offers or provides sexual services for consideration, or exercises control, direction or influence over the movements of that person" (s. 286.3(1)(2)). Given that sex work is assumed to be inherently exploitative in popular discourse, distinction between the two provisions is also largely absent in law enforcement and prosecutorial efforts, and a number of sex work–related criminal cases have been labelled as trafficking (Roots, 2013, 2022). Although human trafficking is intended to capture exploitation across a broader spectrum, the vast majority of anti-trafficking enforcement is enacted against the sex trade, thereby further erasing the distinction (Millar et al., 2015; Roots, 2013, 2022).

Further, Canadian anti-trafficking legislation is itself inconsistent and contradictory. On the one hand, the law is limited to exploitation (it does not capture the comprehensive provisions set out by international law) and focuses on behaviours that "in all the circumstances, could reasonably be expected to cause the other person to believe that their safety or the safety of a person known to them would be threatened if they failed to provide, or offer to provide, the labour or service" (*Criminal Code*, 1985, s. 279.04). In application, exploitation in general is reduced to sexual exploitation, though the language of the law appears to capture a broader set of labour and services. This focus displaces the exploitation and safety concerns of workers outside the sex trade, within a socioeconomic and political climate that structurally manufactures unsafe and exploitative conditions in tandem with abuse, coercion, control, force, and deception. This is particularly the case among migrant workers with precarious immigration status (e.g., see Hastie, 2012; Kaye & Hastie, 2015). On the other hand, trafficking legislation expands in application to subsume many activities in the sex trade and intimate relationships under the category of sexual exploitation. Among other things, this allows those who conflate sex work and trafficking to argue that in addition to physical safety, concerns over emotional and psychological safety should be factored into determining whether exploitation has taken place (see Roots, 2022; Sibley & van der Meulen, 2023).

The same range of "fear for safety" concerns is not generally afforded to circumstances outside the sex trade. Fear for economic safety, for instance, does not qualify someone as a victim of trafficking, though it can cause significant emotional and psychological distress for those living in poverty and precarity or working in deplorable conditions. If it did, an argument could be made that many migrants who travel to Canada to work in often exploitative conditions, including within the Temporary Foreign Worker Program (TFWP), are victims of trafficking. Yet, as discussed in the final section of this introduction, the exploitation, violence, abuse, coercion, deception, and fear for safety experienced by migrant workers, particularly within the government-run TFWP, are rarely categorized under human trafficking. These tensions and contradictions are brought to light and further unpacked in this collection.

The application of trafficking laws and resulting criminal charges are taking place almost exclusively within the sex trade, which raises numerous questions about why other forms of trafficking or trafficking-like conditions are not being considered within the anti-trafficking framework or in the interpretation of human trafficking legislation. While a few cases of transnational labour trafficking have gone through Canadian courts since the enactment of federal laws, most have resulted in acquittal. The high rate of acquittals is not limited to labour trafficking cases but is also evident with domestic sex trafficking cases, the charges for which are frequently withdrawn, stayed, or acquitted, raising questions about police overzealousness to lay trafficking charges in the first place. However, Katrin Roots (2022) found in her study of 123 cases of trafficking in Ontario that a relatively high proportion (25 percent) of those charged with trafficking pleaded guilty to the offence. This finding is surprising given the serious consequences that accompany convictions, including mandatory minimum and high maximum penalties, numerous collateral consequences, and immigration penalties for those with unsecured immigration status. Yet, as chapters in this book explain, without adequate legal representation, those charged with trafficking may be eager to plead to avoid a possible sentence of fourteen years of imprisonment for non-aggravated and life imprisonment for aggravated forms of trafficking.

Legal governance of trafficking is problematic not only at the federal level but also at the provincial and municipal levels, which all together form a carceral web of laws that results in diverse impacts for sex-working, migrant, and racialized people (Fudge et al., 2021). At the provincial level, British Columbia, Manitoba, and Ontario have instituted anti-trafficking strategies with notable resources. The most substantial funding has been provided in Ontario, first with the allocation of $72 million in June 2016 and then $307 million over five years beginning in 2020. A key component of the provincial investment is the development of an extensive surveillance apparatus through a "new intelligence-led joint forces investigations team from police agencies across Ontario" (Ministry of Children, Community and Social Services, 2021, n.p.), which includes municipal police, First Nations police, and the Ontario Provincial Police. Ontario also passed the *Combating Human Trafficking Act* (enacting the *Anti-Human Trafficking Strategy Act*) in 2021 and before that the *Anti-Human Trafficking Act* in 2017. In government debates on this latter legislation, provincial parliamentarians urged an escalation in anti-trafficking action embedded within a trafficking narrative that invalidated the sex trade through invocations of childhood innocence and humanitarian rescue, yet this had no effect in making the legislation and its application less punitive for people in the sex trade (De Shalit et al., 2023).

At the municipal level, cities have implemented bylaws and licensing measures to regulate sex work establishments, such as holistic centres and body rub parlours, under the guise of anti-trafficking. Municipalities use their powers to govern sex work within their own cities as well as across other cities, with concerned residents sometimes acting in cooperation with police and bylaw enforcement officers as gatekeepers and "protectors" of public space (Laing, 2012). The consequence of bylaws targeting the sex trade is that working conditions for sex workers become more unsafe, thereby introducing more, not fewer, opportunities for abuse (Lam, 2018b; van der Meulen & Durisin, 2008, 2018). Elene Lam (2018b) explains the impacts of bylaw enforcement on Toronto massage parlours that employ Asian sex workers: "[Bylaw officers] investigated 400 massage parlours more than 2,600 times a year in order to find trafficking or other criminal issues, investigating sex workers. So we can see the municipal law oppression is huge and it also makes people in the workplace not safe" (p. 20).

Lam's (2018b) work and other studies with migrant sex workers in Toronto show that they do not characterize themselves as trafficked and instead increasingly experience unwarranted investigations, charges, arrests, tickets, and fines, as well as physical, verbal, and sexual harassment by municipal bylaw inspectors and police officers as a result of anti-trafficking mandates (see also Chu et al., 2019; Malla et al., 2019). As one Asian spa owner said, "They don't ask me if I am trafficked…. They are very clear that the purpose of the investigation is to issue tickets" (Chu et al., 2019, p. 15). Here again is a glaring contradiction — an overzealous intrusion into sex work spaces coupled with a reluctancy to view migrants as deserving of adequate supports. Research suggests that white sex workers are more readily offered "help" by law enforcement (Chu et al., 2019) and more frequently deemed as legitimate victims in trafficking prosecutions (Roots, 2022) than migrant sex workers are. In contrast, migrants are defined by their immigration status and perceived criminality, and their supposed victimhood is used to ignite action against trafficking.

Chapters in the book's second section provide a further exploration of human trafficking laws and prosecutions. In Chapter 5, Tamara O'Doherty and Hayli Millar explore the national legal framework and draw attention to trafficking prosecutions across Canada. They show that the enforcement of laws against purported domestic sex trafficking through an ideological framing of sex work as exploitation constrains access to justice for sex workers as well as survivors of violence and abuse. In Chapter 6, Sandra Ka Hon Chu and Robyn Maynard examine the racialized and gendered impacts of provincial level policy by examining Ontario's *Anti-Human Trafficking Strategy Act* (2021), which gives law enforcement broad powers to question and investigate individuals involved in sex work. In Chapter 7, Elene Lam reveals the harms caused by the combined impact of anti-Asian sentiments and municipal anti-trafficking enforcement against massage parlours in Toronto, suggesting that contrary to popular belief, Asian women in these workplaces are not trafficked but instead require labour protections. Chapter 8 is a firsthand narrative by Mash Frouhar, a criminal defence lawyer in Ottawa who has defended people charged with human trafficking. Her chapter provides insight into how police, Crown attorneys, judges, and the media treat those accused of the offence. And finally, Chapter 9 is an anonymously written narrative piece that describes the author's experience within the criminal legal system after being charged with human trafficking for his work as a manager of an escort business. Drawing on a range of contexts, the chapters in this section showcase how the enforcement of anti-trafficking laws impacts a diversity of people in various capacities within the sex trade, particularly migrant, poor, and racialized people.

Trafficking Policing and Surveillance

Police are seen as key agents responsible for enforcing the law and tackling the trafficking problem. Human trafficking, and especially what has become known as sex trafficking, is often characterized as a new and pressing criminal issue that requires novel methods of policing. The United Nations and Canada have both emphasized the need for innovative and aggressive police practices to combat what is described as a new global threat, with a particular focus on the enhancement and extension of surveillance capabilities. Recent years have seen massive increases in anti-trafficking funding, with federal and provincial governments investing heavily in police services. At the federal level, the 2012 National Action Plan to Combat Human Trafficking provided $25 million over four years to, among other things, promote police cooperation and target organized crime networks domestically and internationally, and the 2019–2024 National Strategy to Combat Human Trafficking invests a further $75 million (Public Safety Canada, 2012, 2019). As noted earlier, provincial governments make similar contributions, and in some cases even greater ones, to this cause, with significant portions of funds going to anti-trafficking policing.

Led by the Royal Canadian Mounted Police and supported by the Canada Border Services Agency, anti-trafficking policing efforts have expanded through all levels of government, in part by stressing the multi-jurisdictionality of trafficking, and in the process promoting cooperation across law enforcement agencies. Police forces often display this through various sting and "raid-and-rescue" operations, which are collaborative initiatives aimed at "rescuing" victims of trafficking by forcibly entering sex work businesses unannounced or by posing as clients and arranging meetings with sex workers at hotels or other locations, and then detaining the workers in order to conduct inspections and interrogations. Such efforts are widely covered in news media and are frequently mentioned in government reports on anti-trafficking activities. One of the largest annual cross-Canada operations, Operation Northern Spotlight, ran from 2015 to 2018 (according to the Ontario Provincial Police, it continues to be an ongoing operation, although no raids have taken place since 2018). Following Northern Spotlight raids, newspapers often ran updates reporting on the large number of police forces involved from all levels of government and the extensive geographic areas covered (across provinces or the country). These media reports convey the importance of multilevel anti-trafficking policing, justifying the large-scale funding assigned to the cause and creating an image of a heroic rescuer of a suffering woman or youth. Yet rescue efforts have wide-scale negative impacts. The Canadian Alliance for Sex Work Law Reform (2018) states that the harms stemming from Operation Northern Spotlight's deceptive approach of police posing as clients constituted intimidation and harassment of sex workers and of the sex trade industry more broadly. This deception reduces sex workers' trust in police services even further.

Despite the negative effects and harms caused, the way that police present their actions allows them to assume the role of "white saviour," a term used to describe a seemingly heroic, white Westerner who has tasked themselves with saving the often racialized individual or group from complex situations (Cole, 2021). The activities of white saviours result in dichotomizing expressions of humanitarian care that construct racialized people as unable to care for themselves and, as Kamala Kempadoo (2015) explains, place the burden of saviourhood on the white (wo)man. In the context of trafficking, the white saviour role is taken up by the Western/Northern colonial state and nonstate actors in their efforts to "save" racialized women in the Global South (Heynen & van der Meulen, 2022; Hua, 2011; Hua & Nigorizawa, 2010; Soderlund, 2005). Domestic victims of trafficking in this context come to be filtered through the lens of racial Othering, requiring intervention and saving by police officers and social service providers.

Anti-trafficking surveillance and security apparatuses thus expand beyond police to include NGOs (De Shalit, 2021; De Shalit & Roots, 2023; Heynen & van der Meulen, 2022), capturing what Jennifer Musto (2010) calls carceral protectionism — governance that focuses on the protection of the "good" or "deserving" victim while criminalizing those who fail to meet the criteria for such protection (see also Rodriguez et al.,

2020). In Ontario, the growing role played by NGOs has been attributed to the increased government funding that is allocated to them for anti-trafficking efforts (De Shalit, 2021). In addition to cooperation between governments, the police, and NGOs, various other sectors and industries, such as health care, education, tourism and hospitality, trucking and transportation, and finance, are providing training for their respective workforces on how to spot the signs of human trafficking. These workers are then responsibilized to report to police any suspicions about trafficking. Yet the unsound or unclear anti-trafficking indicators that are noted within the various training materials are broadly inclusive of sex work activities and intimate relationships (De Shalit, 2021). The resulting profiles of trafficking victims individualize trafficking while invisibilizing complex systemic conditions, such as racism, colonialism, sexism, and classism, as well as people's own understanding of their victimhood, or lack thereof. Nevertheless, these indicators contribute to the construction of the trafficking victim.

The general public is also invited to participate in anti-trafficking initiatives through a plethora of public awareness campaigns that have emerged in recent years. One such example is the Shoppable Girls campaign launched in 2020 by Covenant House Toronto and the Toronto Police Service. The campaign depicts young women as products to be purchased, with captions such as "shop this season's most unsettling collection today" and "some things shouldn't be for sale" (O'Neil, 2020, n.p.). The physical manifestation of this campaign included images of young women as items displayed on storefronts at a popular shopping destination on Queen Street in the city's downtown. Posters depicting the same were displayed across the subway system. The goal was to train the public, in particular young people, to be able to notice the signs of trafficking, and therefore become anti-trafficking experts, so they could identify and report such instances to police and avoid being trafficked themselves.

As Ann De Shalit (2021) explains, public awareness campaigns tend to focus their messaging on young women involved in sex work, and sometimes simply in intimate relationships, thus increasing emotional investment by inviting the public to imagine the victim as their daughter, their sister, their niece, or their granddaughter. The public is then encouraged to surveil their neighbours and communities and report their suspicions to the national human trafficking hotline developed by the federal government in 2019 or to law enforcement directly. Elena Shih (2016) describes such surveillance and responsibilization strategies as "backyard abolition," in which members of the public are assigned to be the eyes and ears of the police in a collective aim to prohibit sex work (see also Schwarz, 2020). This neoliberal and paternalistic approach to trafficking, in which the public and purported or potential victims themselves are responsibilized to carry out the functions of state security and surveillance, is not only harmful but it is also undemanding of systemic change, including meaningful protections for people experiencing workplace or intimate partner abuse and violence, undignified labour conditions and withheld compensation, lack of sustainable resource (e.g., housing) allocation, or irregularization of immigration status (De Shalit, 2021). The same extension of surveillance and carcerality emerges from social media portrayals of human trafficking as involving kidnappings at malls, airports, and other public places. Not only do such accounts often rely on stranger danger myths but they also invite the "securitization of society" (Schuilenburg, 2015) along with increased surveillance and augmented police budgets.

An emerging body of scholarship indicates that the growth of anti-trafficking surveillance and security has had inequitable and often counterproductive impacts. Existing studies, including chapters in this book, point to a number of concerns and adverse effects of current anti-trafficking policing. For one, while criminal charges for trafficking have increased over the last decade, a majority of those are stayed, withdrawn by Crown attorneys, or acquitted by judges, as noted above (Millar & O'Doherty, 2020a; Millar et al., 2015; Roots, 2022), suggesting unwarranted and overzealous charging practices by police. Second, officers overwhelmingly lay trafficking charges against racialized people and especially young, low-income Black men, contributing to the criminalization of race and poverty (Millar & O'Doherty, 2020a; Roots, 2022). This finding is not exclusive to Canada, as scholars have found parallel outcomes in the United States (Bernstein, 2012; Williamson & Marcus, 2017). The more generalized police targeting of racialized people has been well documented by critical race scholars (Alexander, 2010; Davis, 2017; Maynard, 2017; Wortley, 2019), and it is reflected in the context of the sex trade by way of anti-trafficking efforts. Third, anti-trafficking policing has resulted in the surveillance of the sex industry writ large; the criminalization and harassment of Indigenous, racialized, and low-income sex workers (Kaye, 2023; Lam, 2018a; Raguparan, 2023); and the deportation of migrant sex workers (Bernstein, 2010, 2012; Lam & Lepp, 2019; Lester et al., 2017; Roots & De Shalit, 2015). Sex workers report feeling traumatized by the intimidating spectacle of police forcing entry into their workplaces, hotel rooms, and apartments.

Examining policing and surveillance in more depth, the chapters in the third section of the book detail the consequences of these efforts, particularly for marginalized, racialized, and Indigenous people. In Chapter 10, Robert Heynen discusses intelligence-led policing, which involves bringing together a large number of police forces, government organizations, NGOs, and the public in what he calls a "whole-of-society" approach to target trafficking. Chapter 11 by Alison Clancey and Julie Ham describes the work of SWAN Vancouver, a sex worker rights organization, and the abject failure of police to respond to a series of violent robberies against Asian im/migrant sex workers in the Greater Vancouver area. In Chapter 12, Julie Kaye and Cerah Dubé examine anti-trafficking policing in Manitoba, showing that the dominant and infantilizing discourse of Indigenous women and girls as vulnerable to trafficking places an emphasis on individual risks, divorcing the issue from the larger ongoing context of settler colonialism. And last, Chapter 13 features a narrative piece about working in both the street-based and indoor sex trade. Victoria Erin Flett recounts her experiences as an Indigenous trans woman in Winnipeg and describes the impacts of settler colonialism and abuse, which are exacerbated by anti–sex work and transphobic police practices in the city.

Trafficking and Migrant Labour Exploitation

Migration is only infrequently addressed in contemporary mainstream anti-trafficking efforts in Canada. Yet studies have repeatedly demonstrated the impacts of the anti-trafficking framework on migrant communities (e.g., see Chu et al., 2019; Lam, 2018a; Malla et al., 2019). The pursuit of economic and other opportunities by migrants who come to Canada for work, which at times involves sex work, is written off as a site of victimization or criminalization. It is not commonly situated in the larger context of globalization and the seemingly borderless movement of capital, or in the increasing poverty and deplorable labour practices of Western/Northern capitalist corporations that move their operations to the Global South for cheap servitude and more lenient human rights and labour standards. Instead, migrants, particularly women, who leave parts of the world that have been dubbed trafficking centres are positioned as helpless victims at risk of falling into the sex trade, from which their inherently "injured bodies" must be saved (Doezema, 2001; Woods, 2013). And while appeals to victimhood on the individual level can be used to "mobilize and claim rights" (Aradau, 2003, p. 56), their deployment in the context of anti-trafficking has proven to be based on essentializing categories that mute the complexities of labour and migration.

Indeed, as this introductory chapter has emphasized, trafficking is assigned to overly simplified criminal legal solutions. We can see how such politics unfold in a notable example from a national study on human trafficking conducted from February to May 2018 by the House of Commons Standing Committee on Justice and Human Rights. At one of the committee meetings, Philippe Massé (2018) from Employment and Social Development Canada (ESDC) explained:

> We know that workers coming into Canada under low-wage streams — caregivers and primary agriculture workers — are the most vulnerable to exploitation … because of language barriers, isolation, and lack of access to accurate information on rights and protections. Some also fear retribution, including the threat of being returned to their home country if they speak out. (n.p.)

Massé went on:

> ESDC has the authority to conduct administrative inspections to ensure that employers meet certain requirements when they first apply for the program, and continue to meet them while the TFWs [temporary foreign workers] are here in Canada. However, ESDC has no jurisdiction over criminal matters such as human trafficking, and it refers such cases to the CBSA [Canadian Border Services Agency] and to the RCMP [Royal Canadian Mounted Police]. (n.p.)

Here, inadequacies in the current immigration system are recognized by a government actor but are distinguished from trafficking, and the latter is seen as requiring the intervention of law and border enforcement measures.

As Massé notes, the TFWP, which houses the Seasonal Agricultural Worker Program and the Live-in Caregiver Program, along with others, is dependent on low-wage and so-called "low-skilled" migrant labour. The federal government promotes the TFWP to fuel the country's economic growth and fulfill the needs of various employers (Fudge & MacPhail, 2009). Evidence demonstrates that the government is far less concerned with the needs and safety of the migrant labourers themselves. A substantial body of research on the TFWP shows that temporary migrant workers experience extremely long hours of work, unpaid overtime, inadequate and overcrowded housing, a lack of health care, confiscation of passports and other identifying documents, threats of deportation, and physical, psychological, and emotional abuse by employers (Bhuyan et al., 2018; Cajax et al., 2022; Landry et al., 2021; Strauss & McGrath, 2017; Vosko, 2022; Zwaigenbaum et al., 2021). The lack of redress for these issues is unsurprising, given that Canada has failed to ratify the international conventions that specifically safeguard the rights of migrant workers, including the 2001 *International Convention on the Protection of the Rights of All Migrant Workers and Members of Their Families* (United Nations), and the 1949 *Convention on Migration for Employment* and its 1975 *Migrant Workers* subprovision (International Labour Organization). This seeming disregard for migrant worker protections stands in direct contradiction to the state's eagerness in ratifying the *Trafficking Protocol*.

Academic and grassroots investigations have specifically named the closed nature of federal government work permits, under which workers are tied to their employers, as contributing to and facilitating the kinds of exploitation, abuse, coercion, deception, and control mentioned above. According to Nandita Sharma (2012), the status of temporary migrants in Canada is dependent on their employability; thus, the lack of status afforded to migrants outside of the workplace renders them unfree (Basok, 2002; LeBaron & Phillips, 2019; Lenard & Straehle, 2012) and leaves them vulnerable to structural conditions that result in potential and confirmed exploitation, abuse, coercion, deception, control, and so on (Hennebry & McLaughlin, 2012; Weller & Cohen, 2018). Nevertheless, such cases are rarely labelled as human trafficking. Here we are highlighting the inequitable enforcement of trafficking laws, despite evidence of rampant exploitation and abuse documented in various industries, rather than advocating for an expansion of the anti-trafficking apparatus and the labelling of more activities and offences as human trafficking. As chapters in this book argue, widening the anti-trafficking net to other labour sectors will only result in more marginalized people experiencing the harms of anti-trafficking legislation and policing.

A notable exception to the typical disregard of labour exploitation is the case of *R. v. Domotor* (2011), in which the exploitation of migrant workers in the construction industry led to trafficking convictions (through guilty pleas), long prison sentences (only partially served), and ultimately deportation of the employers/perpetrators who were permanent residents (as opposed to citizens) and therefore subject to removal orders due to "serious criminality." The case involved the recruitment, transportation, and exploitation of several Hungarian men brought to Canada by two Hungarian families, the Domotors and the Kolompars, who ran a construction business in Hamilton, Ontario. This case is often referenced as evidence that transnational trafficking is taking place in Canada and that courts and the federal government are taking a tough stance. Interestingly, the offenders in this case were prosecuted under the *Criminal Code* human trafficking provisions, which tend to govern domestic trafficking, rather than section 118 of the *Immigration and Refugee Protection Act* (2001), despite the cross-border transportation of the complainants. Notwithstanding the rigour with which the Domotor-Kolompar case was handled, migrant exploitation does not often see such responses from Canada's criminal legal system, particularly if these cases take place within the TFWP. Indeed, the prosecution of the Domotor case was empowered by the fact that the exploitation was carried out by individuals for their own benefit, rather than via a state-approved program such as the TFWP, thus allowing the state to position itself as the saviour rather than the perpetrator.

To mitigate experiences of exploitation and abuse, migrant workers and advocates across the country have called for open work permits for migrant labourers, a strategy that informs practice within the boundaries of the capitalist business model of which exploitation is part and parcel. In 2019, as a direct result of migrant justice organizing, the federal government introduced open work permits for vulnerable workers. Albeit with concerning gaps in reach and scope, the permits allow migrant workers with closed or employer-restricted permits who are experiencing abuse to leave their employers and embark on a temporary search (6 to 12 months) for work elsewhere (Migrant Workers

Alliance for Change, 2020a). Organizers have also long campaigned for permanent status for all migrants on arrival. On December 14, 2023, Immigration Minister Marc Miller tabled a promise to consider a broad and comprehensive regularization program, as proposed by the Migrant Rights Network (2023). Organizations such as the Migrant Rights Network (2023) and the Migrant Workers Alliance for Change (2020b) insist that efforts seeking to address exploitation and abuse should not be tied to law enforcement and must instead enforce anti-racist, access-without-fear, and status-for-all policies across the board. State-coordinated policies, although recognized for their shortcomings in overhauling and regulating global capitalism, can be useful points of intervention in such instances.

Nevertheless, most anti-trafficking efforts continue to focus on the expansion or redefinition of criminal legislation and victim protection or rehabilitation. They fail, for example, to "grapple with how state immigration and labour policies combine with labour market institutions and actors to create a range of different types and degrees of labour exploitation" (Fudge, 2020, n.p.). Even if the anti-trafficking framework is only concerned with extreme forms of exploitation, abuse, coercion, deception, control, force, and threats to safety (Weitzer, 2020), consideration must still be given to how normalized and "everyday" forms of such conditions in capitalist societies give way to those more extreme cases. Questions remain about what will be considered extreme and what will not, according to law. Anti-trafficking efforts suggest that most activities that take place as part of, or alongside, trading or selling sex will be rendered extreme and addressed through concerted anti-trafficking policing and legal efforts, whereas those involving migrant labourers will fall through legislative cracks. In these instances, the threshold of severity is preestablished and often unrelated to practical working conditions.

In the fourth and final section of the book, chapter authors provide compelling accounts of the politics of trafficking and exploitation in relation to the labour and migration of temporary residents in Canada. In Chapter 14, Jessica Templeman's investigation of temporary resident permits for victims of trafficking reveals the governing of migrants through notions of "illegality and fraud" and "foreignness and temporariness," which in the process lead to the denial of their permit applications. In Chapter 15, lawyer Shane Martínez similarly examines the interpretation of migrant experiences in relation to trafficking and trafficking-like conditions, though here focusing specifically on the Seasonal Agricultural Worker Program, under which labourers face systematic and persistent exploitation while being denied "victim" status. To close the book, in Chapter 16, Chris Ramsaroop, a long-time organizer with Justicia for Migrant Workers, provides a first-person narrative of struggling alongside agricultural and other migrant labourers who seek redress from systemic and often state-sanctioned forms of exploitation. Chapters in this section demonstrate the inadequacies of the anti-trafficking framework in addressing the exploitation and abuse experienced by migrant workers, especially within the programs developed and regulated by the Canadian federal government.

Conclusion

As we grapple with the assumptions, undercurrents, operations, and impacts of anti-trafficking efforts, we are also confronted with the many resulting harms. Accounts written from various points of experience and knowledge converge to reveal the contradictions and tensions of anti-trafficking representations and discourses, enforcement and prosecutions, and policing and surveillance, all of which neglect migrant exploitation and abuse. Indeed, as the chapters in this book demonstrate, the existing approach to trafficking suppresses the collective labour, bargaining power, and agency of sex workers, migrant workers, and others. We can see clearly the difficulty but also the urgent necessity of abandoning the contemporary anti-trafficking framework and replacing it with alternative interventions that meaningfully reduce problematic labour conditions, workplace violations, and human rights abuses. Such a context will only be achieved, however, if the individuals who are most directly impacted by the anti-trafficking apparatus, along with their supporters, play a determining role in charting the path forward — these include the authors of the chapters to come.

References

Abel, G., Fitzgerald, L., Healy, C., & Taylor, A. (2010). *Taking the crime out of sex work: New Zealand sex workers' fight for decriminalisation*. The Policy Press.

Alexander, M. (2010). *The new Jim Crow: Mass incarceration in the age of colorblindness*. The New Press.

Anderson, B., & Andrijasevic, R. (2008). Sex, slaves and citizens: The politics of anti-

trafficking. *Soundings*, 40: 135–145.
Aradau, C. (2003). Trafficking in women: Human rights or human risks? *Canadian Woman Studies*, 22, 3, 4: 55–59.
Bales, K. (2005). *Understanding global slavery: A reader*. University of California Press.
Basok, T. (2002). *Tortillas and tomatoes: Transmigrant Mexican harvesters in Canada*. McGill-Queen's University Press.
Bernstein, E. (2007). *Temporarily yours: Intimacy, authenticity, and the commerce of sex*. University of Chicago Press.
———. (2010). Militarized humanitarianism meets carceral feminism: The politics of sex, rights, and freedom in contemporary antitrafficking campaigns. *Signs: Journal of Women in Culture and Society*, 36, 1: 45–71.
———. (2012). Carceral politics as gender justice? The "traffic in women" and neoliberal circuits of crime, sex and rights. *Theoretical Sociology*, 41: 233–259.
Beutin, L. (2023). *Trafficking in antiblackness: Modern-day slavery, white indemnity, and racial justice*. Duke University Press.
Bhuyan, R., Valmadrid, L., Panlaqui, E.L., Pendon, N.L., & Juan, P. (2018). Responding to the structural violence of migrant domestic work: Insights from participatory action research with migrant caregivers in Canada. *Journal of Family Violence*, 33: 613–627.
Bruckert, C. (2018a). Who are third parties? Pathways in and out of third-party work. In C. Bruckert & C. Parent (eds.), *Getting past the 'pimp': Management in the sex industry* (pp. 36–55). University of Toronto Press.
———. (2018b). Introduction: Revisioning third parties in the sex industry. In C. Bruckert & C. Parent (eds.), *Getting past the 'pimp': Management in the sex industry* (pp. 3–18). University of Toronto Press.
Bumiller, K. (2008). *In an abusive state: How neoliberalism appropriated the feminist movement against sexual violence*. Duke University Press.
Bunting, A., & Quirk, J. (2017). Contemporary slavery as more than rhetorical strategy? The politics and ideology of a new political cause. In A. Bunting & J. Quirk (eds.), *Contemporary slavery: Popular rhetoric and political practice* (pp. 5–35). UBC Press.
Canadian Alliance for Sex Work Law Reform. (2018, October 9). Sex worker human rights groups oppose police operation Northern Spotlight [press release]. https://sexworklawreform.com/press-release-operation-northern-spotlight-october-2018/
Chapkis, W. (1997). *Live sex acts: Women performing erotic labor*. Routledge.
Choudry, A., & Smith, A.A. (eds.). (2016). *Unfree labour? Struggles of migrant and immigrant workers in Canada*. PM Press.
Chu, S., Clamen, J., & Santini, T. (2019). The perils of "protection": Sex workers' experiences of law enforcement in Ontario. https://www.powerottawa.ca/wp-content/uploads/2019/09/2807_HIVLegalNetwork_SexWorkerDocumentation_Report_English_FINAL-1.pdf
Chuang, J.A. (2014). Exploitation creep and the unmaking of human trafficking law. *The American Journal of International Law*, 108, 4: 609–649.
Cole, T. (2012, March 21). The white-saviour industrial complex. *The Atlantic*. https://www.theatlantic.com/international/archive/2012/03/the-white-savior-industrial-complex/254843/
Davis, A. (2017). Introduction. In A. Davis (ed.), *Policing the Black man* (pp. xi–2). Pantheon Books.
De Shalit, A. (2021). Neoliberal paternalism and displaced culpability: Examining the governing relations of the human trafficking problem [unpublished doctoral dis-

sertation]. Toronto Metropolitan University.
De Shalit, A., & Roots, K. (2023). The anti-trafficking security assemblage: Examining police and NGO cooperation, negotiation, and knowledge production in Ontario, Canada. *Feminist Legal Studies*. https://doi.org/10.1007/s10691-023-09536-7
De Shalit, A., Roots, K., & van der Meulen, E. (2023). Knowledge mobilization by provincial politicians: The united front against trafficking in Ontario, Canada. *Journal of Human Trafficking*, 9, 4: 568–586.
Department of Justice Canada. (2014, June 4). Statement by the Minister of Justice regarding legislation in response to the Supreme Court of Canada ruling in Attorney General of Canada v. Bedford et al. [news release]. https://www.canada.ca/en/news/archive/2014/06/statement-minister-justice-regarding-legislation-response-supreme-court-canada-ruling-attorney-general-canada-v-bedford-al-.html
Doezema J. (2001). Ouch! Western feminists' "wounded attachment" to the third world prostitute. *Feminist Review*, 67, 1: 16–38.
___. (2010). *Sex slaves and discourse masters: The construction of trafficking*. Zed Books.
Durisin, E.M. (2023). Global white supremacy and anti-trafficking: Race, racism and the politics of human trafficking. In K. Kempadoo & E. Shih (eds.), *White supremacy, racism and the coloniality of anti-trafficking* (pp. 79–91). Routledge.
Durisin, E.M., & Heynen, R. (2015). Producing the "trafficked woman": Canadian newspaper reporting on Eastern European exotic dancers during the 1990s. *Atlantis: Critical Studies in Gender, Culture, and Social Justice*, 37.2, 1: 8–24.
Durisin, E.M., & van der Meulen, E. (2021). The perfect victim: "Young girls", domestic trafficking, and anti-prostitution politics in Canada. *Anti-Trafficking Review*, 6: 145–149.
Durisin, E.M., van der Meulen, E., & Bruckert, C. (2018). Contextualizing sex work: Challenging discourses and confronting narratives. In E.M. Durisin, E. van der Meulen, & C. Bruckert (eds.), *Red light labour: Sex work, regulation, agency, and resistance* (pp. 3–26). UBC Press.
Ferguson, J.A. (2012). International human trafficking in Canada: Why so few prosecutions? [doctoral dissertation]. University of British Columbia. https://commons.allard.ubc.ca/theses/62/
Fudge, J. (2020, November 19). Twenty years after Palermo, can we stop discussing labour exploitation and start fixing it? *openDemocracy: Beyond Trafficking and Slavery*. https://www.opendemocracy.net/en/beyond-trafficking-and-slavery/twenty-years-after-palermo-can-we-stop-discussing-labour-exploitation-and-start-fixing-it/
Fudge, J., Lam, E., Chu, S.K.H., & Wong, V. (2021). Caught in the carceral web: Anti-trafficking laws and policies and their impact on migrant sex workers. *HIV Legal Network*. https://www.hivlegalnetwork.ca/site/caught-in-the-carceral-web-anti-trafficking-laws-and-policies-and-their-impact-on-migrant-sex-workers
Fudge, J., & MacPhail, F. (2009). Temporary Foreign Worker Program in Canada: Low-skilled workers as extreme form of flexible labour. *Comparative Labour Law & Policy Journal*, 31, 1: 5–46.
Global Alliance Against Traffic in Women. (2007). *Collateral damage: The impact of anti-trafficking measures on human rights around the world*. https://gaatw.org/Collateral_Damage_Final/singlefile_CollateralDamagefinal.pdf
Gould, A. (2002). Sweden's laws on prostitution: Feminism, drugs and the foreign threat. In S. Thorbek & B. Pattanai (eds.), *Transnational prostitution: Changing global patterns* (pp. 201–217). Zed Books.
Hastie, B. (2012). Doing Canada's dirty work: A critical analysis of law and policy to address labour exploitation trafficking. In A. Quayson & A. Arhin (eds.), *Labour*

migration, human trafficking and multinational corporations: Commodification of illicit flows (pp. 121–137). Routledge.
Hennebry, J., & McLaughlin, J. (2012). The exception that proves the rule: Structural vulnerability, health risks, and consequences for temporary migrant farm workers in Canada. In P.T. Lenard & C. Straehle (eds.), *Legislated inequality: Temporary labour migration in Canada* (pp. 117–138). McGill-Queen's University Press.
Heynen, R., & van der Meulen, E. (2022). Anti-trafficking saviors: Celebrity, slavery, and branded activism. *Crime, Media, Culture*, 18, 2: 301–323.
Hill-Collins, P. (2004). *Black sexual politics: African American gender and the new racism*. Routledge.
Horning, A., & Marcus, A. (2017). Introduction: In search of pimps and other varieties. In A. Horning & A. Marcus (eds.), *Third party sex work and pimps in the age of anti-trafficking* (pp. 1–13). Springer International Publishing.
Hua, J. (2011). *Trafficking women's human rights*. University of Minnesota Press.
Hua, J., & Nigorizawa, H. (2010). US sex trafficking, women's human rights and the politics of representation. *International Feminist Journal of Politics*, 12, 3–4: 401–423.
Hunt, S. (2013). Decolonizing sex work: Developing an intersectional Indigenous approach. In E. van der Meulen, E.M. Durisin, & V. Love (eds.), *Selling sex: Experience, advocacy, and research on sex work in Canada* (pp. 82–100). UBC Press.
____. (2015). Representing colonial violence: Trafficking, sex work and the violence of law. *Atlantis: Critical Studies in Gender, Culture & Social Justice*, 37.2, 1: 25–39.
Jeffrey, L.A. (2005). Canada and migrant sex work: Challenging the "foreign" in foreign policy. *Canadian Foreign Policy*, 12, 1: 33–48.
Jeffrey, L.A., & MacDonald, G. (2006). *Sex workers in the Maritimes talk back*. UBC Press.
Kalunta-Crumpton, A. (1998). The prosecution and defence of Black defendants in drug trials. *British Journal of Criminology*, 38, 4: 561–591.
Kapur, R. (2005). Cross border movements and the law: Negotiating the boundaries of difference. In K. Kempadoo, J. Sanghera, & B. Pattanaik (eds.), *Trafficking and prostitution reconsidered: Perspectives on migration, sex work and human rights* (pp. 25–41). Paradigm Publishers.
Kara, S. (2009). *Sex-trafficking: Inside the business of modern slavery*. Columbia University Press.
Kaye, J. (2017). *Responding to human trafficking: Dispossession, colonial violence, and resistance among Indigenous and racialized women*. University of Toronto Press.
____. (2023). Anti-trafficking and settler-colonial discourses of protection: The coloniality of racialized interventions. In K. Kempadoo & E. Shih (eds.), *White supremacy, racism and the coloniality of anti-trafficking* (pp. 119–135). Routledge.
Kaye, J., & Hastie, B. (2015). The Canadian Criminal Code offence of trafficking in persons: Challenges from the field and within the law. *Social Inclusion*, 3, 1: 88–102.
Kempadoo, K. (2005). From moral panic to global justice: Changing perspectives on trafficking. In K. Kempadoo, J. Sanghera, & B. Pattanaik (eds.), *Trafficking and prostitution reconsidered: New perspectives on migration, sex work and human rights* (pp. vvii–xxxiv). Paradigm Publishers.
____. (2015.) The modern day white (wo)man's burden: Trends in anti-trafficking and anti-slavery campaigns. *Journal of Human Trafficking*, 1, 1: 8–20.
Kempadoo, K., & Doezema, J. (1998). *Global sex workers: Rights, resistance, and redefinition*. Routlege.
Kulick, D. (2003). Sex in the new Europe: The criminalization of clients and Swedish fear of penetration. *Anthropological Theory*, 3, 2: 199–218.

Laing, M. (2012). Regulating adult work in Canada: The role of criminal and municipal code. In P. Johnson & D. Dalton (eds.), *Policing sex* (pp. 166–184). Routledge.

Lam, E. (2018a). *Behind the rescue: How anti-trafficking investigations and policies harm migrant sex workers.* Butterfly (Asian and Migrant Sex Workers Support Network). https://tinyurl.com/52fsf75s

____. (2018b). *Survey on Toronto holistic practitioners' experiences with bylaw enforcement and police.* Butterfly (Asian and Migrant Sex Workers Support Network). https://tinyurl.com/44jc3k5h

Lam, E., & Lepp, A. (2019). Butterfly: Resisting the harms of anti-trafficking policies and fostering peer-based organizing in Canada. *Anti-Trafficking Review*, 12, 12: 91–107.

Landry, V., Semsar, K., Tjong, J., Alj, A., Darnley, A., Lipp, R., Guberman, G. (2021). The systemized exploitation of temporary migrant agricultural workers in Canada: Exacerbation of health vulnerabilities during the COVID-19 pandemic and recommendations for the future. *Journal of Migration and Health*, 3: 1–5.

LeBaron, G., & Philips, N. (2019). States and the political economy of unfree labour. *New Political Economy*, 24, 1: 1–21.

Lenard, P.T., & Straehle, C. (2012). Introduction. In P.T. Lenard & C. Straehle (eds.), *Legislated inequality: Temporary labour migration in Canada* (pp. 3–25). McGill-Queen's University Press.

Lester, J., Pates, R., & Dolemeyer, A. (2017). The emotional leviathan — How street-level bureaucrats govern human trafficking victims. *Digithum*, 19: 19–36.

Levy, J., & Jakobsson, P. (2014). Sweden's abolitionist discourse and law: Effects on the dynamics of Swedish sex work and on the lives of Sweden's sex workers. *Criminology & Criminal Justice*, 14, 5: 593–607.

Malla, A., Lam, E., van der Meulen, E., Peng, H-Y. (2019). *Beyond tales of trafficking: A needs assessment of Asian migrant sex workers in Toronto.* Butterfly (Asian and Migrant Sex Workers Support Network). https://tinyurl.com/kr52896x

Marcus, A., Horning, A., Curtis, R., Sanson J., & Thompson, E. (2014). Conflict and agency among sex workers and pimps: A closer look at domestic minor sex trafficking. *Annals of the American Academy of Political and Social Science*, 653, 1: 225–246.

Massé, P. (2018, February 27). *Mr. Philippe Massé (director general, Temporary Foreign Worker Directorate, Skills and Employment Branch, Department of Employment and Social Development) at the Justice and Human Rights Committee.* https://openparliament.ca/committees/justice/42-1/88/philippe-masse-1/only/

Maynard, R. (2017). *Policing Black lives: State violence in Canada from slavery to the present.* Fernwood Publishing.

____. (2018). Do Black sex workers' lives matter? Whitewashed anti-slavery, racial justice, and abolition. In E.M. Durisin, E. van der Meulen, & C. Bruckert (eds.), *Red light labour: Sex work regulation, agency, and resistance* (pp. 281–292). UBC Press.

Mensah, M. N. (2018). The representation of the "pimp": A barrier to understanding the work of third parties in the adult Canadian sex industry. In C. Bruckert & C. Parent (eds.), *Getting past the "pimp": Management in the sex industry* (pp. 19–35). University of Toronto Press.

Migrant Rights Network. (2023, December 14). Migrant Rights Network welcomes minister's commitment to a broad & comprehensive regularization program, demands end to deportations and status for all without delay [news release]. https://migrantrights.ca/migrant-rights-network-welcomes-ministers-commitment-to-a-broad-comprehensive-regularization-program-demands-end-to-deportations-and-status-for-all-without-delay/

Migrant Workers Alliance for Change. (2020a). Fact sheet: Open work permit for vulnerable workers. https://migrantworkersalliance.org/wp-content/uploads/2020/12/OWP-VW-Factsheet.pdf

———. (2020b). *Unheeded warnings: COVID-19 & migrant workers in Canada.* https://migrantworkersalliance.org/wp-content/uploads/2020/06/Unheeded-Warnings-COVID19-and-Migrant-Workers.pdf

Millar, H., & O'Doherty, T. (2020a). *Canadian human trafficking prosecutions and principles of fundamental justice: A contradiction in terms? International centre for criminal law reform.* https://icclr.org/publications/canadian-human-trafficking-prosecutions-and-principles-of-fundamental-justice-a-contradiction-in-terms/

———. (2020b). Racialized, gendered, and sensationalized: An examination of Canadian anti-trafficking laws, their enforcement and their (re)presentation. *Canadian Journal of Law and Society*, 35, 1: 23–44.

Millar, H., O'Doherty, T., & SWAN Vancouver Society. (2015). *The Palermo Protocol & Canada: The evolution and human rights impacts of anti-trafficking laws in Canada (2002–2015).* https://icclr.org/publications/the-palermo-protocol-canada-the-evolution-and-human-rights-impacts-of-anti-trafficking-laws-in-canada-2002-2015

Miller, R., & Baumeister, S. (2013). Managing migration: Is border control fundamental to anti-trafficking and anti-smuggling interventions. *Anti-trafficking Review*, 2: 15–32.

Ministry of Children, Community and Social Services. (2021). *Ontario's anti-human trafficking strategy 2020–2025.* https://www.ontario.ca/page/ontarios-anti-human-trafficking-strategy-2020-2025

Mountz, A. (2010). *Seeking asylum: Human smuggling and bureaucracy at the border.* University of Minnesota Press.

Musto, J.L. (2010). The NGO-ification of the anti-trafficking movement in the United States: A case study of the coalition to abolish slavery and trafficking. In T. Zheng (ed.), *Sex trafficking, human rights, and social justice* (pp. 23–36). Routledge.

———. (2016). *Control and protect: Collaboration, carceral protection and domestic sex trafficking in the United States.* University of California Press.

O'Connell Davidson, J. (2015). *Modern day slavery: The margins of freedom.* Palgrave Macmillan.

O'Neil, L. (2020). Teen girls for sale in Toronto storefront as a part of sex trafficking awareness campaign. BlogTO. https://www.blogto.com/city/2020/02/teen-girls-sale-toronto-storefront-raise-awareness-sex-trafficking/

Perrin, B. (2010). *Invisible chains: Canada's underground world of human trafficking.* Penguin Random House Canada.

Pickering, S., & Ham, J. (2014). Hot pants at the border: Sorting sex work from trafficking. *British Journal of Criminology*, 54, 1: 2–19.

Pratt, A. (2005). *Securing borders: Detention and deportation in Canada.* UBC Press.

Public Safety Canada. (2012). *National action plan to combat human trafficking.* https://www.publicsafety.gc.ca/cnt/rsrcs/pblctns/ntnl-ctn-pln-cmbt/index-eng.aspx

———. (2019). *National strategy to combat human trafficking 2019–2024.* https://www.publicsafety.gc.ca/cnt/rsrcs/pblctns/2019-ntnl-strtgy-hmnn-trffc/2019-ntnl-strtgy-hmnn-trffc-en.pdf

Raguparan, M. (2023). Is it because I'm not young and white with blue eyes? Canadian police response to sex workers of colour's experiences of exploitation and trafficking. In K. Kempadoo & E. Shih (eds.), *White supremacy, racism, and the coloniality of anti-trafficking* (pp. 170–186). Routledge.

Rodriguez, S.M., Ben-Moshe, L., & Rakes, H. (2020). Carceral protectionism and the perpetually (in)vulnerable. *Criminology & Criminal Justice*, 20, 5: 537–550.

Roots, K. (2013). Trafficking or pimping: An analysis of Canada's human trafficking law and its implications. *Canadian Journal of Law and Society*, 28: 21–40.

___. (2022). *Domestication of human trafficking: Law, policing and prosecution in Canada*. University of Toronto Press.

Roots, K., & De Shalit, A. (2015). Evidence that evidence doesn't matter: The case of human trafficking in Canada. *Atlantis: Critical Studies in Gender, Culture & Social Justice*, 37.2, 1: 65–80.

Schuilenburg, M. (2015). *The securitization of society: Crime, risk, and social order*. New York University Press.

Schwarz, C. (2020). "I can be big sister, even if you can't be big brother: Spectatorship and punishment in anti-trafficking efforts." *Critical Criminology*, 29: 613–632.

Sharma, N. (2012). The "difference" that borders make: "Temporary foreign workers" and the social organization of unfreedom in Canada. In P.T. Lenard & C. Straehle (eds.), *Legislated inequality: Temporary labour migration in Canada* (pp. 26–47). McGill-Queen's University Press.

Shelley, L. (2010). *Human trafficking: A global perspective*. Cambridge University Press.

Shih, E. (2016). Not in my "backyard abolitionism": Vigilante rescue against American sex trafficking. *Sociological Perspectives*, 59, 1: 66–90.

Sibley, M. (2020). Attachments to victimhood: Anti-trafficking narratives and the criminalization of the sex trade. *Social & Legal Studies*, 29, 5: 699–717.

Sibley, M., & van der Meulen, E. (2023). Courting victims: Exploring the legal framing of exploitation in human trafficking cases. *Canadian Journal of Law and Society*, 37, 3: 409–429.

Soderlund, G. (2005). Running from the rescuers: New U.S. crusades against sex trafficking and the rhetoric of abolition. *NWSA Journal*, 17, 3: 64–87.

Strauss, K., & McGrath, S. (2017). Temporary migration, precarious employment and unfree labour relations: Exploring the "continuum of exploitation" in Canada's Temporary Foreign Worker Program. *Geoforum*, 78: 199–208.

Suchland, J. (2015). *Transnational feminism, postsocialism, and the politics of sex trafficking*. Duke University Press.

van der Meulen, E., & Durisin, E.M. (2008). Why decriminalize? How Canada's municipal and federal regulations increase sex workers' vulnerability. *Canadian Journal of Women and the Law*, 20, 2: 289–311.

___. (2018). Sex work policy: Tracing historical and contemporary developments. In E.M. Durisin, E. van der Meulen, & C. Bruckert (eds.), *Red light labour: Sex work regulation, agency, and resistance* (pp. 27–47). UBC Press.

Vosko, L. (2022). Temporary labour migration by any other name: Differential inclusion under Canada's "new" international mobility regime. *Journal of Ethnic and Migration Studies*, 48, 1: 129–152.

Vuolajärvi, N. (2019). Governing in the name of caring—the Nordic model of prostitution and its punitive consequences for migrants who sell sex. *Sexuality Research and Social Policy*, 16: 151–165.

___. (2022). *Criminalising the sex buyer: Experiences from the Nordic region*. London School of Economics, Centre for Women, Peace and Security. https://www.lse.ac.uk/women-peace-security/assets/documents/2022/W922-0152-WPS-Policy-Paper-6-singles.pdf

Weitzer, R. (2007). The social construction of sex trafficking: Ideology and institutionalization of a moral crusade. *Politics and Society*, 35, 30: 447–475.

___. (2011). Sex trafficking and the sex industry: The need for evidence-based theory and legislation. *The Journal of Criminal Law and Criminology*, 101, 4: 1337–1370.

___. (2020). Modern slavery and human trafficking. *Great Decisions*, 2020: 41–52.

Weller, A., & Cohen, A. (2018, May 1). Migrant farm workers vulnerable to sexual violence. *The Conversation*. https://theconversation.com/migrant-farm-workers-vulnerable-to-sexual-violence-95839/

Williamson, K., & Marcus, A. (2017). Black pimps matter: Racially selective identification and prosecution of sex trafficking in the United States. In A. Horning & A. Marcus (eds.), *Third party sex work and pimps in the age of anti-trafficking* (pp. 177–196). Springer International Publishing.

Woods, T.P. (2013). Surrogate selves: Notes on anti-trafficking and anti-Blackness. *Social Identities*, 19, 1: 120–134.

Wortley, S. (2019). *Halifax, Nova Scotia: Street checks report*. Nova Scotia Human Rights Commission. https://humanrights.novascotia.ca/sites/default/files/editor-uploads/halifax_street_checks_report_march_2019_0.pdf

Zwaigenbaum, J., Salami, B., & Tulli, M. (2021). *The ongoing exploitation of temporary foreign workers*. https://doi.org/10.7939/r3-t035-ge65

Cases

Canada (Attorney General) v. Bedford, 2013 SCC 72, [2013] 3 SCR 1101.

R. v. Domotor, 2011 ONSC 626.

Legislation

Anti-Human Trafficking Strategy Act, 2021, SO 2021, c. 21, Sched. 2 (Ontario).

Anti-Human Trafficking Act, 2017, SO 2017, c. 12 (Ontario).

Canadian Charter of Rights and Freedoms, Part 1 of the *Constitution Act*, 1982, Sched. B to the *Canada Act* 1982 (UK), 1982, c. 11.

Combating Human Trafficking Act, 2021, SO 2021, c. 21 (Ontario).

Convention on Migration for Employment, July 1, 1949, https://www.ilo.org/dyn/normlex/en/f?p=NORMLEXPUB:12100:0::NO::p12100_instrument_id:312242

Criminal Code, RSC 1985, c. C-46.

Immigration and Refugee Protection Act, SC 2001, c. 27.

International Convention on the Protection of the Rights of All Migrant Workers and Members of Their Families, December 18, 1990, https://www.ohchr.org/en/instruments-mechanisms/instruments/international-convention-protection-rights-all-migrant-workers

Migrant Workers (Supplementary Provisions) Convention, June 24, 1975, https://www.ilo.org/dyn/normlex/en/f?p=NORMLEXPUB:12100:0::NO::p12100_instrument_id:312288

Protection of Communities and Exploited Persons Act, SC 2014, c. 25.

Protocol to Prevent, Suppress and Punish Trafficking in Persons, Especially Women and Children, supplementing the United Nations Convention against Transnational Organized Crime, November 15, 2000, https://www.unodc.org/res/human-trafficking/2021the-protocol-tip_html/TIP.pdf

Section One

TRAFFICKING DISCOURSES AND REPRESENTATIONS

2

Beyond Carceral Humanitarianism

Antiblackness as the Structure of Anti-Trafficking Discourse

Lyndsey P. Beutin

In anticipation of Frederick Douglass's two hundredth birthday, Frederick Douglass Family Initiatives joined with the Antiracist Research and Policy Center at American University to generate a list of two hundred individuals who "embody the work and spirit of Douglass" (*The Guardian*, 2018, n.p.). Fifty people were recognized as "modern-day abolitionists" for the project. These activists worked in a range of areas, from racial justice and immigrant rights, to LGBT rights, to ending poverty and police brutality. Prison abolitionist Angela Y. Davis and Black Lives Matter cofounders Patrisse Cullors, Alicia Garza, and Opal Tometi were all honoured — as was one anti-trafficking advocate, Minh Dang. The list's celebration of anticarceral politics was paradoxical because Frederick Douglass Family Initiatives has primarily been involved with campaigns to end human trafficking, which are notorious for their use of policing, prisons, and border control in the name of ending exploitation. Such contradictions are made possible through anti-trafficking discourse: Frederick Douglass Family Initiatives links Douglass's abolitionist legacy to anti-trafficking advocacy by promoting the widely circulating claim that "human trafficking is modern-day slavery."

The terms "modern-day slavery" and "modern-day abolition" are used in many contemporary campaigns to support a wide-ranging set of political agendas that are often at cross-purposes. In this chapter, I first walk through the terms' variable meanings within two popular, but rarely overlapping, spheres: campaigns to end human trafficking and campaigns for prison abolition. Since the June 2020 uprisings for racial justice, the popularity of defunding the police, ending mass incarceration, and abolishing prisons has skyrocketed, and the terms have quickly been co-opted into a variety of reform-based initiatives. In this same period, anti-trafficking advocates issued numerous Black Lives Matter solidarity statements and rhetorically aligned themselves with racial justice campaigns. This shift marks a major change in their rhetoric; however, their carceral politics remain hostile to the Movement for Black Lives' platform of divesting from policing and investing in community. In the midst of a mainstream media reframing of "modern-day abolition" to mean carceral abolition (e.g., see Kolhatkar, 2021) instead of anti-trafficking efforts (e.g., see Mehdi, 2017), anti-trafficking organizations are suggesting that because they use the same language and historical imaginaries, they too are concerned with racial justice. In so doing, the deep-rooted racism of anti-trafficking discourse purports to have always been on the side of racial justice, but only once it is (relatively) politically fashionable to be.

Within this cultural and rhetorical milieu, critical anti-trafficking scholars have begun to more regularly identify the anti-Black racism present in anti-trafficking discourse by emphasizing its investment in carceral solutions. This development is important as it brings two fields — critical prison studies and critical anti-trafficking studies — closer together. I suggest, though, that as critical anti-trafficking scholars, we need to move beyond calling out carceral humanitarianism in our critiques, even though doing so is an efficient way to highlight the racial harms of anti-trafficking discourse. Limiting our understanding of the anti-Black racism of anti-trafficking to carcerality obscures how, I argue, anti-trafficking discourse is *constituted by* antiblack logics and narratives (Beutin, 2023; see also Saucier & Woods, 2014; Woods, 2013). Ultimately, I aim to show that the anti-trafficking apparatus cannot be redeemed, because it works to undermine racial justice movements that target structures of oppression. In other words, anti-trafficking discourse and its use of the language of slavery and abolition developed as a political solution to quell movements aimed at dismantling the structural legacies of transatlantic slavery and European colonialism.

Throughout the chapter, I distinguish antiblackness from racism, following João H. Costa Vargas and Moon-Kie Jung (2021), as it is crucial to understand that antiblackness is "an ontological condition of possibility of modern world sociality, whereas racism is an aspect of sociality" (p. 7). I further distinguish anti-Black racism — a specific type of racism against Black people, where "Black" is capitalized because it is an identity — from antiblackness, which refers to the relation of the construction of Blackness to the structuring forces of modernity and its arsenals of power, including the creation of the category of the Human through European liberal modernity's Enlightenment thought. If we follow this theoretical line, then it might seem that antiblackness structures *all* dominant discourse, but tracing it through anti-trafficking discourse provides a concrete example of what that means and why it matters.

The Many Abolitions: Antiprison, Anti-Trafficking, and Their Feminisms

For the past two decades, anti-trafficking discourse has made human trafficking visually, legally, and discursively synonymous with "modern-day slavery." The visual economy of anti-trafficking relies on slavery aesthetics, where images of suffering victims reference the dominant images of transatlantic slavery in the public imagination (Beutin, 2017; De Shalit et al., 2014). In the *Bellagio-Harvard Guidelines on the Legal Parameters of Slavery* (Research Network on the Legal Parameters of Slavery, 2012), anti-trafficking advocates and scholars created their own legal definition of slavery by broadening the definition of ownership to include the types of social control present in the narrowly circumscribed cases of human trafficking that the US State Department and transnational anti-trafficking organizations focus on (such as forced marriage in the Global South). The circularity of the discourse is compounded by the countless organizations that simply assert human trafficking is modern-day slavery on fact sheets and website FAQs. Alongside references to slavery, anti-trafficking advocates aggrandize themselves as modern-day abolitionists, often drawing explicitly on white abolitionist figures such as Abraham Lincoln and William Wilberforce.

Contemporary activists and scholars who envision a world without prisons and who work to eradicate the punitive criminal legal system often refer to themselves as prison abolitionists. The term invokes the history and memory of the fight to end slavery in the United States. It builds from W.E.B. Du Bois's (1935) notion of an "abolition democracy," a term popularized by scholar and antiprison activist Angela Y. Davis (1998, 2003, 2007), which refers to the unfinished and ongoing fight for full Black enfranchisement and self-determination within US democracy (see also Dilts, 2019; Rojas & Naber, 2022). Prison abolitionists anchor their analysis of the violence of the prison in structures of domination: white supremacy, antiblackness, capitalism, liberalism, and neoliberalism. By resisting carceral reforms, which ultimately strengthen carceral logics and infrastructures (Gilmore, 1998/99), prison abolitionists seek to create new worlds that re-envision what safety means (Abolition Collective, 2018; Petitjean, 2018). In the words of Mariame Kaba (2021),

> prison-industrial complex [PIC] abolition is a political vision, a structural analysis of oppression, and a practical organizing strategy.... PIC abolition is a vision of a restructured society in a world where we have everything we need: food, shelter, education, health, art, beauty, clean water, and more things that are foundational to our personal and community safety. (p. 2)

Far from anti-trafficking advocates' desire to abolish exploitation by incarcerating perpetrators, Kaba and others imagine what safety from state violence and its carceral institutions could look like.

The term "modern-day slavery" has been used to describe conditions within prison and to describe the structure of the prison itself. For example, the list of demands accompanying the 2018 national prison strike in the United States, coordinated by Jailhouse Lawyers Speak, included "an immediate end to prison slavery" (Michigan Abolition and Prisoner Solidarity, 2018, n.p.; see also Ware, 2018). Narratives of prison slavery have similarly been promoted by the Incarcerated Workers Organizing Committee, a prisoner-led project of the Industrial Workers of the World. The Incarcerated Workers Organizing Committee (n.d.) describes prison slavery as both the existential conditions of incarceration ("they feed us like animals ... and when [we're] sick leave us to die," n.p.) and the labour structure (unpaid work to keep jails and prisons running, and low-paid work for subcontracted private corporations). The discursive frame of prison slave labour has gained traction within the media, and many news outlets included the phrase "modern-day slavery" in headlines of the strike coverage. Critical prison scholars, who often identify as prison abolitionists in their activism, have helpfully delineated the limitations of the prison-is-slavery metaphor for understanding both what racial chattel slavery was and how the contemporary political economy of prisons functions. In particular, the use of the discursive frame of slave *labour* reduces the full scope of both prison and racial chattel slavery's investment in racialized social control (including control over enslaved and incarcerated women's reproduction)¹ to the narrow frame of unpaid or extremely low wages, which forestalls deeper understanding of how prisons also function as warehouses for a postindustrial racialized labour force now deemed surplus (Berger, 2016; Gilmore, 2007; Hinton, 2018; Kilgore, 2013; Stark, 2018).

The intersection of feminism and abolition has long been central to antiviolence and prison abolitionist organizing led by women of colour. It is grounded in the late 1990s and early 2000s collaborations between INCITE! Women of Color Against Violence and anticarceral group Critical Resistance that sought to "buil[d] a world without prisons and policing *and* buil[d] a world free of gender and sexual violence" (Davis et al., 2022, p. ix). The term "abolition feminism" has been re-energized within activism and public scholarship of late, in part because the popularization of carceral abolition has overlooked the foundational contributions of women of colour to its praxis, necessitating correctives. Recent publications have worked to correct the record by explicating what abolition feminism means within anticarceral activism (e.g., Bierria et al., 2022; Davis et al., 2022) and by situating the term in longer activist genealogies of both "anticarceral feminist politics" (Thuma, 2019, p. 2) and "anti-imperialist abolition feminism" (Rojas & Naber, 2022, p. 17). Within anticarceral orientations, abolition feminism refers to "the relationality of state and individual violence" (Davis et al., 2022, pp. 2–3), which requires the simultaneous dismantling of state violence, gender and sexual violence, policing, heteropatriarchy, and racial capitalism. This meaning and usage, though, is in opposition to conceptualizations of "abolition feminists" within critical anti-trafficking studies and sex work studies.

Within the critical scholarly fields of anti-trafficking and sex work, scholars use the term "abolitionist feminists" to refer to anti-prostitution feminists who want to abolish or eradicate all forms of sex work. So-called abolitionist feminists got this title through their metaphorical sloganeering at the United Nations about "ending sexual slavery" (Kang, 2020), which was itself an invocation of the memory of transatlantic slavery and abolition. Although the term "abolition" follows from their appropriated use of slavery, Mechthild Nagel (2015) suggests using the more precise descriptor "prohibitionists" for anti-prostitution and anti–sex work advocates, since their agendas rely on "outlawing desires" (p. 9), upholding paternalism, and activating moral panics, rather than advancing anything akin to feminism (see also Durisin et al., 2018, p. 7). Further, anti-trafficking advocates who have been labelled abolitionist feminists endorse carceral approaches to ending sex work, including completely illegalizing prostitution and criminalizing those who purchase sexual services. For decades, sex worker activists and feminist scholars critical of anti-trafficking policy have delineated the many harms that result from what Elizabeth Bernstein (2010) terms "carceral feminism," where carceral solutions are used to help women (see also Whalley & Hackett, 2017). In response to these critiques, some anti-trafficking organizations have begun to champion approaches that seem to move away from overtly carceral solutions, such as focusing on survivor services or generating data from reporting apps. Yet the reforms they endorse ultimately reinforce what Judah Schept (2015) calls "carceral habitus," which refers to how carcerality can be rhetorically rejected but materially replicated because its hegemonic logics structure what is imagined as common sense about care, crime, and responsibility (pp. 10–11). According to Annie Fukushima, Annie Hill, and Jennifer Suchland (2021), "What may appear as a softer or more humane side of the anti-trafficking movement continues to be linked to punitive systems and can result in the criminalisation of survivors and precarious labourers" (p. 6).

Across two modern-day slaveries (trafficking and prison), two modern-day abolitions (ending trafficking and ending prisons and policing), and two abolition feminisms (one for carcerality and one against), we see the same terms are used to advance different historical imaginaries about freedom and different political visions for futures of freedom. In her essay on the uses of abolition in contemporary politics, Robyn Maynard (2018) writes, "As Black, feminist anticarceral activism reaches new heights, it is now more than ever essential to intervene in any invocations of abolition that participate in the resubjugation of Black people, particularly of Black women" (p. 282). Maynard is highlighting how anti-trafficking policies advance the criminalization of Black women sex workers and call it "abolition feminism." The incongruence is striking: anti-trafficking discourse invokes the historic fight to end racial slavery and Black unfreedom in order to advocate for contemporary carceral solutions that promote Black captivity and social control.

Naming the feminist principles and commitments of carceral abolition has been especially important for differentiating it from carceral feminism because of "carceral feminism's paradoxical insistence that safety from gendered violence can only be achieved through … carceral control" (Bierria et al., 2022, p. 3). While prison abolitionists position feminism as central to the work of ending all punitive systems, critical anti-trafficking scholars too often refer to people who pursue carceral approaches to women's safety domestically and internationally as abolitionist feminists. Understanding the opposite meanings of the term in two related fields is crucial as critical prison studies and critical anti-trafficking studies scholars begin to engage each other more frequently in multidisciplinary exchange in pursuit of their shared investment in dismantling carceral humanitarianism.

Carceral Humanitarianism

James Kilgore (2014) coined the term "carceral humanism" to describe the phenomenon whereby prisons are rendered as social service providers or forms of care. Rebranding prisons as care increases public funding for them, expands carceral logics of justice, and redeems criminal legal systems amid growing protest against police, jails, prisons, and detention centres. For me, carceral humanism also draws attention to how liberalism itself is a racial project that was constituted through what Charles Mills (2008) has termed the "intrawhite agreement," where white people recognized one another's so-called universal human rights by relegating nonwhite people to an inferior status (p. 1386). Within the context of critical anti-trafficking studies, though, I prefer to use the closely related term "carceral humanitarianism" because it builds from critical prison studies while streamlining critical anti-trafficking's oft-invoked phrase, "militarized humanitarianism meets carceral feminism" (Bernstein, 2010). It does so in three important ways: first, it drops the confounding use of "feminism" since ultimately "prison is not feminist" (Mariame Kaba, quoted by Thuma & Hankins, 2022, p. 61); second, it acknowledges how deeply entwined national, international, corporate, imperial, and state projects of social control are; and third, it provocatively draws attention to how contemporary carcerality *continues*, rather than sullies, humanitarianism's long tradition of offering benevolent rhetorical cover to racializing and colonizing projects. Both "carceral humanism" and "carceral humanitarianism" articulate the function of carceral reform within contemporary *neo*liberalism, but these dynamics of "penal benevolence" (Schept, 2015, p. 29) have been around as long as the prison itself.

Within contemporary anti-trafficking discourse, policy, and practice, carceral humanitarianism takes many forms. Elena Shih (2021b), for instance, has shown how new licensing requirements for Asian massage parlours appear to be anti-trafficking policy reforms designed to reduce sensationalized police stings and raids, but nevertheless strengthen the "trafficking-deportation pipeline" through policing. The activist push to decriminalize sex work has led to anti-trafficking organizations adopting the so-called Swedish model, which in theory criminalizes sex buyers rather than sellers, but many sex work organizations have demonstrated how this approach makes sex work less safe (Lepp & Gerasimov, 2019). Jennifer Musto (2016) has documented how forms of "carceral protection" intended to be victim-centred, less harmful interventions in sex workers' lives have only created new forms of carcerality for workers to navigate and resist.

The carceral humanitarianism of anti-trafficking has been most commented upon in its relationship to sex work, but it extends far beyond this context. For instance, major US-based international anti-trafficking nongovernmental organizations (NGOs) collaborate with and train police in different countries to arrest whom they refer to as "modern-day slaveholders" — in particular, small cacao farmers in the Ivory Coast (e.g., see Woods & Blewett, 2000) and small owners of brick and carpet businesses in India (e.g., see Free the Slaves, 2017). Some anti-trafficking organizations use drones to aerially surveil rural communities in Africa and Asia in order to spot "slavery from space" (Jackson & Wardlaw, 2017, n.p.) or collaborate with defence contractors and geospatial intelligence corporations to use satellite imagery to rescue "children from enslavement" (International Justice Mission, 2020, p. 16). Anti-trafficking NGOs are known to collaborate with the Ghanaian police to arrest parents of children who fish in rural communities in Lake Volta (Okyere et al., 2021). Ethnographic research with the affected families revealed a string of violent arrests of parents (who were later released without charges) and kidnapping of children by NGOs (Okyere et al., 2021). The notoriously militarized organization Operation Underground Railroad proclaims that arresting Black sex-working women in Haiti is freeing child sex slaves from their pathological mothers and culture (Beutin, 2022). These arrests in both Ghana and Haiti provide the humanitarian imagery that reinforces the long-standing antiblack narratives of Enlightenment liberal philosophy that Africans (and African diasporic subjects) are not capable of remaining in freedom when left to their own self-governance and, without white oversight, will slip back into their natural state of slavery, including by enslaving each other (Beutin, 2023).

All of these examples are part of the larger anti-trafficking apparatus, which is bolstered and underpinned by the US Department of State, which, through its annual Trafficking in Persons Report, operates as global sheriff (Chuang, 2014) by policing all other states' anti-trafficking policies to ensure they align with the US minimum standards. The anti-trafficking apparatus, beyond any one intervention or example, is a thoroughly carceral apparatus. Understanding this larger framework of carcerality is important because some anti-trafficking organizations, such as Freedom United (n.d.), have begun to adopt decriminalization strategies in regard to sex work and promote petitions to "abolish prison slavery in the U.S." (n.p.), while continuing to promote campaigns and imagery that derive from Trafficking in Persons Reports and anti-trafficking organizations, such as the paradigmatic image of child trafficking on cacao farms in the Ivory Coast.

Anti-Trafficking and Solidarity with Black Lives Matter: Three Approaches

Amid so many blatant examples of the anti-trafficking industry's carceral humanitarianism, it is not hard to see how anti-trafficking modern-day abolition is at cross-purposes with carceral abolition, and how policing in order to "free slaves" will negatively affect Black and racialized people globally. It should be clear that anti-trafficking organizations are not aligned with the platform of the Movement for Black Lives. Yet, in June 2020, many anti-trafficking organizations issued statements in support of Black Lives Matter. The arguments in these statements centred on several recurring themes that can be summarized in three threads: anti-trafficking is already concerned with racial justice because trafficking is modern-day slavery (a rhetorical sleight of hand), more attention needs to be paid to the specific vulnerabilities of Black populations to trafficking, and multicultural reforms to existing anti-trafficking initiatives are needed.

The first ruse of solidarity comes from anti-trafficking organizations that are deeply embedded in the carceral apparatus of anti-trafficking and use carceral solutions to end trafficking, such as International Justice

Mission, Polaris, and Stop the Traffik. For instance, Polaris (2020), one of the most prominent anti-trafficking NGOs in the US, issued the following statement:

> Polaris stands in solidarity with all who are protesting the violence against Black Americans and the systemic injustice in our communities. We mourn the many incidents of police brutality that overwhelmingly plague Black communities. This violation of human rights affects us, our families, our friends, and our neighbors — and victims and survivors of human trafficking we serve. (n.p.)

The organization, though, has a long history of collaborating with the police through its National Human Trafficking Hotline. Through its program targeting Asian massage businesses, it also has a history of promoting racial profiling. Elena Shih (2021a) has shown how even when Polaris tries to distance itself from its police collaborations by encouraging citizens to "spot the signs" of trafficking and call the hotline rather than the police, the citizen surveillance interventions still result in notification to police services. An organization that has long contributed to the criminalization of sex work, that has promoted racial profiling as a strategy to end trafficking, and that profits from collaborations with the police erroneously (and opportunistically) configures itself in solidarity with Black Lives Matter.

Other anti-trafficking organizations sought to connect their work to racial justice and Black Lives Matter solidarity by describing the relationship between race and trafficking. In statements and articles, they emphasized Black vulnerability to being trafficked. It's a Penalty (2020), a UK-based organization that uses anti-trafficking advertising at major world sporting events to "end modern slavery," drew on the historical racial imaginaries of slavery to connect trafficking to race, proclaiming in one statement, "Victims of human trafficking and exploitation are typically treated as chattel property; these crimes strongly resonate as a contemporary legacy of the colonial past" (n.p.). By invoking colonialism but leaving it unspecified, the organization implicitly draws on the highly sensationalized assumption that sex workers are being "bought and sold." The statement goes on to describe how systemic racism makes Black people more vulnerable to sex trafficking, but frames vulnerability in ways that pathologize, and ultimately blame, Black families themselves. It specifically identifies "household issues: exposure to sexual exploitation, substance abuse, childhood abuse" and being "raised within the child-welfare system" as examples of risk factors. Doing so builds on narratives and stereotypes that have been mobilized to blame Black families for the harms caused by structural racism. This framing continues a long line of anti-trafficking narratives that indict Black families for "enslaving" or harming their own children and disregards the racial harms caused by anti-trafficking organizations.

Still, it is notable that some anti-trafficking organizations connect their work to Black Lives Matter by naming what they see as the relevance of race to trafficking crimes. For two decades the anti-trafficking apparatus has gone to great lengths to do just the opposite: to distance so-called modern-day slavery from race (Hua, 2011; Woods, 2014). By previously arguing that "today, anyone can be a slave," anti-trafficking advocacy minimized historical injustice against Black people in order to maximize its appeal to philanthrocapitalists (see Chuang, 2015). Now, though, anti-trafficking organizations connect race and trafficking to take advantage of the media popularization of abolition as a racial justice discourse.

Some anti-trafficking advocates took a different approach: to identify the racism within anti-trafficking organizations themselves. In an op-ed for the Thomson Reuters Foundation (which specializes in covering anti-trafficking advocacy with funding from the Omidyar Network), UK-based anti-trafficking advocate Debbie Ariyo (2020) explains that although most victims of trafficking are racialized and are immigrants, most anti-trafficking organizations are predominately white or otherwise not culturally competent. She calls for more racially diverse staff at organizations and more cultural competency training for the police. Naming the racial identities of anti-trafficking staff members helps broader publics understand some of the white saviour and white burden dynamics at play in the most powerful and well-funded anti-trafficking organizations (see Baker, 2019; Heynen & van der Meulen, 2022; Kempadoo, 2015). However, it also limits understanding of the scope of the role that race and racism play in the anti-trafficking apparatus. In so doing, the potential for radical change is reduced to a set of relatively easily incorporable multicultural reforms. The deeper connections between anti-trafficking discourse and white supremacy are elided and rendered into multicultural actions that, especially in the case of police training, end up giving more funding and legitimacy to the police, not less.

The Limits of the Critique of Carceral Humanitarianism

Several critical anti-trafficking scholars responded to the paradox of anti-trafficking organizations' Black Lives Matter solidarity statements in real time. In a blog post for the critical anti-trafficking group Global Alliance Against Traffic in Women, Jennifer Suchland (2020) describes how the carcerality of anti-trafficking policy and discourse undermines such attempts at solidarity. Drawing on the work of Black and Indigenous feminists, activists, and prison abolitionists, she aptly describes how criminal legal approaches to ending trafficking continue to dominate and underpin anti-trafficking efforts, which perpetuates rather than ameliorates state violence. Similarly, several critical anti-trafficking researchers interviewed for another Thomson Reuters Foundation article about racial bias within anti-trafficking criticized the industry's reliance on the criminal legal system, which prioritizes longer prison sentences over addressing structural causes and is itself a system that is "biased against Black people" (Murray, 2020, n.p.). While these critiques are important, I would like to urge us as critical scholars to move beyond relying on carceral humanitarianism to point out the racism of the anti-trafficking apparatus. Although expedient, it nevertheless reduces our understanding of how antiblackness fundamentally *constitutes* the entire enterprise of anti-trafficking.

The stakes of moving beyond the critique of carceral humanitarianism become apparent when contemplating the solutions that critical scholars have proposed. According to the Reuters article, several researchers suggested that "organizations should consider allying with groups looking at broader structural problems related to trafficking from poverty to prison reform and immigration to domestic violence" (Murray, 2020, n.p.). Indeed, important critical scholars have recommended that anti-trafficking organizations "work in alliance and solidarity" with organizations focused on structural oppressions (Suchland, 2020), or complicate, but maintain, the historical analogy of modern-day slavery to stretch the anti-trafficking analysis of the relations among borders, prison, property, migration, and the legacies of slavery (Duane &

Meiners, 2021). Unfortunately, these proposed solutions fundamentally miss what anti-trafficking discourse and policy accomplishes within the overarching global sociopolitical context. There is no room to reform the anti-trafficking industry precisely *because* it operates as a political solution to contain the social movements such critical authors argue anti-trafficking advocates should align with. For anti-trafficking to be in solidarity with movements to end structures of oppression would require the complete dismantling, destruction, and defunding of the anti-trafficking apparatus.

Long-term media ethnographic discourse analysis of the anti-trafficking apparatus allows us to see the meta-register of the political project of anti-trafficking (Beutin, 2023). Anti-trafficking discourse, policy, and practice are not broken. The limitations of the anti-trafficking apparatus exist because it is a discursive political solution designed to maintain the status quo. The political agenda of the anti-trafficking apparatus is unquestionably counterrevolutionary on all fronts. The anti-trafficking apparatus has been effective at garnering widespread support from powerful actors because it offers state-friendly and corporate-friendly solutions to the myriad problems that racial capitalism and racial liberalism create. Far from being a coincidence of overlapping terminology, anti-trafficking policy and discourse came about in the 1990s and early 2000s in ways that solved political problems for states and corporations, entities whose legitimacy was being actively challenged and undermined by transnational and anticorporate globalization social movements organizing to end sweatshops, abolish prisons, and fight for reparations for slavery. As present-day anti-trafficking organizations increasingly incorporate the language of decriminalization, police reform, and racial justice into their work, it is imperative that critical scholars articulate with precision and depth what makes anti-trafficking carceral and what makes anti-trafficking structurally antiblack. It is, I argue, the union of anti-trafficking's antiblack logics and carcerality that make it a flexible and durable *political solution* that upholds corporate and state interests amid changing discursive contexts and transnational agitation for a better world.

Conclusion: How Antiblackness Structures Anti-Trafficking Discourse

In *White Reconstruction*, Dylan Rodríguez (2021) describes how humanitarianism co-opted Black revolutionary movements in the 1960s and 1970s in ways that reconstituted white dominance in new forms. Humanitarianism, in other words, was a response to the threat to white hegemony that civil rights and Black Power movements posed. Rodríguez is concerned with the buildup of carceral logics and infrastructure in the United States and the ways that humanitarianism and philanthropy further carcerality's same political agenda — to maintain the status quo of white power — but in different guises. He writes that post–civil rights, humanitarianism

> across corporate, state, and civil society institutions was not only "designed to counter the potentially revolutionary thrust of the recent [B]lack rebellions in major cities across the country," [Allen, 1969, p.17] but was also a defense of the integrity of White Being in-and-of-itself at a historical conjuncture in which its hemispheric ascendancy was destabilized by the successful overthrow of the Jim Crow apartheid social form. (Rodríguez, 2021, p. 5)

In other words, white reconstruction was necessary for "white self-vindication" in the aftermath of 1970s national racial reckoning. Humanitarianism provided a path for this reconstruction, undermining the actual revolutionary social movements in its midst.

Anti-trafficking discourse and policy fit neatly into this theoretical matrix and provide a hefty empirical case for understanding how carcerality, humanitarianism, and the reconstitution of a guilt-free white sense of self work together in the present, through a combination of political agendas and narrative structures. Anti-trafficking discourse is much more than harmful to migrants and sex workers. It is *helpful* to those it ultimately is designed to serve: powerful state and nonstate actors invested in maintaining the status quo of white supremacy (Kempadoo, 2015). Anti-trafficking discourse helps these entities and actors in several ways, including by creating tax breaks, securing billionaire control of global governance, and providing absolution for corporate greed and capitalism's depravations. Notably, it also produces "white indemnity," a rhetorical insurance policy against being held liable for slavery's racial dispossessions (see Beutin, 2023).

Anti-trafficking discourse does this work through two strategies: (a) mobilizing the rhetoric of modern-day slavery to describe contemporary trafficking, and (b) relying on, and reproducing, several key narrative structures that sutured whiteness to human freedom and Blackness to unfreedom in liberal modernity. For instance, anti-trafficking discourse is underpinned by the narrative that Africans have always enslaved and continue to enslave themselves. Having traced how the terms "modern-day slavery" and "modern-day abolition" offer rhetorical cover for the anti-trafficking industry's racism and carcerality amid the popularization of defunding the police and racial justice movements more broadly, I conclude this chapter by summarizing some of my findings from long-term media ethnographic research of anti-trafficking discourse in order to illustrate my larger claim that antiblackness is the structure of anti-trafficking discourse. The antiblackness of anti-trafficking, in other words, cannot be reduced to its carceral humanitarianism alone.

Anti-trafficking discourse uses the term "modern-day slavery" to suggest that slavery is anti-modern and thus has no place in the modern world. This usage promotes the long-standing European and North American alibi that racial chattel slavery was a premodern system reflecting the unenlightened, premodern views of colonial ancestors, which was phased out once capitalism's more efficient, race-neutral, and profitable modes took over. It minimizes the historical importance of transatlantic slavery to the world economy and social structures and attempts to rhetorically reduce the culpability of former slaving nations and empires. "Modern-day slavery" is further used to suggest that slavery in the United States, Canada, and Europe reflected outdated racial views that Western nations overcame long ago through nineteenth-century abolition movements, which continued through twentieth-century civil rights movements transnationally. In so doing, former slaving nations render themselves as harbingers of freedom, who have long fought to end slavery and will continue to do so in places "where slavery is worst" today (Free the Slaves, n.d.). Astoundingly, Haiti and Ghana — historical locations of a successful slave revolt and an African anticolonial independence movement, respectively — are also two common places where anti-trafficking organizations invoke this discourse. Selecting these sites as evidence of where slavery is worst turns some of the most spectacular wins for Black freedom into empirical proof that Black freedom leads to chaos and re-enslavement, and importantly, that Black people have no one to blame for it but themselves.

Such rhetorical maneuvers attempt to provide visual evidence, backed by NGO metrics and accounting, for the white slavers' alibi that slavery in Africa predated transatlantic slavery, continued after the British imperial abolition of slavery, and continues (or re-emerges) today. These temporal layers compound within the discourse to uphold Enlightenment-era ideologies — to prove, once and for all, with so-called empirical evidence gathered by anti-trafficking NGOs — that African and African diasporic people are naturally slaves, that they are incapable of self-governance (see Lowe, 2015), that left to their own devices they will revert to their natural state of slavery and of enslaving each other, that they have and always will enslave each other without white oversight and intervention, and that they are incapable of imagining their own freedom (see Trouillot, 1995) and therefore are not entitled to it. Each of these scripts are the building blocks of the overarching idea and narrative of "Black unfitness for freedom" that justified the enslavement of Africans and naturalized the contradistinction between Black pathology and white rationality, and thus the exclusively white right to self-determination and freedom (Silva, 2007). These logics were invented to justify transatlantic slavery and global white supremacy in their inception, and anti-trafficking discourse leverages them in the name of ending slavery today. Doing so preserves the status quo of racial unfreedom and calls it abolition.

Yet even when anti-trafficking attaches modern-day slavery to non-Black populations and geographies, such as the paradigmatic Indian brick kiln worker, the discourse is structured through antiblackness. Asian workers are rendered as incorporable subjects who need simple technological fixes (such as recorded messages about human rights on their cell phones) to help them "mature" beyond lingering backward ways (Free the Slaves, 2016). When anti-trafficking organizations find modern slaves that are not Black, the injustice is presented as *beyond racial* in an attempt to multiculturalize slavery, severing the legacy of slavery from the "black-white binary" and redistributing the blame for past and present injustice.

Understanding how epistemological and ontological antiblackness structures anti-trafficking discourse allows us to see that the antiblackness of anti-trafficking is not reducible to instances of anti-Black racism within anti-trafficking organizations, nor to racial asymmetries in vulnerability to trafficking crimes, nor to a carceral agenda. Building on Christina Sharpe's (2016) work, antiblackness must be understood as the total climate in which anti-trafficking discourse gains widespread popularity among diverse constituencies and extensive institutional support from multilateral organizations, universities, corporations, and former slaving nations. The predecessors of these actors and entities legitimated European liberal modernity's racial narratives that naturalized and institutionalized global white supremacy through legal, social, and scientific discourses and thought. Their successors now mobilize the narratives to escape culpability for a past of racial injustice and, most recently, to claim solidarity with racial justice movements of the present.

Acknowledgment

Thanks to Rose Houglet for her assistance in gathering documents that supported this chapter.

Note

1. For an excellent analysis of how control of Black women's reproduction under racial chattel slavery differs from that under post-Emancipation carceral regimes, but in ways that continue to suit state and market agendas, see LeFlouria (2015).

References

Abolition Collective. (2018). Manifesto of the Abolition Journal. *Abolition: A Journal of Insurgent Politics*, 1: 4–7.

Ariyo, D. (2020, June 17). Opinion: Black Lives Matter and the UK's anti-trafficking sector. *Thomson Reuters Foundation News*. https://news.trust.org/item/20200616141000-y3ec4/

Baker, C. (2019). Racialized rescue narratives in public discourse on youth prostitution and sex trafficking in the United States. *Politics & Gender*, 15: 773–800.

Berger, D. (2016, November 18). Rattling the cages. *Jacobin*. https://jacobinmag.com/2016/11/prison-strike-slavery-attica-racism-incarceration/

Bernstein, E. (2010). Militarized humanitarianism meets carceral feminism: The politics of sex, rights, and freedom in contemporary antitrafficking campaigns. *Signs*, 36, 1: 45–71.

Beutin, L.P. (2017). Black suffering for/from anti-trafficking advocacy. *Anti-Trafficking Review*, 9: 14–30.

———. (2022). There's a trafficking jam on the Underground Railroad: Black abolitionist

icons and anti-trafficking media. *Feminist Media Studies.* https://doi.org/10.1080/14680777.2022.2149592
___. (2023). *Trafficking in antiblackness: Modern-day slavery, white indemnity, and racial justice.* Duke University Press.
Bierria, A., Caruthers, J., & Lober, B. (2022). *Abolition feminisms: Vol. 1. Organizing, survival, and transformative practice.* Haymarket Press.
Chuang, J. (2014). Exploitation creep and the unmaking of human trafficking law. *American Journal of International Law,* 108, 4: 609–649.
___. (2015). Giving as governance? Philanthrocapitalism and modern-day slavery abolitionism. UCLA *Law Review,* 62, 6: 1516–1556.
Davis, A.Y. (1998). Race and criminalization: Black Americans and the punishment industry. In W. Lubiano (ed.), *The house that race built* (pp. 264–279). Vintage Books.
___. (2003). *Are prisons obsolete?* Seven Stories Press.
___. (2007) *Abolition democracy: Beyond empire, prisons, and torture.* Seven Stories Press.
Davis, A.Y., Dent, G., Meiners, E.R., & Richie, B.E. (2022). *Abolition. Feminism. Now.* Haymarket Books.
De Shalit, A., Heynen, R., & van der Meulen, E. (2014). Human trafficking and media myths: Federal funding, communication strategies, and Canadian anti-trafficking programs. *Canadian Journal of Communication,* 39, 3: 385–412.
Dilts, A. (2019). Crisis, critique, and abolition. In B.E. Harcourt & D. Fassin (eds.), *A time for critique* (pp. 230–251). Columbia University Press.
Du Bois, W.E.B. (1935). *Black reconstruction in America, 1860–1880.* Free Press.
Duane, A.M. & Meiners, E.R. (2021). Working analogies: Slavery now and then. In G. LeBaron, J. Pliley, & D. Blight (eds.), *Fighting modern slavery and human trafficking* (pp. 56–72). Cambridge University Press.
Durisin, E.M., van der Meulen, E., & Bruckert C. (2018). Contextualizing sex work: Challenging discourses and confronting narratives. In E.M. Durisin, E. van der Meulen, & C. Bruckert (eds.), *Red light labour: Sex work regulation, agency, and resistance* (pp. 3–26). UBC Press.
Free the Slaves. (2016, August 23). *How mobile phones provide hope for slaves in India.* https://www.freetheslaves.net/how-mobile-phones-provide-hope-to-slaves-in-india/
___. (2017, February 27). *What freedom looks like.* [Video]. Agape Visuals. https://www.youtube.com/watch?v=kdVKcIZlumo&t=100s
___. (n.d.). *Training and capacity building.* https://www.freetheslaves.net/our-work/community-liberation-initiative/
Freedom United. (n.d.). *End child exploitation in cocoa.* https://www.freedomunited.org/advocate/chocolate-companies/
Fukushima, A.I., Hill, A. & Suchland, J. (2021). Editorial: Anti-trafficking education: Sites of care, knowledge, and power. *Anti-Trafficking Review,* 17: 1–18.
Gilmore, R.W. (1998/99). Globalization and US prison growth: From military Keynesianism to post-Keynesian militarism. *Race & Class,* 40, 2/3: 171–188.
___. (2007). *Golden gulag: Prisons, surplus, crisis, and opposition in globalizing California.* University of California Press.
The Guardian. (2018, July 5). Frederick Douglass 200. https://www.theguardian.com/commentisfree/ng-interactive/2018/jul/05/the-frederick-douglass-200
Heynen, R., & van der Meulen, E. (2022). Anti-trafficking saviors: Celebrity, slavery, and branded activism. *Crime, Media, Culture: An International Journal,* 18, 2: 301–323.
Hinton, E. (2018, November 2). *"Prison slavery?"* [Presentation]. Gilder Lehrman Center

for the Study of Slavery, Resistance, and Abolition, Yale University, New Haven, CT.

Hua, J. (2011). *Trafficking women's human rights*. University of Minnesota Press.

Incarcerated Workers Organizing Committee. (n.d.). About. https://incarceratedworkers.org/about

International Justice Mission. (2020). *2020 Year in Review*. https://www.ijm.org/2020-year-in-review-full-report

It's a Penalty. (2020). *Solidarity statement: Black Lives Matter*. https://itsapenalty.org/2020/06/30/solidarity-statement-black-lives-matter/

Jackson, B., & Wardlaw, J. (2017, June 1). *Slavery from space*. The Rights Lab. https://blogs.nottingham.ac.uk/rights/2017/06/01/walkfree5/

Kaba, M. (2021). *We do this 'til we free us: Abolitionist organizing and transforming Justice*. Haymarket Books.

Kang, L.H.Y. (2020). *Traffic in Asian women*. Duke University Press.

Kempadoo, K. (2015). The modern-day white (wo)man's burden: Trends in anti-trafficking and anti-slavery campaigns. *Journal of Human Trafficking*, 1: 8–20.

Kilgore, J. (2013, August 9). The myth of prison slave labor camps in the U.S. *Counterpunch*. https://www.counterpunch.org/2013/08/09/the-myth-of-prison-slave-labor-camps-in-the-u-s/

___. (2014, June 6). Repackaging mass incarceration. *Counterpunch*. https://www.counterpunch.org/2014/06/06/repackaging-mass-incarceration/

Kolhatkar, S. (2021, November 15). Abolition through the ages: Reform versus transformation, then and now. *Yes Magazine*. https://www.yesmagazine.org/social-justice/2021/11/15/abolition-reform-vs-transformation

LeFlouria, T. (2015). *Chained in silence: Black women and convict labor in the New South*. UNC Press.

Lepp, A., & Gerasimov, B. (2019). Gains and challenges in the global movement for sex workers' rights. *Anti-Trafficking Review*, 12: 1–13.

Lowe, L. (2015). *The intimacies of four continents*. Duke University Press.

Maynard, R. (2018). Do Black sex workers' lives matter? Whitewashed anti-slavery, racial justice, and abolition. In E.M. Durisin, E. van der Meulen, & C. Bruckert (eds.), *Red light labour: Sex work, regulation, agency, and resistance* (pp. 281–292). UBC Press.

Mehdi, A. (2017, February 9). The modern-day abolitionist movement. *Forbes*. https://www.forbes.com/sites/stratfor/2017/02/09/the-modern-day-abolitionist-movement/

Michigan Abolition and Prisoner Solidarity. (2018, June 4). National prison strike: Jailhouse Lawyers Speak [press release]. https://michiganabolition.org/national-prison-strike-jailhouse-lawyers-speak-press-release/

Mills, C.W. (2008). Racial liberalism. *PMLA*, 123, 5: 1380–1397.

Murray, C. (2020, June 25). Victims and villains: Anti-trafficking movement urged to tackle racial bias. *Thomson Reuters Foundation*. https://www.reuters.com/article/us-usa-race-trafficking-trfn-idUSKBN23W30S

Musto, J. (2016). *Control and protect: Collaboration, carceral protection, and domestic sex trafficking in the United States*. University of California Press.

Nagel, M. (2015). Trafficking with abolitionism: An examination of anti-slavery discourses. *Champ pénal/Penal field*, 12: 1–20.

Okyere, S., Agyeman, N., & Saboro, E. (2021). "Why was he videoing us?": The ethics and politics of audio-visual propaganda in child trafficking and human trafficking campaigns. *Anti-Trafficking Review*, 16: 47–68.

Petitjean, C. (2018, August 2). Prisons and class warfare: An interview with Ruth Wilson Gilmore. *Verso*. https://www.versobooks.com/blogs/3954-prisons-and-class-warfare-an-interview-with-ruth-wilson-gilmore

Polaris. (2020, June 3). *Polaris statement on protests after the murder of George Floyd.* https://polarisproject.org/press-releases/polaris-statement-on-protests-after-the-murder-of-george-floyd/

Research Network on the Legal Parameters of Slavery. (2012). *The Bellagio-Harvard guidelines on the legal parameters of slavery.* https://glc.yale.edu/sites/default/files/pdf/the_bellagio_harvard_guidelines_on_the_legal_parameters_of_slavery.pdf

Rodríguez, D. (2021). *White reconstruction: Domestic warfare and the logics of genocide.* Fordham University Press.

Rojas, C., & Naber, N. (2022). Genocide and "US" domination liberation, only we can liberate ourselves: Toward an anti-imperialist abolition feminism. In A. Bierria, J. Caruthers, & B. Lober (eds.), *Abolition feminisms: Vol. 1. Organizing, survival, and transformative practice* (pp. 11–57). Haymarket Press.

Saucier, P.K., & Woods, T.P. (2014). Ex aqua: The Mediterranean Basin, Africans on the move, and the politics of policing. *Theoria: A Journal of Social and Political Theory,* 61, 141: 55–75.

Schept, J. (2015). *Progressive punishment: Job loss, jail growth, and the neoliberal logic of carceral expansion.* NYU Press.

Sharpe, C. (2016). *In the wake: On Blackness and being.* Duke University Press.

Shih, E. (2021a). The fantasy of human trafficking: Training spectacles in racist surveillance. *Wagadu: A Journal of Transnational Women's and Gender Studies,* 22: 105–137.

___. (2021b). The trafficking deportation pipeline: Asian body work and the auxiliary policing of racialized poverty. *Feminist Formations,* 33, 1: 56–73.

Silva, D. F. (2007). *Toward a global idea of race.* University of Minnesota Press.

Stark, A. (2018, September 7). Like a game of chess: The prison strike and abolitionist strategy. *Abolition Journal.* https://abolitionjournal.org/like-a-game-of-chess/

Suchland, J. (2020, June 8). Anti-trafficking, policing, and state violence. GAATW. http://gaatw.org/blog/1055-anti-trafficking-policing-and-state-violence

Thuma, E.L. (2019). *All our trials: Prisons, policing, and the feminist fight to end violence.* University of Illinois Press.

Thuma, E.L. & Hankins, J. (eds.). (2022). Caring collectively: Twenty-five years of abolition feminism in California. In A. Bierria, J. Caruthers, & B. Lober (eds.), *Abolition feminisms: Vol. 1. Organizing, survival, and transformative practice* (pp. 58–85). Haymarket Press.

Trouillot, M-R. (1995). *Silencing the past: Power and the production of history.* Beacon Press.

Vargas, J.H.C. & Jung, M-K. (2021). Antiblackness of the social and the Human. In M-K. Jung & J.H.C. Vargas (eds.), *Antiblackness* (pp. 1–14). Duke University Press.

Ware, J. (2018, August 16). "I'm for disruption": Interview with prison strike organizer from Jailhouse Lawyers Speak. *Shadowproof.* https://shadowproof.com/2018/08/16/im-for-disruption-interview-with-prison-strike-organizer-from-jailhouse-lawyers-speak/

Whalley, E., & Hackett, C. (2017). Carceral feminisms: The abolitionist project and undoing dominant feminisms. *Contemporary Justice Review,* 20, 4: 456–473.

Woods, B., & Blewett, K. (2000). *Slavery: A global investigation* [film]. True Vision.

Woods, T. (2013). Surrogate selves: Notes on anti-trafficking and anti-Blackness. *Social Identities,* 19, 1: 120–143.

___. (2014). The anti-Blackness of "modern day slavery" abolitionism. *openDemocracy.* https://www.opendemocracy.net/en/beyond-trafficking-and-slavery/antiblackness-of-modernday-slavery-abolitionism/

3

Emergence and Convergence of the Pimp and Trafficker in Media Discourse

Creating a New Super Folk Devil

Stacey Hannem and Chris Bruckert

Stanley Cohen (1972) defined folk devils as figures depicted in media and folklore as deviant monsters who can be blamed for a host of social problems. According to Cohen, folk devils are symbolically and stereotypically constructed, the facts about them are exaggerated or fabricated, and they are expected to continue their immoral and dangerous behaviour, which must be stopped. In many ways, the pimp is a classic folk devil. Mere mention of the word "pimp" conjures up images of predatory men exploiting vulnerable and naive young women, who are lured or tricked into prostitution and controlled through violence, manipulation, drugs, or some combination of these factors. The perception that pimps are despicable parasites is, at least in part, conveyed and affirmed through media representations that "rely on a negative image of the 'pimp' as a male tyrant who profits from coercing his female victims into prostitution" (Mensah, 2018, p. 32). In Canada, as elsewhere, he is also often constituted as Black. As Leslie Ann Jeffrey and Gayle MacDonald (2006) document in their groundbreaking analysis of the moral panic fomented by the *Halifax Chronicle Herald*, the arrest of a few Black men from North Preston, Nova Scotia, on prostitution-related charges quickly grew into a "pimping panic" (p. 158) characterized by evocative images and detailed descriptions of violence featuring young white victims and brutal Black predators. Their research demonstrates that "the media failed to make any attempt to refute the easy racist assumptions that ... all pimps are black and ... that North Preston was full of black male sexual predators" (p. 160). Similarly, Maria Nengeh

Mensah's (2018) media analysis of the pimp uncovered key themes of gangsterism and sadistic violence while drawing attention to the ways "representations of the 'pimp' are also notable for racial stereotyping and stigmatic marking notes" (p. 31).

By contrast, the modern human trafficker[1] is a much more recent and decidedly more shadowy and undefined figure — vilified, but not ascribed a character profile. Perhaps this is not surprising given that "narratives of victims and saviours dominate media representations of trafficking" (De Shalit et al., 2014, p. 390). Of course, "it is difficult to see the trafficker as anything other than male, as somehow 'foreign' to Canada … and as irredeemably evil" (De Shalit et al., 2014, p. 403). Moreover, some (vague) attributes can be deduced from the narratives — including that the trafficker is savvy, profit-oriented, ruthless, and a member of a criminal organization (Durisin & van der Meulen, 2021). It is this very fluidity that, we argue, facilitates the mapping of the pimp trope onto the trafficker to the point that media routinely deploy the terms interchangeably. In this chapter we draw on the Canadian news media coverage from 1980 to 2022 to examine the evolution of the pimp trope before exploring shifts in the framing of human trafficking to tease out the process by which the "trafficker" came to be first discursively linked to, and then conflated with, the "pimp." Subsumed by old stereotypes, steeped in racism, ethnocentrism, classism, and gendered assumptions, the pimp/trafficker emerges as a super folk devil.

Methodology

This chapter draws on David L. Altheide and Christopher J. Schneider's (2012) method of qualitative media analysis and engages ethnographic content analysis to identify key discursive moments and thematic narratives around "pimps" and "traffickers" in Canadian print news media. We used the Factiva database to search "pimp*" and "sex traffick*" (both separately and together), resulting in a data set of 25,951 articles published in Canadian media sources from January 1, 1980, to July 31, 2022 — an astounding total of approximately 33,762 PDF pages.

Using the advanced search function in Adobe Acrobat, we conducted keyword searches of "pimp," "sex traffic," and "domestic human traffic" and reviewed the line-by-line context to identify relevant articles and references for more careful analysis.[2] In analyzing the data, we noted the timelines and points of discursive emergence, identifying the first times that certain terms appeared in Canadian media and the ways in which the terms were framed and presented in media or by key spokespeople (e.g., law enforcement, politicians, advocates, academics, and people with lived experience in the sex industry). Through comparisons across the data set, we were able to sketch the ways the pimp and the trafficker are constructed over time and shed light on the process of their discursive linkage.[3]

The Pimp Discourse

When we examine the media construction of the pimp from the 1980s into the 2000s, several consistent themes speak to the entrenched nature of the trope — pimps are underclass (affirmed through descriptions such as "drifter" and "of no fixed address"), often implicitly or explicitly described as Black,[4] and always men. Notably, while police casually mention that pimps "got the flash, they're dripping in gold chain and wear expensive color co-ordinated outfits" (Canadian Press, 1993, p. B6), for the most part, stigmatic assumptions about the "kind of person who" is a pimp are implied and pivot on so-called common knowledge. Indeed, so entrenched is the assumed shared knowledge that it functions as a foil to those who do not conform to the stereotype. When women or white middle-class men are charged under third-party anti–sex work provisions of the *Criminal Code*, the media carefully notes their markers of respectability (e.g., a former lawyer, a firefighter) and almost inevitably highlights that they are atypical — for example, "Blakely hardly looked the part of a madam or pimp" (Willcocks, 2014, p. D4). However, while the demographic profile of the pimp remains remarkably consistent, several significant, and intertwined, shifts in the discursive framing pivot on the modus operandi of pimps, their sophistication and effectiveness, and the nature of their relationship to sex workers. In the process, the agency ascribed to sex workers who are associated with pimps dissipates and eventually (virtually) disappears.

In 1986 the laws prohibiting communication for the purposes of engaging in prostitution (then s. 195.1 of the *Criminal Code*, now s. 213) were enacted, largely in response to gentrification and the subsequent mobilization by community groups who argued that they were the victims of (street) prostitution (van der Meulen & Durisin, 2018). In this context, and in the face of continued mobilization by these groups, individuals associated with the sex industry were framed as social problems that posed a threat to the (new) residents of established strolls. What is striking, seen through the lens of time, is the extent to which pimps and sex workers (and sometimes clients) were seen as a conjoined threat to communities and their inhabitants. Over the decade following the implementation of the communicating laws, newspapers make repeated reference to "prostitutes and their pimps" (Gorrie, 1996, p. A14) or, more often, "hookers and pimps" (Editorial Board, 1995, p. B2). Moreover, throughout the 1980s and into the 1990s, pimps are assumed to use violence to "control [women] for immoral purposes" (Thomas, 1987, p. A4) but are also understood to afford (much-needed) protection to workers. Several assumptions exist in uneasy tension. At the same time that pimps are thugs and despicable "parasites," there is a recognition that young sex workers have escaped families "that are physically, sexually or emotionally abusive" and may also be "fleeing from child welfare agencies" (Editorial Board, 1990, p. A14). Moreover, young women in the sex industry are not absolved of blame. This ascription of responsibility and disrepute (and, implicitly, agency) is particularly remarkable given the media's focus on so-called teen prostitutes, including, for example, a 14-year-old girl whom a judge described as "prostituting herself" (Darroch, 1987, p. F22).

Over a decade, from the mid-1980s to the mid-1990s, it appears — at least according to police and other claims makers quoted in the sources we examined — that the sex industry's profits increased remarkably. In 1986, income was pegged at $200/day (Darroch, 1986, p. H12); by 1994, one former street-based sex worker allegedly had "hundreds of thousands of dollars [pass] through her fingers every year" (Brazao & Welsh, 1994, p. C1). Concurrently, by the mid-1990s the pimp who was said to have talked young runaways escaping violence-filled homes into prostitution (e.g., see *Toronto Star*, 1989) is replaced by a much more sophisticated, organized, and professional character. At this point the narrative emerges that pimps are addicting young women to illicit substances to maximize control, but that is not all. "Badder pimps up prostitution ante" (Canadian Press, 1993, p. B6), proclaims a 1993 headline in the *Hamilton Spectator*. These "badder pimps" are simultaneously exceptionally violent and also skilled manipulators who systematically seduce before "turning out" their hapless victims:

> These men prey upon girls whom they identify as unhappy and vulnerable, initially showering them with affection and gifts — clothes, drugs, alcohol, expensive restaurants and clubs — until the young teenagers fall in love with their new "boyfriends." The girls are then turned out onto the street with orders to recoup the pimp's investment by selling their bodies — sometimes in fly-by-night trick pads where they may service literally scores of men a night. Girls who attempt to defy their captors are routinely tortured with a "pimp stick," a wire coat hanger unravelled and heated to red-hot on a stove. Their lives and those of their family members are routinely threatened. (*Canada NewsWire*, 1994, p. B6)

Interestingly, in the 1990s the pimp is still not, for the most part, envisioned as the cause of women's involvement in prostitution, but instead as someone who exploits opportunities rooted in childhood sexual and physical abuse or the deeply flawed child welfare system. The "failure of society" theme continues throughout the decade. That said, as the master manipulator pimp who lures young women becomes more present, we see the threat of exploitation slowly expand beyond runaways to include (any) young women — it is the beginning of the "anybody's daughter is at risk" trope. Not only do pimps continue to troll bus stations but they now lurk in shopping malls and even schools where non-runaways congregate: "Pimps can walk right into the school yard, they can spot somebody who has a problem and is off by themselves…. The kids are just pigeons and these guys come off acting really friendly and worried about what is wrong — they just hit on these kids" (Cox, 1993, p. A5). As the culpability of sex workers is mitigated by the predatory nature of the pimp, the framing of sex workers begins a metamorphosis and the agency ascribed (or perhaps over-ascribed, in the case of young teens) to them starts to erode.

Over the 2000s, several discursive shifts set the stage for the revisioning of sex workers as (agentless) victims (and, as discussed in the next section, trafficked women and girls). First, pimps are presented not only as manipulating, threatening, and coercing young women though violence, but as evil individuals who first groom and then "brainwash" (Hanes, 2004) the women until they fall under the pimp's "spell" (Banerjee, 2003). The "failure of society" theme disappears from the media at the same time as the threat posed by the pimp expands into middle-class homes.[5] In 2008, for example, there is a great deal of breathless press coverage about a young woman, meticulously described as a "straight-A" student and the daughter of "professionals":

> "You may be wondering to yourselves how is it possible that a 17-year-old straight-A high school student who lives at home with her family making $5 a day washing dishes, with aspirations to go to university, could possibly be working at an escort agency," the Crown said. "Mr. Mfizi is the reason. All of the evidence points to him and him alone, opening each and every door to the sex trade industry," Ms. Jenkins said. "Mr. Mfizi preyed on her." (Small, 2008, p. A14)

Furthermore, over the course of the decade, young women in the sex industry are increasingly referred to as children or young girls (even if seventeen years old), and, by the mid-aughts, teen prostitutes are (for the most part) "sexually exploited children" (Reynolds, 2007) and adult sex workers are increasingly (albeit not consistently) framed as "victims of the sex trade" (Agrell, 2005). At this point, the shift from active agent to victim is, if not complete, then well underway.

These discursive changes not only legitimate punitive police action against third parties and punitive protective action against young women in the sex industry (Bittle, 2018), but they are also reflected in law. In 2005, the Harper government sought to increase the federally legislated age of consent from fourteen to sixteen to address children's "risk of exploitation from much older sexual predators" (Toews 2005, n.p.), including "pimps" (Bailey, 2006).[6] In 2007 Alberta renamed its *Protection of Children Involved in Prostitution Act* the *Protection of Sexually Exploited Children Act*. As described next, the framing of pimps as sexually abusive predators and the erasure of sex worker agency coincides temporally with the emergence of the discourse of the "domestic sex trafficker."

The Trafficking (and Trafficker) Discourse

The earliest reports in Canadian media of human trafficking linked to sexual exploitation frame human trafficking as an international problem and perpetrators and victims as residing outside of Canada. In our data set, the first mention appears in a 1986 *Toronto Star* article, which references the work of American sociologist and anti-prostitution advocate Kathleen Barry, who described international human trafficking as "female sexual slavery" (Sweet, 1986, p. B1). Throughout the late 1980s and early 1990s, sporadic reports concerned with "trafficking in women" make claims regarding large numbers of Asian women trafficked into prostitution in places such as Bangladesh and Thailand, and Eastern European women trafficked into prostitution in the Netherlands. Media reports focus on estimates of the scope of the trafficking problem and on its foreign roots. Curiously, individual traffickers are absent from the narrative; they are stereotypically and generically framed as profit-motivated Asian or Eastern European men involved in large-scale organized crime and gangs. One 1990 *Toronto Star* article states that "police point to Chinese criminal triad societies as being responsible for much of the Asian sex trade in North America" (Kelly, 1990, p. H3). Occasionally, a nod is given to the unequal distribution of global wealth. A handful of media articles featuring interviews with purported victims of trafficking, or with police and advocates who had "rescued" trafficking victims, paint a picture of women and children forced into the hands of traffickers by extreme poverty and lack of opportunities in their countries of origin.

In 1996, the *Toronto Star* published a lengthy front-page investigative report on the child sex trade in Asia, which details accounts from victims of trafficking and forced prostitution. What is clear in this article and others is the discursive distinction being maintained between traffickers and pimps. While both are said to exercise control though violence, traffickers initially purchase or steal women and girls, or coerce or persuade them into migrating, and then transport and sell them to pimps; meanwhile, pimps purchase women and children from traffickers and exploit them by forcing them into prostitution (Watson, 1996). In this context, North American sex tourism is portrayed as exacerbating trafficking by fuelling demand for the sex industry. Articles repeatedly refer to demand and (relatedly) the massive profits generated; however, the extent of that profit appears to have undergone significant inflation (echoing the trend seen in relation to pimping). For example, in August 1996, the sex industry in Thailand is described by the *Toronto Star* as earning "millions" (Watson, 1996, p. A1), and by the *Hamilton Spectator* as a "$1.5 billion a year industry" (Canadian Press, 1996a, p. A8). Sixteen months later, the *Hamilton Spectator* claims that "the trafficking of women and children for sexual purposes has, for some years, been big business in Southeast Asia. It brings in an estimated $27 billion annually in Thailand alone" (Galloway, 1997, p. A1).

During this time, isolated articles begin making sweeping claims that the problem of sex trafficking is becoming a domestic one. A Canadian Press (1996b) article, referencing an international congress hosted in Ottawa on the problem of "Child Sex Trafficking in Asia," claims that "the growing market for child sex and kiddie porn is as much a Canadian problem as it is abroad" (p. A7). Beginning in 1997, well-publicized police raids on strip clubs in Ontario and New Brunswick shifted the focus to women from Eastern Europe and other poor regions being brought to Canada to work in the sex trade (Jiminez & Bell, 2000; see also Durisin & Heynen, 2015). Migrant women found in strip clubs were arrested and charged with "prostitution-related offences"; some were also subject to immigration charges and deportation. Media discussions of migrant women acknowledge that while some were persuaded to come to Canada under false pretences, attracted by promises of good jobs and wages, many were aware that they would be engaging in sex work. In short, these women are ascribed a measure of culpability while the economic contexts they navigated are made invisible. A 1999 article in the *Hamilton Spectator* quotes a York Regional Police detective as saying, "There's more savvy participants than people who are unaware of what's going on" (Prete et al., 1999, p. A1).

While the media, politicians, advocates, and police claimed that trafficking in women was a "burgeoning" problem in Canada, they also acknowledged that "information on trafficking in women at the federal level is very limited" (Bell & Jiminez, 2000, p. A01), as outlined in a front-page story in the *National Post* on May 17, 2000. This same article goes on to highlight claims of "anecdotal evidence" that the problem was increasing, stating paradoxically, "Current estimates of the number of women brought to Canada by traffickers vary from 8,000 to 16,000, although there is 'little hard data' to document the problem, according to one federal report" (Bell & Jiminez, 2000, p. A01). Importantly, the definition of trafficking in women used in the news media at the time is broad and unclear. While trafficking was implicitly linked to prostitution and other forms of sex work, there was a concerted push by government officials, police, and advocacy groups quoted in the sources we examined to expand the conceptual scope of the problem by including "mail-order brides and domestic workers lured by false promises of wealth" (Bell & Jiminez, 2000, p. A01).

On the surface, this more expansive definition appears to be a move to frame the problem of trafficking as an issue of unfree labour (rather than one of sex work). However, the effect of this definition is to increase estimates of the size of the problem, without breaking the entrenched discursive link to prostitution and sexual exploitation. Moreover, while many advocates acknowledged trafficking as a broad issue, a victim hierarchy emerged wherein greater emphasis was placed on sex trafficking as a serious problem while other kinds of labour abuses were minimized. As a spokesperson for the Global Alliance Against Traffic in Women said, "Trafficking in women in Canada ranges from mild cases of overworking nannies to 'extreme exploitation, being held in brothels.... [and] in Canada, the brothels tend to be called massage parlours'" (McInnes, 1997, p. A6).

Media depictions and descriptions of the pimp and trafficker begin to blur together in the first decade of the 2000s. While the focus remains on vulnerable women from poor countries who are trafficked and sold to pimps, the media increasingly highlight that many trafficked victims are teenagers or young women. In tandem with the shift illustrated above in relation to pimping, it is at this point that these young victims become discursively linked to the "child sex trade." Moreover, the use of the term "sex trade" — previously used to refer to consensual sex work — to describe an industry fuelled by trafficking muddies the conceptual waters between sex work and exploitation. Media reports of large numbers of trafficked women and girls flooding into Canadian strip clubs and massage parlours give the impression that many people working in the industry during that period are coerced, and implicitly bring up questions about the existence of a "voluntary" sex industry.

Beginning in late 2004, journalists, politicians, and advocates have raised the issue in media reports of an exemption within the federal Temporary Foreign Worker Program that allowed women to work as "exotic" dancers in Canada without a specific work permit (Durisin & Heynen, 2015; Macklin, 2003). Opponents of the special exemption suggested that it was being used to "traffic" women legally into Canada and that the women working in strip clubs had come to Canada out of desperation and were vulnerable to exploitation and forced prostitution. However, the federal minister of citizenship and immigration at the time, Judy Sgro, insisted that "she has seen no evidence the program is a front for sex trafficking" (Sallot & Freeze, 2004, p. A9). While this work permit exemption was extended to migrant workers in a wide range of labour sectors, opinion pieces and news stories focus almost exclusively on migrant erotic dancers, and numerous articles on the subject appeared in newspapers across the country at the end of November and early December 2004. In a representative excerpt, a *Montreal Gazette* editorial from November 30 suggests that "the Canadian government has signed on as state pimp for desperate women around the world.... Our government makes much of its opposition to global trafficking in women as part of the sex trade. Except when it's a participant" (Willcocks, 2004, p. A1). Nearly all the opinion pieces use the word "pimp" to refer to the government's role in permitting women to enter Canada for the purposes of working in strip clubs.

The federal government caved to pressure and ended the special exemption for erotic dancers on December 1, 2004; however, media coverage of the issue continued to the end of the year, firmly entrenching the discursive link between international human trafficking for prostitution, organized crime, the domestic strip industry, and exploitation in the sex industry in Canada.[7] This linkage sensitized the Canadian public to issues of exploitation in the sex industry and created a platform for moral crusaders to propose legal solutions.

The Emergence of the Pimp/Trafficker

The discourse of the "domestic sex trafficker" — Canadian traffickers coercing Canadian women and girls into the Canadian sex industry — emerges in the media first as speculation in late 2003. A researcher with the Quebec Council on the Status of Women is quoted in the *Montreal Gazette* as saying, "We don't know if kidnappings for the sex trade happen here in Canada. But why would Quebec and Canada be excluded from a network that exists elsewhere?" (Carroll, 2003, p. A4). Importantly, in 2005, anti-trafficking provisions were added to the *Criminal Code*. These included a different definition of human trafficking than had been previously set out in the *Immigration and Refugee Protection Act*, which required movement across an international border. The new broader *Criminal Code* understanding of trafficking opened the door for prosecution of anyone who "recruits, transports, transfers, receives, holds, conceals or harbours a person, or who exercises control or influence over the movements of a person, for the purposes of exploiting them or facilitating their exploitation" (*Criminal Code*, s. 279.01(1)). This expanded legal definition of human trafficking set the stage for a significant change in media discussions of pimps and traffickers after 2005. Driven by anti-trafficking advocates and law enforcement spokespersons' descriptions of sex trafficking in Canada, the formerly distinct roles become blurred and conceptually linked in the public discourse and imagination.

The next mention of domestic trafficking in our data set comes in 2006 with the release of a Status of Women Canada–funded report entitled *From the Curb: Sex Workers' Perspectives on Violence and Domestic Trafficking* (Matas, 2006). While the prevailing narrative is still that traffickers coerce, move, and sell women while pimps carry out the actual exploitation and forced labour in the sex industry, and the report continues to link domestic trafficking to movement, it is here that we see the beginning of the discursive linkage of pimps and traffickers:

> Sex workers say they are moved quietly, put in cars and taken on "road trips." Pimps and traffickers buy bus and plane tickets for them and escort them to their new locations. At times, they are drugged, bound and abducted by rival pimp families or crime organizations, and wake up in new locations across the country.... In Canada, everyone thinks international trafficking of women means women from Asia or Eastern Europe. They do not realize it is Canadian women from Toronto, who are taken to Calgary for the Stampede, or others who are moved around the country.... There is lots of movement of sex workers across Canada. (Matas, 2006, p. S1)

A year later, reporting on the release of another Status of Women report, *Turning Outrage into Action to Address Trafficking for the Purpose of Sexual Exploitation in Canada* (Standing Committee on the Status of Women, 2007), articles draw links between sex work and human trafficking and present anti–sex work advocates' arguments that if clients (and third parties) were criminalized, the industry would be less attractive for traffickers. Maria Minna, a Liberal member of Parliament, is quoted in one article explaining, "Traffickers will look for the country that has the least protection and the least stringent laws.... If Canada is going to be charging the customer, chances are the demand is going to go down" (Greenaway, 2007, n.p.). This discursive strategy continues to draw a link between human trafficking and the consensual sex industry, framing the latter as a driving force of the former, and in the process opening a space to treat "trafficker" and "pimp" as interchangeable terms for "exploiter" in the sex industry.

At the end of the first decade of the 2000s and throughout the 2010s, the conflation becomes even further entrenched. In 2009, University of British Columbia professor Benjamin Perrin referred to "sex traffickers and pimps" in a discussion of the recruitment of teenage girls into prostitution via the internet and social media. Perrin described this kind of recruitment as "online sex trafficking" and the "new kiddie stroll" (Iype, 2009, p. A10). Notably, there is no discussion of forced or coerced movement as part of the modus operandi of these traffickers — only sexual exploitation. The following year, retired RCMP officer Marty Van Doren, at the time the RCMP's human trafficking awareness coordinator for Ontario, is quoted as saying,

> Human trafficking involves recruitment, transport and exploitation.... But the victim doesn't have to be transported very far. If a pimp recruits a young girl in a food court in a shopping mall ... he might be pimping her out in an apartment or condo across the street.... The phrase 'human trafficking' is a 21st-century term for exploitation. (Petricevic, 2010, p. B6)

By 2012, the language of domestic human trafficking is being used to describe scenarios that are reminiscent of discourses on women exploited by pimps in the sex industry two decades earlier — that is, the "badder pimp" (Canadian Press, 1993, p. B6), who skilfully manipulates and seduces his victim into believing he is her boyfriend before turning violent and exploitative:

> [She] explained that a boyfriend, whom she met through friends "with ulterior motives" ... soon turned on her, forcing her to perform sexual acts while collecting all the money she made as a dancer. She said she met several women in the same position, one of them who was trafficked by her brother. "We all called them our boyfriends," she said of their captors.... Alienated and alone, and hooked on crack provided by her boyfriend, she wanted to leave but could not. "At one point I had all 10 toes

broken," she said. "I've got cigarette burns all over me." He also used emotional blackmail. (Rivers, 2012, p. 1)

The rhetoric explicitly links the trafficker/pimp to the use of drugs to incentivize the victims' cooperation:

> To find their victims, human traffickers may approach a young woman in a bar to pursue a relationship.... He may encourage her to try drugs, get her addicted, expose her "to sex situations," then share her out.... Next thing you know, the pimp owns them. Traffickers often take the women to Toronto and farm them out as escorts or in massage parlours.... The women are frequently hooked on crystal meth or cocaine. (Wood, 2012, p. A1)

At the same time, spokespeople for police and anti-trafficking advocates suggested that "pimps and traffickers will pose as potential boyfriends, hoping to lure youth to cities with the promise of a lavish lifestyle" (Mcquarrie, 2021, p. A6). Increasingly, media coverage and rhetoric from police and anti-trafficking advocates frame the pimp/trafficker as a danger to "good girls" from "good homes" who may become swept up in sex trafficking if parents are not vigilant:

> "It looks like a normal relationship — a boyfriend being sweet and endearing and very attentive," she [Carly Kalish, Victim Services of Durham Region] said. "They are listening to your child, looking for things that are missing in your child. If someone is feeling bullied, and has no friends, a trafficker will offer friendship, or if a teen is upset that mom won't let her go to a party or buy that sexy dress, a trafficker will be there to give a shoulder." (Moodie, 2021, p. A1)

By 2015, the discursive linkage of pimps/traffickers in media discourse has been firmly entrenched, supported by the analyses that law enforcement, advocates, and politicians offered to media. At this point, we begin to see the manufacture of narrative distinctions between types of pimps/traffickers in the form of a typology, based on a diagnosis of the techniques that they use to control their victims. Importantly, this typology of the trafficker/pimp draws heavily on the well-established framings detailed above:

> The "Romeo" pimp will draw a young person into their lives with promises of love and affection and access to a more glamorous lifestyle. On the other hand, the "gorilla" pimp finds young victims and uses violence and sexual assault as a way to break that individual and gradually bring them into trafficking circles. (Ellis, 2019, n.p.)

In short, at this time the trope of the manipulative pseudo-boyfriend who seduces hapless young women re-emerges as the "Romeo pimp" narrative (albeit now linked to traffickers). Romeo pimps, who "pose as boyfriends and gain the girls' trust and love" are described as "smart, skilled and looking for vulnerabilities" (Monteiro, 2018, p. A3). By contrast, the "gorilla pimp," which emerges in the mid- to late 2010s, uses violence and aggression as a means of controlling victims; he is a thug who snatches women from the streets and from other pimps/traffickers to exploit them for his own profit. His victims need not be the kinds of women and girls who are lured in by false promises of romance or money — the victims of the gorilla pimp are "truly innocent" women and girls who are kidnapped and held captive, which plays on the fear that, indeed, *anyone* can be a victim of this heinous crime and erases the complex intersecting vulnerabilities of class, race/ethnicity, gender, addiction, and isolation.

Not only does the term "gorilla pimp" evoke deep-seated, racist stereotypes, it is explicitly used in media to describe a group of Black men in Halifax termed "North Preston's Finest." For example, an *Ottawa Citizen* headline proclaiming, "North Preston's Ugly Reputation; Community Battles Its Portrayal as a Breeding Ground for Ruthless Gangs and Sex Traffickers" goes on to quote Natasha Falle, anti-trafficking activist and founder of SexTrade 101, as saying, "The typical profile of a North Preston pimp leans toward the 'Gorilla pimp' — someone prone to get what he wants through violence and threats" (Quan, 2016, p. N1).

The connection of the pimp and trafficker discourses has significant implications for the representation and understandings of the women who fall into the grasp of presumed pimps/traffickers. Whereas early narratives of victims of trafficking in the 1980s and 1990s painted the women as, at least initially, voluntarily compliant with their migration and even their entrance into the sex industry, and some sex workers were understood to work with and for pimps, the "new domestic trafficker" of the 2010s and beyond is purely an exploiter, victimizing hapless and vulnerable women and girls who have no agency in the situation:

> Pimps were seen as pimps, and only charged with crimes such as procuring and living on the avails of a prostitute. When human trafficking is the charge, the dark corners are made less grey; the pimp is the sole criminal — the one prostituted is the victim. Ideally, this framework allows sex-trade workers to escape.... Prosecuting their cases [as] "human trafficking" helps with this by more clearly defining the relationship of pimp and prostitute as criminal and victim. (Shaughnessy, 2010, n.p.)

Conclusion: The New Super Folk Devil

We began this chapter with Stanley Cohen's (1972) foundational work on folk devils and moral panics, which alerted us to the process by which outsiders are responsibilized for social malaise and envisioned as posing a widespread danger to society. Importantly, both the presumed characteristics and widespread acceptance of folk devil tropes are contingent on normative congruence. For example, the contours of the pimp/trafficker trope pivot on well-entrenched scripts of young women as gullible and passive, and racialized men as sly, seductive, hypersexual, and, above all, violent. Recognizing these problematic stereotypes still leaves open the question of how the pimp/trafficker evolved into at once a super folk devil and interchangeable personas.

Tracing the pimp and trafficker discourses sheds light on the significant discursive shifts that created a space for the pimp/trafficker super folk devil — a framing put forth by police as well as anti-sex work and anti-trafficking activists — to rapidly become unquestioningly reproduced in media to the point that news articles today deploy the terms "pimp" and "trafficker" interchangeably and readers accept them as such. The pimp and the trafficker have become synonymous. In some ways, the lack of an articulated trafficker persona (save vague descriptions that could be extrapolated from discussions of trafficking) coupled with readily available pimp tropes may have created a space for them to merge.

Our research highlights several important elements of the convergence of these narratives, which has implications for the social framing of, and response to, both human trafficking and sex work. First, context disappears. Early reporting on sex workers and trafficking victims attended to push factors including economic pressures, social disadvantage, dysfunctional families, the failure of the child welfare system, the unequal distribution of global wealth, and women's economic plight engendered by global events (e.g., the dissolution of the Soviet Union). However, over time that nuance dissipates, and the pimp/trafficker becomes *the* responsible party. The folk devil of the pimp/trafficker becomes a useful scapegoat to assuage any social responsibility that might come from the recognition of global systemic inequities and frames the appropriate response to human trafficking as the individual criminalization of pimps/traffickers.

Second, the (presumed) efficacy of the pimp/trafficker increases exponentially as he is envisioned as increasingly savvy and successful. The thuggish pimp and the organized criminal are replaced by an entity that is at once more ruthless and violent, and also more sophisticated and calculated. So clever is this new predator that even children from middle-class and implicitly white families (often referred to as "good homes" in the media we reviewed), are vulnerable.

Finally, the agency of both Canadian and international sex workers is eroded; they receive absolution, and are freed from all culpability and responsibility (or at least complicity), but at the cost of having all vestiges of agency stripped away. In short, the sex industry is bad and pimps/traffickers — and only pimps/traffickers — are responsible. It is a framing that eliminates the need to consider the interlocking systems of oppression (e.g., colonialism, patriarchy, capitalism) that many sex workers, regardless of country of origin, navigate. The erasure of agency conflates all sex work with exploitation and thus also serves to undermine the voices and advocacy of sex workers who fight for decriminalization of their work to improve safety, security, and autonomy. The ensuing moral panic not only distracts from the experiences of individuals who, as a function of social location, legal context, and intersecting identities, are vulnerable to exploitation, it also lends itself to surveillant and carceral solutions that, ironically, do further harm to vulnerable women in the sex industry.

Notes

1. Here we are focusing on the framing of the trafficker that emerged post-1980, not the incarnation at the turn of the twentieth century in the context of what became known as the white slave trade (Valverde, 2008).
2. Not all mentions of "pimp" in the data set were relevant; in the first decade of the 2000s, the television show *Pimp My Ride* popularized "pimp" as a cultural reference for making something stylish, resulting in a number of playful mentions and variations (e.g., "pimp my apartment," "pimp my style").
3. The careful reader will note that many of the examples in this chapter are drawn from print news media published in southern Ontario (particularly Toronto and Hamilton) and, to a lesser extent, Montreal, Quebec. While the data contained reports from across Canada, there was more representation from these regions, which might be explained by several factors. First, the number of daily newspapers in these regions led to increased coverage of social issues and particular cases of alleged exploitation and trafficking. Second, editorial policies and interests at some major papers such as the *Toronto Star* focused a great deal of coverage on specific controversial concerns, such as the proposed development of a "red light district" in Toronto in the mid-1990s. Lastly, these regions appeared to have more concern about the likelihood of trafficking and directed greater provincial funding to anti-trafficking police, campaigns, and other efforts, resulting in greater public awareness and media coverage. That said, the rhetorical strategies and framing of the issues were relatively consistent, regardless of the provincial or local context.
4. At times the reference is explicit, as in the coverage by the *Globe and Mail* of "North Preston's Finest," which carefully noted, "Most of these young prostitutes, virtually all of them white, work for a loosely organized community of Nova Scotia black men" (Jones, 1993, p. D1; for more on this issue, see Jeffrey & MacDonald, 2006). More often Blackness is conveyed — but not articulated — by authors noting when individuals accused of being pimps hail from countries such as Haiti or Jamaica, which are predominantly Black.
5. Jeffrey and MacDonald (2006) also point out the rise of "the story of young white girls being snatched by black pimps and forced into a life of prostitution through painful beatings and threat of death, and then being shipped to other locations in Canada and the United States. This story of evil pimping rings and innocent children was much more interesting to the public than was the earlier, careful Children's Aid Society reporting, which linked youth prostitution to abusive parents, runaways, and homelessness" (p. 158).
6. The federal, legal age of consent for heterosexual sex was increased from fourteen to sixteen in 2008 with the passing of the *Tackling Violent Crime Act*.
7. In fact, Canada's human trafficking criminal laws were first used to charge the owner of a legal massage parlour in Vancouver (*Vancouver Sun*, 2005).

References

Agrell, S. (2005, February 28). Peel police go online to track pimps: Child prostitution. *National Post*, A9.

Altheide, D.L., & Schneider, C.J. (2013). *Qualitative media analysis* (2nd ed.). Sage.

Bailey, S. (2006, June 23). Age of consent would rise to 16 under bill. *Toronto Star*, A04.

Banerjee, S. (2003, February 15). Street workers split on aid for young hookers: Alberta uses protective custody. Dans la Rue executive favours 'safe houses' but other workers skeptical about value. *The Montreal Gazette*, A6.

Bell, S., & Jimenez, M. (2000, May 17). Ottawa helpless to stop global sex traffic: Thousands of women and children bought and sold [Toronto edition headline]. Canada a hub for global sex traffickers: Ottawa has no policy to deal with issue [All but Toronto headline]. *National Post*, A01.

Bittle, S. (2018). Protecting victims sexually exploited through prostitution? Critically examining youth legal and policy regimes. In E.M. Durisin, E. van der Meulen, & C. Bruckert (eds.), *Red light labour: Sex work, regulation, agency and resistance* (pp. 134–156). UBC Press.

Brazao, D., & Welsh, M. (1994, November 21). The happy ex-hooker. *Toronto Star*, C1.

Canada NewsWire. (1994, July 22). Prostitution's sickening trade in children. B6.

Canadian Press. (1993, January 18). 'Gorillas' rule vice jungle: Bigger, badder pimps up prostitution ante. *Hamilton Spectator*, B6.

Canadian Press (1996a, August 26). Nations ready to combat child porn: Child sex worth billions. *Hamilton Spectator*, A8.

Canadian Press (1996b, August 27). Child sex trade thriving in Canada, experts warn. *Hamilton Spectator*, A7.

Carroll, A. (2003, October 23). Exploited women suffer in silence: Few statistics exist on illegal business. *Montreal Gazette*, A4.

Cohen, S. (1972). *Folk devils and moral panics*. Routledge.

Cox, K. (1993, January 21). Halifax parents fight pimps who prey on young. *Globe and Mail*, A5.

Darroch, W. (1986, October 22). Man, 25, guilty of raping, procuring teens. *Toronto Star*, H12.

___. (1987, June 18). Pimp jailed 3 years for living off teen, putting her in trunk. *Toronto Star*, F22.

Durisin, E.M., & Heynen, R. (2015). Producing the "trafficked woman": Canadian newspaper reporting on Eastern European exotic dancers during the 1990s. *Atlantis: Critical Studies in Gender, Culture, and Social Justice*, 37.2, 1: 8–24.

Durisin, E. M., & van der Meulen, E. (2021). Sexualized nationalism and federal human trafficking consultations: Shifting discourses on sex trafficking in Canada. *Journal of Human Trafficking*, 7, 4: 454–475.

De Shalit, A., Heynen, R., & van der Meulen, E. (2014). Human trafficking and media myths: Federal funding, communications strategies, and Canadian anti-trafficking programs. *Canadian Journal of Communications*, 39, 3: 385–412.

Editorial Board. (1990, August 2). To provide help that street kids will accept. *Globe and Mail*, A14.

Editorial Board. (1995, June 24). Red light district. *Toronto Star*, B2.

Ellis, C. (2019, October 29). Modern slavery: The human trafficking issue. *UWire*.

Galloway, G. (1997, December 4). Asian sex trade: Story of poverty and tradition. *Hamilton Spectator*, A1.

Gorrie, M. (1996, March 18). Facts & Arguments. Strike fires: The view from the street; The homeless, the chronically mentally ill, prostitutes and their pimps, and public-sector workers: We share the street now, the 1990s detritus of market economics. *Globe and Mail*, A14.

Greenaway, N. (2007, February 28). Criminalize pimps, johns, not prostitutes: Commons committee recommends ways to combat human trafficking. *Ottawa Citizen*.

Hanes, A. (2004, July 28). Alleged pimps refused bail, ordered not to talk to young hookers: Tears from the cheering section. Key figures in juvenile prostitution case will remain behind bars, judge rules. *Montreal Gazette*, A7.

Iype, M. (2009, July 11). Police work to curb underage sex ads; Craigslist online service co-operating with efforts to ID, weed out offenders. *Montreal Gazette*, A10.

Jeffrey, L.A., & MacDonald, G. (2006). *Sex workers in the Maritimes talk back*. UBC Press.

Jiminez, M., & Bell, S. (2000, June 16). Police charge 80 in strip club raids: 300 officers involved: Foreign women main target of exploitation. *National Post*, A23.

Jones, D. (1993, April 24). Prostitution skirmishes in the skin trade Halifax police have set their sights on black pimps who are sending hundreds of local teen-agers to sell their bodies on streets across Canada. *Globe and Mail*, D1.

Kelly, F. (1990, April 15). Breaking the bonds of Asian sex slaves a daunting task. *Toronto Star*, H3.

Matas, R. (2006, May 1). Canadian prostitutes bought, sold and forcibly moved; study shows. *Globe and Mail*, S1.

Macklin, A. (2003). Dancing across borders: "Exotic dancers," trafficking, and Canadian immigration policy. *International Migration Review*, 37, 2: 464–500.

McInnes, C. (1997, April 30). Two delegates to conference denied visas. *Globe and Mail*, A6.

Mcquarrie, J. (2021, December 22). Human trafficking is happening across the country. *Peace River Record Gazette/PostMedia*, A6.

Mensah, M.N. (2018). The representation of the "pimp": A barrier to understanding the work of third parties in the adult Canadian sex industry. In C. Bruckert & C. Parent (eds.), *Getting past the "pimp": Managers in the sex industry* (pp. 19–55). University of Toronto Press.

Monteiro, L. (2018, September 1). Girls as young as 12 victims of sex trafficking. *Waterloo Regional Record*, A3.

Moodie, J. (2021, November 6). Accent: 'We have to meet our teens where they are at.' *Sudbury Star*, A1.

Petricevic, M. (2010, February 27). Slavery's modern face. *Waterloo Region Record*, B6.

Prete, C., Wells, C., & Galloway, G. (1999, July 22). Sex-slave charges for club operator Burlington strip club owner accused of confining women. *Hamilton Spectator*, A1.

Quan, D. (2016, August 20). North Preston's ugly reputation; Community battles its portrayal as a breeding ground for ruthless gangs and sex traffickers. *Ottawa Citizen*, N1.

Reynolds, L. (2007, September 5). Another child of the streets gone forever no 17-year-old should fall victim to city's roaming sex predators. *Winnipeg Free Press*.

Rivers, H. (2012, September 10). Former sex slave recounts nightmare. *Woodstock Sentinel-Review*, 1.

Sallot, J., & Freeze, C. (2004, November 24). Exotic-dancer program on Sgro hit list; "My concern is the exploitation of women." *Globe and Mail*, A9.

Shaughnessy, B. (2010, March 27). The most dangerous game; She was lured to Canada with hollow promises of work, held captive in strip clubs and massage parlours — and then she walked away. *Globe and Mail*, GMBN.

Small, P. (2008, June 18). Man gets 8 years for turning teen into prostitute; Another name put on sex offender registry. *Toronto Star*, A14.

Standing Committee on the Status of Women. (2007). *Turning Outrage into Action to Address Trafficking for the Purpose of Sexual Exploitation in Canada: Report of the Standing Committee on the Status of Women*. https://www.ourcommons.ca/Content/Committee/391/FEWO/Reports/RP2738918/feworp12/feworp12-e.pdf

Sweet, L. (1986, January 24). Society spawns horrific sexual assaults. *Toronto Star*, B1.
Thomas, G. (1987, March 3). BC Man Looking for work robbed in first hour. *Toronto Star*, A2.
Toews, V. (2005, September 29). Vic Toews on age of consent. *Open Parliament*. https://openparliament.ca/debates/2005/9/29/vic-toews-1/only
Toronto Star. (1989, February 8). Markham man jailed as pimp after runaway turned prostitute. A16.
Valverde, M. (2008) *The age of light, soap, and water: Moral reform in English Canada, 1885–1925*. University of Toronto Press.
Vancouver Sun. (2005, April 25). Victims must be enlisted to help thwart human traffickers. A10.
van der Meulen, E., & Durisin, E.M. (2018). Sex work policy: Tracing historical and contemporary developments. In E.M. Durisin, E. van der Meulen. & C. Bruckert (eds.), *Red light labour: Sex work, regulation, agency, and resistance* (pp. 27–47). UBC Press.
Watson, P. (1996, August 3). The scandal of Asia's child sex trade: Thousands sold into brothels Girls raped, tortured in industry that generates millions. *Toronto Star*, A1.
Willcocks, P. (2004, November 30). Need a stripper? Call the federal government: Pimping for the nation; Immigration department is helping to keep strip clubs well stocked with fresh flesh. *Montreal Gazette*, A25.
___. (2014, October 12). The politician and the madam; How a B.C. cabinet minister's career crashed after an ill-advised telephone call. *Victoria Times Colonist*, D4.
Wood, D. (2012, June 15). Human trafficking along 401, police say. *Waterloo Region Record*, A1.

Legislation
Criminal Code, RSC 1985, c. C-46.
Protection of Children Involved in Prostitution Act, SA 1998, c. P-19.3 (Alberta).
Protection of Sexually Exploited Children Act, RSA 2000, c. P-30.3 (Alberta).
Tackling Violent Crime Act, SC 2008, c. 6.

4

A Narrative on Anti-Trafficking Discourse and Advocacy in Newfoundland

Laura Winters

I became involved in Newfoundland's sex worker rights movement while I was in university. As part of a course, I volunteered at a community organization in St. John's that was running the Coalition Against the Sexual Exploitation of Youth. They were doing great work and trying to open up conversations across the province. However, I found that nobody was talking about adults and their experiences; all of the focus was on youth. This led me to become interested in the adult sex industry. I started volunteering outside of school with some frontline community organizations that were doing outreach and meeting women who were engaged in sex work, many of which were advancing a sex workers' rights perspective. It was very different from the youth-based approach. I later went on to do PhD research in St. John's with sex workers, interviewing over thirty people about their responses to sex work stigma.

Over a decade ago, when I was first getting involved in the movement, Newfoundland had no collective advocacy around the human rights of sex workers and no community-based services specifically for people engaged in the industry. We did not have anything like the fabulous Stella in Montreal, or Stepping Stone in Halifax, or Maggie's in Toronto. Fortunately, in 2013, the St. John's Status of Women Council, a local women's centre and frontline feminist organization, received a small donation to build a resource for sex workers. I completed my doctoral research and was hired to start SHOP — the Safe Harbour Outreach Project. It was founded on explicitly feminist and advocacy-oriented principles, which directly informed its operation as a frontline service delivery program. As part of that work, I visited staff teams across the city's community sector, giving presentations, building relationships, and finding family doctors and health care professionals who were supportive of sex workers. I worked as the coordinator of SHOP for three years and then decided to step away, given the desire to move the program toward a peer-support and peer-led model with current and former sex workers as employees and volunteers. During my time with SHOP, I learned a lot from people engaged in sex work, and I feel lucky to have been the person originally hired to help build the program.

Later, in 2019, after working in a number of different roles in St. John's community sector, I became the executive director of the city's Status of Women Council. By that time, SHOP had grown and become a more established program, and a human rights approach to sex work was written into the council's bylaws and constitution. I especially appreciated that the council had board members with sex work experience. This meant that the human rights of sex workers were embedded in the fabric of the organization.

Currently, I am the CEO of Stella's Circle, which operates many programs including the Just Us Women's Centre, a program for women with involvement in the criminal justice system. As we know, sex workers are hugely overrepresented in the system. Stella's Circle also houses the only shelter for young women (under thirty years old) in St. John's, called the Naomi Centre. The shelter sees lots of women with involvement in the sex industry, so a priority for me is ensuring that the shelter environment is comfortable for sex workers, that staff have a harm reduction and human rights–based approach to sex work, and that it is safe for women to disclose their history there. In the same way that we ensure the shelter is inclusive of trans women, sex workers too need to be part of the ongoing conversation.

Conflating Sex Work and Trafficking

I have been fortunate to work at organizations that politically and discursively distinguish sex work from human trafficking. At the St. John's Status of Women Council, for instance, the bylaws and constitution clearly and prominently stated that it was a feminist organization that supported the human rights of sex workers. Other groups operating in the city did not advance the same perspective. One example was the Coalition Against Human Trafficking, which was mostly a faith-based group. I tried to connect with the group about how dangerous it was to conflate human trafficking with sex work but was not successful in changing their minds. For the most part, people in Newfoundland's anti-trafficking movement were not open to the idea that selling sex could be a consensual activity. They certainly held a saviour stance, and I think it brought to light the division within the feminist community around this issue.

The many inaccurate and harmful media representations and public perceptions about sex work create challenges. Not everyone can adopt a critical lens and tease the issues apart, particularly when they concern something as morally laden as sex. Discourses on the sex industry can be highly salacious when advanced by people who know little about what the work actually entails. It is especially difficult when sex workers themselves say, "That's not my reality," and outsiders with no lived experience reply, "Yes, it is." People need to understand that although exploitation and trafficking do happen, those are very different from sex work. They should not be conflated.

Another thing that further complicates the issue is that I have worked with lots of women who have had both experiences — sexual exploitation and sex work. When that kind of situation arises, conversations with people who only understand the anti-trafficking discourse and mentality become even more difficult. For them, the priority is police enforcement to combat human trafficking, not improvement of labour rights and protections so that people do not have to work in exploitative conditions to begin with. What is encouraging, though, is people educating themselves and listening to sex workers' own perspectives and narratives. I find this learning occurs especially among the strong movement of young feminists connected to the Status of Women Council in St. John's.

Anti-Trafficking Funding

When the *Protection of Communities and Exploited Persons Act* was passed in 2014 and federal anti-trafficking funding became readily available, a group in St. John's received a grant to start a program to help people exit the sex industry, which was called Blue Door. SHOP made a conscious decision not to apply for and access that pool of funding. Although the organization certainly could have used the funds, we felt it would limit our harm reduction work and compromise our values.

We also felt the women and nonbinary folks we served would not appreciate us taking anti-trafficking money that could lead to a change in SHOP's overall direction. We did, however, write a letter of support for Blue Door, as we recognized the work was valid, even though it was not in line with our mandate or approach.

The organization that received funds to start Blue Door was doing harm reduction work in a range of areas long before getting the federal grant. It was a robust organization with great services, but unfortunately it did not advance a human rights approach to sex work. The organization strengthened a one-sided, anti-trafficking, anti-exploitation discourse in St. John's, refusing to recognize consensual engagement in the sex industry or the complex nuances of people's experiences within it. The partnership between SHOP and the organization suffered because of the contentious politics involved, even though many people accessed both programs simultaneously. SHOP did support women who wanted to change their involvement in the sex industry; they were a great fit for Blue Door. However, some women were coming to SHOP to get supports and services as sex workers and were also on the caseload at Blue Door. They reported hiding the fact that they were still engaged in sex work when they went there. The two programs were operating from different philosophies and perspectives. Some of this conflict played out in damaging ways in the media as SHOP and Blue Door were publicly pitted against each other. It was not good for the social service sector in St. John's, for the community members who were being served by the organizations, or for public understanding of the realities of sex industry involvement.

Currently, the Newfoundland and Labrador government's Office of Women and Gender Equality (WAGE) funds SHOP. Though at times representatives of WAGE may mention human trafficking when they speak publicly, in actuality, by providing funding they support SHOP and its approach to sex workers' rights. WAGE was also responsive during the COVID-19 pandemic in recognizing that many of the financial benefits that were available to the general public, such as the Canada Emergency Response Benefit, were not available to sex workers. WAGE gave a fairly significant amount of money to SHOP to create a sex worker relief fund, which was an invaluable source of aid for sex workers in the community.

Relationships with Police

When I worked with SHOP, we tried to develop relationships with the Royal Newfoundland Constabulary, the city's police force, because they were intimately involved in the lives of our service users. We tried, from a harm reduction lens, to work with the police department's assigned liaison officers. If a woman needed to report an assault, we thought it would be beneficial if she could call a specific liaison officer who was knowledgeable about the myths and realities of sex work. Unfortunately, however, that relationship began to deteriorate when police treatment of sex workers created harm for the communities that SHOP served. In particular, they often treated sex workers who contacted them for support or to report violence as informants about drug trafficking or other crimes — as if sex workers must be regular witnesses to organized crime and did not deserve support and system navigation on the basis of their own experiences within or outside of the sex industry. The relationship further deteriorated when the police started to advance the anti-trafficking discourse and engage in harmful activities such as Operation Northern Spotlight, which contributed to broken trust and put sex workers in harm's way.

Later, when I became the executive director of the Status of Women Council, the staff at SHOP told me that they felt the police were continuing to act in harmful ways. So, as the organization running the SHOP program, the council made the decision to cut ties between SHOP and the police and hold the police accountable, in part by going public and telling the larger community that the police force was not serving sex workers. At the same time, however, the police claimed to have a strong relationship with SHOP, saying in the media, "We're doing right by people. We support X, Y, and Z programs" — including SHOP. In response, we told the police that they were part of an inherently harmful institution that needed to do major internal work and they needed to educate themselves better on sex work. For us, it was about listening to the voices of people accessing our services and responding to those voices by challenging powerful institutions that were doing harm.

SHOP and the Status of Women Council tried hard to make the relationship with police work, but we could not resolve fundamental political, social, and discursive differences. When we officially ended our collaboration, the liaison officers were upset. But I was clear with the chief of police that the issue was about his leadership and the organizational culture of the institution rather than individual frontline officers. There were further issues with the police force as well, such as the officer who sexually assaulted a woman while he was on duty, which was widely reported in the media. The Newfoundland police's inability to serve women from a gender-appropriate lens, especially those engaged in sex work, is directly linked to its misogynistic culture and leadership.

Police Anti-Trafficking Efforts

SHOP used to train all new police officers on stigma reduction for sex workers. However, as anti-trafficking discourses and narratives expanded across St. John's, the police developed an internal training program and also began to receive training from staff at Blue Door. The lack of opportunity for SHOP to offer training to police further contributed to the relationship breakdown. They could work more easily within the "victim" framework than with our human rights perspective. Their narrative of "saving" sex workers aligned much better with an exploitation and trafficking approach than it did with SHOP's harm reduction work. Before Blue Door ended up losing its federal anti-trafficking funding in early 2022, it facilitated a large-scale project highlighting its relationships with the police, showing the ways that officers were supposedly supporting Blue Door service users. CBC radio even aired a documentary about how great the police were in serving this population, which was very much at odds with the lived experiences of many people who were accessing SHOP. Some mutual participants of SHOP and Blue Door were closely connected to this project, but for others the Blue Door project and the subsequent documentary were difficult to see, since they had such a different experience with the police.

In addition to collaborating with Blue Door on anti-trafficking activities, the police in Newfoundland also participated in a major national anti-trafficking (and anti–sex work) "raid-and-rescue" effort called Operation Northern Spotlight. This was, and still is, an organized operation that involves numerous police services across the country targeting local escort agencies and independent sex workers in an effort to find and rescue victims of trafficking and arrest exploiters. I was working at SHOP when the first round of Operation Northern Spotlight occurred in the province in 2015. At that time, SHOP's relation with the police was a bit more positive because SHOP was working with the liaison officers. I received a call from a woman who was scared of being arrested. She had booked an appointment with someone she thought was a client, but when she arrived at the hotel room, the police were waiting for her. They eventually let her go after intensely questioning her about her "trafficking." She was really shaken up, and the experience broke her trust in the police. It also broke her trust in general. She was wary of booking appointments for a long time, which caused her financial hardship. For her and the other women caught up in the St. John's stings, the experience was traumatic. When SHOP brought that feedback to the police, they did not understand why someone would be concerned about walking into a hotel room full of officers, once again showing their lack of willingness to listen to sex workers. Even though SHOP wrote reports explaining how the anti-trafficking stings were actually harming, not helping, sex workers and people experiencing exploitation, the police went ahead and participated in the second round of Operation Northern Spotlight in 2017.

Conclusion

The biggest issue with normative discourses on anti-trafficking is that they take away from a human rights approach to sex work and deny sex workers' capacity to define their lives and their work. It is harmful to exert power and try to describe someone else's reality. At a deep level, it is about who gets to define experience, who gets to have a voice. The anti-trafficking movement in St. John's and elsewhere has taken so much from sex workers and their supporters, who are already fighting harmful laws, stigma, and more. They should not also have to spend their time fighting a group of people who are trying to "save" them. In my experience, sex workers do not want or need saving; they want access to human rights, safety at work, and the ability to live in their communities free from stigma and discrimination.

Section Two

TRAFFICKING LAWS AND PROSECUTIONS

5

Prosecuting Trafficking in Persons Offences

Problems and Pitfalls in the Post-PCEPA Era

Tamara O'Doherty and Hayli Millar

Critical sociolegal scholarship, including the contributions of several authors in this volume, has documented the politicized evolution of human trafficking law in Canada, its ideological underpinnings, and the adverse effects of the deliberate conflation of sex work and human trafficking.[1] Persons with lived experience, scholars, and activists have been calling not only for attention to be paid to the flawed empirical basis for Canadian anti-trafficking law but also for action to rectify the highly racialized and gendered patterns of such criminalization. In this chapter, we present data that affirm these concerns: we report prosecution trends in Canada over the past twenty years since the country first enacted an anti-trafficking law, including legislative expansionism (net widening) that differently impacts some — especially racialized and marginalized — members of society. We then note that the criminalization of commercial sex work via human trafficking law raises deeply troubling questions about fundamental principles of justice by potentially infringing the rule of law and principles of res judicata. Finally, we discuss the impact of the politicized and unidimensional narratives regarding victimhood, which can create significant barriers to justice for those whose victimization is doubted in court. Our research reveals that continuing on the current path of ideologically motivated and empirically flawed criminalization will only exacerbate inequities and facilitate further vulnerabilities to exploitation. It is clear to us that rather than addressing the serious issues of labour exploitation and victimization across especially precarious and migrant work sectors, Canada's enforcement of anti–human trafficking law sustains unequal access to justice and creates the very conditions in which labour and other forms of exploitation flourish.

Our Study

Since 2013, we have examined the evolution, implementation, and impacts of Canadian anti-trafficking laws. Our initial study (Millar & O'Doherty, 2015), conducted in partnership with SWAN Vancouver Society, comprised a legislative and case analysis, interviews with key stakeholders in the legislative and law enforcement realms, and focus groups with SWAN staff. Our findings affirmed enforcement patterns and concerns raised by many other Canadian and international critical sociolegal scholars (Alexander, 2012; Bruckert & Hannem, 2013; Burke, 2018; Chu et al., 2019; Faulkner, 2018; Hunt, 2015; Kaye, 2017; Kempadoo, 2016; Kinney, 2015; Krüsi et al., 2016; Lam, 2018; Lam & Lepp, 2019; Maynard, 2017, 2018; Nagel, 2015; O'Brien, 2016; Roots, 2018, 2022; Shih, 2016; Soderlund, 2005; Srikantiah, 2007; Sterling & van der Meulen, 2018; Weitzer, 2011; Williamson & Marcus, 2017): there is inadequate evidence to support the forms of criminalization and immigration regulation that Canada has elected to implement, ostensibly to prevent and combat human trafficking. Further, our research findings indicated there are serious adverse human and labour rights consequences associated with the highly politicized, unempirical, and unidimensional narrative about human trafficking in Canada, its conflation with all forms of commercial sex work, and the racialized, gendered, and sensationalized patterns of law enforcement.

Our first study contributed evidence of the patterns of legislative expansionism and law enforcement evident in Canadian prosecutions from 2002 to 2015. Our second study (Millar & O'Doherty, 2020a) extended this legal analysis to 2018. Here, we update these two reports with data up to and including June 2022, and discuss twenty years of legal data about Canadian anti-trafficking law enforcement and prosecutions. Each of the studies has employed the same method. We regularly search legal databases for trafficking in persons judgments as well as maintain alerts for Canadian news reports on alleged cases, for which we then try to obtain official case data to confirm which trafficking in persons charges are actually prosecuted and the legal outcomes in those cases. We have previously attempted access to information requests without success; however, we have been able to triangulate and confirm our case lists with other scholars and with Canadian justice data.

Taken together, we now have data for 159 prosecuted Canadian trafficking cases. We report our data on the basis of a primary defendant who is named in the criminal or immigration enforcement court proceedings to provide a case or incident-based analysis, acknowledging that some cases involve multiple defendants, not all of whom are necessarily charged or convicted on trafficking-specific charges. We also provide police charging data to compare patterns of law enforcement (number of persons charged) with patterns of prosecution (number of persons prosecuted, convicted, and sentenced). In this way, we hope to provide as holistic a picture as possible, knowing the various limitations of each type of data source.[2]

Prosecution Patterns Pre- and Post-PCEPA

Canada enacted a federal immigration trafficking in persons offence in 2001 and subsequently introduced a criminal trafficking in persons offence in 2005, which now is the main provision used to charge and prosecute trafficking cases. Since 2005, the Canadian government has amended the criminal trafficking offence several times to "strengthen" the law, with further amendments proposed in 2021 (and still in consideration in 2023) to make it easier to prosecute this offence. The former Conservative government introduced one of these legislative amendments in response to the landmark 2013 Supreme Court of Canada decision in *Bedford* that struck down certain sex work offences because they undermined the constitutionally protected personal security rights of sex workers. The 2014 *Protection of Communities and Exploited Persons Act* (PCEPA) criminalized commodified sex for the first time in Canada by focusing mostly on those who purchase sex and third parties who profit from sex work. Significantly, PCEPA also changed the legislative objectives associated with the criminalization of sex work. It seeks to end all commercial sex work and repositions sex workers as "victims," aiming, in particular, to "protect" women and girls from harm.

Due to the simultaneous amendment of the commercial sex (commodification of sexual services) and trafficking in persons offences under the umbrella of "protecting exploited persons," these two categories of offences are now legislatively and jurisprudentially fused. Most trafficking cases involve co-charges for commodification offences, and the available jurisprudence reflects both trafficking *and* commodification case law, some of which is exceptionally dated (more than twenty years old) and connected to offences that have since been found to be unconstitutional. In fact, human trafficking is prosecutorially and judicially characterized as "pimping" plus some element of exploitation (see *R. v. D'Souza*, 2016, para. 39). This legislative overlap is problematic for several reasons, including that sex work is caught up in a resulting carceral web (see especially Fudge et al., 2021) and attention is directed away from other forms of unfree labour and sexual exploitation that take place in other labour contexts. It also invites police to surveil sex workers and overcharge third parties with two or more charges for what is essentially the same conduct.

What do the 159 prosecuted cases tell us about Canada's anti-trafficking efforts? Canadian anti-trafficking laws are overwhelmingly used to prosecute what has been labelled as domestic sex trafficking. International (cross-border) prosecutions are rare. Nonsexual labour trafficking prosecutions are infrequent and have rarely been successful in securing a conviction. Since the enactment of PCEPA, the number of persons charged and the number of prosecuted cases have increased. The prosecuted cases are increasingly legally complex. A prosecution often involves multiple pretrial and voir dire applications and may take many years to proceed through the courts from the point of charging through to appeals.[3] Most of the prosecuted cases involve multicount indictments, including co-charges for commodification offences. Many of the prosecuted cases involve persons who were in an intimate partner relationship and show evidence of increasing coercive control and violence across the relationship as reflected by frequent co-charges for physical and sexual violence (e.g., see *R. v. Casanova*, 2020). Some of the cases would be more aptly described as child exploitation or as sexual violence cases in which the human trafficking charges are subsidiary to these other charges (e.g., *R. v. S.C.*, 2019). Because sex work is a criminalized economy, many of the prosecuted cases involve charges for firearms offences (e.g., *R. v. Antoine*, 2019; *R. v. Leduc*, 2019), are connected to persons involved in the illicit drug trade (e.g., *R. v. Davidson*, 2020; *R. v. Shahinian [Chahinian]*, 2018), or include allegations that the accused used drug dependency as a form of inducement or control for complainants to provide commercial sexual services (e.g., *R v. Casanova*, 2020; *R. v. Clayton*, 2021).

There continues to be limited evidence of serious organized criminal involvement in the form of organized crime charges across the prosecutions. Most of the prosecuted cases involve one (usually male) accused and one (almost always female) complainant. A significant portion of the prosecuted cases comprise minor complainants who legally cannot consent to engage in commercial sex work *or* multiple complainants for whom similar fact evidence potentially can be introduced (in other jurisdictions these cases have been described as "low-hanging fruit"; see Godziak, 2020). There continue to be few accused youths (only five cases). However, in several cases (at least 31 of 159 cases) women were the primary accused or co-accused. In these cases, we echo other sociolegal scholarship and jurisprudence in asserting that alleged victim-offender intersectionality may not be given sufficient attention in court proceedings (British Columbia Civil Liberties Association, 2010; Chan & Chunn, 2014; Gittens & Cole, 1995; Jiwani, 2016; Lewis, 1992; Maynard, 2017; McNeilly, 2018, 2019; Monchalin, 2010; Ontario Human Rights Commission, 2003, 2017, 2018; *R. v. Barton*, 2019; *R. v. Le*, 2019; *R. v. Spence*, 2005; *R. v. Williams*, 1998; Sinclair, 2018; Tanovich, 2008; Tulloch, 2018; Wortley, 2019). While restitution orders are rarely applied, we also

Table 5-1. Summary of prosecuted trafficking cases in Canada, 2006–2022

Type of trafficking	Cases (n)	Defendants (n)	Complainants (n)
Domestic sex trafficking	150	221	218
Only adult complainants	82		
Only minor complainants	46		
Mix of adult and minor complainants	10		
Unknown or contested complainant age	12		
Domestic labour trafficking	–	–	–
International sex trafficking	2	2	3[a]
International labour trafficking	6	22[b]	23[c]
International forced marriage	1	1	1
Total	**159**	**246**	**245**

Note: These numbers should be interpreted with some caution as we do not have comprehensive complainant/victim/survivor information for all cases. Most cases (110) involved a solo complainant, forty-two cases involved more than one complainant, and the number of complainants for the remaining seven cases is unknown. With the exception of the *Domotor* (2011) case, all complainants, where known, were women and girls, including one transgender woman. Multidefendant cases are difficult to characterize since there may be defendants in addition to those indicated as primary or co-accused and we may lack corroborating court judgments. [a] Includes two adults and one minor. [b] Includes multidefendant *Domotor* case. [c] Includes multivictim *Domotor* case and an unknown number of victims in another case.

note potential gender disparities between female and male accused.[4] Ongoing racial disparities are seen across the prosecuted cases in which a disproportionate number of the accused appear to be Black and racialized persons and many of the complainants are white women and girls.

Pitfalls in Prosecutions

As is well articulated by several authors in this volume and reported in other critical sociolegal scholarship, a clear lack of empirical evidence underlies the enactment and subsequent amendment of Canadian anti-trafficking law. Further, overt ideological goals are embedded in the legislation and applied in practice. In addition to this troubling foundation, post-PCEPA case prosecution based on Canadian anti-trafficking law has several alarming implications that ought to be central in discussions regarding legislative reform.

First, the prosecuted cases demonstrate an alarming narrowing of enforcement to sex industries while widening enforcement within sex industries to capture almost all activities and relations within them, making it virtually impossible to practise sex work collectively. Indeed, our findings reveal that the criminal trafficking offence is overwhelmingly used to police domestic commercial sex work. Rather than targeting a new or previously underinvestigated, hard-to-reach type of activity such as cross-border trafficking in persons, most of the trafficking cases involve procuring (previously known as "pimping" and "living on the avails") and the commercial sexual exploitation of young female adults and female persons under the age of eighteen years in Canada. This legislative expansionism and the convergence of federal criminal and immigration laws and their enforcement (so-called crimmigration) to regulate domestic commercial sex work are reinforced and augmented by a variety of other laws that are also used to punitively regulate those who work in the commercial sex sector — including family laws (DeWolf, 2021), municipal bylaws (Craig, 2011; Lam, 2016; Sterling & van der Meulen, 2018), residential tenancy laws, taxation laws, and a growing number of provincial anti-trafficking laws and policies. In effect, as Figure 5-1 demonstrates, Canada has simply renamed previously domestically criminalized activities, "trafficking."

Legislative expansionism is accompanied by increased surveillance of those involved in the commercial sex work sector by persons (especially

88 TRAFFICKING HARMS

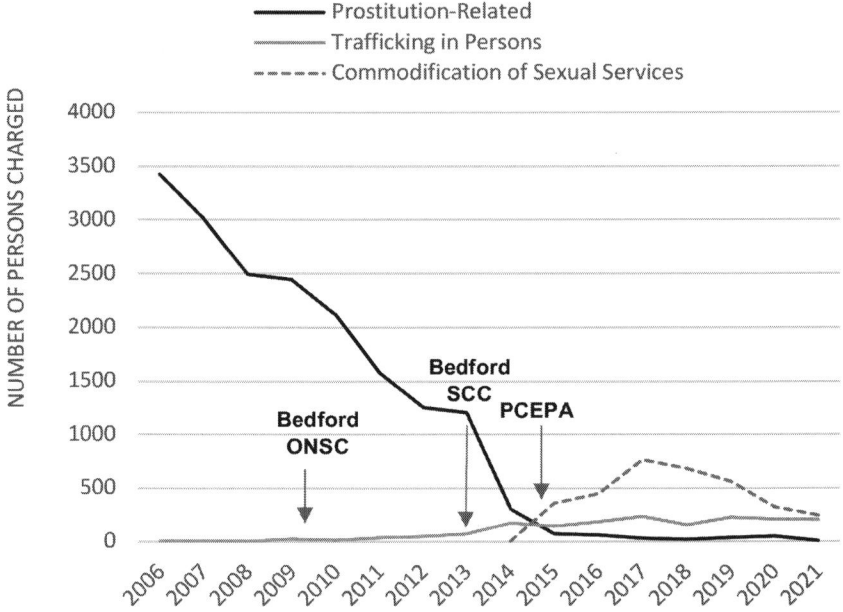

Figure 5-1. Police-reported charges for prostitution-related, trafficking in persons, and commodification offences in Canada, 2006–2021

Note: ONSC = Ontario Superior Court of Justice, PCEPA = *Protection of Communities and Exploited Persons Act;* SCC = Supreme Court of Canada.
Source: Statistics Canada. Table 35-10-0177-01 Incident-based crime statistics, by detailed violations, Canada, provinces, territories, Census Metropolitan Areas and Canadian Forces Military Police. DOI: https://doi.org/10.25318/3510017701-eng.

in the social service, health care, hospitality, transportation, and education sectors), through artificial intelligence of "at-risk" communities, and by means of proactive law enforcement campaigns through what is known as "preventive policing." The negative impacts of police and border enforcement–based and protectionist undercover sting operations and workplace "raid-and-rescue" campaigns, along with progressively more expansive in-person and technological surveillance, are well documented (Brayne, 2018; Lam & Lepp, 2019; Law Commission of Ontario, 2020; Maynard, 2018; Robertson et al., 2020; Sterling & van der Meulen, 2018). They include adverse consequences for those subjected to intensified legal intervention, as evidenced by the Supreme Court of Canada granting leave to appeal in both *R. v. Haniffa,* 2021, and *R. v. Dare,* 2021, although ultimately rejecting the doctrine of entrapment (e.g., see *R. v. Haniffa,* 2022) and several constitutional challenges to provisions enacted in PCEPA. Crucially, this legislative conflation and expansionism serves to invisibilize many other forms of exploitation, including victimization of transgender, nonbinary, and queer individuals, and a range of other labour and human rights violations that occur in other — especially precarious and migrant — labour sectors and global supply chains extending to international students. As is demonstrated in Table 5-2, Canada has prosecuted very few transnational cases or cases involving organized crime.

Second, there are intersectional inequities in the enforcement of human trafficking and commodification offences, and the available evidence suggests that human trafficking offences are enforced in ways that are highly racialized, gendered, and sensationalized (Kaye, 2017; Lam, 2018; Maynard, 2017; Millar & O'Doherty, 2020b; Roots, 2022). As other contributors in this volume discuss, racialized Canadians face both intensified policing and underprotection. This is especially apparent in the context of anti-trafficking law enforcement. Analysis of case law demonstrates the same harmful villain/victim dichotomy that has been reported in numerous other countries (see Faulkner, 2018; Kinney, 2015; Shih, 2016; Soderlund, 2005; Srikantiah, 2007) and a stereotype that perpetrators of trafficking are cisgender racialized men[5] while the victims of trafficking are "innocent and therefore deserving" white cis-

Table 5-2. Types of prosecuted trafficking cases in Canada, 2006–2014, 2015–2022

Trafficking characteristic	Cases (n)		
	Pre-PCEPA 2002–2014	Post-PCEPA 2015–2022	Total
Geographic location			
Domestic	31	119	150
International	4	5	9
Type			
Sex (domestic)	31	118	149
Sex (international)	1	1	2
Labour (international)	3	3	6
Forced marriage (international)	—	1	1
Unknown	—	1	1
Total	35	124	159

Note: PCEPA = *Protection of Communities and Exploited Persons Act*.

gender women and girls. Increasing surveillance raises the likelihood of criminalization for members of racialized communities, yet Indigenous, Black, and other racialized persons are not often able to safely access protective police services, particularly when they distrust police involvement in their lives due to potential criminalization, precarious migration status, or histories of systemically biased policing.

Third, our data indicate geographic and economic disparities in the enforcement of human trafficking and commodification offences. Although some provinces (Alberta, Saskatchewan, Manitoba, Ontario, Quebec, and Nova Scotia) have prioritized human trafficking enforcement, investing serious resources to police and prosecute these offences, other provinces and territories have not. This prioritization illustrates both the impact of political support on funding, as well as the effect of politicization on prosecution and investigation rates: when a province invests millions toward such law enforcement, the official statistics indicate more cases. The economic incongruities are not limited to discrepancies among provinces and territories: the monetary and personnel resources invested in anti-trafficking investigations do not match the degree to which human trafficking is believed to exist in any region. While keeping in mind that only some alleged criminal incidents come to the attention of the police, the annual charges data reveal that human trafficking is consistently a very small fraction of police-reported crime in Canada — the large amount of resources devoted to these investigations is well out of alignment with the small proportion that human trafficking offences represent of total criminal incidents committed in a given year. The amount of money devoted to these investigations is simply unwarranted.

For example, in 2020, more than 2.2 million alleged criminal incidents were reported by the police and more than 567,000 persons were charged. In the same year, there were 385 alleged incidents of human trafficking resulting in 210 persons charged, and 756 alleged commodification offence violations resulting in 326 persons charged. Despite these very small numbers of alleged trafficking cases, the mainstream media, academics, various levels of government, and civil society organizations continue to promote a fear-based narrative about human trafficking, recently suggesting, for instance, that it is Canada's "best hidden crime" (CBC News, 2022; Public Safety Canada, 2022) and that police-reported incidents of trafficking represent actual "victims" (Taschner, 2022).

Fourth, legislative amendments over the past fifteen years have increased the penality of anti-trafficking laws. In 2010 and 2014, the government adopted mandatory minimum sentences for trafficking in persons offences. Such sentences are known to perpetuate systemic racism on their own — when combined with an established pattern of racialized policing and prosecution, the data eliminate any doubt of the consequence of increased criminalization for predominantly Black and other racialized men and some women. These mandatory minimum sentences have been successfully challenged in several trafficking and commodification cases as violating a defendant's right not to be subjected to cruel and unusual punishment, as outlined in section 12 of the *Charter of Rights and Freedoms* (*R. v. Abara and Kulafofski*, 2018 [see Dubinski, 2018]; *R. v. Ahmed et al.*, 2019; *R. v. Antoine*, 2020; *R. v. Charboneau*, 2019; *R. v. Chisholm*, 2018; *R. v. Faroughi*, 2020; *R. v. Finestone*, 2017; *R. v. J.G.*, 2021; *R. v. J.L.M.*, 2017; *R. v. Joseph*, 2020; *R. v. Kassongo*, 2019; *R. v. Lopez*, 2018; *R. v. Mercer*, 2017; *R. v. Reginald Louis Jean*, 2020; *R. v. Robitaille*, 2017; *R. v. Safieh*, 2018; *R. v. Strickland-Prescod*, 2019; *R. v. Webber*, 2019).

Finally, the legislative conflation of human trafficking and commodification has produced the judicial conflation of case precedents in which so-called "pimping" or "pimping plus" offences are viewed as interdependent and indivisible, not only in interpretation of elements of the trafficking offence but also in sentencing (see, e.g., Millar & O'Doherty, 2020a, pp. 32, 54–61; see also Sibley & van der Meulen, 2022, for an insightful discussion of the judicial interpretation of the trafficking in persons offence elements). Troublingly, the legal framework has reproduced the application of outdated stereotypes about commercial sex work, including paradoxical ideas about consent: courts refuse to accept that consent can occur in a commercial setting, but then also allow for implied consent in some commercial sex cases by refusing to accept that someone could consent to some sexual acts but not others. These prevailing attitudes about sex workers exist in spite of an emerging body of case law, government inquiry, and other anecdotal and empirical evidence challenging the problematic use of discredited yet pervasive and deeply harmful gendered myths and stereotypes about sexualized violence in the criminal law.[6] The stereotypes take on a distinctly racist sentiment when the victim or witness is an Indigenous (First Nations, Métis, or Inuit) person or is otherwise racialized.

Table 5-3. Minimum and maximum imprisonment sentences for trafficking, 2002–2014, 2015–2022

Offence	Imprisonment Sentences	
	Pre-PCEPA 2002–2014	Post-PCEPA 2015–2022
Trafficking in persons		
279.01(a) Aggravated trafficking adult	Maximum life	Maximum life; minimum 5 years
279.01(b) Non-aggravated trafficking adult	Maximum 14 years	Maximum 14 years; minimum 4 years
279.011(a) Aggravated trafficking minor (offence and penalties added in 2010)	Maximum life; Minimum 6 years	Maximum life; minimum 6 years
279.011(b) Non-aggravated trafficking minor (offence and penalties added in 2010)	Maximum 14 years; Minimum 5 years	Maximum 14 years; minimum 5 years
Material benefit trafficking in persons		
279.02(1) Material benefit trafficking adult (offence amended in 2019 to allow Crown prosecutors to elect to proceed summarily or by indictment)	Maximum 10 years	Maximum 2 years less one day if Crown proceeds summarily; maximum 10 years if Crown proceeds by indictment
279.02(2) Material benefit trafficking minor (offence added in 2014)	Not applicable	Maximum 14 years; minimum 2 years
Withholding documents trafficking in persons		
279.03(1) Withholding documents trafficking adult (offence amended in 2019 to allow Crown prosecutors to elect to proceed summarily or by indictment)	Maximum 5 years	Maximum 2 years less one day if Crown proceeds summarily; maximum 5 years if Crown proceeds by indictment
279.03(2) Withholding documents trafficking minor (offence added in 2014)	Not applicable	Maximum 10 years; minimum 1 year

Problematic Dismissal of Fundamental Justice

In addition to the trends noted above, we have identified three implications of Canada's approach to anti-trafficking criminalization that contradict fundamental principles of justice. Much of the discussion relating to exploitation currently centres on victim and survivor experiences of trauma. We agree that this is a necessary centring; however, in order to maintain public confidence in Canadian legal institutions, they must also continue to uphold principles of fundamental justice whenever the state wields its power (Locke, 2021). Fundamental principles of fairness, the rule of law, and equality under and before the law — including equal protection and benefit of the law — are all vital mechanisms for ensuring that the state does not impede individual rights and freedoms, particularly for those who are targeted disproportionately by state apparatuses such as criminal law. Where evidence exists of racialized patterns of prosecution and conviction, the infringements of equality rights and fundamental principles of justice described below ought to take on heightened concern for the government and for equity-seeking individuals and groups.

Our research findings expose a troubling reality of overcharging and multiple trafficking-related convictions for essentially the same conduct. Given the significant overlap between some of the new commodification offences — especially procuring and financially or materially benefiting from sexual services — and the criminal trafficking in persons offences, not only can charges be used interchangeably based on the discretion of the police or Crown, but in some cases, the accused are dually convicted for trafficking and procuring or materially benefiting.[7] This charging practice brings two mirror components of fundamental justice into play via the protection against double jeopardy: protection against multiple prosecutions for the same conduct and protection against double punishment for the same conduct. Protections against double jeopardy are enshrined in various ways under Canada's *Criminal Code* (ss. 607 and 609), under the *Charter* (s. 11(h)), within the common law as res judicata (in Canada, the *Kienapple v. R.*, 1975, principle), and in international conventions such as article 14(7) of the *International Covenant on Civil and Political Rights* (1966). These fundamental principles of justice have such a solid basis in law because they are designed to guard against abuse of state power and to bring a standardized level of fairness in state actions against accused persons. However, the Canadian jurisprudence related to anti-trafficking law reveals serious problems with the jurisprudential conflation of the trafficking and commodification charges, in spite of legislative and constitutional protections.[8]

Further, the degree of politicization of, and the lack of an empirical basis for, both the law and the approach of targeting human trafficking via criminalization of the entire sex industry raises potential violations of the rule of the law. As Hamish Stewart (2016) and Sandra Ka Hon Chu and Rebecca Glass (2016) argue, mutually inconsistent objectives in the legislation, such as seeking to prosecute and protect victims of exploitation, can lead to findings of arbitrariness. For example, prosecuting third parties as traffickers removes a venue option that sex workers suggest actually functions to increase their safety and not subject them to exploitation (*R. v. Anwar*, 2020; *R. v. Kloubakov*, 2021). Likewise, the clearly ideological definitions of harm that form the basis of human trafficking and commodification laws (such as the purchase of sex alone constituting an expression of harm against all women and children) and the funding offered to law enforcement agencies to find human trafficking (regardless of whether a case is actually a material benefits charge) compound concerns about arbitrariness. When combined with patterns of racialized law enforcement and increased penalty for trafficking convictions in comparison to commodification convictions — as we found in our review of Canadian cases and have written about elsewhere (see Millar & O'Doherty, 2020b) — the arguments regarding arbitrary state conduct ought not to be ignored.

While the rule of law is a convoluted concept lacking a clear and widely accepted definition, legal scholars appear to understand the principle as forming the basis of accountability in the context of state lawmaking and law enforcement powers. As Cara Locke (2021) writes, fundamental principles of fairness require the state to hold firmly to transparency and accountability in its use of power over citizens. Locke argues that provisions such as section 213(1.1) of the *Criminal Code*, which is used to empower police to detain sex workers (ostensibly for their own good, or as a way to increase their likelihood of testifying against third parties) rather than charge workers with a criminal offence, remove sex workers' access to trial processes and accountability for police conduct, thereby raising concern about arbitrariness. Likewise, we argue that the use of law for ulterior purposes, such as surveilling sex workers in order to access victims of human trafficking, raises serious concerns about fairness and the arbitrary use of law. Where laws are used in these indirect manners and do not result in charges against the primary person, who is used by police, there is no trial process. Thus, the very citizens over whom the state wields its power have no or a limited opportunity to challenge the law that allows for their surveillance and detention, which creates a serious violation of principles of fundamental justice.

Finally, our research supports the extant literature in the finding that sex workers and victims of sexualized violence do not have equal access to justice in Canada (Durisin & van de Meulen, 2021; Hunt, 2015; Jiwani, 2016; Kaye, 2017; Maynard, 2015; Raguparan, 2019; United Nations Special Rapporteur on the Rights of Indigenous Peoples, 2014). Not only do sex workers rarely benefit from state protection, but recent jurisprudence, social science, national inquiry, and government reports all indicate that victims of sexualized violence have cause to be concerned about the deeply harmful, sexist, and often racist treatment they receive in court processes and investigations (*R. v. Barton*, 2019; Canadian Judicial Council, 2016; National Inquiry into Missing and Murdered Indigenous Women and Girls, 2019). The criminal laws against human trafficking and commercial sex work operate together to decrease sex workers' ability to employ health and safety-enhancing strategies within their work. Then, when victimization does occur — and victimization occurs along specific racialized and gendered lines and comes from not only predators masquerading as clients or abusive third parties, but also from police and others in positions of power[9] — sex workers often report having their credibility doubted in court simply because they work in the sex industry, as well as judges, lawyers, police, and others all seeming to accept implied consent even when express consent is the only consent that meets Canadian legal standards. This latter point was a central focus of the *Barton* (2019) case, wherein the Supreme Court of Canada felt it necessary to remind judges and future juries to avoid using racist and sexist stereotypes about Indigenous women who perform sex work. The court laid out basic expectations that should never have to be vocalized: that Indigenous women who sell sex are entitled to respect, humanity, and dignity; that their decision to sell sexual services does not reduce their credibility; and that they do not deserve any victimization because they chose to take a risk (arguably a risk created by societal constructions in a colonial state, including using asymmetric criminalization to abolish sex work) that others may not have. These 2019 directives are clear indicators of the depth of the systemic issues that are present — particularly for racialized sex workers — when victims of violence seek protection from the state via police services that are supposed to serve and protect all persons or via court processes that are supposed to provide "justice."

Conclusion

In everyday narratives, trafficking in persons is widely used simply to refer to commercial sex irrespective of whether there is any element of coercion, force, fraud, deception, or abuse of power, let alone transnational movement of persons, which the parent convention (*United Nations Convention against Transnational Organized Crime and the Protocols Thereto*) is designed to combat. This is deeply problematic for both its contribution to the surveillance and criminalization of targeted and often racialized groups in Canada as well as its significant negative impacts on victims of violence, including state violence and neglect. In the case of our anti-trafficking in persons law, not only is the law itself ideologically based, but it is also enforced and wielded through ideological mechanisms that seek to make use of vulnerable groups for access to potential victims of human trafficking. This use of sex workers as "collateral damage" in an effort to root out exploitation is a misguided strategy that not only causes harm to the individuals involved but also serves to sustain inequitable access to justice and erode fundamental principles of justice. Post-PCEPA, there is no evidence that the state's anti-trafficking efforts have produced effective results in reducing exploitation. Instead, evidence is mounting that anti-trafficking efforts, especially when conjoined with the enforcement of anticommodification offences, are creating harm across several communities while sustaining barriers to justice for victims of violence.

The path to securing justice for those who are exploited in their labour necessitates careful use of state power to support rights and inclusion in the civic realms. The goal of creating a more equitable society cannot be met without a rejection of racialized and gendered criminalization based on outdated and nonempirically based myths and stereotypes. Where such patterns appear not only to exist but also to be growing, we must take a hard look at how state mechanisms are driving inequity and act to dismantle structural oppression in the criminal justice system and its enforcement.

Notes

1. We use the terms "human trafficking" and "trafficking in persons" interchangeably and define human trafficking using Canadian legal definitions. The specific legal charges on which our work is based include sections 279.01–279.04 of the *Criminal*

Code and section 118 of the *Immigration and Refugee Protection Act*.
2. See especially Katrin Roots (2023), who methodically tracked all human trafficking cases in Ontario from charging through to prosecution and sentencing and who speaks to the complexities of this method.
3. These include various types of *Charter* challenges — for example, in relation to contesting the police search of cell phones and statements given to police, lengthy delays in the trial of trafficking cases, and multiple section 276 applications as a defence by an accused seeking to prove a complainant's volitional engagement in commercial sex work.
4. See, for example, *R. v. Senoubari Abedini*, 2020, in which the sentence for a female accused included a $185,000 fine in lieu of forfeiture, versus the sentences imposed for male accused in *Chahinian c. R.*, 2022, which included a $10,000 fine in lieu of forfeiture, and *R. c. Valcourt*, 2017, in which a Mercedes and $10,565 were confiscated and forfeited to the state as proceeds of crime. The sentences in *Abedini* and *Chahinian* were both upheld on appeal.
5. In the words of our courts, these men are "parasitic." See, especially, Sibley and van der Meulen (2022), pp. 413–414, for a discussion of the parasite as a metaphor for exploitation and its origins in the constitutionally impugned and repealed offence of living on the avails.
6. See *R. v. Barton*, 2019, for a detailed discussion of the existence of these myths and their prevalence throughout the criminal justice system.
7. For example, thirty-five of seventy-two conviction cases from 2015 onward feature convictions for both types of offences.
8. It should be noted that prosecutors and judges are increasingly recognizing the offence overlap, applying the *Kienapple* principle, and staying charges.
9. For example, former Vancouver police officer James Fisher was found guilty of sexually assaulting two minor victims during the course of his work as a counterexploitation officer. See also O'Doherty and Waters (2019) regarding the differential gender-based impacts of criminalization on sex workers generally, and Burke (2018) on the intersecting effects of citizenship, gender, and sex work.

References

Alexander, M. (2012). *The new Jim Crow: Mass incarceration in the age of colorblindness*. The New Press.

Brayne, S. (2018). The criminal law and law enforcement implications of big data. *Annual Review of Law and Social Science*, 14, 1: 293–308.

British Columbia Civil Liberties Association. (2010). *Racial profiling*. https://bccla.org/wp-content/uploads/2012/03/2007-BCCLA-Report-Racial-Profiling.pdf

Bruckert, C., & Hannem, S. (2013). Rethinking the prostitution debates: Transcending structural stigma in systemic responses to sex work. *Canadian Journal of Law and Society/ La revue canadienne droit et société*, 28, 1: 43–63.

Burke, N.B. (2018). Double punishment: Immigration penalty and migrant trans women who sell sex. In E.M. Durisin, E. van der Meulen, & C. Bruckert (eds.), *Red light labour: Sex work regulation, agency, and resistance* (pp. 203–212). UBC Press.

Canadian Judicial Council. (2016). *In the matter of an inquiry pursuant to s. 63(1) of the* Judges Act *regarding the Honourable Justice Robin Camp: Report and recommendation of the Inquiry Committee to the Canadian Judicial Council*. https://cjc-ccm.ca/

cmslib/general/Camp_Docs/2016-11-29%20CJC%20Camp%20Inquiry%20Committee%20Report.pdf
CBC News. (2022, July 18). *AI helps researchers identify victims of human trafficking.* https://www.cbc.ca/news/canada/british-columbia/human-trafficking-survivor-new-study-flags-likely-victims-using-ai-1.6516085
Chan, W., & Chunn, D. (2014). *Racialization, crime, and criminal justice in Canada.* University of Toronto Press.
Chu, S.K.H., Clamen, J., & Santini, T. (2019). *The perils of "protection:" Sex workers' experiences of law enforcement in Ontario.* Canadian HIV/AIDS Legal Network. http://www.aidslaw.ca/site/the-perils-of-protection/?lang=en
Chu, S.K.H., & Glass, R. (2013). Sex work law reform in Canada: Considering problems with the Nordic model. *Alberta Law Review*, 51, 1: 101–124.
Craig, E. (2011). Sex work by law: *Bedford's* impact on municipal approaches to regulation of the sex trade. *Review of Constitutional Studies*, 16, 1: 205–225.
Daly, R. (2017). Canada's relationship with women migrant sex workers: Producing "vulnerable migrant workers" through "protecting workers from abuse and exploitation" [master's thesis]. Wilfred Laurier University. https://scholars.wlu.ca/etd/1934/
DeWolf, J. (2021). Sex workers and the best interests of their children: Issues faced by sex workers involved in custody and access legal proceedings. *Windsor Yearbook of Access to Justice*, 37, 2: 312–336.
Dubinski, K. (2018, December 20). Judge rejects mandatory minimum sentence, gives human traffickers less time. *CBC News.* https://www.cbc.ca/news/canada/london/human-trafficking-mandatory-minimum-sentence-london-1.4954200
Durisin, E.M., & van der Meulen, E. (2021). Sexualized nationalism and federal human trafficking consultations: Shifting discourses on sex trafficking in Canada. *Journal of Human Trafficking*, 7, 4: 454–475.
Faulkner, E. (2018). The victim, the villain and the rescuer: The trafficking of women and contemporary abolition. *The Journal of Law, Social Justice and Global Development*, 21: 1–14.
Fudge, J., Lam, E., Chu, S.K.H., & Wong, V. (2021). *Caught in the carceral web: Anti-trafficking laws and policies and their impact on migrant sex workers.* HIV Legal Network. https://www.hivlegalnetwork.ca/site/caught-in-the-carceral-web-anti-trafficking-laws-and-policies-and-their-impact-on-migrant-sex-workers
Gittens, M., & Cole, D. (1995). *Report of the Commission on Systemic Racism in the Ontario Criminal Justice System.* Government of Ontario.
Godziak, E.M. (2020). Low hanging fruit: How domestic minor sex trafficking erased foreign-born victims of child trafficking from anti-trafficking efforts in the United States. *Journal of Human Trafficking*, 6, 2: 1–8.
Hunt, S. (2015). Representing colonial violence: Trafficking, sex work, and the violence of law. *Atlantis: Critical Studies in Gender, Culture and Social Justice*, 37.2, 1: 25–39.
Jiwani, Y. (2016). Mediations of race and crime: Racializing crime, criminalizing race. In B. Perry (ed.), *Diversity, crime and justice in Canada* (2nd ed.; pp. 43–62). Oxford University Press.
Kaye, J. (2017). *Responding to human trafficking: Dispossession, colonial violence, and resistance among Indigenous and racialized women.* University of Toronto Press.
Kempadoo, K. (2016). The war on humans: Antitrafficking in the Caribbean. *Social and Economic Studies*, 65, 4: 5–32.
Kinney, E. (2015). Victims, villains, and valiant rescuers: Unpacking sociolegal constructions of human trafficking and crimmigration in popular culture. In M. J. Gui (ed.),

The illegal business of human trafficking (pp. 87–108). Springer.
Krüsi, A., Kerr, T., Taylor, C., Rhodes, T., & Shannon, K. (2016). "They won't change it back in their heads that we're trash": The intersection of sex work related stigma and evolving policing strategies. *Sociology of Health and Illness*, 38, 7: 1137–1150.
Lam, E. (2016). Inspection, policing and racism: How municipal by-laws endanger the lives of Chinese sex workers in Toronto. *Canadian Review of Social Policy*, 75: 87–112.
___. (2018). *Behind the rescue: How anti-trafficking investigations and policies harm migrant sex workers*. Butterfly (Asian and Migrant Sex Workers Support Network). https://tinyurl.com/52fsf75s
Lam, E., & Lepp, A. (2019). Butterfly: Resisting the harms of anti-trafficking policies and fostering peer-based organising in Canada. *Anti-Trafficking Review*, 12: 91–107.
Law Commission of Ontario. (2020). *The rise and fall of AI and algorithms in American criminal justice: Lessons for Canada*. https://www.lco-cdo.org/wp-content/uploads/2020/10/Criminal-AI-Paper-Final-Oct-28-2020.pdf
Lewis, S. (1992). *Report on race relations in Ontario*. Ontario Legislative Assembly. http://www.ontla.on.ca/library/repository/mon/13000/134250.pdf
Locke, C. (2021). Debating the rule of law: The curious re-enactment of the solicitation offence. *Alberta Law Review*, 58, 3: 687–738.
Maynard, R. (2015). Fighting wrongs with wrongs? How Canadian anti-trafficking crusades have failed sex workers, migrants, and Indigenous communities. *Atlantis: Critical Studies in Gender, Culture and Social Justice*, 37.2, 1: 40–56.
___. (2017). *Policing Black lives: State violence in Canada from slavery to the present*. Fernwood Publishing.
___. (2018). Do Black sex workers' lives matter? Whitewashed anti-slavery, racial justice, and abolition. In E.M. Durisin, E. van der Meulen, & C. Bruckert (eds.), *Red light labour: Sex work regulation, agency, and resistance* (pp. 281–292). UBC Press.
McNeilly, G. (2018). *Broken trust: Indigenous people and the Thunder Bay Police Service*. Office of the Independent Police Review Directorate.
___. (2019). *Breaking the rule: A review of police strip searches in Ontario*. Office of the Independent Police Review Directorate.
Millar, H., & O'Doherty, T. (2015). *Key findings: The Palermo Protocol & Canada: The evolution and human rights impacts of antitrafficking laws in Canada (2002–2015)*. ICCLR. https://icclr.org/publications/the-palermo-protocol-canada-the-evolution-and-human-rights-impacts-of-anti-trafficking-laws-in-canada-2002-2015/
___. (2020a). *Canadian human trafficking prosecutions and principles of fundamental justice: A contradiction in terms?* https://icclr.org/publications/canadian-human-trafficking-prosecutions-and-principles-of-fundamental-justice-a-contradiction-in-terms/
___. (2020b). Racialized, gendered, and sensationalized: An examination of Canadian anti-trafficking laws, their enforcement, and their (re)presentation. *Canadian Journal of Law and Society*, 35, 1: 23–44.
Monchalin, L. (2010). Canadian Aboriginal peoples victimization, offending and its prevention: Gathering the evidence. *Crime Prevention and Community Safety*, 12, 2: 119–132.
Nagel, M. (2015). Trafficking with abolitionism: An examination of anti-slavery discourses. *Champ pénal/Penal field*, 12.
National Inquiry into Missing and Murdered Indigenous Women and Girls. (2019). *Reclaiming power and place: The final report of the National Inquiry into Missing*

and Murdered Indigenous Women and Girls. Government of Canada. https://www.mmiwg-ffada.ca/final-report/

O'Brien, E. (2016). Human trafficking heroes and villains: Representing the problem in anti-trafficking awareness campaigns. *Social & Legal Studies*, 25, 2: 205–224.

O'Doherty, T., & Waters, I. (2019). Gender, victimization, and commercial sex: A comparative study. *Atlantis: Critical Studies in Gender, Culture and Social Justice*, 40, 1: 18–31.

Ontario Human Rights Commission. (2003). *Paying the price: The human cost of racial profiling inquiry report*. http://www.ohrc.on.ca/sites/default/files/attachments/Paying_the_price%3A_The_human_cost_of_racial_profiling.pdf

____. (2017). *Under suspicion: Research and consultation report on racial profiling in Ontario*. http://ohrc.on.ca/sites/default/files/Under%20suspicion_research%20and%20consultation%20report%20on%20racial%20profiling%20in%20Ontario_2017.pdf

____. (2018). *A collective impact: Interim report on the inquiry into racial profiling and racial discrimination of Black persons by the Toronto Police Service*. http://ohrc.on.ca/sites/default/files/TPS%20Inquiry_Interim%20Report%20EN%20FINAL%20DESIGNED%20for%20remed_3_0.pdf

Public Safety Canada. (2022). *Public Safety Canada's webinar series 2022: Education and awareness of human trafficking*. Government of Canada. https://www.publicsafety.gc.ca/cnt/rsrcs/pblctns/2022-dctn-wrnss-ht/index-en.aspx

Raguparan, M. (2019). "So it's not always the sappy story": Women of colour and Indigenous women in the indoor sectors of the Canadian sex industry speak out [doctoral dissertation]. Carleton University. https://curve.carleton.ca/a33b09b7-81cd-4457-9287-ddbe93b10963

Robertson, K., Khoo, C., & Song, Y. (2020). *To surveil and predict: A human rights analysis of algorithmic policing in Canada*. Citizen Lab and International Human Rights Program. https://citizenlab.ca/2020/09/to-surveil-and-predict-a-human-rights-analysis-of-algorithmic-policing-in-canada/

Roots, K. (2018). The human trafficking matrix: Law, policy and anti-trafficking practices in the Canadian criminal justice system [doctoral dissertation]. York University. https://yorkspace.library.yorku.ca/xmlui/handle/10315/35510

____. (2022). *The domestication of human trafficking: Law, policing, and prosecution in Canada*. University of Toronto Press.

Shih, E. (2016). Not in my "backyard abolitionism": Vigilante rescue against American sex trafficking. *Sociological Perspectives*, 59, 1: 66–90.

Sibley, M., & van der Meulen, E. (2022). Courting victims: Exploring the legal framing of exploitation in human trafficking cases. *Canadian Journal of Law and Society*, 37, 3: 409–429.

Sinclair, M. (2018). *Thunder Bay Police Services Board investigation: Final report*. https://tribunalsontario.ca/documents/ocpc/TBPSB_Investigation_Final_Report_-_EN-FINAL-1.pdf

Soderlund, G. (2005). Running from the rescuers: New U.S. crusades against sex trafficking and the rhetoric of abolition. *National Women's Studies Association Journal*, 17, 3: 64–87.

Srikantiah, J. (2007). Perfect victims and real survivors: The iconic victim in domestic human trafficking law. *Boston University Law Review*, 87: 157–211.

Sterling, A., & van der Meulen, E. (2018). "We are not criminals": Sex work clients in Canada and the constitution of risk knowledge. *Canadian Journal of Law and Society*, 33, 3: 291–308.

Stewart, H. (2016). The constitutionality of the new sex work law. *Alberta Law Review*, 54, 1: 69–88.
Tanovich, D. (2008). The charter of whiteness: Twenty-five years of maintaining racial injustice in the Canadian criminal justice system. *Supreme Court Law Review*, 40: 655–686.
Taschner, E. (2022, July 22). Officials in North Bay launch initiative to combat human trafficking. CTV *News*. https://northernontario.ctvnews.ca/officials-in-north-bay-launch-initiative-to-combat-human-trafficking-1.5999102
Tulloch, M. (2018). *Report of the independent street checks review*. https://www.ontario.ca/page/report-independent-street-checks-review
United Nations Special Rapporteur on the Rights of Indigenous Peoples. (2014). *Report of the special rapporteur on the rights of Indigenous Peoples, James Anaya. Addendum: The situation of Indigenous peoples in Canada* (HRC/27/52/Add.2). Human Rights Council.
Weitzer, R. (2011). The social construction of sex trafficking: Ideology and institutionalization of a moral crusade. *Politics and Society*, 35, 3: 447–475.
Williamson, K.G., & Marcus, A. (2017). Black pimps matter: Racially selective identification and prosecution of sex trafficking in the United States. In A. Horning & A. Marcus (eds.), *Third party sex work and pimps in the age of anti-trafficking* (pp. 177–196). Springer International Publishing.
Wortley, S. (2019). *Halifax, Nova Scotia: Street checks report*. Nova Scotia Human Rights Commission. https://humanrights.novascotia.ca/sites/default/files/editor-uploads/halifax_street_checks_report_march_2019_0.pdf

Cases

Canada (Attorney General) v. Bedford, 2013 SCC 72, [2013] 3 SCR 1101.
Chahinian c. R., 2022 QCCA 499.
Kienapple v. R., [1975] 1 S.C.R. 729.
R. v. Ahmed et al., 2019 ONSC 4822.
R. v. Antoine, 2019 ONSC 3843.
R. v. Anwar, 2020 ONCJ 103.
R. v. Barton, 2019 SCC 33.
R. v. Casanova, 2020 QCCQ 9101.
R. v. Charboneau, 2019 ABQB 313.
R. v. Chisholm, 2018 ONSC 7802.
R. v. Clayton, [2021] OJ No. 6732.
R. v. Dare, 2021 ONCA 327.
R. v. Davidson, 2020 ONSC 2775.
R. v. Domotor, 2011 ONSC 626.
R. v. D'Souza, 2016 ONSC 2749.
R. v. Faroughi, 2020 ONSC 780.
R. v. Finestone, 2017 ONCJ 22.
R. v. Haniffa, 2021 ONCA 326.
R. v. Haniffa, 2022 SCC 46.
R. v. J.G., 2021 ONSC 1095.
R. v. J.L.M., 2017 BCCA 258.
R. v. Joseph, 2020 ONCA 733.
R. v. Kassongo, [2019] O.J. No. 6689.
R. v. Kloubakov, 2021 ABQB 960.

R. v. Le, 2019 SCC 34.
R. v. Leduc, 2019 ONSC 6794.
R. v. Lopez, 2018 ONSC 4749.
R. v. Mercer, 2017 NSPC 20.
R. v. Reginald Louis Jean, 2020 ONSC 624.
R. v. Robitaille, 2017 ONCJ 768.
R. v. Safieh, 2018 ONSC 4468.
R. v. S.C., 2019 ABQB 793.
R. v. Senoubari Abedini, 2020 ONCA 520.
R. v. Shahinian [Chahinian], 2018 QCCQ 20771.
R. v. Spence, 2005 SCC 71.
R. v. Strickland-Prescod, 2019 ONCJ 755.
R. c. Valcourt, 2017 QCCQ 6798.
R. v. Webber, 2019 NSSC 147.
R. v. Williams, [1998] 1 S.C.R. 1128.

Legislation

Canadian Charter of Rights and Freedoms, Part 1 of the *Constitution Act*, 1982, Sched. B to the *Canada Act* 1982 (UK), 1982, c. 11.
Criminal Code, RSC 1985, c. C-46.
Immigration and Refugee Protection Act, SC 2001, c. 27.
International Covenant on Civil and Political Rights, December 16, 1966, https://www.ohchr.org/en/instruments-mechanisms/instruments/international-covenant-civil-and-political-rights
Protection of Communities and Exploited Persons Act, SC 2014, c. 25.
Protocol to Prevent, Suppress and Punish Trafficking in Persons, Especially Women and Children, supplementing the United Nations Convention against Transnational Organized Crime, November 15, 2000, https://www.unodc.org/res/human-trafficking/2021the-protocol-tip_html/TIP.pdf
United Nations Convention against Transnational Organized Crime and the Protocols Thereto, November 15, 2000, https://www.unodc.org/unodc/en/organized-crime/intro/UNTOC.html

6

Human Trafficking Law and Policy

Exacerbating Racial and Gendered Violence in Ontario

Sandra Ka Hon Chu and Robyn Maynard

Sex workers face an alarming web of punitive laws and policies from all levels of government, which are crushing the measures and networks that keep them safe (Fudge et al., 2021). In *Canada v. Bedford*, sex workers from across the country supported a successful court challenge to repeal criminal prohibitions on bawdy-houses, "living on the avails" of prostitution, and communicating in public for purposes of prostitution. The 2013 Supreme Court of Canada ruling on the case accepted long-standing claims by communities who sell or trade sex that the criminalization of sex work fuels violence against sex workers and undermines their ability to facilitate their own and one another's safety (Belak, 2018). The federal Conservative government of the day, however, disregarded decades of evidence supporting decriminalization, and in 2014 passed the *Protection of Communities and Exploited Persons Act*, which effectively recriminalized most activities related to sex work under the guise of preventing exploitation. In addition to reintroducing prohibitions on working in public spaces, "materially benefiting from" sex work, and "procuring" someone to offer or provide sex, the legislation added new layers of criminalization. For the first time in Canadian history, purchasing sexual services (as well as communicating for that purpose) and advertising sexual services became crimes (Durisin et al., 2018).

These sex work laws function alongside federal legislation that criminalizes human trafficking by prohibiting actions "for the purpose ... of exploitation" (*Criminal Code*, 1985, s. 279.01(1)), and prevents, via immigration regulations, migrants from working in the sex industry. While the criminal regulation of sex work and human trafficking is rooted in federal state powers, a growing number of provincial anti-trafficking laws have been advanced under the claim of promoting awareness of human trafficking and facilitating its investigation.[1] Yet the experiences of Black, racialized, Indigenous, and migrant sex workers show that despite such nominally benevolent aims, these laws and their enforcement are frequently a source of harm rather than support for sex workers, particularly those most marginalized (Chu et al., 2019; Lam, 2018a).

This chapter considers the impacts of Ontario's recent venture into the space first taken up by federal powers. We begin by briefly outlining recent anti-trafficking efforts in the province, as implemented and supported by the provincial government, focusing on the introduction in 2021 of the *Anti-Human Trafficking Strategy Act*. We then provide a detailed analysis of current anti-trafficking approaches and the ways in which the new policy contributes to existing harms. By way of conclusion, we argue that efforts to address racial violence, gendered violence, and labour exploitation experienced by people who sell sex must move away from carceral systems and instead focus on listening to affected communities, granting permanent status for all migrants, decriminalizing sex work, and repealing anti–sex work immigration regulations.

Ontario's Sociolegal Anti-Trafficking Context

In 2020, the Ontario government announced an investment of $307 million over five years in an alleged strategy to combat human trafficking and sexual exploitation. The unprecedented scale of this financial investment coincided with some of the most comprehensive budget cuts (e.g., to legal aid and childcare) as well as privatization of services (e.g., health care) in Ontario's history. Part of the massive anti-trafficking investment has been funnelled into sweeping investigations by police. One such high-profile campaign is Operation Northern Spotlight, a yearly initiative undertaken by the Royal Canadian Mounted Police, Ontario Provincial Police, and numerous municipal police forces that has involved police posing as clients and intruding on sex workers in their workplaces. While these initiatives purportedly protect the safety and security of potentially vulnerable women, they have resulted in the arrests of Black, racialized, and migrant people for sex work and immigration offences, and the laying of numerous bylaw infraction charges. As migrant sex worker organization Butterfly (2018) has described, "The current 'Rescue Model,' as reproduced by Operation Northern Spotlight, not only harms sex worker communities, but increases the surveillance, arrest, detainment and deportation of sex workers, particularly migrant sex workers. Police and city bylaw enforcement officers actively share information with [the Canada Border Services Agency]" (p. 3; see also Shih, 2021).

In 2021, the provincial moral panic fuelling anti-trafficking initiatives culminated in the introduction of Bill 251, the *Combating Human Trafficking Act*, which, once passed later that same year, enacted the *Anti-Human Trafficking Strategy Act*.[2] The law was justified on the grounds of sensationalist and unfounded allegations, such as thirteen is the average age of recruitment into sex trafficking (see Smith & Hale, 2021) and "human trafficking is one of the fastest-growing crimes worldwide" (Ministry of Children, Community and Social Services, 2021, n.p.). The *Anti-Human Trafficking Strategy Act* requires the province to maintain an anti–human trafficking strategy; enables regulations necessitating unspecified persons, whose employers are required to provide them with training, to report instances of suspected human trafficking; and imposes various obligations on advertisers of sexual services, including keeping records, reporting, and making specific information available to the public. While the Act nominally combats human trafficking, sex workers have highlighted that the lack of clarity in the definition of "trafficking" has resulted in the wholesale surveillance, investigation, and punishment of the entire ecosystem of sex work (Butterfly & HIV Legal Network, 2021). Perhaps most troublingly, the law expands the ever-growing net of law enforcement powers to investigate and respond to suspected cases of human trafficking in the province, including by deputizing a new category of inspectors to ensure compliance with the legislation.

Under the Act, inspectors may, without a warrant or notice, and at any time, enter and inspect any place, including a dwelling, to determine compliance with the legislation as long as they have "the consent of the occupant" (*Anti-Human Trafficking Strategy Act*, 2021, s. 7(4)) notwithstanding obvious disparities in power between an inspector and the person being inspected. Inspectors are also granted unfettered powers to examine, demand, remove, or copy records and question a person on any matter that may be relevant to the inspection. Noncompliance is a punishable offence subject to a fine of $50,000 or $100,000 for an individual or corporation, respectively. The broad authority granted to inspectors — arguably broader than the search-and-seizure powers that police already have under emergency circumstances — give them frighteningly wide latitude based on their sole discretion in determining what may be relevant to an inspection. At the same time, an individual is not permitted to refuse to answer questions on any matter that is or may be relevant to the inspection. This potentially requires sex workers, who face an array of negative consequences for engaging in criminalized labour (including stigma, discrimination, eviction, travel bans, child apprehension, criminal charges, and loss of immigration status), to disclose details of their work with little knowledge as to whether an inspector's questions are relevant to a human trafficking investigation. Importantly, this interrogation occurs in a context of extraordinarily uneven power relationships between law enforcement and sex workers, especially those who are Black, Indigenous, Asian, or migrant. Sex workers may feel compelled to let people into their residences or workplaces and to participate in an interrogation that risks criminalizing their coworkers, friends, family, and community more broadly. The coercive possibility of heavy-handed fines for not cooperating is compounded for migrant workers who may not understand or speak English.

Curiously, the Act acknowledges that "certain populations may be disproportionately impacted by human trafficking, such as women and girls and racialized groups including Indigenous and Black communities" (*Anti-Human Trafficking Strategy Act*, 2021, preamble), and lists among its foundational principles the need to promote and protect "human rights" and be guided by "diverse sources of evidence" (s. 5). Yet, as we detail further below, this sweeping surveillance will lead to various harms borne by Black, Indigenous, Asian, and migrant sex workers, including major and unwarranted intrusions on privacy and racial profiling, driving sex workers into more isolated spaces on the basis of blurry understandings of human trafficking that too often conflate it with sex work.

Imprecise Understandings of Trafficking and the Impacts of Current Approaches

As others have noted, "human trafficking" is a loaded term used to describe everything from sex work to intimate partner violence to labour exploitation (De Shalit & van der Meulen, 2019; Hunt, 2015; Kempadoo,

2005; Roots, 2013, 2022; Sibley, 2020). Among policymakers, law enforcement, and community-based services for survivors of human trafficking, the term is almost always associated with sex trafficking, given the pervading view that sex work is an illegitimate form of labour and that people who sell or trade sexual services are all victims of sexual exploitation (De Shalit, 2021; Durisin & van der Meulen, 2021; Sibley, 2020). Illustrating the amorphous nature in which human trafficking is framed, the Ontario government's list of "signs that someone may be trafficked" (Ministry of Children, Community and Social Services, 2017, n.p.) is meaninglessly broad. Routinely, police construe all third parties who work with and support sex workers as human traffickers — a position many social service providers also adopt, at the expense of sex workers and their networks of support. This misconstruing, in turn, falsely inflates statistics on human trafficking victims, which suggest "approximately two-thirds of police reported human trafficking cases in Canada occur in Ontario" (Ministry of Children, Community and Social Services, 2022, n.p.). Similarly, the *Anti-Human Trafficking Strategy Act* imprints the notion that sexual services are equivalent to human trafficking, subjecting advertisers of these services to additional surveillance and reporting requirements.

In a context in which sex work and trafficking are often understood to be one and the same, the Act's deputization of provincial inspectors to determine compliance with the law via expansive access to workplaces means that people who are working in a wide assortment of sex work establishments will be subject to unwanted surveillance, abuse, and possibly violence. The Black Legal Action Centre (2021), an Ontario-based community legal clinic with the mandate of combating systemic anti-Black racism in the province, told the Standing Committee on Justice Policy during the debates on Bill 251 that it "has the potential to increase the criminalization of sex work and sex workers, by distorting the lived realities of sex workers," which can produce "particularly debilitating consequences for Black, Indigenous and racialized people more generally" (p. 2). Already, research shows how existing human trafficking initiatives have been exploited as a pretext to invade sex workers' workplaces (Butterfly, 2018; Chu et al., 2019; Lam, 2018a). In particular, Black, Indigenous, Asian, and migrant women have been subject to heightened police profiling and targeting, including presumption of involvement in sex work (Hunt, 2015; Kaye, 2017; Maynard, 2017, 2018). Due to sexualized stereotypes about them, Black women are often assumed to be involved in sex work merely by walking in public spaces, and Indigenous and Black sex workers have been accused of human trafficking when they work collectively (Crenshaw & Ritchie, 2015; Maynard, 2017; Ontario Human Rights Commission, 2003). Asian women and their networks of support have been racially profiled by law enforcement variously as human trafficking victims and members of so-called criminal organizations, then ticketed for municipal bylaw infractions or detained for immigration infractions, often resulting in deportation (Lam, 2018a).

One sweeping commonality among sex workers' experiences is of law enforcement as a source of repression, not protection (Ade Kur & Duffy, 2022; Bruckert & Hannem, 2013; Chu et al., 2019). As Black women's experiences make clear, policing is a form of racial and gendered violence. Black feminists in Canada have mobilized around the issue of police harassment and assault of Black women since at least the 1980s (Mugabo, 2016; Rocha, 2005, as cited in Tator & Henry, 2006). The police shooting of Sophia Cook in 1989 brought the issue, at least momentarily, into the spotlight, as Black women — including Cook, who survived the shooting — organized to address the injustice (Holden, 1990; *Windsor Star*, 1990). Available data suggest that Black women are policed at rates significantly higher than those for white women. In one study based in Kingston, Black women were *more than two times* more likely than white women to have been stopped by police (Owusu-Bempah & Wortley, 2014). A Montreal-based study found that Black girls were three times more likely than white girls to have been arrested two or more times (Bernard & McAll, 2008). A 2019 report on street checks in Halifax, commissioned by the Nova Scotia Human Rights Commission, found that Black women are "significantly over-represented" in such interactions (519 per 1,000), being stopped more than white men (481 per 1,000) and at a rate 3.6 times greater than white women (143 per 1,000) (Wortley, 2019).

In the United States, a significant body of research has addressed the policing of Black sex workers (e.g., McTighe & Haywood, 2017; Ritchie & Mogul, 2008), but no such study has yet been published in Canada. Historical data suggest racially disproportionate forms of policing vis-à-vis prostitution-related arrests and charges. Notably, in the nineteenth and early twentieth centuries, Black women were disproportionately impacted by prostitution-related arrests and charges in many Canadian cities (see Backhouse, 1985; Mosher, 1998). Existing research further demonstrates that law enforcement officers continue to associate Black women with prostitution. As Robyn Maynard (2017) has written elsewhere, "The mere presence of a Black female body in public space is sexualized, and prostitution is frequently assumed" (p. 138). Black women have described incidents to researchers in which the police harassed them due to an assumption they were involved in sex work (see Bernard, 2001; Ontario Human Rights Commission, 2003). The high-profile cases of Audrey Smith and Stacy Bonds illustrate this dynamic; in 1993 and 2008, respectively, these Black women were subject to abusive strip searches by Canadian police officers under the pretext that they may have been involved in prostitution (see Lawson, 2002; Maynard, 2017; Tanovich, 2011). The Ontario Human Rights Commission (2017) also reported on the experiences of racialized women whose presumed engagement in sex work contributed to police profiling of them and their associates. In one such case, a Black woman and her white boyfriend were stopped by police officers who thought she was a sex worker and he was a client. The Nova Scotia report that found Black women are overrepresented in street checks in Halifax also found that Black residents are 4.5 times more likely to be involved in a "prostitution-related" check than are white residents (Wortley, 2019). It is safe to conclude that Black women in Canada are subject to intensive rates of policing, informed by assumptions about their involvement in sex work.

Given the ongoing criminalization of Black life, policing is more likely to cause harm than to prevent or disrupt it for Black sex workers, just like for Black women more generally. Police have failed to provide support and even been the source of harm for Black women who are involved in sex work, such as Moka Dawkins, a trans sex worker who was criminally charged and incarcerated for protecting herself from violence, and those believed to be involved in sex work, such as Alloura Wells, a homeless transgender woman whose disappearance was not prioritized for investigation. These cases fit within a broader pattern documented in the United States by sociologist Beth Richie (2012): when criminal laws are brought in under the guise of protecting women, it is Black women who are disproportionately and predominantly criminalized (see also, Davis, 1997; Mirchandani & Chan, 2005; Sudbury, 2002).

Butterfly, the migrant sex worker organization, has repeatedly documented migrant sex workers' experiences of human rights violations at the hands of law enforcement who are purportedly upholding various laws (Lam, 2018a). Migrant sex workers have been subjected to harassment and discrimination, arbitrary arrests, and detention. They even report having false evidence used against them to justify their ongoing detention. They have also reported being prevented from accessing legal representation and support while in the custody of anti–human trafficking investigators, and many have lost their immigration status and been deported. In a 2018 study by Butterfly of Asian migrant massage and holistic centres in Toronto, more than one-third of workers reported having been abused or harassed by bylaw enforcement or police officers during anti–human trafficking investigations. The study found no instances of trafficking or forced labour among the sixty-one workers surveyed (Lam, 2018b; see also Malla et al., 2019).

In a 2018 submission to a federal parliamentary committee studying human trafficking, Butterfly described the arrests and deportations of twenty-three of its members since 2015. The workers reported degrading experiences of detention along with confiscation of money (up to $50,000) and other personal belongings by law enforcement officers during human trafficking investigations. One worker described being locked up in chains even though she had been identified as a suspected victim of trafficking. Another worker reported her exploitative boss to the authorities. The information she provided was shared with an anti-trafficking team and a raid was carried out at her workplace, resulting in the arrest and deportation of her coworkers, and eventually the worker herself, after it was revealed to immigration authorities that she was working in Canada without status.

Such anti-Asian racism has significant historical precedent. The first ban in Canadian immigration law on the grounds of race and gender was implemented in 1885 through the *Chinese Immigration Act*, which directed that "no permit to land shall be granted ... to any Chinese woman who is known to be a prostitute" (s. 9). The 1885 report from the Royal Commission on Chinese Immigration had noted that "the Chinese are the only people coming to the continent the great bulk of whose women are prostitutes" (p. lxxix) and "Chinese prostitutes are more shameless than white women who follow the same pursuit, as though the former had been educated for it from their cradle" (p. lxxviii) — marking Chinese women as legitimate targets for state surveillance because of their racialized inclination for sex work.

In research conducted by the HIV Legal Network, Indigenous sex workers also shared their experiences of pervasive racial profiling, as well as arrest, incarceration, and physical assault by police investigating sex work, including an instance where an Indigenous worker was charged with human trafficking and running a "prostitution ring" merely for working with other sex workers in a shared workplace (Chu et al., 2019). The Vancouver Sex Workers Rights Collective (2018), which describes itself as a "diverse collective of Indigenous individuals who participate or participated in sex work or trade or provide sexual services in the Downtown Eastside of Vancouver" (p. 2), made the following submission to the National Inquiry into Missing and Murdered Indigenous Women and Girls:

> The use by academics, activists, the media and governments of human trafficking as *the* framework or lens through which responses to murdered and missing Indigenous women and girls are considered is inappropriate, ineffective and harmful. The focus on human trafficking shifts attention away from the systemic colonial factors that created and maintain the circumstances and structures of violence. This approach focuses resources and responses to violence into increased policing and away from programs and services that may help individuals that are facing specific types of violence that are conflated into human trafficking (child exploitation, sexual exploitation or violence experienced when participating in sex work). Police attention on individuals who participate in sex work reclassified as victims in the human trafficking framework puts these individuals at risk. (p. 8)

The extension of law enforcement powers also facilitates the racial profiling of Black men. In a recent study, Hayli Millar and Tamara O'Doherty (2020) found that after the passage of the *Protection of Communities and Exploited Persons Act* in 2014, law enforcement in Canada continued to treat sex work and trafficking interchangeably and to associate Black communities in particular with sex work, specifically vis-à-vis the stereotype of Black men as "pimps." The same study found that anti-trafficking prosecutions have steadily increased, and Black and Caribbean men comprised at least 40 percent of primary or co-accused in over eighty-seven trafficking cases prosecuted from 2006 to 2017.

Researchers also found media coverage related to human trafficking saturated with images of accused Black men in a manner that was not seen when the accused was white (Millar & O'Doherty, 2020). Katrin Roots (2022) analyzed 123 court documents of individuals charged with human trafficking in Ontario and found that the primary target of human trafficking investigations in Canada has become the prototypical "Black pimp," a figure easily resurrected and redeployed as part of Canada's anti–human trafficking efforts. In the United States, Kathleen Williamson and Anthony Marcus (2017) described the enforcement of anti-trafficking laws as a form of "Black criminalization" and a serious and systemic human rights violation, finding that 62 percent of national sex trafficking prosecutions involved Black people (see also Bernstein, 2012).

As these experiences with anti-trafficking law and policing make clear, racial and gendered violence will be exacerbated by Ontario's recent passage of the *Anti-Human Trafficking Strategy Act*. The legislation will undoubtedly contribute to profound harm to Black, Indigenous, and migrant sex workers, while failing to address many forms of gender-based violence and exploitative working conditions that currently fall under the umbrella term of "human trafficking."

Conclusion

Contemporary state-led anti-trafficking efforts effectively obscure and exacerbate the root causes of social, racial, and economic disenfranchisement that create the conditions for exploitation and abuse of all kinds — anti-Black criminalization, the racialization of poverty, housing precarity, "current and historical colonialism [and] the criminal and immigration laws that place people in a rights-vacuum" (Maynard, 2015, p. 41) in the first place. From the creation of programming by and for sex workers to antiviolence programs to legal challenges, sex workers in Ontario have been at the helm of movements to eradicate the laws and practices that contribute to racism and exploitative working conditions, and they have established organizations that provide education around safer sex and HIV prevention — all while demanding labour and citizenship rights for all. In effect, communities of people who sell and trade sex have been and continue to organize in their own communities to address the myriad harms that are increasingly lumped under the catch-all term of "trafficking" (see, e.g., Native Youth Sexual Health Network, Black Sex Workers Collective, and Butterfly). The *Anti-Human Trafficking Strategy Act*, framed as ending exploitation, effectively undercuts this organizing, and minimizes the ability of different communities to undertake meaningful, community-led antiviolence work.

The Act's introduction of more law enforcement and investigations, largely unchecked, into Black, Indigenous, racialized, and migrant communities, under a provincial government that has committed only nominally to addressing systemic anti-Black and anti-Indigenous racism, will only exacerbate the crisis of policing in Black, Indigenous, racialized, and migrant people's lives. By further equipping law enforcement to terrorize people in their everyday lives and work, the *Anti-Human Trafficking Strategy Act* is counter to what people living and working in precarity need to be safe. Vulnerable communities will have more to fear from policing, from traumatizing raids of workplaces, and from excessive surveillance, particularly when people are working with one another or in indoor settings, which is far safer for those who sell or trade sex.

Sex workers are best positioned to observe situations of violence and exploitation within the industry, but the criminalization of sex work and the terrifying experiences of sex work and human trafficking investigations, among other forms of criminalization, only serve to further distance them from supports in times of need. Increasing surveillance and criminalization do nothing to end racial violence, gendered violence, and labour exploitation experienced by people who sell or trade sex. If provincial politicians are truly concerned about these abuses, they must address structural barriers such as poverty, precarious immigration status, and lack of access to affordable housing, health care, and social services. They should support the repeal of the *Anti-Human Trafficking Strategy Act* as well as the federal anti–sex work offences and immigration regulations that make it more difficult for sex workers and migrants to work safely. Further, policymakers can support access to permanent status for migrants so that they are not forced into vulnerable positions where they could be exploited in any industry where human trafficking — that is, forced labour — occurs. The decriminalization of sex work and the regularization of immigration status would be meaningful steps toward ending labour abuses.

For sex workers, for Black, Indigenous, and migrant communities, and for others, problematic laws and the corresponding increase of policing cannot be understood as the solution when they are instead the cause of harm and violence. There has been an unprecedented wave of support spanning labour, health, and housing movements across North America for a racial and gender justice movement geared toward the "abolition of all carceral systems" (American Public Health Association, 2020, n.p.). This movement, oriented toward more meaningful forms of safety, has forwarded demands for the repeal of unjust laws, an immediate and significant divestment from policing, and a dramatic decrease in the scale, scope, and powers of policing over our communities. Necessary measures include the decriminalization of sex work, the decriminalization of drugs and the creation and scale-up of a safe supply, the decriminalization of poverty-related offences, and the divorce of law enforcement from mental health, overdose, and all other forms of health care, as crucial steps on the path toward abolitionist futures (Black Lives Matter, n.d.; Choosing Real Safety, n.d.; Ritchie et al., n.d.). Also needed is a concurrent investment in noncarceral forms of security, including decent and affordable housing for all, restorative and transformative justice initiatives, and community-based antiviolence programs geared toward preventing gendered violence and supporting survivors. While all sex workers and all communities in Ontario and beyond require protection from harm, current state-led anti-trafficking legislation cannot and will not deliver this much-needed safety.

Notes

1. Examples include Alberta, *Protecting Survivors of Human Trafficking Act*, 2020; Manitoba, *The Child Sexual Exploitation and Human Trafficking Act*, 2011; and Saskatchewan, *Protection from Human Trafficking Act*, 2012.
2. At the time of writing, sections 6 to 10 of the *Anti-Human Trafficking Strategy Act*, featuring the regulations related to inspectors and inspections, had yet to come into force.

References

Ade Kur, E., & Duffy, J. (2022). Sex worker justice—by us, for us: Toronto sex workers resisting carceral violence. In S. Pasternak, K. Walby, & A. Stadnyk (eds.), *Disarm, defund, dismantle: Police abolition in Canada* (pp. 98–112). Between the Lines.

American Public Health Association. (2020). *Advancing public health interventions to address the harms of the carceral system*. https://www.apha.org/policies-and-advocacy/public-health-policy-statements/policy-database/2021/01/14/advancing-public-health-interventions-to-address-the-harms-of-the-carceral-system

Backhouse, C. (1985). Nineteenth-century Canadian prostitution law reflection of a discriminatory society. *Social History*, 18, 36: 387–423.
Belak, B. (2018). Bedford v Canada: A breakthrough in the legal discourse. In E.M. Durisin, E. van der Meulen, & C. Bruckert (eds.), *Red light labour: Sex work, regulation, agency, and resistance* (pp. 48–56). UBC Press.
Bernard, L., & McAll, C. (2008). La surrepresentation des jeunes noirs Montrealais. *Revue du CREMIS*, 1, 3: 15–21.
Bernard, W.T. (2001). *Including Black women in health and social policy development: Winning over addictions — empowering Black mothers with addictions to overcome triple jeopardy.* Maritime Centre of Excellence for Women's Health.
Bernstein, E. (2012). Carceral politics as gender justice? The "traffic in women" and neoliberal circuits of crime, sex and rights. *Theoretical Sociology*, 41: 233–259.
Black Legal Action Centre. (2021). *Submission to the Standing Committee on Justice Policy.* https://www.blacklegalactioncentre.ca/wp-content/uploads/2021/05/BLAC-Bill-251-submissions-March-13-2021.pdf
Black Lives Matter. (n.d.). *BLM demands.* https://blacklivesmatter.com/blm-demands/
Bruckert, C., & Hannem, S. (2013). To serve and protect? Structural stigma, social profiling, and the abuse of police power in Ottawa. In E. van der Meulen, E.M. Durisin, & V. Love (eds.), *Selling sex: Experience, advocacy, and research on sex work in Canada* (pp. 297–313). UBC Press.
Butterfly (Asian and Migrant Sex Workers Support Network). (2018). *Brief to the House of Commons Standing Committee on Justice and Human Rights on Human Trafficking in Canada: How migrant sex workers are harmed by anti-trafficking initiatives and policies.* https://www.ourcommons.ca/Content/Committee/421/JUST/Brief/BR10005482/br-external/ButterflyAsianAndMigrantSexWorkersSupportNetwork-e.pdf
Butterfly & HIV Legal Network. (2021). *Joint Submission on Bill 251, Combating Human Trafficking Act, 2021.* https://www.hivlegalnetwork.ca/site/joint-submission-on-bill-251-combating-human-trafficking-act-2021
Choosing Real Safety. (n.d.) *Choosing real safety: A historic declaration to divest from policing and prisons and build safer communities for all.* https://www.choosingrealsafety.com/declaration
Chu, S.K.H., Clamen, J., & Santini, T. (2019). *The perils of "protection": Sex workers' experiences of law enforcement in Ontario.* Canadian HIV/AIDS Legal Network.
Crenshaw, K., & Ritchie, A. (2015). *Say her name: Resisting police brutality against Black women.* African American Policy Forum.
Davis, A. (1997). Race and criminalization: Black Americans and the punishment industry. In W. Lubiano (ed.), *The house that race built: Original essays by Toni Morrison, Angela Y. Davis, Cornel West, and others on Black Americans and politics in America today* (pp. 264–279). Vintage Books.
De Shalit, A. (2021). Neoliberal paternalism and displaced culpability: Examining the governing relations of the human trafficking problem [unpublished doctoral dissertation]. Toronto Metropolitan University.
De Shalit, A., & van der Meulen, E. (2019). Thinking critically about human trafficking claims: Definitional and conceptual challenges. *Justice Report*, 34, 3: 33–36.
Durisin, E.M., & van der Meulen, E. (2021). Sexualized nationalism and federal human trafficking consultations: Shifting discourses on sex trafficking in Canada. *Journal of Human Trafficking*, 7, 4: 454–475.
Durisin, E.M., van der Meulen, E., & Bruckert, C. (eds.). (2018). *Red light labour: Sex work, regulation, agency, and resistance.* UBC Press.

Fudge, J., Lam, E., Chu, S.K.H., & Wong, V. (2021). *Caught in the carceral web: Anti-trafficking laws and policies and their impact on migrant sex workers*. Butterfly & Canadian HIV/AIDS Legal Network. https://www.hivlegalnetwork.ca/site/caught-in-the-carceral-web-anti-trafficking-laws-and-policies-and-their-impact-on-migrant-sex-workers

Holden, A. (1990, March 4). Sophia Cook was given a standing ovation. *Toronto Star*.

Hunt, S. (2015). Representing colonial violence: Trafficking, sex work, and the violence of law. *Atlantis: Critical Studies in Gender, Culture, & Social Justice*, 37.2, 1: 25–39.

Kaye, J. (2017). *Responding to human trafficking: Dispossession, colonial violence, and resistance among Indigenous and racialized women*. University of Toronto Press.

Kempadoo, K. (2005). From moral panic to global justice: Changing perspectives on trafficking. In K. Kempadoo, J. Sanghera, & B. Pattanaik (eds.), *Trafficking and prostitution reconsidered: New perspectives on migration, sex work, and human rights* (pp. vii–xxxiv). Paradigm Publishers.

Lam, E. (2018a). *Behind the rescue: How anti-trafficking investigations and policies harm migrant sex workers*. Butterfly (Asian and Migrant Sex Workers Support Network). https://tinyurl.com/52fsf75s

____. (2018b). *Survey on Toronto holistic practitioners' experiences with bylaw enforcement and police*. Butterfly (Asian and Migrant Sex Workers Support Network). https://tinyurl.com/44jc3k5h

Lawson, E. (2002). Images in black: Black women, media and the mythology of an orderly society. In N. Wane Njoki, K. Deliovsky, & E. Lawson (eds.), *Back to the drawing board: African Canadian feminism* (pp. 199–223). Sumach Press.

Malla, A., Lam, E., van der Meulen, E., & Peng, H-Y. (2019). *Beyond tales of trafficking: A needs assessment of Asian migrant sex workers in Toronto*. Butterfly (Asian and Migrant Sex Workers Support Network). https://tinyurl.com/kr52896x

Maynard, R. (2015). Fighting wrongs with wrongs? How Canadian anti-trafficking crusades have failed sex workers, migrants, and Indigenous communities. *Atlantis: Critical Studies in Gender, Culture and Social Justice*, 37.2, 1: 40–56.

____. (2017). *Policing Black lives: State violence in Canada from slavery to the present*. Fernwood Publishing.

____. (2018). Do Black sex workers' lives matter? Whitewashed anti-slavery, racial justice, and abolition. In E.M. Durisin, E. van der Meulen, & C. Bruckert (eds.), *Red light labour: Sex work regulation, agency, and resistance* (pp. 281–292). UBC Press.

McTighe, L., & Haywood, D. (2017). "There is no justice in Louisiana": Crimes against nature and the spirit of Black feminist resistance. *Souls*, 19, 3: 261–285.

Millar, H., & O'Doherty, T. (2020). Racialized, gendered, and sensationalized: An examination of Canadian antitrafficking laws, their enforcement, and their (re)presentation. *Canadian Journal of Law and Society*, 35, 1: 23–44.

Ministry of Children, Community and Social Services. (2020). *Recognizing human trafficking*. Government of Ontario. https://www.ontario.ca/page/about-human-trafficking

____. (2022). *Ontario's anti-human trafficking strategy 2020–2025*. Government of Ontario. https://www.ontario.ca/page/ontarios-anti-human-trafficking-strategy-2020-2025

Mirchandani, K., & Chan, W. (2005). *The racialized impact of welfare fraud control in British Columbia and Ontario*. Canadian Race Relations Foundation.

Mosher, C.J. (1998). *Discrimination and denial: systemic racism in Ontario's legal and criminal justice systems, 1892–1961*. University of Toronto Press.

Mugabo, D.I. (2016). Geographies and futurities of being: Radical Black activism in a context of anti-Black Islamophobia in 1990s Montreal [master's thesis]. Concordia University. https://spectrum.library.concordia.ca/id/eprint/981936/

Ontario Human Rights Commission. (2003). *Paying the price: The human cost of racial profiling.* https://www.ohrc.on.ca/en/paying-price-human-cost-racial-profiling

———. (2017). *Under suspicion: Research and consultation report on racial profiling in Ontario.* https://www.ohrc.on.ca/en/under-suspicion-research-and-consultation-report-racial-profiling-ontario

Owusu-Bempah, A., & Wortley, S. (2014). Race, crime, and criminal justice in Canada. In S.M. Bucerius & M. Tonry (eds.), *The Oxford handbook of ethnicity, crime, and immigration* (pp. 281–320). Oxford University Press.

Richie, B. (2012). *Arrested justice; Black women, violence, and America's prison nation.* New York University Press.

Ritchie, A.J., Kaba, M., & Ervin, W. (n.d.). *#Defundpolice, #Fundthepeople, #Defendblacklives: Concrete steps toward divestment from policing & investment in community safety.* https://www.interruptingcriminalization.com/defundpolice-toolkit

Ritchie, A.J., & Mogul, J.L. (2008). In the shadows of the war on terror: Persistent police brutality and abuse of people of color in the United States. *DePaul Journal for Social Justice*, 1, 2: 175–250.

Roots, K. (2013). Trafficking or pimping? An analysis of Canada's human trafficking legislation and its implications. *Canadian Journal of Law and Society*, 28, 1: 21–41.

———. (2022). *Domestication of human trafficking: Law, police and prosecution in Canada.* University of Toronto Press.

Royal Commission on Chinese Immigration. (1885). *Report of the Royal Commission on Chinese Immigration: Report and evidence.* Government of Canada, Privy Council Office. https://publications.gc.ca/site/eng/9.823869/publication.html

Shih, E. (2021). The trafficking deportation pipeline: Asian body work and the auxiliary policing of racialized poverty. *Feminist Formations*, 33, 1: 56–73.

Sibley, M. (2020). Attachments to victimhood: Anti-trafficking narratives and the criminalization of the sex trade. *Social & Legal Studies*, 29, 5: 699–717.

Smith, A., & Hale, A.S. (2021, July 9). PC's human trafficking statistic based on withdrawn reports. *Politics Today.* https://www.politicstoday.news/queens-park-today/pcs-human-trafficking-statistic-based-on-withdrawn-reports/

Sudbury, J. (2002). Celling Black bodies: Black women in the global prison industrial complex. *Feminist Review*, 70: 57–74.

Tanovich, D.M. (2011). Gendered and racialized violence, strip searches, sexual assault and abuse of prosecutorial power. *Criminal Reports*, 79: 132–150.

Tator, C., & Henry, F. (2006). *Racial profiling in Canada: Challenging the myth of "a few bad apples."* University of Toronto Press.

Vancouver Sex Workers Rights Collective. (2018). *Written submissions: National Inquiry into the Murdered and Missing Indigenous Women and Girls.* https://www.mmiwg-ffada.ca/wp-content/uploads/2019/06/Van-Sex-Worker-Rights-Collective-Final-written-submission.pdf

Williamson, K., & Marcus, A. (2017). Black pimps matter: Racially selective identification and prosecution of sex trafficking in the United States. In A. Horning & A. Marcus (eds.), *Third party sex work and pimps in the age of anti-trafficking* (pp. 177–196). Springer International Publishing.

Windsor Star. (1990, January 29). Crippled by police, woman vows to walk.

Wortley, S. (2019). *Halifax, Nova Scotia: Street checks report.* Nova Scotia Human Rights Commission. https://humanrights.novascotia.ca/sites/default/files/editor-uploads/halifax_street_checks_report_march_2019_0.pdf

Cases
Canada (Attorney General) v. Bedford, 2013 SCC 72, [2013] 3 SCR 1101.

Legislation
Anti-Human Trafficking Strategy Act, 2021, SO 2021, c. 21, Sched. 2 (Ontario).
The Child Sexual Exploitation and Human Trafficking Act, 2011, CCSM, c. C94 (Manitoba).
Chinese Immigration Act, SC 1885, c. 71.
Combating Human Trafficking Act, 2021, SO 2021, c. 21 (Ontario).
Criminal Code, RSC 1985, c. C-46.
Protecting Survivors of Human Trafficking Act, SA 2020, c. P-26.87 (Alberta).
Protection of Communities and Exploited Persons Act, SC 2014, c. 25.
Protection from Human Trafficking Act, SS 2021, c. 23 (Saskatchewan)

7

Targeting Asian Massage Parlours in the Name of Anti-Trafficking
Experiences of Asian Women in Toronto

Elene Lam

Moon had worked in massage parlours[1] across Canada for more than twenty years. In 2015 and 2016, after the police conducted anti-trafficking raids in Ottawa and Montreal, her workplace was shut down and her friends and coworkers were arrested and deported. She moved to Toronto and found work in a spa. She enjoyed the income and the working conditions but often worried about investigations by law enforcement. She was right to worry. In a one-year period, she was investigated over twelve times by police and bylaw enforcement officers, who told her she was not allowed to work because she did not have a holistic licence and identification. Moon received six tickets and paid over $1,500 in fines. She was also told by police that she would be reported to immigration officials if they saw her again. The spa where she worked was shut down and she was forced to stop working even though she loved her job. Moon started taking clients in an apartment and a hotel room in a small town in Ontario but felt isolated and less supported. She was robbed, assaulted three times in one week, and arrested after a hotel worker reported her to the police for providing sexual services. The police expressed concern about her and asked if she was trafficked. They told her not to leave the hotel in order to protect her own safety. Two hours later, immigration officers from the Canada Border Services Agency (CBSA) arrested her. The officers took $2,000 cash and a ring, which were never returned to her. During the detention review, she found out that the police had reported her to the CBSA.

On March 16, 2021, eight people were killed in three spas in Atlanta, Georgia. Among the dead were six Asian women who worked in the spas. The murderer claimed he wanted to punish and kill people in the sex industry (Fausset, 2021). This was not an isolated incident; in 2020, a massage worker was stabbed and killed in Toronto by a teenager who said the workers "weren't very clean people" (Freeze, 2022, n.p.). Misogyny, racism, xenophobia, and whorephobia were all at play in these murders (Lam et al., 2021; Red Canary Song, 2021; Shih, 2021a). As Elena Shih (2021a) notes, anti–sex work sentiments are often directed at massage workers, whether or not they offer sexual services. Indeed, many spa workers have been violently attacked because of the racism, stigma, moral panic, and overpolicing directed at sex work generally and Asian massage businesses specifically.

In the last few decades, massage parlours, particularly those with nonaccredited or nonregistered massage therapists, have become seen as unprofessional and illicit businesses. Often deemed a public nuisance and associated with deviance, immorality, and criminality, massage parlours — which include holistic, body rub, and other personal wellness centres — are a target of new bylaws and law enforcement officers. While Asian massage workers have been overpoliced for years, the rise of the anti-trafficking movement has increased the moral panic surrounding Asian massage parlours. Exploitation of and violence involving sex workers is often cited by anti-trafficking organizations, especially those that advance white saviour and carceral approaches (Bernstein, 2010), and religious organizations with anti–sex work agendas, to justify anti-trafficking laws and campaigns that target Asian massage parlours (Butterfly, 2022; Red Canary Song et al., 2022; Shih, 2021b).

Anti-trafficking narratives frequently frame Asian women as ignorant, naive victims available for saving, or as "illegals" and criminals whose businesses should be controlled or closed, thus justifying the punitive regulation and policing of Asian parlours. Some pro-carceral anti-trafficking organizations urge city governments to investigate, fine, raid, and close massage parlours by applying existing bylaws or instituting new ones that make these businesses difficult to operate (Butterfly, 2021). They argue that in doing so, they are protecting innocent non-English-speaking trafficked victims. For example, in 2019, the Canadian Centre to End Human Trafficking, which received over $14.5 million in government funding to operate an anti-trafficking hotline and collect data for police and others, lobbied the government to impose stronger regulations and shut down massage parlours in Toronto (CityNews, 2019). Without any supportive evidence, founder and former CEO Barbara Gosse claimed that "the victims of human trafficking are sold within body rub parlours and holistic centres" (Canadian Centre to End Human Trafficking, 2018, p. 1). Gosse had been fighting to increase the investigation and prosecution of massage parlours and strip clubs since 2012, when she was working with the Canadian Women's Foundation.

In recent years, law enforcement officers have raided massage parlours in Ontario, and the workers, particularly Asian women, have been charged, arrested, detained, and deported. They have also faced racial attacks and unfair treatment by city staff (Paradkar, 2020). Criminal, immigration, and municipal laws have been used by law enforcement to raid and shutter businesses (Butterfly, 2021; Lam, 2018a, 2023; Lam et al., 2021; Red Canary Song et al., 2022). The City of Toronto has drawn on other policies as well, including those related to public health and financial assistance, to target massage parlours. While these efforts reputedly tackle human trafficking and help its victims, the workers — like many racialized and migrant women who experience high rates of gender-based violence — are left feeling revictimized by the criminal legal system (Lam, 2018a; McBride et al., 2019).

As this chapter shows, municipal bylaws in Toronto are frequently used to target massage parlours under the guise of anti-trafficking efforts. I begin by offering a brief history of regulation of massage parlours with a particular focus on how narratives about police raids have shifted from immorality to protection of women. I then present the findings from my primary research with Asian massage parlour workers, exploring their everyday practices and experiences with municipal bylaw and police officers. Instead of offering protection, repressive bylaw practices and anti-trafficking raids have increased the vulnerability of these women and put them at greater risk of violence.

Background

The social and moral values of the 1960s in Canada were such that the adult sex industry (e.g., massage parlours, strip clubs, pornographic bookstores, escort agencies) operated openly along Toronto's Yonge Street (Brock, 1998). This situation started to change in the 1970s when massage parlours, particularly those near the significant city thoroughfare, became municipally regulated (Ross, 2022). Politicians, middle-class citizens, and evangelicals advocated for a government crackdown to "clean" Yonge Street of its "sinful" sex-related businesses. Along with being subjected to federal sex work and immigration laws, massage parlours, particularly those offering body rub or sexual services, became regulated by the *Toronto Municipal Code*'s Chapter 545, the licensing bylaw, in 1975. The bylaw targeted owners, operators, and workers, and allowed only twenty-five licences to be granted to body rub parlours (Cook, 2018).

Shortly after, in 1977, massage parlours, strip clubs, and other adult entertainment venues began to experience heightened police raids following the sexual assault and murder of a twelve-year-old boy named Emanuel Jaques in a building that also housed a massage parlour. Over two hundred inspections were carried out in a single month, resulting in owners and workers facing criminal charges and municipal fines, as well as many massage parlours being shut down. At least five parlours within one block were closed (Fraser, 2017).

While the crusade against massage parlours was animated by ideas of "sinfulness" in the 1970s, beginning in the mid- to late 1990s, raids became justified by the growing moral panic over human trafficking. Rather than "immoral" and "sinful," massage parlours were framed as sites of exploitation of vulnerable women. And though the stated goal of anti-trafficking campaigns at the time was the rescue of Asian women from traffickers, in practice they resulted in migrant women being treated like criminals and illegal migrants. Consequently, Asian massage workers became entangled in a carceral web (Fudge et al., 2021) of increased surveillance, fines, charges, arrests, workplace closures, and deportation. For example, in 1997, twenty-three Malaysian migrant women working in massage parlours in Toronto were arrested in anti-trafficking raids as part of Project Orphan. A year later, as part of Project Trade, police again conducted raids and arrested sixty-eight people, the majority of whom were Asian women (Brock et al., 2000; Toronto Network Against Trafficking in Women et al., 2000). Similar raids have been carried out across Canada, including in Vancouver, Markham, Ottawa, Montreal, and Hamilton.

In addition to the earlier massage parlour bylaw, Toronto implemented a holistic centre bylaw in 1998 that allowed some holistic practitioners to provide therapeutic treatment, but it significantly controlled sexual and body rub services. The fervour of the late 1990s eventually quieted, only to be revived again in 2012 following the lobbying of women's, religious, and anti-trafficking organizations. The City of Toronto passed a motion to develop a strategy to increase investigations and prosecutions of strip clubs, body rub parlours, and holistic centres. From 2013 to 2018, the number of investigations and prosecutions grew by a factor of more than 3.5 (Lam, 2018b; Lam & Wong, 2020). In a survey conducted in 2017–2018 with sixty-one massage workers in Toronto, almost half reported they had been charged and fined, and over 65 percent conveyed fear of law enforcement. They also reported a significant increase in excessive investigations and abuse of power (Lam, 2018b).

By 2019, over two thousand holistic practitioners who were not registered massage therapists were working in holistic centres in Toronto (Holistic Practitioners' Alliance et al., 2019). The majority were, and still are, Asian migrant women. In practice, the licensing bylaw, along with other laws and procedures, is enforced as an anti-trafficking tactic, generating harmful impacts for Asian migrant massage workers including excessive and punitive legal ramifications and violence, harassment, and misconduct from law enforcement officers themselves (Lam et al., 2020).

Method of Inquiry

This chapter is based on research collected for a larger study that aims to uncover how investigations of massage parlour workers are organized and how they impact the workers.[2] The study participants are key knowledge producers who have used the results to advocate for social justice and an end to the harmful policies being applied in their lives (Bowen & O'Doherty, 2014; Dewey & Zheng, 2013; van der Meulen, 2011). In the following, I report on the results of semistructured interviews conducted from 2019 to 2023 with twenty-five Asian migrant women in Toronto who identified as massage or sex workers. Participants were recruited through sex worker organizations and snowball sampling methods. Interview questions focused on workers' everyday lives and experiences with colleagues, clients, and law enforcement. The workers generously shared their experiences as well as documents related to investigations, such as licences, tickets, and court case details, and the actions they have taken to advocate for their rights. The participants were all cisgender women, ranging in age from thirty to sixty-eight years old, who had worked in massage parlours for one to fifteen years. All were migrants; twenty came from China, two from Hong Kong, one from South Korea, one from India, and one from Taiwan. They had a range of immigration statuses as permanent residents, refugee claimants, sponsored spouses, international students, and undocumented persons. Pseudonyms are used for confidentiality.

Working in Massage Parlours

The Asian migrant women with whom I spoke generally called themselves "massage workers" and referred to their workplaces as "spas" or "massage parlours," though they were mostly licensed as holistic practitioners or body rubbers (outside of Toronto, massage workers may also be licensed as "personal wellness practitioners"). Despite popular perceptions that their work is illicit or illegal, or involves human trafficking, they identified themselves as workers and their massage parlours simply as places where they worked and earned a living. The women came from a variety of countries, held different immigration statuses, and varied widely in terms of English-language skills and support networks. For example, workers from China had the strongest social networks and supports. Workers with precarious immigration status, regardless of country of origin, had fewer options for employment as well as more difficulty improving their working conditions or seeking help when they experienced violence.

None of the workers reported being trafficked; on the contrary, many found working in massage parlours rewarding and empowering. The reasons women decided to engage in massage work included the decent income, flexible hours, work that was less demanding than other types, and the opportunity to take a break while waiting for the next client. Although most said they needed to share their income with their boss, they could still earn three to ten times more than they would working at a restaurant, factory, or grocery store. Some workers said they would not be able to afford the expensive immigration legal fees, pay rent, or purchase a home if they did not work in the sex industry. Some also found they were less isolated and had better social supports by working with others who spoke the same language. And some expressed pride in their ability to support themselves and help others. Lin, for example, said, "I am a massage worker. I use my hands to earn a living and support myself." Many talked about the contributions they made by helping others and the satisfaction they received from making clients feel good or alleviating their pain.

Most participants noted that massage work helped them overcome the challenges they faced as non-English-speaking, racialized, migrant, and working-class women (e.g., racism in employment, language barriers, difficulties accessing supports). Davy, an international student, found that working in massage parlours allowed her to earn a living while managing her demanding schoolwork and paying high international student fees. The flexible work hours also allowed her to participate in volunteering and an internship program, increasing her chances of getting a job and permanent residency upon graduation. Although the women mostly spoke favourably about their massage work, they also acknowledged the challenges. For example, some described sacrificing their own health to serve others. Yuen, who had worked in massage parlours for eight years, talked about work-related injuries, saying, "My thumb, wrist, and my back all got injured and often feel pain." Others spoke about long working hours, bad employers, stigma, and the double discrimination resulting from anti-Asian racism and the stigmatization of massage parlours, which are often associated with sex work. Many talked about the challenges they faced with the licensing process and safety concerns arising from forced adherence to the licensing bylaw.

Navigating the Licensing Bylaw

All the participants I interviewed said they could not become registered massage therapists because they did not meet the English-language requirements or could not afford the time and expense of training. Therefore, they were required to obtain a city licence (i.e., body rubber licence or holistic practitioner licence) to offer massage services in Toronto, which also posed a number of challenges. Body rub parlours are regulated as adult services and the licensing bylaw is highly restrictive (Butterfly et al., 2019). For instance, body rubbers are prohibited from receiving or holding clients' money or belongings. Though the bylaw does not mention a sexual aspect of services, body rubbers are required to undergo a medical exam and provide proof that they are free of communicable diseases. Further, zoning restrictions on body rub parlours, along with a high licensing fee of $14,526.85 for these establishments (City of Toronto, n.d.b) and a limit on the number allowed, create barriers to accessing a body rub licence. The majority of massage parlour workers therefore work in holistic centres rather than body rub parlours.

Of the twenty-five women I interviewed, fourteen had a holistic licence and two had a body rub licence. The rest were unlicensed. Four workers were not able to obtain or renew their licences because they could not provide a valid work permit or proof of residency. Requirements for proof of immigration status violate Toronto's claim to be a sanctuary city (City of Toronto, n.d.a). The licensing process in Toronto also requires proof of membership in a professional holistic association in the case of holistic practitioners, and intrusive medical examinations for "communicable diseases" in the case of body rub workers, as noted earlier. In both cases, workers must have a criminal record check and pay an application and licensing fee.

Because the women I spoke with had limited English-language skills, none had read the licensing bylaw, nor did they know how or where to locate it online. Instead, many reported that their massage parlour boss, their coworkers, or others helped them apply for a licence and develop practices to avoid being ticketed and fined. For example, the women understood they needed to obtain a licence, post the licence in a public space, keep client records, include their licence number in advertisements, keep their massage table in good repair, cover specific parts of clients' bodies, regulate their own clothing, close their business at 9 p.m., and keep the door unlocked, all of which are mandated by the bylaw. Chui said that learning about the bylaw's many requirements had been stressful:

> It was very hard at the beginning. I not only need to learn how to do massage and handle the clients, I also need to know how to handle the licence [bylaw enforcement] officers. My boss kept reminding me to wear the "working clothes" [robe], fill in the record, and other rules. I tried to learn because I don't want to be charged or have any trouble.

Although the bylaw does not require workers to wear a robe, it has nevertheless become common practice because workers think it will prevent them from being charged for not being "properly dressed" or "neat and clean" (*Toronto Municipal Code*, 2022, s. 545-357).

Many workers argued that the regulations are problematic and undermine their safety. Conflicts can arise, for instance, when women request personal and identifying information from their clients. Many clients are reluctant to give their names and take receipts because they do not want to be charged for purchasing a sexual service, as per the *Criminal Code*, or be surveilled by police and others. However, when workers do not record their clients' names and details about the services rendered, or issue and keep receipts, they can be charged under the bylaw. The protection of privacy is a significant consideration for both clients and workers. Indeed, the women I spoke with found that posting their licence in a public place exposed their personal information, including their home address. Mui and Lok Shan talked about clients seeing their home addresses and harassing them and their families.

Most of the workers further expressed great concern about the requirement that their door remain unlocked, noting that locking the door was an important safety measure. Yo Yo, for example, explained that she had been robbed and assaulted — violence that could have been avoided if she had been allowed to lock the door. In order to protect their own and each other's safety, workers often share information about robbers and abusers. Yo Yo had recognized the robber when he arrived at her door from a picture her friends had shown her. As she described it:

> I tried to turn him away, but he was able to come in because the door was unlocked. He grabbed my head and pushed it down, then pointed a knife at me and forced me to give him my money. Afterwards, he sexually assaulted me and also took my phone.

Angel shared a similarly terrifying and violent situation:

> Three young men rushed into my spa. I tried to flee but they stopped me. One man pointed a gun at my head. Then they searched the spa and took my money and the money from the spa. I was very frightened and did not want them to hurt me, so I complied with their demands.... One of the men forced me to sit on the floor and sexually assaulted me, while the other men looked at me and laughed. I was humiliated and insulted, but I continued to collaborate because I was afraid that they would

> hurt me more. At this point, I was about to collapse from fear and the trauma of the situation. I kneeled down and begged them to let me go. I saw a chance to run out the door, which I took. I ran in bare feet to the store next door and sat down on the floor, shaking. Someone called the police for me. They [the robbers] were able to enter in this way because the bylaw enforcement officers ordered me to keep my door unlocked. I had previously been charged, and already had a $240 fine in court. I would have been able to avoid being assaulted if I had been allowed to lock the door.

Only a few workers had reported violence against them to police because they felt intimidated and feared they or others would be penalized for violating the bylaw or other laws. Many had previous traumatizing and frustrating experiences with police, which generated feelings of helplessness because they could not protect their safety. Lui shared her experience:

> Around ten in the morning, not long after the spa opened, a man came in and chose the forty-dollar massage. I started the massage, and when I had almost finished, he suddenly got up and pressed me onto the massage table. He tore off my clothes until I was almost naked, and then he tried to rape me. It took all my effort to get away and run outside.... I ran to the convenience store next to the spa. Since I had nothing with me, I asked the store owner to help me call 911, but he was afraid of getting in trouble. He didn't want his business to be affected, so he refused. After I begged him, he finally let me use his phone to call my friend. I asked my friend to call 911 for me right away.... When the police arrived, they confronted the man. Now I had to face the other nightmare that I never expected. The female police officer who was on duty hinted to me in Chinese that I should give up and withdraw my case, as the odds were against me in the sense that the judge would not believe or sympathize with my words because I was a holistic practitioner. Later on, I heard that the man was released the next day. Additionally, I received a ticket for unprofessional clothing despite [the fact that] my clothes were torn because of the sexual assault.

For Nikki, the violence she encountered was unforgettable:

> I wished for nothing but death in those terrifying, awful moments. With my eyes closed, I suddenly thought about my children. I couldn't die. Who would take care of them if I died? I could only endure his disgusting actions. When he was finally done, I desperately begged him not to hurt or kill me. I was only a single mom, an ordinary worker who didn't even own a car. I swore to him I would not call the police. I begged him for almost three hours until he let me go. He dragged me to the basement and locked me in there before he left.... The heavy discrimination against my profession by law enforcement officers makes me reluctant and afraid to call the police even when I am in danger.

Importantly, testimonies such as Nikki's demonstrate how current licensing bylaw expectations exacerbate the vulnerability of massage parlour workers to violence and prevent them from being able to protect themselves. As the next section shows, law enforcement efforts further compound this vulnerability.

Impacts of Law Enforcement

Both police and bylaw enforcement officers are authorized to investigate and charge massage parlour workers, clients, managers, and owners. As my interviewees relayed, some of the law enforcement officers that attended their places of work did not wear a uniform, show identification, or otherwise identify themselves, and workers often did not know who was inspecting them or what they were being charged for. They explained that they encountered excessive and punitive legal ramifications, including fines, tickets, arrests, and deportation, as well as violence, harassment, and misconduct from law enforcement officers. These mechanisms notably contradict the protections the bylaw supposedly offers, especially when rolled out under the guise of anti-trafficking.

Excessive and punitive legal ramifications
As noted earlier, workers reported a rising number of workplace inspections beginning in 2013, after the city passed a motion to increase investigations and prosecutions, and the number continued to climb as

anti-trafficking sentiments grew. Several interviewees reported being investigated more than ten times per year. Most described being excessively interrogated, humiliated, discriminated against, and insulted by police and bylaw officers. Among other things, officers ordered them to face the wall and did not allow them to move, sit, talk, answer the phone, or even use the bathroom. Mui, who was investigated by law enforcement over twenty times in three months, explained, "I was not allowed to sit down. I was ordered to face the wall. They searched every corner, and even my personal belongings." Siu Mei shared that when bylaw enforcement officers learned she was a dancer in China, they ordered her to sing and dance and laughed while she performed. Ming described how a bylaw enforcement officer requested the owner of the spa she worked at to identify anyone who was receiving Ontario Works; the officer then reported them to social assistance for fraud. During the COVID-19 pandemic, bylaw officers issued five tickets in two days to Fung for violating mandatory closure orders, despite the fact that she did not open or operate her business.

Many of the workers feared being ticketed or fined. As Lui explained, "I often cannot sleep after being charged. I am afraid they [bylaw enforcement officers] will come back again and find whatever reason to charge me." They also worried that family members, landlords, and neighbours would find out they were working in a massage parlour if the ticket was sent to their home address. The workers described being ticketed for minor reasons and the lengths to which officers went to find bylaw infractions. Donna, for example, explained how law enforcement spent an hour searching every corner of the spa where she worked, including her personal belongings, until they found something they could use to lay a charge. According to Donna, "If massage practitioners like us cannot quickly open the door within three seconds, or another delay of five seconds, we will get a ticket for not opening the door." Similarly, Siu recounted how she put three layers of towels on top of the massage bed to ensure it was clean and comfortable, but law enforcement officers flipped the towels off the bed. She was charged for not keeping her massage table in good repair due to a small crack they found. She was subsequently convicted and received a $1,500 fine.

For some, the fear of having to go to court led them to just pay the bylaw fine rather than try to fight it. As Ming said:

> I have never been to court in my life. I was so scared. I just want to resolve it as soon as possible. I don't want to get into more trouble. They want to have money, and I would pay whatever they ask. I just want to end this case.

Other workers reported receiving a court notice a few months or even a year after an investigation. Very few of them had fought tickets in court because of the expensive legal fees, which can run into the thousands of dollars. Some also said they were threatened by the Crown prosecutor, who told them they would have to pay $50,000 if they lost their case. As a result, most workers pleaded guilty to the bylaw infraction and paid the $100 to $1,500 ticket instead. Workers explained that, on some days, ten to fifteen workers would be queued in the courtroom to deal with their tickets. For them, being charged under the bylaw and paying a fine was preferable to being investigated and arrested by police. As Chui noted:

> They came to us because they want to get something. They want to charge you [with a bylaw infraction] and give you fine. You must let them charge you and give them money. Otherwise, they would be angry and try harder to punish you. If they do not send bylaw, they may send police and it would be more problematic.

While many tickets are for various minor offences, the accumulation of tickets can become a significant financial burden, impacting workers' ability to renew their licence, and possibly forcing them to shut down their business. At the same time, the large number of convictions for bylaw infractions is used to create the impression that some — namely Asian-run — licensed massage parlours are problematic, unprofessional, and illegal, justifying the excessive investigations of Asian women's workspaces.

Those with precarious immigration status are also worried that investigations may affect their application for permanent residency and lead to arrest and deportation. As Donna noted:

> Bylaw enforcement came very often. They not only ask us to show them the licence, they also ask us to show our ID.... I do not have a work permit to renew the licence. The bylaw enforcement officers told me that they would call immigration if they see me again. I really believe they would do so.

Another worker, Shu Yi, explained that after her refugee claim was rejected, she could not renew her licence because she did not have a work permit. This made her feel "like a mouse who must hide at all times." As an unlicensed worker, it was difficult for her to find another parlour to work at, and when she did, she was often paid much less than her coworkers because her boss could be charged if Shu Yi was found to be working. Shu Yi's fears were validated when she saw bylaw enforcement officers call the CBSA and arrest her undocumented coworker. She also witnessed a colleague get arrested while trying to renew a licence at the city's licensing office. Similarly, Micky and her coworkers were arrested after a neighbour reported a robbery at her spa. Upon learning that the workers did not have immigration status, the police called the CBSA. Other workers shared that they were de facto forced to stop working in massage parlours in Toronto to avoid being investigated, charged, and reported to the CBSA. Instead, they started to work in hotels or moved to small towns, where they did not have the same support networks as they did in the large city.

Violence, harassment, and misconduct
In addition to the problematic experiences recounted above, some workers reported that law enforcement officers themselves (both bylaw and police) were a major source of violence in their lives, and they expressed concerns about abuse, misconduct, harassment, and human rights violations. The workers described law enforcement officers as often rude and disrespectful, acting like gangsters, dehumanizing workers, and treating them like criminals or animals. They characterized investigations into their workspaces as intimidating and disturbing, not only for the business but also for workers, neighbours, and customers. Some noted that investigations of spas suspected of offering sexual services were more aggressive and excessive. They described feeling discriminated against because of their race and ethnicity, pointing out that spas run by Chinese and other Asian people were especially targeted. According to Shan, "This is racism.... Why do they come to our place so often? They are targeting us because we do not speak English. They think that we are not Canadian. Would they treat white people like this? Of course not." A law enforcement officer told her that she should not stay in Canada if she could not speak English. Other workers who had been employed in parlours run by English-speaking white people had not been inspected

in their time there. Ching Yin explained, "White people are the mainstream, and their English is good. Plus, they know how to protect their rights by knowing the laws and use them as weapons. If the massage parlours were run by the whites, then things would be different."

Ron described the behaviour of police and bylaw enforcement officers as similar to that of robbers: "Some officers opened the door and entered the treatment room. They were very rude, and many clients felt embarrassed and angry." She detailed an incident during which three male officers entered a room where a female client was undressed and lying on a massage bed. Another worker, Linda, described a similar experience during an inspection:

> I was offering the massage service to a couple with my colleague. It was almost finished. However, the licence [bylaw enforcement] officers ordered me to come out from the [treatment] room, and they didn't allow us to continue with the service. The clients were so angry and left without paying.

Many workers were also sexually harassed and abused as law enforcement officers examined their clothing. Some were even charged in relation to their clothes, including for wearing a V-neck T-shirt, shorts, or a dress. As noted earlier, wearing a robe has become common practice among workers; however, some explained that officers would order them to remove their robe to show them what they were wearing underneath. Depending on what the workers were wearing, law enforcement would lay charges and take pictures. Ling described such a situation: "They are very rude. Some of them asked us to take off the robe or pull up our dress to show what we wear underneath. I was issued a ticket when they saw I wear a black lace dress inside the robe. I was so scared."

According to the workers, these kinds of practices are not a matter of individual officers' behaviour. They are systemic and commonplace. Ling, for example, detailed how one police officer repeatedly asked her to have sex with him outside her place of work and even requested she pay for the hotel room. He promised her she would not receive any more tickets for violating the bylaw if she did what he told her. Yee had a similar experience in which an undercover bylaw enforcement officer took off his clothes and lay down on the massage bed, requesting a hand job. After giving him the hand job he requested, Yee was charged. Lok Shan described how one particular law enforcement officer frequently came by to inspect her place, sometimes staying for hours, lying on her massage bed or watching TV. She was forced to work in another city to avoid being stalked and harassed by him.

Mui shared that four officers, some bylaw and some police as she later found out, came to her parlour when she and some coworkers were working. They did not identify themselves and only one flashed his identification. She described the events that followed:

> After they came, they shout at us, "Face the wall!" They wouldn't allow us to say anything. They said to a coworker, "Shut up! Don't say anything." … After that, the police found two pornography video [discs] left behind by a client. The officers used my notebook to play it and forced us to watch the movie with them…. After they searched, they asked me to go outside the store on the street. Outside the store is a garbage bin, and I was standing next to the garbage bin with four officers around me, so everyone on the street could see us. In front of everybody, the licensing officer … broke the [disc] … and forced me to put it in the garbage bin.

The officers also searched every room, including inside drawers. They went to the private staff area and searched Mui's purse, flipped open her notebook, and looked through her underwear. After the inspection, she received three tickets for not keeping patient records, not having a massage table in good repair, and not providing safekeeping for customers. Mui said the police called her garbage. She felt insulted and humiliated and continued to cry even after the inspection. She was so angry that she went to the police station and the bylaw enforcement office to make a complaint. Later, she found out no formal complaint had been recorded. Instead, the officers came back to her workplace twice in two weeks, ordered a client to leave, and laid five more charges against her.

Most of the workers felt they were forced to accept the violence they faced from law enforcement and did not file any complaints for fear of retaliation. Only a few of the workers spoke up or raised their concerns to management. When they did, the complaints were ignored, and some workers even experienced retaliation. Chiu shared that not only did bylaw enforcement officers harass her but uniformed bylaw officers also went to her home and issued her a ticket. They told her roommates and family members about her work in the massage parlour. This tactic was common among bylaw officers seeking to intimidate the women, especially those who wanted to challenge officers or advocate for themselves.

The workers' many experiences with law enforcement — of being targeted and overpoliced, physically and sexually harassed, humiliated and insulted, and discriminated against — demonstrate clearly why Asian massage parlour workers believe the licensing bylaw is designed to harm and control them. In order to push back against the damaging discourses of trafficking and illegality, as well as punitive bylaw enforcement, the workers have been organizing since 2017 to learn more about the bylaw, write letters to policymakers, and arrange community meetings. Over three hundred workers participated in a series of city meetings reviewing the body rub parlour and holistic centre sections of the licensing bylaw in 2019. They continue to organize community events and petitions; educate the public, policymakers, and city staff; and advocate for their rights. They have found that the fight is not easy, but the process is empowering.

Conclusion

Human trafficking has become a significant concern in Canadian society. Millions of dollars have been allocated to anti-trafficking initiatives, and federal, provincial, and municipal governments have introduced various anti-trafficking policies to protect trafficked victims. Though Toronto's municipal bylaw regulating massage parlours was established prior to the contemporary anti-trafficking movement, its enforcement has become entangled in the human trafficking rubric. The City of Toronto is applying the anti-trafficking framework via licensing requirements and enforcement that target massage parlours and practitioners, racialized women, and migrants in the name of protection. However, human trafficking is not what workers are concerned about. Instead, they worry about the licensing and safety challenges posed by the bylaw, and being targeted and discriminated against by law enforcement officers who violate their civil and human rights.

The insights shared in this chapter provide important threads for an inquiry into institutional processes, with consideration for how massage parlour workers' experiences are shaped by the licensing bylaw and law enforcement, how the bylaw itself is activated by anti-trafficking logics and used to investigate and charge massage parlour workers, and how anti–sex work sentiments are institutionalized and embedded within these practices. The experiences and voices of the workers showcased here make an important contribution not only to racial justice and migrant and sex worker movements, but also to critical anti-trafficking studies. Their collective voices and actions challenge institutional discourses that depict Asian massage parlour workers as passive, innocent trafficked victims who need to be rescued or as illegal, immoral criminals who need to be punished. Through their words and actions, they demonstrate that they are workers who contribute to their families, their communities, and their society, and they deserve to be treated with respect and dignity.

Notes

1. Massage parlours run by nonregistered massage therapists are often called and licensed as body rub parlours, holistic centres, or personal wellness centres, depending on the municipality. The terms "massage parlour" and "massage worker" are used in this chapter to reflect how workers identify their workplaces and themselves.
2. This chapter reports part of the findings of my doctoral research titled *The Regulation and Policing of Asian Migrant Sex Workers in Canada: A Critical Inquiry*. The study is informed by the methodological approaches of institutional ethnography and participatory action research. The aim is to better understand how the everyday lives of Asian and migrant sex workers (including massage workers) are organized institutionally and uncover the day-to-day implications of legal and policy frameworks adopted and enabled at multiple levels. The research was approved by the McMaster Research Ethics Board and financially supported by the Social Sciences and Humanities Research Council.

References

Bernstein, E. (2010). Militarized humanitarianism meets carceral feminism: The politics of sex, rights, and freedom in contemporary antitrafficking campaigns. *Signs: Journal of Women in Culture and Society*, 36, 1: 45–71.

Bowen, R., & O'Doherty, T. (2014). Participant-driven action research (PDAR) with sex workers in Vancouver. In C.R. Showden, & S. Majic (eds.), *Negotiating sex work: Unintended consequences of policy and activism* (pp. 53–74). University of Minnesota Press.

Brock, D.R. (1998). *Making work, making trouble: Prostitution as a social problem*. University of Toronto Press.

Brock, D., Gillies, K., Oliver, C., & Sutdhibhasilip, M. (2000). Migrant sex work: Roundtable analysis. *Canadian Woman Studies*, 20, 2: 84–91.

Butterfly (Asian and Migrant Sex Workers Support Network). (2021). *Call to action: Stop racist attacks from harmful antitrafficking organizations against Asian massage parlours and sex workers*. https://www.butterflysw.org/stop-racist-attacks

___. (2022). *Town of Newmarket: End racism against Asian massage businesses and workers*. https://www.butterflysw.org/newmarket-end-racism

Butterfly, Maggie's, Canadian HIV/AIDS Legal Network, Migrant Sex Work Project, Sterling, A., & Gillies, K. (2019). *Submission to the City of Toronto's review of body-rub parlour and holistic centre bylaws*. https://www.butterflysw.org/_files/ugd/5bd754_8 8c231dd09ba49e9afc26d44f0db1813.pdf

Canadian Centre to End Human Trafficking. (2018, April 10). *Comments for Toronto Municipal Licensing and Standards Committee*. https://www.toronto.ca/legdocs/mmis/2018/ls/comm/communicationfile-79532.pdf

City of Toronto. (n.d.a). *Access to city services for undocumented Torontonians*. https://www.toronto.ca/city-government/accountability-operations-customer-service/long-term-vision-plans-and-strategies/access-to-city-services-for-undocumented-torontonians/

___. (n.d.b). *Body rub parlour — Fee*. https://www.toronto.ca/services-payments/permits-licences-bylaws/body-rub-parlour-and-body-rubber/body-rub-parlour/

CityNews. (2019, May 20). *Changes to body rub parlour rules prompt trafficking concerns* [video]. https://www.youtube.com/watch?v=qEvl6aeKxw0

Cook, T. (2018). *Work plan for review of Chapter 545, licensing, body rub parlours and holistic centres*. City of Toronto. https://www.toronto.ca/legdocs/mmis/2018/ls/bgrd/backgroundfile-113619.pdf

Dewey, S., & Zheng, T. (2013). *Ethical research with sex workers: Anthropological approaches*. Springer Science & Business Media.

Fausset, R. (2021, July 27). Suspect in Atlanta-area spa shooting pleads guilty to 4 counts of Murder. *New York Times*. https://www.nytimes.com/2021/07/27/us/spa-shooting-robert-long-charges.html

Fraser, L. (2017 June 22). Murder of Emanuel Jaques changed the face of Yonge Street and Toronto. *CBC News*. https://www.cbc.ca/news/canada/toronto/emanuel-jaques-yonge-street-sex-work-1.4172511

Freeze, C. (2022, September 15). Toronto man pleads guilty in 2020 massage parlour attack. *Globe and Mail*. https://www.theglobeandmail.com/canada/toronto/article-toronto-man-pleads-guilty-in-2020-massage-parlour-attack/

Fudge, J., Lam, E., Chu, S.K.H., & Wong, V. (2021). *Caught in the carceral web: Anti-trafficking laws and policies and their impact on migrant sex workers*. HIV Legal Network. https://www.hivlegalnetwork.ca/site/caught-in-the-carceral-web-anti-trafficking-laws-and-policies-and-their-impact-on-migrant-sex-workers

Holistic Practitioners' Alliance, Coalition Against Abuse by Bylaw Enforcement, Butterfly (Asian and Migrant Sex Workers Support Network), & Wong, V. (2019). *City of Toronto body rub parlours and holistic centres bylaw review—joint submissions*. https://www.butterflysw.org/_files/ugd/5bd754_1c05641b2ec7421fa32b79 8e22437854.pdf

Lam, E. (2018a). *Behind the rescue: How anti-trafficking investigations and policies harm migrant sex workers*. Butterfly (Asian and Migrant Sex Workers Support Network). https://tinyurl.com/52fsf75s

___. (2018b). *Survey on Toronto holistic practitioners' experience with bylaw enforcement and police*. Butterfly (Asian and Migrant Sex Workers Support Network). https://tinyurl.com/44jc3k5h

___. (2023). How laws regulate migrant sex workers in Canada: To protect or to harm? *Canadian Review of Social Policy*, 82: 22–57.

Lam, E., Gallant, C., & Wong, V. (2020, May 29). A terrorism charge isn't the solution to violence against women. *Chatelaine*. https://www.chatelaine.com/opinion/incel-terrorism-sex-work/

Lam, E., Shih, E., Chin, K., & Zen, K. (2021). The double-edged sword of health and safety: COVID-19 and the policing and exclusion of migrant Asian massage workers in North America. *Social Sciences*, 10, 5: Article 157.

Lam, E., & Wong, V. (2020, March 11). Punitive bylaw enforcement increases risk of violence for massage workers. *Ricochet*. https://ricochet.media/en/2976/punitive-bylaw-enforcement-increases-risk-of-violence-for-massage-workers

McBride, B., Shannon, K., Duff, P., Mo, M., Braschel, M., & Goldenberg, S.M. (2019). Harms of workplace inspections for im/migrant sex workers in in-call establishments: Enhanced barriers to health access in a Canadian setting. *Journal of Immigrant and Minority Health*, 6: 1290–1299.

Paradkar, S. (2020, July 9). 'Why am I being treated this way?' Between the pandemic and city bylaws, massage parlour workers are struggling. *Toronto Star*. https://www.thestar.com/opinion/star-columnists/2020/07/09/why-am-i-being-treated-this-way-between-the-pandemic-and-city-bylaws-massage-parlour-workers-are-struggling.html

Red Canary Song. (2021). *Rapid response to Atlanta shooting*. https://www.redcanarysong.net/atlanta

Red Canary Song, Massage Parlor Outreach Project, Butterfly, in collaboration with Bowen Public Affairs & Brown University Center for the Study of Slavery and Justice Human Trafficking Research Cluster. (2022). *Un-licensed: Asian migrant massage licensure and the racialized policing of poverty*. https://www.redcanarysong.net/resources

Ross, D. (2022). *The heart of Toronto: Corporate power, civic activism, and the remarking of downtown Yonge Street*. University of British Columbia Press.

Shih, E. (2021a, March 26). How to protect massage workers. Policing and criminalization of sex work hurts massage workers, even when they aren't sex workers. *New York Times*. https://www.nytimes.com/2021/03/26/opinion/politics/atlanta-shooting-massage-workers-protection.html

———. (2021b). The trafficking deportation pipeline: Asian body work and the auxiliary policing of racialized poverty. *Feminist Formations*, 33, 1: 56–73.

Toronto Network Against Trafficking in Women, Multicultural History Society of Ontario, & Metro Toronto Chinese and Southeast Asian Legal Clinic. (2000). *Trafficking in women including Thai migrant sex workers in Canada*. http://www.mhso.ca/mhso/Trafficking_women.pdf

van der Meulen, E. (2011). Action research with sex workers: Dismantling barriers and building bridges. *Action Research*, 9, 4: 370–384.

Legislation

Toronto Municipal Code, 2022, Chapter 545, Licensing, https://www.toronto.ca/legdocs/municode/1184_545.pdf

8

A Narrative on Defending People Charged with Human Trafficking

Mash Frouhar

When I went to law school, I never thought I would represent people charged with crimes such as human trafficking, but here we are. A little about me: I was called to the Ontario Bar in 2009 and have since worked in criminal law as both an assistant Crown attorney and a defence counsel. However, since 2010, I have focused my practice solely on criminal defence. That's right, I defend individuals accused of crimes, often serious, such as murder, attempt to commit murder, human trafficking, sexual assault, and more. Before you frown and wonder why anyone would want to provide that kind of defence, bear with me; I hope that after reading this chapter you will understand the importance of criminal defence within the legal system. In Canada, one of the main pillars of our criminal justice system is the presumption of innocence and the need for the Crown to prove their case beyond a reasonable doubt. This is where I come in!

Experience with Human Trafficking Cases

While there have not been many human trafficking cases in recent years within the Ottawa region, where I am located, I have represented a handful of individuals accused of trafficking or related offences since the federal government changed the prostitution laws in 2014 through the *Protection of Communities and Exploited Persons Act*. Once the new regulations were implemented, the number of human trafficking charges by police spiked in various larger jurisdictions such as Ottawa and Toronto. The activities for which police are now laying human trafficking charges would have been considered "procuring" or "living on the avails of prostitution" before 2014. Since the repeal of these offences through the new legislation, the charge of human trafficking is used as a back door to otherwise unprovable offences.

Officers within the special human trafficking task forces almost seemed to stretch their reasonable grounds findings to lay a human trafficking charge.[1] For example, in one of my cases, a woman was working as a sex worker and stored the money that she collected in a jar. Her partner, who became my client, also worked odd jobs and added money into the same pot when possible. They would then use the communal cash to pay for rent, food, and other necessities. However, when my client was charged with domestic assault following an argument, the police, in speaking with the complainant, wrote a synopsis of the case that read as though my client was exploiting her by using the money in the jar. He was subsequently charged with human trafficking.

Until recently, a human trafficking conviction came with a mandatory minimum sentence of five years, which meant that the person would surely be serving a penitentiary sentence.[2] Just by way of example, someone could get a similar sentence for manslaughter or for serious drug trafficking charges. In the case of the money jar, I was unsure how the police linked a woman who engaged in sex work of her own volition to human trafficking.

When people are informed that they could face a minimum sentence of five years in jail if convicted of human trafficking, they often understandably become anxious and may accept deals, pleading guilty to almost anything if the Crown agrees to withdraw the human trafficking charge. In such situations, the role of a defence counsel is essential. For a defence counsel to be effective, they must be knowledgeable and willing to do the work. Their first responsibility is to reassure clients and explain that being charged with human trafficking does not automatically mean that the Crown will be able to prove the charge beyond a reasonable doubt, nor does it mean that they must accept any offer being made.[3] I have never had a client who was charged with human trafficking plead guilty. Although the charge may seem daunting, the case becomes less straightforward upon examination of the elements that the Crown must prove beyond a reasonable doubt for a conviction.

Following the prostitution law changes in 2014, numerous cases emerged in Ottawa in which police appeared to be overcharging individuals. Defendants were brought before the court on multiple charges, many of which had little chance of leading to conviction. These charges included forcible confinement, uttering threats, extortion, sexual assault, and various prostitution or criminal organization offences, including human trafficking. Some defence lawyers believed that the human trafficking charge was a ploy to give the Crown more bargaining power during settlement discussions with defence lawyers. The Crown would offer a deal where the defendant would plead guilty to all charges except human trafficking, as most accused individuals would not want to risk going to trial for it, given the mandatory jail sentence.

During bail hearings, defence counsel often found themselves fighting the idea that the charges were merely allegations. Even for a client with no criminal record, simply being charged with forcible confinement or kidnapping was a grave matter. Just the mention of "human trafficking" seemed to lead to the presumption of innocence being disregarded. And this is where many people fail to realize the gravity of being accused of human trafficking, even if the allegations are baseless.

The Ottawa Police Service has established a specialized unit dedicated to addressing cases of human trafficking and sexual exploitation. However, in my experience, their approach involves a narrow focus on finding evidence that fits a human trafficking charge, rather than objectively examining all available evidence. This approach can potentially impact the accuracy and fairness of their findings.

In speaking with some complainants and other sex workers, I was advised that some officers would corner them by pretending to be customers. They would then continually suggest to the sex workers that there was no way they were choosing to engage in such activities willingly and pressure them to disclose who was forcing them to do so. My initial question was "How do you, as an officer, know unequivocally that the workers have been forced into the sex trade?" The idea that they may want to be sex workers was completely disregarded, and the possibility that they had not been forced was dismissed. In my experience, this narrative frequently underlies how all human trafficking investigations are conducted. If a person decides to sell sex, they are often assumed to be doing it against their will and thus must be saved. I am not suggesting that this type of coercion never happens; I am simply pointing out that it is dangerous to paint everyone's experiences with the same brush.

In the early 2010s, many sex workers posted advertisements for their services on websites such as Backpage for a nominal fee. These platforms offered workers more freedom to choose the customers they wanted to meet, and to set the location and pricing of their services in advance. However, there was a drawback — payments for posting an advertisement could be made only through credit cards, which most street-based workers did not possess. As a result, they would request a friend, colleague, or someone else who had a credit card to post the advertisement on their behalf and to rent the room. In some cases, they would even compensate that person a small amount to remain on-site in case of any complications with the customer. Generally, this arrangement was mutually advantageous.

It was, and still is, a common tactic for male undercover police officers to respond to job ads by pretending to be a client and arranging a meeting with sex workers, only to try and convince them that they need to be rescued. Officers would suggest that a worker was not there by choice and needed help with issues like drug addiction. In exchange for information on their supposed exploiter, the workers would be offered assistance from programs such as the Victim/Witness Assistance Program, which could help them access resources like housing, treatment, and financial support. Unfortunately, individuals in desperate situations may be subtly or effectively coerced into saying nearly anything to receive the assistance they need to survive.

The Case of the Wrongfully Accused

One case that had a profound impact on me involved a man named Madani Ba. I dedicated many sleepless nights poring over his case and was extremely frustrated with the police for not conducting a thorough investigation before charging my client. To set the stage, the complainant was from a well-to-do white suburban family while Mr. Ba was an international student. In June 2017, the complainant, feeling "bored," decided to post an ad on Backpage out of what she described as curiosity. At the time, Mr. Ba and the complainant were in a casual "friends with benefits" relationship. She alleged that he took pictures of her, helped post them, and monitored client messages in exchange for money. During the trial, it came to light that the complainant made the allegations of being "trafficked" only after Mr. Ba ended their relationship and started seeing her close friend.

Mr. Ba was a law-abiding individual with no prior record. Though there was no indication that he would be armed, dangerous, or a flight risk, he was arrested in a SWAT team–like operation during his permanent resident interview at a Canadian immigration office. This unwarranted tactical decision had an irreversible impact on his life and his chances of becoming a Canadian resident.

Police knew Mr. Ba's whereabouts and could have invited him to the station for questioning. However, they chose to arrest him in a dramatic manner and charge him with human trafficking. Following a bail hearing, he was released under stringent conditions that prevented him from leaving the country. Police also alerted the media, who published his mug shot with the caption "human trafficker." Because of the charges, Mr. Ba was unable to continue his university studies due to potential violations of the institution's code of ethics. This resulted in his study visa becoming invalid, leaving him in the unfortunate position of being an undocumented immigrant through no fault of his own. Moreover, he could not leave the country while he awaited trial for the pending charges against him.

The matter took over two years to be heard in the Ontario Superior Court of Justice, and the trial made evident that the Ottawa Police Service's investigation had been poorly executed. The investigating officer had unquestioningly believed the complainant without any attempt to verify her claims. They had accepted the selective Snapchat videos provided by the complainant without requesting to review the original videos or extract the remainder of the relevant messages and videos with the help of their forensic team. It was clear that the investigating officer had already concluded that my client was guilty and that the complainant, who was privileged and white, would never voluntarily advertise on Backpage. Fortunately, Mr. Ba was acquitted of all charges. The judge was convinced of his innocence based on the cross-examination of the complainant at trial and the inconsistencies in her story as well as the Snapchat videos she had taken but not disclosed to the police.

Nonetheless, this case left me feeling sad about how the actions of a careless officer resulted in long-term consequences for a young Black man with no previous criminal record. Despite his acquittal, my client continues to face the repercussions of his case to this day, as he could not apply for citizenship due to his prolonged illegal status in Canada. In my view, the complainant should have faced charges of obstructing justice, given that she had repeatedly lied to the police during her interview.

After the acquittal, I contacted a journalist who had written an article about Mr. Ba at the time of his arrest and informed him that Mr. Ba had been acquitted of all charges. However, the next day, the same mug shot was published with a new caption that simply stated, "Man found not guilty in human trafficking case," without any further details regarding the wrongful accusations. The article mentioned that he was one of three individuals charged — even though none of the cases were related — but did not provide any information about his acquittal. This treatment highlights a double standard when it comes to reporting court proceedings. An acquittal, it seems, is not as sensational as a conviction.

The Case of the Chanel Purses

Another case I worked on involved a Chinese couple renting rooms to individuals who used the premises to sell sexual services. This operation could be likened to a high-end Airbnb, offering amenities and towels to the renters. Although the couple had no criminal records, law enforcement conducted a raid, resulting in the couple's arrest on charges of human trafficking. The sex workers using the premises for their business were of Asian descent and had limited English proficiency. The Crown's main argument at the bail hearing was "Do you know how much money they have? The officer, who knows her name brands, told me that Chanel bags were everywhere in that apartment, along with other designer stuff, and they were all real. It is over $200,000 worth of stuff!"

At the time, I remember asking if the officer had seen and verified the serial numbers within each Chanel piece to confirm their authenticity. But once again, I was told that the officer "knows her name brands." In the end, all the bags turned out to be fake; however, during the bail hearing, the Crown leaned on this narrative to convince the judge not to release my clients because they supposedly had access to a considerable amount of money and were, therefore, a flight risk. Thankfully, they were released, but only on a high cash bond. Perhaps the most interesting part of the proceedings is that the woman presented by the Crown as the "victim" came forward to present herself as a surety for the couple. She also offered to pay both bonds as well as the legal fees. In this instance, the complainant did not view herself as a victim. Fortunately, the case was assigned to a highly knowledgeable and senior assistant Crown attorney who agreed to a peace bond within four days of the arrest and withdrew the charges. Despite the attorney's fair position given the facts of this case, he ultimately had to answer to his superiors for his decision.

Specialized Crowns, Victim Services, and Police

In Ontario, the Crown Policy Manual provides directives that all Crowns are expected to follow. In practice, however, how Crown offices operate can vary from jurisdiction to jurisdiction. Some offices have a reputation for being strict with their assistant Crown attorneys, requiring management approval for every decision made on a file. This type of supervision can cause delays, slowing down the progress of a case and prolonging the remand stage. Unfortunately, such internal roadblocks can adversely affect clients, forcing them to remain on strict bail conditions while awaiting trial on baseless accusations.

When a client is charged and brought in for questioning, they often feel vulnerable and at a disadvantage when questioned by a trained professional. Interrogation tactics, such as invading personal space and slowly moving closer to the accused during the interview, can be used to make them feel uncomfortable. Usually, interrogations must be audio and videotaped. As a lawyer, I advise my clients to repeatedly vocalize any feelings of uneasiness about the proximity of the interrogator. Usually, my advice is "Keep your mouth shut and don't say a word. And trust me, I will know if you spoke when I watch the video." Unfortunately, some clients do not follow this advice.

Another police tactic — not limited to human trafficking cases — is to create a rapport and claim they "want to hear your side of the story." Often, police officers will say things like "We already know what happened, but we want to hear your side as well." Police can make the person believe they have more information than they actually possess, for example, by showing the person a photo or some documents and leaving the room while the cameras continue to roll to capture any motions, comments, or reactions. Unless a person is under arrest, they can leave at any time during questioning. Still, walking out the door can be challenging, especially for individuals unfamiliar with the legal system and police questioning tactics.

And then there is my all-time favourite tactic, which I call the "Your lawyer isn't here, but I am" tactic. The officer will say, "You had a chance to speak to your lawyer? Okay. I do not need to know what your lawyer said, but remember that she is currently at home living her life, and you are here. She is not the one here in this mess. I can help you if you help me understand what happened."

When an officer tells an individual of their right to call counsel, it usually means that the officer has already decided to charge them with a criminal offence. In such situations, anything the accused says to the officer is unlikely to change this decision. I always tell my clients to ask the police: "If I talk, will this affect your decision to charge me?" Officers will almost never agree to not charge the individual, which is why lawyers advise clients to exercise their right to silence. The only words a person under questioning should be saying are "On the advice of my lawyer, I have nothing to say. I want to go back to my cell now." I have sometimes advised clients that if the questioning continues despite their repeated requests to return to their cell, they should sit on the ground and roll up in a ball. If it comes to a Charter challenge, it reflects poorly on the officer during trial if the video shows that the questioning continued while the client was in the fetal position.

Concerns about Anti-Trafficking Efforts

The biggest issue with anti-trafficking efforts is the assumption that people do not enter into sex work willingly. This idea that everyone in the industry must be a victim is problematic and sexist. A woman cannot possibly make a conscious decision to sell sexual services and a man assisting her somehow must be trafficking, exploiting, or procuring her — these archaic, sexist, and absurd assumptions are all too prevalent in our society and, at times, within the justice system. That is why women are rarely charged with human trafficking. Most times, the individuals accused of such offences are young Black men. Unfortunately, a great misconception exists about what choices sex workers make and what they willingly decide to do. At times, the various players within the judicial system — police, Crown attorney, judiciary — may look like the "protectors" of these "poor women." However, who are we to tell them what they can and cannot do with their bodies? When women insist that no coercion or violence is involved in their choice to provide sexual services, disagreeing with them dismisses their agency.

Notes

1. In Canadian criminal law, for an individual to be charged with an offence, the officer must establish that they have reasonable grounds to believe that a crime has been committed. This means that the officer must believe, based on their investigation, that all the elements of a specific offence have occurred before charging the individual with a particular crime.
2. A mandatory minimum sentence takes away a judge's discretion to give a sentence they may deem appropriate on a case-to-case basis. One could argue that such mandatory minimums tie the hands of the judge when it comes to "less serious" cases.
3. I would still need to ensure that any offer the Crown gives is discussed with the client, who ultimately must instruct me on what they wish to do.

9

A Narrative on Being Charged with Human Trafficking

Anonymous

I was charged with human trafficking in 2015, when I was twenty-one years old. I am twenty-nine now. On the day of my arrest, I was in a hotel room next to the rooms where the sex workers worked. Two of the sex workers were arguing and fighting, and security was called. The police arrived and laid charges. Everything in my life immediately changed.

I am a biracial man, mixed white and Black, who used to oversee the operations of an escort agency. I organized everything, collected the money, hired people to do various jobs. I employed three sex workers and a driver who booked the hotel rooms and other things under his name. I also had a female friend who answered phone calls and pretended to be a sex worker. To find new employees, I made Facebook profiles that looked like real accounts with friends and pictures. I would tell people on Facebook that I was a sex worker, and say things like "I make this much money, the work is not that bad," etc. Nothing was a lie. There was no sex worker behind those accounts, but all the claims were legit. We would correspond and I would gain their trust. After they said they were okay to work in the sex trade, I would arrange for an old friend of mine to meet them in person.

In the beginning I treated it like a job. I would clock in, clock out, book shifts, and manage two women who worked five days a week. One was in university and the other was about to start. Unless you are very smart, university is expensive, so that was their justification for doing this kind of work. For a whole year, both women worked for me; there was no turnover. I would book a hotel, the girls would take public transit downtown to meet the client, and at the end of their shift they would go home. I never had sex with them. It was strictly a job. I made good money, and so did they. I would get half of their earnings, which is standard in the sex trade, but I would cover all of the administrative costs as well as the hotel and food. There was no drug use and minimal drinking.

Then they both left. One decided she had made enough money and the other got into a relationship. For the next two years, until I was arrested, worker turnover was really high. I hired people more through word of mouth and less through Facebook. A lot of people knew what I was doing. I didn't mind because I treated everybody well. I didn't have anything to hide. I didn't want to hide.

Getting Arrested

On the day of my arrest, hotel security was called because of a noise complaint. We booked multiple rooms that day — one for chilling and relaxing, and two for working. When security came, one of the sex workers was distraught. She'd had enough of the other woman she was working with. They were getting into fights, and I was not paying attention. During that period, I was hands-off when my job needed me to be more hands-on. When security showed up, one of the workers said, "I don't want to be a prostitute anymore" or something like that, and the guard said, "Come with me right away." Then the police were called and that was the end of the show.

The two sex workers who were fighting did not get charged. Three others of us did — a woman, a guy, and me. After I hired others to help run the business, I knew there was an increased risk of being arrested, but I didn't realize how serious human trafficking charges were. I had no idea the case would take five to six years of my life and have long-term implications going forward. Ten charges were laid in total, including human trafficking, procuring, and advertising sexual services. In this trade, when a person is arrested, police will apply a laundry list of charges when, really, the main charge they want to stick is trafficking. Before trial the Crown will magically drop nine out of the ten charges, but trafficking always stays. A win for them is a human trafficking conviction.

During the ride to the police station, I was thinking, "Where am I going to work now? What is a legit job that I can do?" I thought that I would go to the police station, get some paperwork, promise to appear in court, show up on a certain day, and tell the judge "I'm really sorry" and "I'll never do it again." Instead, I spent a month in jail before even getting bail. It was a lot harsher than a slap on the wrist and search for a new job. The more time I did before bail, the more people would say,

"You have no idea what's going on. You're a nice kid, you're young, but you're going to do a lot of time." I learned through the grapevine what was coming for me and what my near future held. It was very different from what twenty-one-year-old me thought it would be.

Being Questioned at the Police Station

When I arrived at the police station, I called a lawyer I had used for previous charges. I talked with someone from his office who said, "They're going to ask you a ton of questions. Answer every question with 'I am not talking about this until my lawyer's here.'" He made clear that the police might say or do things to try to put me at ease, but what they were really trying to do was get as much information from me as possible to help build their case. Unfortunately, my two co-accused were questioned before me and told the police everything. They were not helping themselves; they were only helping the cops. The detectives were thrilled to get so much information from them.

Just like the lawyer's assistant warned me, one of the cops who questioned me kept trying to make small talk. He was wearing sports gear and so we were talking about sports together. I thought, "This guy's pretty cool." He figured I was going to spill the beans, but I said nothing incriminating. I was not trying to deceive anybody; I was just trying to give myself the best opportunity at freedom. The cops were getting frustrated because they knew I was not going to break. They said, "Why don't you tell us now? You can help yourself. Maybe we can give you a lesser sentence so that you can get out earlier." They were making promises that I knew were nonsense. Initially, they were friendly, but once it became clear that I was not going to say anything, they quickly got angry. They didn't get what they wanted. I didn't take it as a win in my books by any means, as I was very lost and very scared. They said, "You're going to go to jail for a long time."

After that they put me in handcuffs and walked me to the cells. When we got there, one of the cops grabbed me very hard and pushed me. He then punched me in the back of the ribs while I was facing the cell wall. I was not in the best state physically. I was very small, kind of tall, and I was not in "workout" shape. I definitely was not thrilled about getting punched while I was in handcuffs, and when I looked up at the CCTV camera right above me I saw that it was conveniently facing the other way.

Pleading Guilty and Being Sentenced

My lawyer advised me to plead guilty because the sentence would then be much lower. Human trafficking, like some other crimes, has a mandatory minimum sentence, which can be pretty serious. I asked the lawyer, "If you had a son and he was in the same shoes, what would you recommend?" He said, "Plead." And that's what sealed the deal. It turned out to be the better route because I did a lot less time. I had evidence to show that I never forced anyone to do something they didn't want to, so I decided to plead guilty and then challenge the mandatory minimum sentence as a form of cruel and unusual punishment. While that seemed like the most mature and respectful thing to do, I still felt like a cowardly cop-out for not fighting the charge itself. At least in the end I did get a lesser sentence, and by not going to trial I saved myself and my family probably another $100,000.

My legal representation was definitely adequate. I was fortunate to get referred to a lawyer who was educated in the field. He was straight up; he was not trying to sugarcoat the situation and give me hugs and coddle me. He charged a lot of money, but you cannot put a cost on freedom. I was very young at the time, and it was very scary. I didn't know what was going to happen, how many years I was going to get, if I was going to die in jail. I was just a lonely guy with a lot coming in the future that I had no control over.

I was lucky to get the shortest sentence for human trafficking in the province's history: just under four years. But there were many other consequences. For example, my passport was taken while I was in custody. I can travel now but not to countries that prohibit entry to people with a criminal record. At least there are no restrictions on where I can go in Canada. I also had to register as a sex offender. I think that's for ten years. When I eventually got parole, the only stipulation was that I could not eat at restaurants where the main source of income was alcohol. The bank also closed my accounts. They gave me my money and said take a hike. Getting them to explain why they did that was frustrating. I assumed the reason was my trafficking conviction, but it took a lot of back and forth to get them to actually admit it. After many emails, they sent me a letter with a copy of my mugshot. It was pretty unprofessional.

Being in the Media

Media coverage was the hardest part of the whole ordeal. You go from doing your thing in relative privacy to suddenly everybody knowing your business and being biased against you because of the way you are portrayed in the news. The media did a good job of making me out to be the worst possible human. But I guess the reason I got such a short prison sentence was because I was not really the monster that I was portrayed to be, which the judge recognized. The story that the media told was not the full story, which was frustrating. The reality was very different. It would have been nice to have a couple of newspaper articles covering the conclusion of my sentencing. All the public heard about was my arrest and charges, along with a lot of unfounded allegations.

Receiving Support from Family and Friends

After I got out of prison, I logged into my Facebook and read everything — all the death threats and hate comments, people saying they were going to kill me and shoot me and stab me. But then I also read a lot of posts from people who had my back, saying: "This guy really messed up but he's a good person, he treated me well." I really appreciated their support, because it is easy in a case like mine to just say "He's a horrible person, write him off for life, throw him in the fire."

My family was also very supportive, which does not happen for everyone going through the legal system. I do not think they fully understood the work that I was doing, but they knew I was engaged in some illegal activities. They were obviously sad when I got arrested and concerned about my well-being. I come from a family where this kind of thing does not happen. I spent a fair amount of time with them while I was out on bail. I was fortunate that I was able to collect ten to fifteen letters from my family and close friends for the judge to consider during sentencing. I felt very lucky that my family not only sent me money while I was in prison but also visited me, phoned me, and mailed letters and magazines. My family continues to support me today, years after my release, because there are things that I am still having to deal with. It is not an easy life when you have a criminal record, especially for human trafficking.

Section Three

TRAFFICKING POLICING AND SURVEILLANCE

10

Anti-Trafficking and Data-Driven Policing

A Whole-of-Society Strategy

Robert Heynen

In 2019, Public Safety Canada inaugurated a five-year National Strategy to Combat Human Trafficking that promised "a new whole-of-government strategy" in the fight against trafficking. It builds on and extends the 2012 National Action Plan to Combat Human Trafficking, which, as Julie Kaye (2017) suggests, "consolidated national anti-trafficking efforts in Canada within a criminal justice framework" (p. 125). The $75 million dedicated to the strategy included $14.51 million for the 2019 launch of the Canadian Human Trafficking Hotline, run by the Canadian Centre to End Human Trafficking, with the remainder supporting collaborations with other government departments including the Canada Border Services Agency; Financial Transactions and Reports Analysis Centre of Canada (FINTRAC); Public Services and Procurement; Immigration, Refugees and Citizenship; and Women and Gender Equality (Public Safety Canada, 2021).

What is striking, then, is that while the strategy cements the primacy of a criminal justice approach, the new funding goes mainly to programs designed to support police rather than to the police themselves. Indeed, police at municipal, provincial, and federal levels, including the Royal Canadian Mounted Police (RCMP), already have extensive anti-trafficking funding and programs. The strategy aims to bring a wide range of government agencies, nongovernmental organizations (NGOs), companies, and other organizations into the fight against trafficking. Provincial and municipal anti-trafficking projects, strategies, and funding envelopes function similarly, providing resources to police but also a range of other actors. In 2022, for example, the Alberta provincial government pledged $20.8 million over four years to implement the recommendations of the Alberta Human Trafficking Task Force. These included the formation of a centre of excellence for research and data collection, as well as extensive funding for community organizations. Anti-trafficking organizations played a key role in the creation and running of the task force, which was chaired by the country singer Paul Brandt, whose anti-trafficking credentials came from spearheading the #NotInMyCity campaign (Drinkwater, 2022). Far more ambitious and expensive is Ontario's anti–human trafficking initiative, which also provides funding for many organizations and initiatives and is set to run from 2020 to 2025 at a cost of $307 million (Ministry of Children, Community and Social Services, 2020). Ontario is thus a key focus in this chapter.

The whole-of-government approach encompasses all the different levels of government, but also extends well beyond. The corporate sector is playing an increasingly important role not only in leading awareness-raising campaigns but also in partnering with police and other agencies to provide information, collaborate in investigations, and train their own staff to identify alleged instances of trafficking (Bernstein, 2016). The most notable example is the Tech Against Trafficking coalition, which includes Amazon, Google, Meta, and Microsoft as leading members. In many respects, however, as seen clearly in the case of Alberta, anti-trafficking advocacy organizations and social service providers have led the fight to expand anti-trafficking interventions, often by partnering and working directly with governments and police. Anti-trafficking organizations also receive a significant share of new funding, which goes almost exclusively to those with anti–sex work politics (Clancy et al., 2014; De Shalit, 2021).

More than whole-of-government, then, anti-trafficking today is perhaps better described as a whole-of-society endeavour. However, while often couched in a rhetoric of care and victim-centred responses, as for example in the 2019 federal strategy, which cites "preventing and addressing gender-based violence, and supporting the safety and security of Indigenous peoples" as key concerns (Public Safety Canada, 2019, p. 3), the whole-of-society approach in fact serves to cement and legitimize the centrality of policing and state security in anti-trafficking interventions. As Jennifer Suchland (2015) puts it, "A prosecutorial antitrafficking apparatus has developed, enlisting a whole host of actors, and yet the state is rarely the object of critique" (p. 55). Writing on transnational labour migration and border securitization more broadly, Nandita

Sharma (2015) argues that "anti-trafficking policies do a great disservice to migrating people, especially the most vulnerable. By diverting our attention away from the practices of nation-states and employers, they channel our energies to support a law-and-order agenda of 'getting tough' with 'traffickers'" (n.p.; see also Mac & Smith, 2018). Not only do these policies produce harm, Sharma (2015) contends, but they in fact "cast nation-states as the 'rescuers' of 'victims of trafficking' instead of showing nation-states to be the *source* of much of their woes" (n.p.).

For police, the turn to anti-trafficking comes with an additional significant added value: it is a way to build legitimacy and budgets at a time when Black Lives Matter, Idle No More, and other movements have highlighted the profound harms that result from addressing complex social issues by deploying police. Yet anti-trafficking provides a strikingly clear case study of the harms produced by policing and criminalizing approaches. Despite the claims made in the 2019 strategy that anti-trafficking promotes Indigenous safety and security, for example, anti-trafficking has in fact long served the projects of Indigenous dispossession and immigration control at the heart of the settler-colonial state (Kaye, 2017). The federal Immigration and Refugee Protection Regulations, which, on the grounds of fighting trafficking, prohibit temporary workers from taking up sex work–related employment, likewise extend the power of various government agencies, including police, over the lives of migrant workers (Chu et al., 2019). In general, anti-trafficking needs to be understood as part of what Loïc Wacquant (2009) calls "a *new government of social insecurity*" (p. 11), in which the criminalization of poverty expands in response to the shrinking of social security and growing labour precarity. The role of the anti–sex work women's movement is crucial in this respect, as it has driven a focus on so-called "sex trafficking" or "trafficking for purposes of sexual exploitation" (to use the more common police formulation). Elizabeth Bernstein (2010) calls this a "carceral feminism" and Jennifer Musto (2016) a "carceral protectionism," ostensibly victim-centred approaches in which arresting or imprisoning "victims," particularly youth, is conceived as a form of help or rescue, a rhetoric of care often deployed in anti-trafficking discourses. Focusing almost exclusively on sex work–related activity, anti-trafficking most often supports a broader anti–sex work agenda. It operates through a conception of community that excludes sex workers, understanding them only as victims to be rescued or as a threat to social order, and mobilizes police as the primary mechanism of community protection (Wright et al., 2015). As other chapters in this volume outline in detail, policing and criminalization produce myriad harms, particularly for sex workers, temporary or nonstatus migrant workers, BIPOC communities and people, trans people, poor people, women, and a range of others already subject to overpolicing.

In this chapter, I examine anti-trafficking policing targeting sex work–related activity, although the problems identified here also extend to the policing of trafficking in other labour sectors. The whole-of-society approach to trafficking, I argue, is linked to broader policing changes associated with the emergence of intelligence-led policing (ILP). ILP relies heavily on new data-based technologies, including in some cases automated systems, and prioritizes broad collaborations between different police forces, government agencies, NGOs, and the corporate sector. The whole-of-society approach to trafficking in Canada has been structured in precisely this way, with NGOs (primarily advocacy and social service agencies) taking on an especially prominent role. Most notable in this respect, as I discuss at greater length later, is the Canadian Centre to End Human Trafficking. Its selection by Public Safety Canada to run the national anti-trafficking hotline means that a key tool used in police investigations across the country has been outsourced and privatized, and the centre's role in anti-trafficking policing has in turn legitimized the NGO as arguably the most sought-after and influential organization when it comes to advising government agencies, companies, and other anti-trafficking organizations.

I begin the chapter by outlining ILP and whole-of-society approaches to human trafficking, and how these have reframed complex social dynamics and inequities as policing problems. I then turn to surveillance and data gathering, which is central to ILP, and look at some of the key data-gathering tools, including automated technologies, that are used to construct trafficking as an object for police intervention. In the final section, I examine more concretely how trafficking is constructed through indicator lists used by police, government agencies, and anti-trafficking organizations. These lists enable the creation of trafficking profiles by police and other anti-trafficking actors, including ordinary citizens, and also form the basis for the design of automated anti-trafficking technologies. This profiling encodes deeply troubling conceptions of trafficking and its alleged victims and perpetrators, cements the conflation of trafficking and sex work, and entrenches and legitimizes policing as the only possible response to trafficking.

Intelligence-Led Policing, Surveillance, and the Work of Anti-Trafficking

ILP involves a shift to what Brendan McQuade (2019) describes as "mass supervision," the continuous monitoring not only of those who are under concrete suspicion or have been convicted of criminal offences but also of larger populations deemed suspect or at risk. In a time of dramatic cuts to social services, wage stagnation, the growth of precarious labour, environmental crises, and the protection of urban property values, ILP enables the management of social order by remaking perceived disorder as a policing problem. Because it relies on data analytics rather than human intervention, ILP is often claimed to be less biased than traditional policing, but studies have shown that the opposite is often true; its reliance on historical racist, gendered, and classed policing data often reinforces existing inequities, including the disproportionate use of force against particular communities such as sex workers (see Ferguson, 2017; Jefferson, 2020). ILP targets predetermined populations, which in the case of trafficking primarily means that sex work–related activities and people are brought under surveillance.

Fusion centres, pioneered in the United States under the leadership of the Department of Homeland Security, have institutionalized the law enforcement collaborations characteristic of ILP. These centres bring together officials from various agencies to coordinate responses to perceived systemic threats, in particular terrorism, the drug trade, or radical political mobilizations like the Indigenous-led protests against the Dakota Access Pipeline and the Black Lives Matter movement (McQuade, 2019). Fusion centres "thrive upon the production and exchange of data and the sorting of individuals based on their assigned risk" (Monahan & Palmer, 2009, p. 619), with their operations prone to "*mission creep*, where their functions expand beyond their originally intended purposes to encompass things like all-hazards preparedness" (Monahan & Palmer, 2009, p. 620). In Canada, the model has influenced a variety of developments. Most prominent are the Integrated Security Units established to protect the G8 and G20 meetings in Ontario and the Vancouver Winter Olympics in 2010 (Monaghan & Walby, 2012), and later to surveil and police Indigenous and environmental protesters allegedly threatening "critical infrastructure" such as pipelines (Crosby & Monaghan, 2018; Dafnos et al., 2016). These Integrated Security Units continued feeding intelligence into the Canadian Security Intelligence Service's Integrated Terrorism Assessment Centre long after the event or situations ended. At a smaller and more local scale, Ontario and Saskatchewan have each developed a Risk-driven Tracking Database, which provides another example of "a collaborative approach to policing called the Hub model that partners cops, school staff, social workers, health care workers, and the provincial government" (Munn, 2019, n.p.; see also Munn, 2022). The database brings together personal information gathered by police and civilian agencies, ranging from drug use to whether one lives in a "negative neighbourhood," to identify those purportedly in need of intervention. Those targeted include youth, and information gathering has been done without consent. Despite the rhetoric of care, then, ILP tends to exacerbate the overpolicing of already marginalized communities.

Anti-trafficking encompasses national, regional, and local collaborations that, in Canada and elsewhere, produce what Elya M. Durisin and Emily van der Meulen (2021) call a "sexualized nationalism" in which the policing of trafficking and sex work, again presented as a form of care, is made central to a purportedly progressive national identity. As the authors stress, in reframing social service provision as a policing problem, this approach produces significant harms for sex workers. These harms were evident from early on in British Columbia, a key early innovator of the ILP approach to anti-trafficking. Raid-and-rescue operations targeting eighteen massage parlours across the province's Lower Mainland in 2006 marked an early instance of collaborative policing, an approach institutionalized in 2007 with the pioneering formation of British Columbia's Office to Combat Trafficking in Persons. These early collaborations between police, government agencies, and NGOs were fraught, not least because during the 2006 raids police very publicly handcuffed and arrested over a hundred people, primarily alleged human trafficking victims. No charges resulted from the raids, but this stigmatizing spectacle brought significant harm for those targeted (Kaye, 2017), and the handcuffing of those allegedly being "rescued" demonstrated the blurred lines between who is deemed "victim" or "threat" in anti-trafficking policing. Again in British Columbia, the 2010 Vancouver Winter Olympics provided a further boost to anti-trafficking policing. A very public, lurid, and often misleading campaign by anti-trafficking and anti–sex work NGOs such as the Salvation Army pushed for greater police attention to trafficking, if with only partial success (Global Alliance Against Traffic in Women, 2011; Lepp, 2013; Matheson & Finkel, 2013).

More recently, Ontario has taken over as the leading jurisdiction in driving anti-trafficking ILP. The Ontario Provincial Police (OPP) Anti-Human Trafficking Investigations Coordination Team and the newly created provincial Intelligence-led Joint Forces Strategy bring together investigators from the OPP and twenty-one municipal and First Nations police forces across Ontario to build anti-trafficking cases. Beginning in 2021, the Intelligence-led Joint Forces Strategy has facilitated several anti-trafficking investigations in partnership with local police services, including Project Wrigg and Project Shamrock in Kingston, Project Harwich in Barrie, and Project Exodus in Ottawa (CityNews Ottawa, 2022; *Kingston Whig-Standard*, 2022; Wilson, 2021). These projects promise to target instances of trafficking, yet few trafficking-specific charges have resulted, and it remains to be seen how many will lead to convictions. As Hayli Millar and Tamara O'Doherty (2020) stress, relative to the scale of the resources brought to bear on trafficking, the number of charges and especially convictions remains quite small.

The Intelligence-led Joint Forces Strategy reflects the fusion centre approach in bringing together not only multiple police forces across Ontario (and, in the case of Project Wrigg, Edmonton police as well), but also federal agencies such as FINTRAC and the Canadian Air Transport Security Authority along with anti-trafficking NGOs. As noted earlier, of the latter organizations, the Canadian Centre to End Human Trafficking is a key contributor to the expansion of these approaches. It has supported Ontario's new strategy while continuing to argue for even more resources for ILP approaches: "We need investments in creating more inter-jurisdictional law enforcement teams that can act quickly and decisively across municipal and provincial jurisdictions, funding of programs and supports in perpetuity and a truly, victim informed [*sic*] pan-Canadian strategy" (Canadian Centre to End Human Trafficking, 2021c, n.p.). Especially crucial, it argues in an extensive report, is monitoring and policing "human trafficking corridors" (Canadian Centre to End Human Trafficking, 2021a, n.p.) that allegedly run along intra- and interprovincial transportation routes, primarily major highways.

The Canadian Centre to End Human Trafficking is not alone in partnering with police in this area. As part of a campaign called #ProjectONroute, the NGO Courage for Freedom ran advertisements in rest stops operated by the ONroute company along Highway 401 in Ontario on National Human Trafficking Awareness Day in 2019, later expanding the campaign to highways nationally as #ProjectMapleLeaf. It sought to enlist citizen surveillance, exhorting people to watch for signs of trafficking along the highway. Courage for Freedom's founder characterized this approach as "a neighbourhood watch for human trafficking" (Balogh, 2019, n.p.) based on the rather startling claim that "60 per cent of human trafficking victims in Canada report that it began in Ontario on the province's 400-series highways" (Balogh, 2019, n.p.). The campaign was amplified by police via the Facebook page of the Woodstock Police Service (2019), which reposted Courage for Freedom's campaign video and proclaimed, "We're heading over to the Woodstock 401 Eastbound onroute to show our support for #ProjectONroute."

The work of the Canadian Centre to End Human Trafficking provides an interesting insight into the contradictions of anti-trafficking politics. Its report on trafficking corridors is based on interviews with key "primary definers" (see Hall, 1982) of trafficking — namely, law enforcement personnel and frontline nongovernmental service providers — buttressed by a review of eighty-five academic and nonacademic publications. Crucially, there is no engagement with those most likely to be caught up in anti-trafficking operations, in particular sex workers or sex worker rights advocates. Despite the centre's strong bias toward policing solutions and, through the anti-trafficking hotline, direct collaboration with police, Executive Director Julie Drydyk acknowledged in her July 6, 2022, testimony before the Senate's Standing Committee on Human Rights on Bill S-224 (an amendment to the trafficking in persons section of the *Criminal Code*) that "bias still exists within the judiciary" (Senate of Canada, 2022, n.p.). Indigenous, Black, racialized, LGBTQI+, poor, and precariously housed people are at greater risk of trafficking, Drydyk stated, and "have also historically and are currently experiencing discrimination and abuse from the very institutions that are supposed to protect them" (Senate of Canada, 2022, n.p.).

Further, the centre's own research suggests that policing is not the obvious response to trafficking. In interviews done for its report on trafficking corridors, it found that police and service provider respondents said that 15 percent of those they identified as trafficked did not self-identify as such, while 15 percent cited lack of housing or shelter as reasons for not leaving their situation, and the largest group, 30 percent, said that they stayed because of the income their work provides. Thus, as the report concludes,

> Social assistance rates and provincial minimum wages provide subsistence income at best and are far less than victims would 'earn' on any given day. Even though victims are often forced to hand over their earnings to traffickers, the idea of working a minimum wage job or relying on social assistance presents significant barriers to exiting. (Canadian Centre to End Human Trafficking, 2021a, p. 39)

What is striking, then, is that while the centre's own evidence points directly to complex socioeconomic dynamics as the context for trafficking, and highlights policing as often harmful, the carceral protectionist impulse is so powerful that the centre still focuses overwhelmingly on policing solutions. Out of its four recommendations, two advocate for increasing police and criminal justice capacities, one calls for incorporating more partners, including industries such as car rentals and hotels, into police-led anti-trafficking collaborations, and only one stresses community service provision (Canadian Centre to End Human Trafficking, 2021a, pp. 49–50). That final recommendation also focuses on organizations that collaborate with police. There is an almost complete absence here of attention to labour-based perspectives foregrounded by sex workers and migrant workers. Instead, reflecting a larger anti–sex work politic as well, these are remade as policing problems.

As Suchland (2015) asks, "Why is the violence of trafficking so visible and the violence of precarious labor not, and why has the affective power of representing trafficking not translated into heightened criticism of the market or economic policy?" (p. 16). Sex workers, migrant workers, and advocates have shown that anti-trafficking interventions produce and exacerbate broader social harms. Those interventions do little to ameliorate conditions of violence and exploitation, and instead foster mass supervision and operate according to an ILP logic of "pacification, or the systematic fabrication of capitalist forms of order" (McQuade, 2019, p. 9).

Data Gathering, Technology, and Intelligence-Led Anti-Trafficking

"Around the world, trafficking can take many different forms and it often begins online," proclaimed Marco Mendicino, the federal minister of public safety, on July 30, 2022. "That is why this year's World Day Against Trafficking in Persons focuses on the role of technology in enabling human trafficking" (Public Safety Canada, 2022, n.p.). Evoking the whole-of-society approach by noting that "combatting it requires urgent action across all levels of government, in close partnership with industry and civil society" (Public Safety Canada, 2022, n.p.), Mendicino builds here on a common contention in anti-trafficking circles that new technologies, particularly social media, facilitate trafficking on the one hand, but on the other provide new tools to address it. The most recent National Strategy to Combat Human Trafficking, for example, emphasizes both growing dangers online and the need to use new technologies to "close data gaps" relating to trafficking, and includes the formation of a working group on "Research, Information Sharing and Data Collection" (Public Safety, 2021, p. 33) to address what the Canadian Centre to End Human Trafficking (2021b) laments as an "absence of data" (p. 12).

The lack of data, however, does not prevent anti-trafficking advocates from making categorical claims about the scale and severity of the problem — those dubious claims are then used to promote and legitimize a dramatic expansion of surveillance and policing. Youth are often framed as those at greatest risk, but in practice the implementation of online and other forms of surveillance has the greatest impact on adult sex workers. As critics have noted, this surveillance often collapses distinctions between sex work and trafficking and increases precarity and risk for those ostensibly being helped (Milivojevic et al., 2020; Musto, 2016; Musto & boyd, 2014).

Technological and other forms of data gathering and analysis are central to anti-trafficking ILP, and many innovations originate in the United States. The US military's Defense Advanced Research Projects Agency, for example, has played a key role in bringing together companies, anti-trafficking organizations, and academic researchers to develop Memex, a suite of tools enabling the surveillance of the deep web in search of trafficking-related activity (Pellerin, 2017). Many other anti-trafficking technologies are developed by NGOs and companies and made available, generally for free, to law enforcement (Mendel & Sharapov, 2022), including Spotlight (developed by the NGO Thorn, established by Ashton Kutcher), IBM's AI-based Traffik Analysis Hub, and Marinus Analytics' Traffic Jam. Most commonly these technologies are designed to scrape data from websites that host advertisements for sex workers' services, sex worker message boards, and other sources, and they often use tools such as face and text recognition systems to track trafficking indicators across the web.

Canadian companies have played a role in these developments as well. The nonprofit subsidiary of the Toronto-based company Uncharted, for example, created TellFinder, the centrepiece tool of the TellFinder Alliance, which partnered with big tech companies like Microsoft (Edge & Larson, 2021) to facilitate global data sharing around trafficking. TellFinder, which ceased operating in May 2023, scraped text and images from the internet to identify people across different platforms and places and to visualize their activities and movements through data visualizations and interactive dashboards in ways that enabled law enforcement intervention. Waterloo- and Ottawa-based Magnet Forensics, a digital forensics company founded by a former police officer, is another example. Through its Auxtera Project, it donates use of its for-profit tools "to those in need—including police agencies, public defenders, charities, and not-for-profits" (Auxtera, n.d., n.p.) that are working to combat trafficking.

Anti-trafficking tools of these kind are generally built on automated systems (what is often referred to as artificial intelligence) that recognize patterns in data ostensibly associated with trafficking. As many critical data scholars argue (see Benjamin, 2019; Crawford, 2021), automated systems frequently reflect and reinforce discriminatory patterns. Sex workers and advocates working from a critical data justice perspective stress that anti-trafficking tools encode the conflation of sex work and trafficking, and reinforce racist, misogynist, and other harmful logics (hacking//hustling, n.d.; Milivojevic et al., 2020; Network of Sex Work Projects, 2021). Such tools are generally "black boxed" (Pasquale, 2016), meaning that their internal workings (i.e., how they identify suspected cases of trafficking) are inaccessible and thus not subject to critical scrutiny.

Researchers and the public also have little sense of how these tools are being used by Canadian police. The designers of TellFinder, Traffic Jam, and other tools trumpet their use by police forces in the United States, Canada, and beyond, but provide no specifics. Anecdotal evidence, including conversations with FINTRAC officials, suggest that these technologies are indeed being used in building anti-trafficking investigations. Information obtained via an access to information request confirms at least one specific instance, as a grant proposal from the London police to fund Project Solstice II explains: "The crime analysis attached to the project will utilize technology in order to assist in identifying victims and perpetrators, as well as track their advertisements in an attempt to identify patterns" (London Police Service). The tools in question are not specified, and while more research is needed to gain a deeper sense of how technological tools are being used, the opacity of police operations makes this research especially challenging.

The impact of these technologies should not be overstated given that research suggests rank-and-file police are often resistant to the use of networked and automated investigative tools (Cotter, 2017). Much anti-trafficking data gathering is not solely or even primarily automated. For example, FINTRAC, established initially to target money laundering and financing of terrorism, also began to target trafficking in 2016 with the BMO-led Project Protect. Currently, FINTRAC investigations focus on trafficking for sexual exploitation and not on any other form of labour trafficking, supported by funding from Public Safety's National Strategy to Combat Human Trafficking. The agency relies primarily on Suspicious Transaction Reports provided by financial institutions. These reports draw on data derived from the automated tracking of financial patterns, but also from bank tellers and other workers flagging suspicious activity. Bank staff are trained on the indicator lists I discuss below, and FINTRAC uses the data they provide to produce intelligence packages that feed into police investigations. Capturing the logic of ILP, the director and CEO of FINTRAC celebrated the agency's collaboration with Ottawa police and other organizations on the 2022 anti-trafficking investigation Project Exodus by proclaiming that "a network assembled to defeat a network" (Paquet, 2022, n.p.).

The network metaphor foregrounds the centrality of new digital and online forms of surveillance to the work of anti-trafficking, but the more prosaic technology of the telephone supports what is perhaps the most significant form of data collection in Canada, the national anti-trafficking hotline that is, as noted earlier, run by the Canadian Centre to End

Human Trafficking. The RCMP and police forces across the country direct victims and witnesses of alleged trafficking to call the hotline, and the gathered data play a dual role: the centre assesses reports and funnels findings to police while also using the data to support its anti-trafficking advocacy more broadly. Like the #ProjectONroute neighbourhood watch approach to trafficking, the national hotline promotes forms of citizen surveillance and data gathering. Sex workers and advocates condemn this approach. As Jenny Duffy of the Toronto-based sex worker organization Maggie's puts it: "This hotline encourages the public to now surveil the movements of this group [sex workers] and report them for further investigation. We can expect that the public will be reporting sex workers, putting them in further harm, and further hindering workers from accessing key services" (Keung, 2019, n.p.).

ILP and whole-of-society approaches to trafficking thus extend webs of surveillance deep into the everyday lives of those deemed "at risk" of trafficking, and sex workers in particular bear the brunt. Digital surveillance builds on and amplifies a wide range of data-gathering practices and police interventions. As a guide for sex workers navigating digital surveillance stresses, "Due to the conflation of sex work and trafficking, algorithms replicate the discrimination embedded in current law enforcement systems and target sex workers" (Network of Sex Work Projects, 2021, p. 9). The question then is how this discrimination works, not only in automated systems but in the larger context of anti-trafficking data-based surveillance.

Trafficking Indicators and the Work of Data-Based Profiling

McQuade's (2019) description of ILP provides a particularly apt framing for current anti-trafficking approaches: "As the central component of mass supervision, the process of intelligence fusion mobilizes the decentralized surveillance capacities of state and private powers to render the complexity of social life legible as 'intelligence'" (p. 15). Looked at in this way, trafficking must be understood not as a stable and self-evident phenomenon, but instead as both a legal construct and the product of data-based profiling practices that bring together a seemingly incommensurate range of activities, people, and characteristics as constituting "trafficking," and thus as a legible object for intervention. Fundamental to anti-trafficking in this respect is the construction of lists of indicators, data patterns, classifications, and profiles. As critical work on ILP and predictive policing highlights, techniques used by police to analyze data tend to reinscribe and reinforce historical and contemporary inequities and enable growing overpolicing of Black, Indigenous, racialized, and poor communities (Benjamin, 2019; Jefferson, 2020). These tendencies are very evident in the policing of human trafficking as well.

Suchland (2015) argues that the focus of anti-trafficking work is primarily "on defining and deciphering the proper individual victim" (p. 5). This is presented as a victim-centred approach, but in practice it renders largely invisible both the complex sociocultural dynamics at play and the self-understanding of those deemed trafficked. It also obscures changing Canadian and global sociolegal understandings of trafficking, its victims, and its perpetrators. For example, as Durisin and van der Meulen (2021) note, during a 2006 Canadian House of Commons standing committee consultation, anti-trafficking advocates conceptualized trafficking primarily as transnational, involving adult victims, and driven by economic factors. By 2018, however, this understanding had shifted dramatically, and in a similar consultation advocates focused instead on domestic trafficking, youth victims, and emotional vulnerability as the main driver of trafficking (Durisin & van der Meulen, 2021). What markers or indicators constitute trafficking or identify its alleged victims and perpetrators, in other words, is far from clear or stable. What is clear is the central role played by anti–sex work ideologies and advocates in shaping how trafficking is understood.

The primary tool through which police and other actors involved in the whole-of-society anti-trafficking apparatus (government agencies, social service providers, advocacy NGOs, banks, airlines, hotels, technology companies) frame the problem they claim to be addressing is trafficking indicator lists. As seen with bank tellers, indicators are used to guide or train everyone brought into the anti-trafficking surveillance project, from police to ordinary citizens, on how to identify trafficking situations, perpetrators, and victims, and they also inform the design of data-based anti-trafficking technologies. Organizations generally produce their own tailored lists, but the intimate sharing of information and approaches across the whole-of-society apparatus means that these lists tend to have common themes. Prominent anti-trafficking organizations such as the Canadian Centre to End Human Trafficking play particularly important roles in advising police, government agencies, and other NGOs on the construction of trafficking indicators. A systematic account is well beyond the scope of this chapter, but in what follows I briefly identify some typical anti-trafficking indicators along with potential issues to which they give rise.

At the national level, the RCMP's (2022) indicator list prioritizes "recognizing human trafficking *victims*" (n.p.; emphasis added). Indicators include signs of violence (e.g., bruises, malnourishment) as well as more ambiguous markers that capture a person who displays unfamiliarity with the neighbourhood in which they are working or living, or who "doesn't speak on their own behalf" (RCMP, 2022). Also included is a list of groups at greater risk of being trafficked: migrant workers, new immigrants, youth, Indigenous persons, women and girls, people living in poverty, people with substance use disorders, survivors of abuse and trauma, people who identify as 2SLGBTQ+, and people experiencing cultural or societal inequities. I return to these socioeconomic factors shortly, but note for the moment the carceral protectionist impulse by which marginalized communities are made more visible and vulnerable to police surveillance and intervention in the name of care.

Trafficking indicator lists include characteristics related to various forms of labour exploitation and not only sex work, but so-called sex trafficking is usually the primary focus. Crucially, sex work is the only form of labour that is in and of itself "deemed a self-evident indicator or symptom of trafficking" (De Shalit et al., 2021, p. 1725; see also Chu et al., 2019). This assumption legitimizes the systematic surveillance of advertising sites for sexual services, for example, and underlies the Toronto Police Service's (n.d.) identification of "slang language that is often used in the sex industry" (p. 12) as a behavioural marker of trafficking in *A Guide for Human Trafficking Survivors*. The OPP's (n.d.) *Human Trafficking Resource Guide* is unambiguous; in its list of charges related to trafficking it includes all the *Criminal Code* provisions on prostitution (purchasing, advertising, receiving a material benefit, procuring, and communicating for the purposes of obtaining sexual services), thus entirely collapsing sex work and trafficking as legal categories. Beyond police, FINTRAC's (2021) indicators include many that target sex workers' routine practices, including "personal account received multiple funds transfers from payment processors" and "frequent payments of premium fees for online escort advertisements" (p. 7). The challenge in analyzing indicator lists, however, is that police and other agencies do not generally identify victims through a single indicator. Their data analysis is black boxed, meaning that researchers and the public cannot know precisely what goes into profiling. What weight is put on the use of sex industry slang, for example, and what other indicators might also need to be present to trigger an anti-trafficking investigation? Much more research is needed to understand police operations in this respect.

What is clear, however, is that indicator lists systematically erase the agency of those deemed potential victims, and in the process enable and legitimize police and other anti-trafficking actors to use data to speak *for* victims and to enact rescue. This perspective dovetails with that of the anti–sex work movement, which considers sex work to be inherently violent and exploitative, and contends that workers who deny this reality are not to be believed. As noted in the OPP's (2021) list: "The individual may not self-identify as a victim of human trafficking" and "The individual may not appear to need community-based social services because they have a place to live, food to eat, medical care and what *they think* is a paying job" (n.p.; emphasis added). The influential indicator list developed by the Canadian Centre to End Human Trafficking (n.d.) is similar: victims may "not know they are being victimized because they have a relationship with their trafficker" or may "not appear to need assistance because they have a place to live, food to eat, nice clothes" (n.p.). The implication is not just that trafficking victims cannot recognize their own condition — *their unwillingness to identify as a victim itself becomes an indicator that they are being trafficked.*

Though denials of victimization are not to be believed, claims of victimization are endorsed even if they do not meet legal definitions of trafficking. Thus, in the Canadian Centre to End Human Trafficking's (2021b) recent annual report on the hotline is a footnote stating, "When a signaller [caller to the hotline] says that they are a trafficking victim/survivor, the case is classified as trafficking even if the signaller doesn't share the action, relationship and purpose elements of the Criminal Code definition" (p. 18). The contradictions here are stark: in the first instance, denial of being a victim is reread as an indicator of being a victim, while in the second, a claim to the status of victim is accepted even when it does not meet the legal threshold. There are of course valid and important reasons for a hotline operator not to challenge the self-understanding of callers in crisis, but the centre is far more than a service provider: its deeply skewed data collection and analysis funnels directly into police investigations across the country and grounds its central role in shaping Canadian anti-trafficking policymaking and policing.

The selective denial of the agency and self-understanding of alleged victims plays an even more insidious role in legitimating policing. Across various police and anti-trafficking indicator lists, mistrust of police is highlighted as another marker of trafficking. The Government of British Columbia's (n.d.) trafficking indicator document makes the reasonable claim that trafficked persons may be reluctant to seek help because they "fear law enforcement and other authorities" and "fear being deported if they are from another country" (n.p.). More typical, however, is the OPP's (n.d.) resource guide, which lists being "fearful, anxious, and nervous of police" (p. 8) as the *first* of its signs that someone is potentially a trafficking victim. Because the trafficker develops a bond with the victim, the OPP guide asserts, "the trafficked person may fear and resist police intervention" (p. 3). The Toronto Police Service (n.d.) gives as a "behavioural indicator" that the victim "seems *coached*/frightened/nervous/paranoid hostile [*sic*] when engaging with persons in authority or the police" (p. 12, emphasis added), while Crimestoppers (n.d.), in a pamphlet funded by Public Safety, suggests that victims may "be *taught* to distrust outsiders, especially law enforcement. They have a sense of fear and distrust toward the government and police. Foreign victims may be afraid they will be detained and deported" (n.p.; emphasis added). In other words, the distrust of police itself cannot be trusted, and the seemingly rational fear articulated by alleged victims can only be the result of manipulation. Fear of police becomes an indicator of being trafficked.

Once again returning to the Canadian Centre to End Human Trafficking's (n.d.) list of indicators is important given its weight in the sector. The list also includes being "taught to distrust and fear the government and law enforcement officers because they [the alleged victims] are afraid they will get arrested or deported (if from another country)," but it goes one rather astonishing step further, categorizing being "fearful of law enforcement or immigration services" under the heading "Mental Health or Signs of Abnormal Behavior" (n.p.). Especially given long histories of deploying psychiatric labels and confinement against marginalized communities, this deeply Orwellian classification of fear of police and other repressive agencies as abnormal fantasy is terrifying. It negates the position put forward by sex workers, migrants, and advocates that the criminalization of sex work and migration is the prime cause of violence and exploitation, and even contradicts the centre's own acknowledgment of the harms produced by policing. Further, it pathologizes the argument often made by sex workers that police are not only major contributors to the stigma, precarity, and violence they face, but are also regular *perpetrators* of such violence, up to and including assault and sexual assault (Ade Kur & Duffy, 2022; Bruckert & Hannem, 2013; Chu et al., 2019), which especially impacts street-based workers. Similarly, it is self-evident and entirely rational why migrant sex workers, especially nonstatus or temporary workers, would fear authorities and deportation. Such legitimate fears are magnified for Black, Indigenous, racialized, disabled, and trans workers. By reframing very real, material reasons for the distrust of authorities as markers of being trafficked, and even as signs of psychological deviance, indicator lists entrench a perverse logic that blocks critical analysis and powerfully legitimizes the further expansion of police intervention.

Conclusion

Indicator lists have become key building blocks through which the whole-of-society and ILP approaches to anti-trafficking have been implemented, used both in training people to identify alleged trafficking and encoded in automated anti-trafficking technologies. While these lists enable trafficking to be made legible and constructed as an object for police intervention, this kind of data-based policing decontextualizes lived experiences and imposes a reductive set of assumptions and classifications that risk enmeshing sex workers and migrant workers in unaccountable systems of surveillance and policing. This is not to suggest, however, that sex workers and migrants are in fact without agency. Remarkable examples of resistance and resiliency in the face of criminalization and policing abound. What happens as trafficking is inscribed in ILP practice, however, is that the possibility for critical scrutiny or political challenge is blocked, with anti-trafficking policing black boxed, encoded in technological fixes, and outsourced to NGOs or corporate actors.

All of this hides the fundamentally contradictory and even incoherent nature of dominant anti-trafficking approaches. We can see this clearly in the Canadian Centre to End Human Trafficking's (2021b) report *Human Trafficking Trends in Canada*, which recapitulates many of the issues discussed in this chapter. Regarding drivers of trafficking, the report acknowledges that "anecdotal evidence from Hotline Response Advocate interviews found significant barriers in Canada's complex web of government and social programs" (p. 22), with access to housing a particular problem. It also explicitly notes that addressing social inequities through criminalization presents myriad problems, most notably for people who are Black, 2SLGBTQI+, or migrating under the Temporary Foreign Worker Program, and includes a special mention of the fact that 2SLGBTQI+ people "have historically been criminalized" (p. 28). In fact, the centre acknowledges that it needs to do better in engaging with Indigenous perspectives and the legacies of settler colonialism. In an effort to address this lack, it gives over the report's foreword to two Indigenous scholar-activists, Shelagh Roxburgh and Candice Shaw, who stress that "rather than offering protection, the criminal justice system often targets Indigenous women and girls through the biased application of the law and through violence perpetuated by police officers" (p. 10).

How are we to square these claims with the Canadian Centre to End Human Trafficking's deep integration into the whole-of-society policing-based approach to trafficking? Coherence is provided to this incoherent approach through the neoliberal logics of ILP and carceral protectionism. The centre is part of the larger not-for-profit anti-trafficking apparatus that, as one recent study of Ontario-based organizations suggests, advocates "a neoliberal project of self-improvement and redemption" (De Shalit et al., 2021, p. 1727) on the part of those deemed victims. To this we can add the rhetoric of care, which, as we have seen, provides a depoliticized and individualized legitimation for anti-trafficking interventions. Thus, the centre's primary response to the reduction of state social service supports is not the reconstitution of those supports, but rather a call for ILP mass supervision and the outsourcing of social services to not-for-profit anti-trafficking organizations that are overwhelmingly anti–sex work in their politics. This approach, typical of the sector, is built on data-based approaches that produce "trafficking" as a field for police intervention, in the process systematically undercutting the agency of those deemed at risk. The erasure of the agency and voices of sex workers and migrant workers from these debates is not accidental but fundamental to a carceral protectionist model.

Acknowledgment

This work is supported by the Social Sciences and Humanities Research Council of Canada (grant number 430-2019-00719)

References

Ade Kur, E., & Duffy, J. (2022). Sex worker justice — by us, for us: Toronto sex workers resisting carceral violence. In S. Pasternak, K. Walby, & A. Stadnyk (eds.), *Disarm, defund, dismantle: Police abolition in Canada* (pp. 98–112). Between the Lines.

Auxtera Project. (n.d.). *United in the pursuit of justice.* https://theauxteraproject.com/

Balogh, M. (2019, August 2). We need a neighbourhood watch for human trafficking. *Kingston Whig-Standard.* https://www.thewhig.com/news/local-news/we-need-a-neighbourhood-watch-for-human-trafficking

Benjamin, R. (2019). *Race after technology: Abolitionist tools for the new Jim Code.* Polity Press.

Bernstein, E. (2010). Militarized humanitarianism meets carceral feminism: The politics of sex, rights, and freedom in contemporary antitrafficking campaigns. *Signs: Journal of Women in Culture and Society*, 36, 1: 45–71.

___. (2016). Redemptive capitalism and sexual investability. In A.S. Orloff, R. Ray, & E. Savci (eds.). *Perverse politics? Feminism, anti-imperialism, multiplicity* (45–80). Emerald Publishing.

Bruckert, C., & Hannem, S. (2013). To serve and protect? Structural stigma, social profiling, and the abuse of police power in Ottawa. In E. van der Meulen, E.M. Durisin, & V. Love (eds.), *Selling sex: Experience, advocacy, and research on sex work in Canada* (pp. 297–313). UBC Press.

Canadian Centre to End Human Trafficking. (2021a). *Human trafficking corridors in Canada.* https://www.canadiancentretoendhumantrafficking.ca/wp-content/uploads/2021/05/CCTEHT-Human-Trafficking-Corridors-ENG-FINAL.pdf

___. (2021b). *Human trafficking trends in Canada, 2019–2020.* https://www.canadiancentretoendhumantrafficking.ca/wp-content/uploads/2021/10/ENG-Human-Trafficking-Trends-in-Canada---2019-20-Report-Final-1.pdf

___. (2021c, February 22). *The government of Ontario's response to sweeping legislation to combat human trafficking falls short in tackling this crisis.* https://www.canadiancentretoendhumantrafficking.ca/the-government-of-ontarios-response-to-sweeping-legislation-to-combat-human-trafficking-falls-short-in-tackling-this-crisis/

___. (n.d.). *Signs of human trafficking.* https://www.canadiancentretoendhumantrafficking.ca/signs-of-human-trafficking/

Chu, S.K.H., Clamen, J., & Santini, T. (2019). *The perils of "protection": Sex workers' experiences of law enforcement in Ontario.* Canadian HIV/AIDS Legal Network.

CityNews Ottawa. (2022, April 14). Ottawa police officers charge four men in relation to human trafficking. *City News.* https://ottawa.citynews.ca/police-beat/ottawa-police-officers-charge-four-men-in-relation-to-human-trafficking-5267195

Clancy, A., Khushrashahi, N., & Ham, J. (2014). Do evidence-based approaches alienate Canadian anti-trafficking funders? *Anti-Trafficking Review*, 3: 87–108.

Cotter, R.S. (2017). Police intelligence: connecting-the-dots in a network society. *Policing & Society*, 27, 2: 173–187.
Crawford, K. (2021). *The atlas of AI: Power, politics, and the planetary costs of artificial intelligence*. Yale University Press.
Crimestoppers. (n.d.). *It's happening here. Together we can make it stop*. https://web.archive.org/web/20230529151200/https://www.canadiancrimestoppers.org/plugins/userData/Blue_Blindfold-English-1.pdf
Crosby, A., & Monaghan, J. (2018). *Policing Indigenous movements: Dissent and the security state*. Fernwood Publishing.
Dafnos, T., Thompson, S., & French, M. (2016). Surveillance and the colonial dream: Canada's surveillance of Indigenous self-determination. In R. Lippert, K. Walby, I. Warren, & D. Palmer (eds.), *National security, surveillance and terror: Canada and Australia in comparative perspective* (pp. 319–342). Palgrave Macmillan.
De Shalit, A. (2021). Neoliberal paternalism and displaced culpability: Examining the governing relations of the human trafficking problem [unpublished doctoral dissertation]. Toronto Metropolitan University.
De Shalit, A., van der Meulen, E., & Guta, A. (2021). Social service responses to human trafficking: The making of a public health problem. *Culture, Health & Sexuality*, 23, 12: 1717–1732.
Drinkwater, R. (2022, October 3). Alberta announces $20.8 million in funding to fight human trafficking. *CBC News*. https://www.cbc.ca/news/canada/edmonton/alberta-human-trafficking-funding-announcement-1.6603930
Durisin, E., & van der Meulen, E. (2021). Sexualized nationalism and federal human trafficking consultations: Shifting discourses on sex trafficking in Canada. *Journal of Human Trafficking*, 7, 4: 454–475.
Edge, D., & Larson, J. (2021, September 23). Real-world evidence and the path from data to impact. *Microsoft Research Blog*. https://www.microsoft.com/en-us/research/blog/real-world-evidence-and-the-path-from-data-to-impact/
Ferguson, A.G. (2017). *The rise of big data policing: Surveillance, race, and the future of law enforcement*. New York University Press.
Financial Transactions and Reports Analysis Centre of Canada. (2021). *Updated indicators: Laundering of proceeds from human trafficking for sexual exploitation*. https://www.fintrac-canafe.gc.ca/intel/operation/oai-hts-2021-eng.pdf
Global Alliance Against Traffic in Women. (2011). *What's the cost of a rumour? A guide to sorting out the myths and the facts about sporting events and trafficking*. https://www.gaatw.org/publications/WhatstheCostofaRumour.11.15.2011.pdf
Government of British Columbia. (n.d.). *Signs that a person might be trafficked*. https://www2.gov.bc.ca/gov/content/justice/criminal-justice/victims-of-crime/human-trafficking/signs
Hacking//hustling. (n.d.). *Online platforms and sex worker discrimination: Sex workers use the internet as a harm reduction tool*. https://hackinghustling.org/online-platforms-sex-worker-discrimination/
Hall, S. (1982). *Policing the crisis: Mugging, the state, and law and order*. Macmillan Press.
Jefferson, B. (2020). *Digitize and punish: Racial criminalization in the digital age*. University of Minnesota Press.
Kaye, J. (2017). *Responding to human trafficking: Dispossession, colonial violence, and resistance among Indigenous and racialized women*. University of Toronto Press.
Keung, N. (2019, May 29). Hotline aimed at helping human trafficking victims may hurt them, advocates are warning. *Toronto Star*. https://www.thestar.com/news/

canada/2019/05/29/hotline-to-help-human-trafficking-victims-educate-public-launches-across-canada.html
Kingston Whig-Standard. (2022, October 4). Police charge Kingston man with 95 offences, seek additional victims. https://www.thewhig.com/news/local-news/police-charge-kingston-man-with-95-offences-seek-additional-victims
Lepp, A. (2013). Repeat performance? Human trafficking and the 2010 Vancouver Winter Olympic Games. In E. van der Meulen, E.M. Durisin, & V. Love (eds.), *Selling sex: Experience, advocacy, and research on sex work in Canada* (pp. 251–268). UBC Press.
Mac, J., & Smith, M. (2018). *Revolting prostitutes: The fight for sex workers' rights.* Verso.
Matheson, C., & Finkel, R. (2013). Sex trafficking and the Vancouver Winter Olympic Games: Perceptions and preventative measures. *Tourism Management,* 36: 613–628.
McQuade, B. (2019). *Pacifying the homeland: Intelligence fusion and mass supervision.* University of California Press.
Mendel, J., & Sharapov, K. (2022). "Stick them to the cross": Anti-trafficking apps and the production of ignorance. *Journal of Human Trafficking,* 8, 3: 233–249.
Milivojevic, S., Moore, H., & Segrave, M. (2020). Freeing the modern slaves, one click at a time: Theorising human trafficking, modern slavery, and technology. *Anti-trafficking Review,* 14: 16–32.
Millar, H., & O'Doherty, T. (2020). *Canadian human trafficking prosecutions and principles of fundamental justice: A contradiction in terms?* https://icclr.org/publications/canadian-human-trafficking-prosecutions-and-principles-of-fundamental-justice-a-contradiction-in-terms/
Ministry of Children, Community and Social Services. (2020). *Ontario's anti-human trafficking strategy 2020–2025.* Government of Ontario. https://www.ontario.ca/page/ontarios-anti-human-trafficking-strategy-2020-2025
Monaghan, J., & Walby, K. (2012). Making up "terror identities": Security intelligence, Canada's Integrated Threat Assessment Centre and social movement suppression. *Policing & Society,* 22, 2: 133–151.
Monahan, T., & Palmer, N.A. (2009). The emerging politics of DHS fusion centers. *Security Dialogue,* 40, 6: 617–636.
Munn, N. (2019, February 27). Police in Canada are tracking people's "negative" behavior in a "risk" database. *Vice.* https://www.vice.com/en/article/kzdp5v/police-in-canada-are-tracking-peoples-negative-behavior-in-a-risk-database
———. (2022, July 28). "Terrifying": Canada's police going all in on "pre-crime" intervention. *The Breach.* https://breachmedia.ca/terrifying-canadas-police-going-all-in-on-pre-crime-intervention/
Musto, J. (2016). *Control and protect: Collaboration, carceral protection, and domestic sex trafficking in the United States.* University of California Press.
Musto, J., & boyd, d. (2014). The trafficking-technology nexus. *Social Politics,* 21, 3: 461–483.
Network of Sex Work Projects. (2021). *Digital security: The smart sex worker's guide.* https://www.nswp.org/sites/default/files/sg_to_digital_security_eng.pdf
Ontario Provincial Police. (2021, February 19). *Human trafficking.* https://www.opp.ca/index.php?id=115&lng=en&entryid=5717c7e38f94ac77337b23c6
———. (n.d.). *Human trafficking resource guide.* https://www.opp.ca/tms/entrydata.php?fnc=3&_id=63906c14dc3c0c0665553a93
Paquet, S. (2022, June 15). *Remarks from Sara Paquet, director and chief executive officer, at the Canadian Institute 21st annual Canadian Forum on Anti-money Laundering and Financial Crime.* https://fintrac-canafe.canada.ca/new-neuf/ps-pa/2022-06-15-eng

Pasquale, F. (2016). *Black box society: The secret algorithms that control money and information*. Harvard University Press.

Pellerin, C. (2017, January 4). DARPA *program helps to fight human trafficking*. U.S. Department of Defense. https://www.defense.gov/Explore/News/Article/Article/1041509/darpa-program-helps-to-fight-human-trafficking/

Public Safety Canada. (2019). *National Strategy to Combat Human Trafficking 2019–2024*. https://www.publicsafety.gc.ca/cnt/rsrcs/pblctns/2019-ntnl-strtgy-hmnn-trffc/index-en.aspx - a08

___. (2021). *National Strategy to Combat Human Trafficking: Annual Report 2020–2021*. https://www.publicsafety.gc.ca/cnt/rsrcs/pblctns/ntnl-strtgy-cmbt-hmn-trffckng-2020/ntnl-strtgy-cmbt-hmn-trffckng-2020-en.pdf

___. (2022, July 30). *Statement by the minister of public safety on world day against human trafficking in persons*. https://www.canada.ca/en/public-safety-canada/news/2022/07/statement-by-the-minister-of-public-safety-on-world-day-against-human-trafficking-in-persons.html

Royal Canadian Mounted Police. (2022, February 15). *Recognizing human trafficking victims*. https://www.rcmp-grc.gc.ca/en/human-trafficking/recognizing-human-trafficking-victims

Senate of Canada. (2022, June 6). The *Standing Senate committee on Human Rights: Evidence*. https://sencanada.ca/en/Content/Sen/Committee/441/RIDR/11EV-55579-E

Sharma, N. (2015, March 30). Anti-trafficking: Whitewash for anti-immigration programs. *OpenDemocracy*. https://www.opendemocracy.net/en/beyond-trafficking-and-slavery/antitrafficking-whitewash-for-antiimmigration-programmes/

Suchland, J. (2015). *Economies of violence: Transnational feminism, postsocialism, and the politics of sex trafficking*. Duke University Press.

Toronto Police Service. (n.d.). *A guide for human trafficking survivors*. https://www.ht-survivors.to/A_Guide_for_Human_Trafficking.pdf

Wacquant, L. (2009). *Punishing the poor: The neoliberal government of social insecurity*. Duke University Press.

Wilson, K. (2021, December 15). Six arrested, 51 charges laid under new human trafficking strategy in Ontario. *CP24*. https://www.cp24.com/news/six-arrested-51-charges-laid-under-new-human-trafficking-strategy-in-ontario-1.5708535

Woodstock Police Service. (2019, July 30). We're heading over to the Woodstock 401 Eastbound [status update]. *Facebook*. https://www.facebook.com/woodstockpolice/videos/projectonroute/461768491325783/

Wright, J., Heynen, R., & van der Meulen, E. (2015). "It depends on who you are, what you are": 'Community safety' and sex workers' experience with surveillance. *Surveillance & Society*, 13, 2: 265–282.

Freedom of Information Request

London Police Service, Freedom of Information Request, File #20-377.

11

Anti-Trafficking Policing in Vancouver

The Denial of Crimes against Asian Sex Workers

Alison Clancey and Julie Ham

In 2017, a string of violent robberies targeted im/migrant Asian women sex workers in the Greater Vancouver area. As the executive director of SWAN Vancouver, a sex worker rights organization that assists im/migrant and racialized women in the sex industry, and a board member of the organization during that period, we struggled to get police to attend to these crimes. Instead, we were continually ignored and marginalized due to law enforcement's almost exclusive focus on human trafficking. SWAN advocated with and provided assistance to these victims of violence, and was subsequently criminalized under the anti–sex work laws set out in the *Protection of Communities and Exploited Persons Act* (PCEPA). The blatant disregard of targeted violence toward Asian women working in the sex trade and the criminalization of a sex worker rights organization occurred against the backdrop of a police anti-trafficking investigation and in relation to criminal laws around sex work.

In this chapter, we begin by outlining the policing and policy context in which SWAN initiated a cautious engagement with law enforcement, before discussing the pattern of violent crimes against Asian sex workers and police reactions (or lack thereof) to it. We then recount the threats that were communicated to SWAN and the organization's response. We conclude by situating SWAN's experience within the broader sociolegal context that Asian women sex workers and their allies must contend with. We share these experiences as a cautionary tale for other community groups working with sex workers, and to help inform sex worker organizations and allies about the risks of engaging with law enforcement within the current legal climate.

Indeed, the anti-trafficking framework has birthed an expansive anti-trafficking industry, involving organizations, programming, and campaigns that have notably produced severe consequences for sex workers and migrants, and limited outcomes for human trafficking victims (Ham, 2020). In this context, SWAN has much more often been contacted by women who have been anti-trafficked rather than trafficked — that is, women harmed or traumatized by anti-trafficking measures such as police surveillance and raids (Mackenzie & Clancey, 2020). The experiences discussed in this chapter show that the myriad harms of anti-trafficking extend to the persistent disregard for sex workers who are the victims of violence as well as to the criminalization of community organizations that assist those workers. We offer our reflections and analysis here to foster a genuine and informed solidarity.

Hoping for Change

SWAN has a long history of advocating against harmful anti-trafficking approaches (Mackenzie & Ham, 2019). As part of this work, the organization has sought police accountability regarding anti-trafficking enforcement and its impact on im/migrant and Asian sex workers. Anti-trafficking efforts and their approach toward Asian women have a troubling history in the Greater Vancouver area. For example, in 2006, law enforcement raids of eighteen Asian massage parlours to identify victims of trafficking resulted in the arrests of seventy-eight women, none of whom were trafficked or in breach of immigration laws (Kari, 2006).

Beginning in 2017, SWAN led advocacy against Operation Northern Spotlight, a national, anti-trafficking operation purportedly created to help police identify and rescue victims of human trafficking, which included undercover sting operations and workplace raids on locations where sex work occurs. Created by the Durham Regional Police in Ontario in 2014 (Public Safety Canada, n.d.), Operation Northern Spotlight involved sixty-two police agencies across the country at its height in 2018 (RCMP, 2018). British Columbia's police agencies did not participate in Operation Northern Spotlight to any great extent. However, based on reports that im/migrant sex workers made to SWAN over the years, anti-trafficking raids were a common occurrence in Greater Vancouver, albeit conducted in a less coordinated, more clandestine manner than those of Operation Northern Spotlight.

British Columbia's police agencies may have decided not to participate in the highly publicized Operation Northern Spotlight because they did not want to alienate sex workers and sex work activists. At the time, the sex worker rights community was still reeling from the police inaction that had enabled serial killer Robert Pickton[1] to target sex workers with impunity (Missing Women Commission of Inquiry, 2012). Following Pickton's conviction, the City of Vancouver acknowledged that a municipal sex worker–led approach had to be implemented to prevent a tragedy of that magnitude from ever occurring again, and to address the ongoing violence that sex workers risked. Part of the City's reckoning included the 2013 *Sex Work Enforcement Guidelines* from the Vancouver Police Department (VPD).

The guidelines stated that "sex work involving consenting adults is not an enforcement priority for the VPD" (VPD, 2013, p. 4).[2] Some sex workers and members of the community at large lauded the guidelines as a progressive step in not enforcing Canada's anti-prostitution laws, while others reported limited changes from law enforcement (Krüsi et al., 2016). However, the guidelines also stated that the "VPD views situations involving violence, exploitation, youth, other criminal associations (e.g., street crimes or gang affiliations) or human trafficking as being high risk and therefore a priority for intervention for the safety of the workers and the community" (VPD, 2013, p. 4). What the community at large and non-im/migrant sex workers did not realize at the time was that the guidelines served as a Trojan horse for the police to continue the surveillance and criminalization of im/migrant sex workers (Peng, 2018). The VPD continued to orchestrate anti-trafficking raids, although it shifted its focus from carrying out visible raids on municipally licensed massage businesses to micro-brothels — in other words, condos where migrant sex workers with temporary or precarious immigration status worked. Despite this, the perception that the VPD's guidelines is an example of progressive policing persists to this day.

Within this unique context of sex work–related policy change and purported non-enforcement of anti-prostitution laws, SWAN began to cautiously engage with the VPD to address the violence that im/migrant sex workers experienced. When the VPD's non-enforcement policy was first introduced, we hoped that police would make genuine efforts to address sex workers' safety and that SWAN could mitigate barriers for im/migrant sex workers reporting violence. For a short period, SWAN had a verbal understanding with the VPD's Counter Exploitation Unit that migrant sex workers could report crimes without their immigration status or work becoming the focus of the investigation. This approach would, in effect, resemble an informal sanctuary policy like those implemented in Vancouver, Edmonton, London, Hamilton, Toronto, Ajax, and Montreal, where immigration enforcement is delinked from municipal and city services (Paquet & Joy, 2022).

Hoping for Help

The VPD's image as somewhat more progressive than other police services across the country was short-lived. When SWAN asked the VPD and two other police agencies to investigate a string of violent robberies predominantly targeting Asian migrant sex workers in 2017, the police quickly proved to be indifferent to crimes against im/migrant sex workers that did not involve trafficking. The investigation of the robberies rapidly turned into an investigation of what the VPD believed to be an international trafficking ring, leaving robbery victims unassisted and traumatized by anti-trafficking raids.

The VPD's zeal to uncover a purported international trafficking case may be better understood in the context of the scrutiny brought upon the police force during this time. In December 2016, Constable Detective Jim Fisher, a decorated veteran officer who worked with the Counter Exploitation Unit, was arrested for breach of trust and sexual exploitation for victimizing young women who had been trafficked by another man, a case that Fisher himself investigated (Lindsay, 2021). Fisher was sentenced to twenty months in jail, and the VPD was under heavy scrutiny not only for his crimes but also the alleged actions of three other Counter Exploitation officers in relation to him (the charges against his counterparts were eventually dropped) (Lindsay, 2020).

Not long after, in early 2017, SWAN began receiving reports that migrant sex workers were being robbed. The robberies targeted sex workers with temporary or precarious immigration status doing sex work in condos across three Greater Vancouver municipalities — Vancouver, Richmond, and Burnaby. Some of the robbery victims and the individuals who managed or operated sex work businesses, often called third-party managers, reported these crimes to SWAN outreach staff since they did not feel that they could report the incidents to police. By March of that year, the frequency of the robberies and reports to SWAN had increased significantly, as had the violence. Women told us that they had to go to the emergency room as a result of the attacks. In SWAN's experience, due to the stigmatization and criminalization of sex work, im/migrant sex workers access the health care system only in extreme cases of injury or illness. One disturbing detail of the attacks was that many women had their hair cut by the assailants. The women reported this action as being more devastating and traumatizing than the robberies themselves. The forcible removal of hair has been used as a technique of shaming, punishment, and social control across different cultures and within institutions (Holton, 2020; Lo et al., 2022). In this way, hair cutting can be understood as an act of gendered violence to humiliate and dehumanize sex workers.

Multiple community members forwarded SWAN the names of the alleged mastermind and the men carrying out the robberies, including their telephone numbers and photos. By then, one community member estimated the number of robberies had reached seventy. SWAN posits that the actual number was much higher, as research has established that 87 percent of im/migrant sex workers do not report their experiences of violence to anyone (Centre for Gender & Sexual Health Equity, 2019). While it was clear to SWAN that the robberies had to be addressed, we also understood the risks for im/migrant sex workers who report crimes to law enforcement: they become targeted as potential suspects in an anti-trafficking investigation, or they are arrested, detained, and possibly deported. This had already proved to be true in one of the robbery cases when the victim called 911. The robber injured the woman's male partner and then fled. Due to a language barrier and with no interpreter provided for the partner, the police initially assumed that the woman was the perpetrator of intimate partner violence, and jailed her overnight. Once it was understood that a robbery had taken place, the police sought the public's help by publishing the alleged robber's photograph and the block where the robbery occurred, without the victim's knowledge. SWAN notified the woman of this careless public announcement so that she could take the necessary precautions to protect herself from possible retribution from the assailant.

Despair and frustration about the robberies grew in the community. Some considered taking the law into their own hands. One third-party manager believed that the police would act only if a murder occurred.

Vancouver police had informed SWAN numerous times over the years that without a formal victim's statement, it could not investigate a situation — what the police referred to as "no victim, no crime." And yet, given previous negative encounters with police, none of the robbery victims felt safe enough to file an official report. It was and remains rare for police to work with community to mitigate barriers to reporting crimes.

After consulting with the community on other ways to address the robberies, and due to the high potential for further violence and fatalities, SWAN received permission to file a general report on the community's behalf. SWAN cautiously moved forward and contacted three police agencies in jurisdictions where the majority of robberies had occurred. The catch-22 was clear. We knew from experience that police use sex work–related reports to gather intelligence, rather than pursue the perpetrators of violence. Therefore, we were careful to share only general information about the robberies and no identifiable details about the victims.

In April 2017, SWAN emailed two Royal Canadian Mounted Police (RCMP) detachments in British Columbia (Burnaby and Richmond) as well as the VPD with reports about the robberies and asked each of them to investigate. Given the lack of police coordination with regard to the murders committed by Pickton through the 1980s and 1990s (Mission Women Commission of Inquiry, 2012), SWAN felt it necessary to include the three police agencies in the email to prevent possible future claims that they were unaware of the situation. SWAN did not receive any significant response to this email. A month later, in May 2017, Alison (as the executive director of SWAN) was able to speak to a Burnaby RCMP officer for the first time. The phone call was memorable for the extent to which she had to plead with the officer to initiate an investigation. Unfortunately, that did not materialize. SWAN was only able to get in-person meetings with police to further urge an investigation in August (Richmond RCMP), September (VPD), and December (Burnaby RCMP) of that year. One of the RCMP detachments confirmed as late as November 2017 that there had been no interagency collaboration in response to SWAN's reports. Meanwhile, one of the police agencies informed SWAN that the Canada Border Services Agency (CBSA) had increased immigration enforcement — something that SWAN had suspected throughout 2017. Among migrant sex workers, the risk of deportation is a major impediment to reporting crimes to police (Mackenzie, 2017).

Regarding the robberies that occurred in the Lower Mainland, the community was left to fend for itself. With no criminal justice recourse to address the violent thefts, and with the added threat of CBSA enforcement, SWAN initiated a comprehensive and multipronged community-based intervention, prevention, and response effort. We participated in online, sex worker–led chat groups to strategize about safety; with permission, we sent out Abuser Alerts (text and email notifications) that informed women of the latest robbery; in our community newsletter, we encouraged women to report incidents to SWAN for tracking; we shared prevention and response strategies the community had shared with us; we provided information to support informed decision-making, explaining, for example, that depositing $10,000 or more in cash in the bank could prompt an anti-trafficking investigation; and we acknowledged the myriad efforts the community itself had made to be safe in the absence of any protection from the criminal (in)justice system. Our desperation was perhaps most evident in an unrelated meeting with the CBSA regarding immigration enforcement. CBSA staff indicated knowledge of a known third-party exploiter and the robberies. When Alison raised concerns about the police's lack of action, the CBSA offered to contact police to advocate for a response to the robberies. Police did not return the CBSA's calls.

SWAN held a tense meeting with the VPD in September 2017, in which the VPD again communicated a "no victim, no crime" approach in the absence of formal victim statements and, notably, failed to strategize on how to overcome these reporting barriers. We met with the VPD again in October. Finally, in November, the police service began investigating the incidents. During that same month, Burnaby RCMP reached out to the VPD stating it was not aware of the many robberies, despite SWAN's numerous communication efforts since the previous April.

From the outset, SWAN had grave concerns that im/migrant sex workers would become targets of immigration or anti-trafficking enforcement as a result of any robbery investigation. However, weighing the risk of further violence, even fatalities, we felt we had no other choice. Once the investigation was finally underway, there was an impressive amount of attention from the VPD's Robbery, Assault and Arson Unit. However, a few short months later, SWAN's hopes for justice were again shattered. The VPD chose to forgo the investigation and instead shifted its focus to an international human trafficking bust in the hopes of adding a jewel in its crown.

This shift resulted in a series of raids on sex worker establishments. On January 31, 2018, three distraught women visited SWAN's office to seek support after anti-trafficking operations at two of their work locations. The women were sent text messages of a sexual nature by VPD officers who had posed as clients for weeks leading up to the raid. According to the women, an officer drew a gun and pointed it at one of the women during the raid, causing her to believe it was another robbery. The women recalled the officers repeatedly asking them if they had been forced to work, along with other questions:

> How many customers do you have in one day? Where do you put your money? Can you show me your bank card? How much do you charge each customer? How much is thirty minutes? Forty-five minutes? One hour? Who sends the customers? Who rents the apartment? How much does the manager keep? How long have you been working? How many customers have you had today?

According to the women, VPD officers also photographed them, stating the reason was "in case something happens to you, you go missing." Before leaving, an officer pulled one of the women aside, slipped her his business card, and told her to call anytime to report her exploiter, illustrating the police's persistent belief that the women were trafficking victims. At the second location, police carried out the raid without language interpreters. A couple of days later, officers paid a repeat visit to one of the women to again determine if she was forced to work and invited her to become a police informant. The trauma caused by law enforcement actions stood in sharp contrast to the VPD's public report of anti-trafficking efforts in April 2018: "The VPD's Counter Exploitation Unit (CEU) received information regarding two male suspects robbing female sex trade workers at apartments in Vancouver, Burnaby, Richmond, and Surrey. Suspects were identified by MCS [Major Crime Section], resulting in the exposure of an international sex trade and human trafficking 'boss'" (p. 20).

The women who visited SWAN's office to report the VPD's anti-trafficking raids were frightened and traumatized. They were too fearful to return to the locations where they had been staying and working in case the police returned. They had concerns about deportation and were unable to work due to fears that undercover police officers would pose as clients. A month later, the VPD raided the second location again and the CBSA arrested one of the women, making their greatest fear come to fruition. One woman told SWAN that the actions of the police were worse than what any robber could do: "At least when you are robbed, it is over with. With the police, now I don't know when they are coming back or if CBSA are coming."

Criminalizing Assistance

As soon as the women who came to report anti-trafficking operations had left SWAN's office on January 31, 2018, SWAN staff called the VPD to request an immediate discussion about why robbery victims were being subjected to anti-trafficking raids. What unfolded on that phone call was shocking given the VPD's public commitment to not enforce criminal laws regarding sex work, as per their own guidelines. The officer stated he had "inquired up the chain of command about charging a community organization" and threatened to charge SWAN with offences in the *Criminal Code*, namely, obstruction of justice (s. 139) and receiving material benefit (s. 286.2) for providing counselling and direction in relation to the alleged exploitation. He stated that SWAN was criminally liable.

The latter of these laws — receiving material benefit — had only been added to the *Criminal Code* a few years earlier by way of PCEPA. Since its implementation, supporters of sex worker rights have uniformly critiqued PCEPA for criminalizing clients and third parties such as managers, owners, and operators, who are purported to receive various benefits from the sale of sexual services, jeopardizing the health and safety of sex workers, limiting access to justice and health care, and presenting a barrier for sex workers who wish to exit the industry (Belak & Bennett, 2016; Benoit et al., 2021; Bowen, 2015; Canadian Alliance for Sex Work Law Reform, 2015, 2021; Centre for Gender & Sexual Health Equity, 2019). Few expected that a sex work support organization could also be liable to arrest and prosecution under that provision. It revealed, in part, the risk that PCEPA posed to stakeholders and allies who work from a sex worker rights perspective. The threats SWAN received from the police were all the more surprising given the strength of the sex worker rights movement in British Columbia, the VPD's supposed sex work non-enforcement guidelines, and actions by the City of Vancouver to implement recommendations from *Forsaken*, the report produced by the province's Missing Women Commission of Inquiry (2012). The facade that the VPD was ever a community partner was shattered as we learned what the police service really thought of the communities supported by SWAN. The VPD revealed an entrenched racist, disempowering view of im/migrant sex workers, saying to SWAN's executive director, Alison, "You got snowed believing the women are not victims [of trafficking]" and "You are gullible to think the women are not coached on what to say before any interactions with SWAN."

We immediately retained a lawyer who had ample experience litigating police as well as knowledge of PCEPA. The threatened charge of receiving material benefit did not make sense. Who provided the material benefit to SWAN? Our funders, including the City of Vancouver, that provide financial support for the programs SWAN offers? Or maybe the women SWAN serves? It was unclear. Understandably, SWAN went into crisis mode. Staff feared that at any moment the VPD would confiscate their phones and records. Working in a street-level, windowed office in a Vancouver neighbourhood frequented by the VPD induced anxiety day after day. Whenever VPD officers walked by or sirens approached, we wondered if that would be the day SWAN was raided.

In early April 2018, the VPD confirmed in a phone call with SWAN's lawyer that SWAN was indeed under an ongoing investigation in relation to section 286.2 of the *Criminal Code*, although the officer could not provide more specific details. The VPD shared that it would likely issue a written warning to SWAN in the near future, which would specify what SWAN was alleged to have done, and noted that if we complied with that warning, there should be no further problems. The officer assured our lawyer that he would contact her if arrest warrants were issued for anyone at SWAN, and that a written warning would be sent prior to the VPD taking that step. Thus, SWAN staff members were in a position of deep uncertainty, and it remained unclear how our frontline support services could amount to the organization receiving a material benefit from the sale of sexual services. Unlike the many other sex work support organizations across the country that hold workshops and trainings on a range of sex work–related topics (e.g., how to effectively work online, how to file taxes from sex work earnings), SWAN had to be extra vigilant about any information we discussed with im/migrant sex workers so as not to be seen as providing counselling or direction.

A month passed and the VPD still had not issued the warning letter, so on May 18, 2018, SWAN's lawyer again reached out for clarity concerning the investigation and requested a response by May 31. The response did not come until June 25: "*At present* the VPD is neither investigating you [Alison] nor SWAN for such an alleged offence" (emphasis added), it stated, in reference to receiving a material benefit. The VPD went on to state that since the "issue of the above-mentioned criminal investigation has been clarified, the VPD and SWAN may re-establish our working relationship." Needless to say, by that point SWAN had realized that the public relations exercise of the non-enforcement clause of the VPD's *Sex Work Enforcement Guidelines* applied only to white sex workers. In our experience, whiteness has often been centred in the sex worker rights community in Canada, and some white, relatively privileged sex workers to this day perpetuate the myth that the VPD is different from and better than any other police agency in Canada. The VPD leveraged the perception of its supposedly progressive approach when representatives sat on committees formed by the City of Vancouver to address sex worker concerns and engaged with the sex worker community (although that has now ceased). In retrospect, the VPD's community engagement appears to have functioned primarily as an information-gathering strategy rather than a means of protecting the safety and well-being of sex workers.

Another valuable lesson we learned during this process is that the police only value sex workers and sex work organizations if they are willing to become informants. This reality was driven home through our numerous observations, stated directly by a non-VPD member of law enforcement, and demonstrated by the VPD itself on more than one occasion when officers inappropriately asked victims of violence to be informants. Indeed, SWAN never observed the VPD empathizing with im/migrant sex workers. Rather, the police service seized opportunities to gather intelligence from im/migrant sex workers whenever possible.

In the end, no assailants were arrested for the robberies. And no trafficking charges were laid as a result of the police raids. Women still report to SWAN (as recently as 2022) that the individuals who were committing the robberies back in 2017 continue to act with impunity, albeit less frequently. To date, im/migrant sex workers must continue to protect themselves in the absence of any legal or labour protections provided by the state.

Conclusion

This chapter was difficult to write. The events discussed here presented some of the toughest challenges that SWAN has faced. Victims of violent robberies should be able to rely on police support, but in this case, no support was given. It was a sickening realization that the robberies were not isolated incidents but a pattern of violence targeting predominantly Asian migrant women sex workers. Despite our best efforts and the increasing calls from the community to do something about the robberies, the police would not take action. Instead, the VPD chose to focus its energies and resources on an anti-trafficking investigation and anti-trafficking raids in sex work establishments. Left with no alternative but to provide the necessary support ourselves, SWAN was criminalized and threatened with criminal charges.

SWAN had internal discussions concerning how much support the organization would get from the broader sex worker rights community in Vancouver and nationally. As one of very few organizations that works specifically with racialized and im/migrant sex workers, predominantly Asian women, SWAN occupies a unique position within the sex worker rights movement in Canada. And while the movement hosts a range of perspectives about whether to collaborate with police and whether police can be an ally in some circumstances, the women who access SWAN's services are dealing with very different social, political, and legal realities than are white sex workers. Accordingly, we were uncertain about whether some sex worker rights organizations, particularly those working mainly with white women, would understand why Asian women had markedly different experiences with, and distrust of, law enforcement. During this time, we consulted with trusted allies to solicit their advice on how to protect SWAN from the threats communicated by law enforcement.

However, we also had a strong sense that we needed to share this story more widely. Here was a clear-cut case of how the anti-trafficking framework enabled the perpetuation of violence through anti-trafficking raids and the dismissal of other forms of violence. SWAN's experience demonstrates that PCEPA, and specifically the law that criminalizes receiving a material benefit, permits police services to deny assistance to sex workers. The question whether criminal charges are actually laid does not capture the far-reaching impacts of criminalization. In SWAN's case, charges were not formally laid, but PCEPA provided a powerful tool to repress assistance to sex workers and to prevent sex worker rights organizations from asking for assistance and accountability from the police.

The events of 2017–2018 fundamentally changed SWAN's approach. Before, the organization cautiously engaged in good faith with police officers who appeared to understand that sex workers who became victims of a crime deserved assistance from police. Since then, however, we no longer do so. SWAN recognizes that as long as any aspect of sex work is criminalized, all sex workers and their allies remain at risk of harm if they seek assistance from law enforcement. For migrant sex workers, or those perceived to be migrants, the persistent association of their work with human trafficking negated the potential value of the VPD's non-enforcement guidelines. In a climate of criminalization, non-enforcement policies may initially appear to be one of the few available options for sex workers' safety, but our experience has shown that police non-enforcement policies can still enable harm produced by the anti-trafficking framework.

Notes

1. In 2001, Robert Pickton was charged with murdering twenty-six women at his pig farm in Greater Vancouver (Coquitlam). Some of the women were involved in the sex trade. In 2007, Pickton was convicted on six charges and sentenced to life in prison.
2. In November 2017, the British Columbia Association of Chiefs of Police and the Missing Women Commission of Inquiry Advisory Committee released the provincial *Sex Work Enforcement Guidelines & Principles*, which supersedes the VPD's (2013) *Sex Work Enforcement Guidelines*.

References

Belak, B., & Bennett, D. (2016). *Evaluating Canada's sex work laws: The case for repeal*. Pivot Legal Society. https://www.pivotlegal.org/evaluating_canada_s_sex_work_laws_the_case_for_repeal

Benoit, C., Unsworth, R., Healey, P., Smith, M., & Jansson, M. (2021). Centering sex workers' voices in law and social policy. *Sexuality Research and Social Policy*, 18, 4: 897–908.

Bowen, R. (2015). Squaring up: Experiences of transition from off-street sex work to square work and duality — concurrent involvement in both — in Vancouver, BC. *Canadian Review of Sociology*, 52, 4: 429–449.

British Columbia Association of Chiefs of Police & Missing Women Commission of Inquiry Advisory Committee. (2017). *Sex work enforcement guidelines & principles*. http://docs.openinfo.gov.bc.ca/Response_Package_PSS-2018-86039.pdf

Canadian Alliance for Sex Work Law Reform. (2015). *Sex work and changes to the criminal code after Bill C-36: What does the evidence say?* http://sexworklawreform.com/wp-content/uploads/2017/05/Laws-General.pdf

____. (2021, March 30). *Sex worker human rights groups launch constitutional challenge* [press release]. https://www.hivlegalnetwork.ca/site/sex-worker-human-rights-groups-launch-constitutional-challenge

Centre for Gender & Sexual Health Equity. (2019). *Harms of end-demand criminalization: Impact of Canada's PCEPA laws on sex workers' safety, health & human rights.* https://www.cgshe.ca/app/uploads/2019/12/Harms_2019.12.16.v1.pdf

Ham, J. (2020). Anti-trafficking in Southeast Asia. In *Oxford Research Encyclopedia of Criminology and Criminal Justice*. Oxford University Press. https://doi.org/10.1093/acrefore/9780190264079.013.612

Holton, M. (2020). On the geographies of hair: Exploring the entangled margins of the bordered body. *Progress in Human Geography*, 44, 3: 555–571.

Kari, S. (2006, December 9). B.C. massage parlours raided. *Globe and Mail*. https://www.theglobeandmail.com/news/national/bc-massage-parlours-raided/article972542/

Krüsi, A., Kerr, T., Taylor, C., Rhodes, T., & Shannon, K. (2016). "They won't change it back in their heads that we're trash": The intersection of sex work-related stigma and evolving policing strategies. *Sociology of Health & Illness*, 38, 7: 1137–1150.

Lindsay, B. (2020, February 28). Deceit and corruption at the heart of allegations against 3 VPD officers, court hears. *CBC News*. https://www.cbc.ca/news/canada/british-columbia/vancouver-police-deceit-corruption-allegations-1.5478913

____. (2021, September 9). "Repugnant behaviour" of former Vancouver cop not enough to overturn pimp's convictions, court rules. *CBC News*. https://www.cbc.ca/news/canada/british-columbia/bc-court-of-appeal-moazami-appeals-rejected-1.6170569

Lo, T.W., Hui, C.Y.T., Guan, X., & Kwok, S.I. (2022). Prisoners' perceived violence and hair regulation in Hong Kong prisons: Gender-based differences. *Frontiers in Psychology*, 13.

Mackenzie, K. (2017). *Barriers to justice for migrant and immigrant sex workers: A community-led research project.* SWAN Vancouver. https://www.swanvancouver.ca/_files/ugd/3a120f_e6cc3cba12c0460da5167e8e6ad5511b.pdf

Mackenzie, K., & Clancey, A. (2020). *Im/migrant sex workers, myths and misconceptions: Realities of the anti-trafficked* (2nd ed.). SWAN Vancouver. https://swanvancouver.ca/wp-content/uploads/2022/09/Im-Migrant-Sex-Workers-Myths-Misconceptions-Realities-of-the-Anti-Trafficked-SWAN-2020.pdf

Mackenzie, K., & Ham, J. (2019). SWAN Vancouver: Supporting immigrant and migrant women in the sex industry. In A. Lebovitch & S. Ferris (eds.), *Sex work activism: Speaking out, standing up* (pp. 104–117). Arbeiter Ring Publishing.

Missing Women Commission of Inquiry. (2012). *Forsaken: The report of the Missing Women Commission of Inquiry. Executive summary.* https://www2.gov.bc.ca/assets/gov/law-crime-and-justice/about-bc-justice-system/inquiries/forsaken-es.pdf

Paquet, M., & Joy, M. (2022). Canadian sanctuary policies in context. *Canadian Public Administration*, 65, 4: 629–646.

Peng, J. (2018, May 2). Your Airbnb could be used for sex work, police say. *Toronto Star*. https://www.thestar.com/vancouver/2018/05/02/your-vancouver-airbnb-could-be-used-for-sex-work-police-say.html

Public Safety Canada. (n.d.). *National Action Plan to Combat Human Trafficking: 2014–2015 annual report on progress.* https://www.publicsafety.gc.ca/cnt/rsrcs/pblctns/ntnl-ctn-pln-cmbt-prgrss-2015/index-en.aspx

Royal Canadian Mounted Police. (2018, October 24). Operation Northern Spotlight VII: Canadian police services continue to work together to stop human trafficking [press release]. https://www.rcmp-grc.gc.ca/en/news/2018/operation-northern-spotlight-vii-canadian-police-services-continue-work-together-stop

Vancouver Police Department. (2013). *Sex work enforcement guidelines.* https://vpd.ca/wp-content/uploads/2021/06/sex-work-enforcement-guidelines.pdf

___. (2018). *Vancouver Police Department 2017 strategic business plan report-back.* https://vancouverpoliceboard.ca/police/policeboard/agenda/2018/0426/1804P03-Strategic-Business-Plan-Report-back-2017.pdf

Legislation

Criminal Code, RSC 1985, c. C-46.

Protection of Communities and Exploited Persons Act, SC 2014, c. 25.

12

Challenging Notions of Benevolence and Protection

Settler-Colonial Anti-Trafficking Policing in Manitoba

Julie Kaye and Cerah Dubé

Critical examinations of anti-trafficking policies, practices, and programs have long established the harmful effects of anti-trafficking mechanisms that prioritize and reinforce police interventions (Lam & Gallant, 2022; Maynard, 2015). In Canada, these interventions often disregard the context of ongoing settler colonialism and the role of police in (re)producing colonial gendered violence. As a result, human trafficking is read as a symptom or legacy of historical violence affecting marginalized populations, thereby compelling interventions that target "at-risk" individuals. Meanwhile, the persistent violence of the settler-colonial state and the structures of oppression that produce risk, including policing and child welfare, escape critical analyses. In contexts of settler-colonial gendered violence, anti-trafficking continues to form discursive linkages to varying forms of marginalization and multiple claims for carceral interventions.

This chapter troubles anti-trafficking policies and practices derived from rescue-driven ideologies by examining the settler-colonial context of the Canadian prairies, with a particular focus on the province of Manitoba. In Manitoba, anti-trafficking responses are explicitly conflated with addressing the sexual exploitation of predominantly Indigenous children and youth and unapologetically provide additional tools and resources of intervention to law enforcement and child welfare officials. By examining such interventions, this chapter makes visible the role that anti-trafficking strategies in Manitoba play in reproducing conditions of structural inequality and ongoing settler-colonial gendered violence.

We first discuss theories of settler-colonial nation-state building and decolonial feminist thought that help situate and make sense of such anti-trafficking interventions in the prairies. We then discuss Manitoba's *Hospitality Sector Customer Registry Act* as a particular example that illustrates how anti-trafficking mechanisms reinforce settler-colonial policing interventions under the guise of benevolence and rescue. As the chapter demonstrates, interventions such as the *Hospitality Sector Customer Registry Act*, in effect, reinforce a culture of surveillance and profiling as well as perpetuate structural forms of violence, such as the continuation of stark overrepresentations of racialized and Indigenous persons as targets of carceral interventions within a context of ongoing colonial gendered violence.

Canadian Anti-Trafficking and the Reproduction of Conditions of Violence

The emphasis on individuals demarked as "at-risk" subjects is evident in Canadian anti-trafficking interventions whereby trafficking has been conflated with the trading and selling of sexual services by Indigenous women as well as the ongoing genocide of Indigenous women, girls, and two-spirit+ persons (WG2S+). Domestic trafficking, particularly for the purpose of sexual exploitation, has been identified as the leading form of trafficking in Canada (Global Slavery Index, 2018). The focus of domestic anti-trafficking efforts on "at-risk" Indigenous women and girls advances interventions as a form of benevolence, and particularly forwards legal and police-driven involvement as a means of protection, which, in effect, reinforce settler-colonial relations of power that position Indigenous bodies as objects of intervention and white saviours as necessary interveners (De Shalit et al., 2014; Kaye, 2022).

Benevolence, and particularly white benevolence, is "a form of paternalistic racism that reinforces, instead of challenges, racial hierarchies, and its presence is found across Canadian institutions" (Gebhard et al., 2022, p. 1). An understanding of white benevolence troubles the dominant national narrative of Canada as a place that is innocent, humanitarian, tolerant, and inclusive (Thobani, 2012). Despite this master narrative, Canada remains a settler society premised on dispossession of land and genocide of Indigenous people, specifically targeting Indigenous women. Maile Arvin, Eve Tuck, and Angie Morrill (2013) further explain that "in order for settlers to usurp the land and extract its value, Indigenous people must be destroyed, removed, and made into ghosts" (p. 12). Contextualizing the foundational narrative of Canada as one of attempted genocide and erasure emphasizes ongoing relations of structured dispossession and resistance of colonial violence. Interrogating benevolent, rescue-oriented interventions into the lives of Indigenous women, such as the anti-trafficking initiatives discussed in this chapter, makes visible mechanisms of dispossession and control that both create and exacerbate the conditions of vulnerability predicating such interventions.

As scholars have noted, responding to social and economic conditions of inequality, harm, and violence with carceral interventions — the policing and prisoning responses of the legal system that are characterized by "intensive surveillance, punitive power, discipline, and imprisonment" (Bird & Kaye, 2020, p. 343) — not only reinforces existing colonial systems of oppression but also undermines the necessary changes required to address colonial gendered violence (Bourgeois, 2015; Deer, 2011; Hunt, 2015; Maynard, 2015). Julie Kaye (2016) explains,

> We have often merely "recognized" Indigenous suffering and abuse without supporting the structural changes required to account for and eliminate ongoing forms of abuse and violence. Violence against Indigenous women, in particular, informs many claims for "recognition" in Canada; yet, such claims continue to reinforce the power of the settler colonial state, reify the state as savior, and undermine alternatives to state mechanisms of justice. (p. 464)

In the context of settler colonialism, this politics of recognition refers to the ways in which the state publicly grants recognition of some of the harms produced by colonial violence, often through public apologies, as a means of championing its commitment to reconciliation (Coulthard, 2014). However, at the same time, it continues to perpetuate violence by criminalizing, violating, and undermining Indigenous sovereignty and moves toward self-determination, actively reproducing the very conditions of oppression and subjugation that shape and uphold the colonial state. This behaviour makes clear how "colonial powers will only recognize the collective rights and identities of Indigenous peoples insofar as this recognition does not throw into question the background legal, political, and economic framework of the colonial relationship itself" (Coulthard, 2014, p. 41). The politics of recognition, in this way, allows for "surface-level acknowledgement of the products and wrongdoings of colonialism while simultaneously leaving the structural and institutional roots of colonialism unchecked and unchallenged" (Dubé, Box 12-1, in Bird & Kaye, 2020, p. 319).

The politics of recognition is particularly evident in Canadian anti-trafficking frameworks (Kaye, 2017; Raguparan, 2023). As Menaka Raguparan (2023) highlights, even in cases when a victimization directly fulfills the *Criminal Code* requirements of demonstrating exploitation and trafficking, an individual's victim status is questioned and not believed, and the victimized individual receives no warranted protection under the law. Hayli Millar and Tamara O'Doherty (2020) similarly find that very few complainants in human trafficking cases in Canada are Indigenous, despite the prevailing rhetorical emphasis on Indigenous women and girls in anti-trafficking efforts. Katrin Roots (2022) further underscores that Indigenous women continue to be perceived as illegitimate victims within these legal frameworks even while being portrayed as the primary victims of human trafficking in Canada.

Far from offering an additional tool of protection in a context of ongoing colonial gendered violence, the human trafficking framework

> reinforces power relations that represent Indigenous women as dependent on the colonial government and the law to be saved and protected from physical and sexual violence. So far, this relationship of dependency has not worked in Indigenous women's favour and, in fact, perpetuates colonial power relations and racist notions of Indigenous moral inferiority. (Hope Restored Canada, 2022, p. 9; see also Hunt, 2015)

Portrayals of Indigenous women as lacking agency and personhood further fortify discourses of their supposed dependency on the state and police for protection from harm and violence. In particular, as Robyn Maynard (2015) details, the victimizing discourse of anti-trafficking "is infantilizing, in that it equates racialized, Indigenous, and sex working women with children, negating their resourcefulness and resilience and their ability to negotiate complex situations" (p. 42). This further invisibilizes the personhood of Indigenous WG2S+ and reproduces the conditions of colonial violence in which Indigenous personhood is denied.

Although anti-trafficking efforts are implemented on the basis of moral outcries and outrage about the need to rescue Indigenous children and "at-risk" Indigenous women and girls, they have yet to translate into "funding programs that support vulnerable ('at-risk') women, children and youth by addressing the root causes of vulnerability: economic, housing and food security for communities" (Hope Restored Canada, 2022, p. 22). Anti-trafficking responses and the moral panic that fuel them have, however, channelled funds into bolstering policing and carceral interventions in the settler-colonial context of Canada. The National Action Plan to Combat Human Trafficking, for example, was launched in 2012 with a significant investment in policing. For the 2013–2014 fiscal year, $8 million was invested in anti-trafficking with $5,375,000 directly allocated to law enforcement (Public Safety Canada, 2012; also see De Shalit et al., 2014; Roots, 2022). National anti-trafficking efforts have also led to increased coordination among police forces, including the establishment of an integrated enforcement team led by the Royal Canadian Mounted Police. Municipal police forces, such as those of Edmonton and Winnipeg, also made shifts from vice units to specialized anti-trafficking units (see Kaye, 2022).

Alongside reproducing structures of inequality, this chapter underscores how anti-trafficking interventions further invisibilize the inherent dignity and agency of the very people deemed "at risk" of human trafficking. Far from centring the "voices, agency, freedom, and mobility" (Hunt, 2013a, p. 84) of women who trade and sell sexual services, anti-trafficking representations of missing women "serve to naturalize particular women's susceptibility to violence, blaming the women themselves for the violence they encounter" (Hunt, 2013a, p. 88). Caroline Doenmez (2016) further underscores how "spatialized logics" imagine both sex workers and Indigenous people "as already belonging to a space of violence and criminality" (p. 120), justifying the use of violent carceral interventions. Rather than address oppressions in criminal legal systems, child welfare and family services, and other settler-colonial institutions, anti-trafficking "blames the sex trade" (Ferris, 2015, p. 45) and facilitates the policing and criminalization of individuals engaged in trading or selling sexual services under the auspices of benevolent protection.

Settler Colonialism and Indigenous Feminist Decolonial Thought

Theorizing about settler colonialism challenges the assumptions of state benevolence and neutrality that form the master narrative of Canadian identity (Thobani, 2012). Such theorizing particularly unsettles conceptions of Canada as a liberal, multicultural, humanitarian, and democratic society (Gebhard et al., 2022; Simpson, 2016; Thobani, 2012). Foregrounding settler colonialism emphasizes the continuities between early doctrines of discovery and the genocidal nature of settler-colonial gendered violence that targets Indigenous WG2S+. As Kahnawà:ke Mohawk scholar Audra Simpson (2014) identifies,

> In spite of the innocence of the story that Canada likes to tell about itself ... that it is a place that reconciles, that apologizes ... Canada is just quite simply a settler society. A settler society whose multicultural, liberal, and democratic structure and performance of governance seeks an ongoing settling of land. This settling is not, of course, innocent either. It is dispossession: the taking of our land from us. And it is ongoing. It is killing our women in order to do so. (n.p.)

Characterized by structured dispossession (Coulthard, 2014; Simpson, 2016), settler colonialism in Canada reproduces violence against Indigenous people and is distinctly gendered (Arvin et al., 2013).

Structured dispossession takes shape through state-sponsored policies and actions aimed at diminishing and eliminating Indigenous people's sovereignty, such as the confinement and control of movements via reserves and pass systems; criminalization and incarceration, areas in which Indigenous people are starkly overrepresented; land theft for purposes of resource extraction and settlement; child apprehension and family separation via residential schools, the Sixties Scoop, and birth alerts; the disappearing of Indigenous WG2S+; and intentionally inaccessible, inadequate services and funding from the state in areas of health, education, and housing for Indigenous people in both rural areas and urban centres (Comack, 2018; Comack et al., 2013; Fontaine, 2014; Hunt, 2013b, 2015; Monture, 2006). Notions of Canada as "humanitarian" and "innocent" — the story Canada likes to tell about itself — invisibilize the pervading nature of colonialism in systems of "benevolent" intervention, including criminal legal systems, public health, education, and social work.

Settler-colonial theorizing renders visible the ongoing colonialism and colonial gendered violence that are reproduced through benevolent and often hegemonic notions of intervention, such as anti-trafficking. Emphasizing the structures of inequality, violence, and oppression that both explicitly and implicitly aim to invisibilize, disappear, and erase Indigenous people, theories of settler colonialism identify the means by which these structures are reinforced and reproduced. As Arvin et al. (2013) detail, settler colonialism "is a persistent social and political formation in which newcomers/colonizers/settlers come to a place, claim it as their own, and do whatever it takes to disappear the Indigenous peoples that are there" (p. 12). Patrick Wolfe (1999) further demonstrates how "elimination" is an "organizing principle of settler-colonial society rather than a one-off occurrence" (p. 338). Elimination tactics particularly target Indigenous WG2S+.

Amid this ongoing action of "eliminating" and "disappearing," the settler-colonial state is conceived as both the provider of humanitarian support and the administrator of carceral interventions. Enacted in a context of neoliberal retrenchment of social services and welfare provisions, carceral responses fuel increased criminalization of marginalized persons (Dhillon, 2017; Pollack, 2009). Rescue-driven responses, such as coordinated anti-trafficking policing projects (see Kaye, 2022), position the state as the sole avenue for rescue and salvation from conditions that create harm, violence, and inequality — for example, insecure housing, food scarcity, and lack of adequate and accessible health services and supports — despite the state itself playing a direct role in manifesting such conditions (Hope Restored Canada, 2022). This creates a context wherein already marginalized persons are forced to rely on state-sanctioned responses to violence and harm. In the face of scarce social supports, such interventions further exacerbate and reinforce rescue-driven dependencies that (re)produce settler-colonial systems of surveillance and control. Government and police strategies continue to rely on recognition politics and protectionism in ways that reinforce racialized patterns of policing and criminalization and maintain a continued state of Indigenous overrepresentation in criminalizing institutions like remand centres, prisons, and jails.

Critical scholars taking their lead from Indigenous feminists have shifted attention to understanding violence against Indigenous WG2S+, as well as rescue-driven antiviolence responses, as sites of ongoing colonialism and continuations of policies and processes of disappearing (Dean, 2015; Hunt, 2015; Kaye, 2017). Critical anti-trafficking approaches focus on colonial gendered violence against Indigenous people, making visible the role of the Canadian state as a trafficker of human beings, and highlighting the problematic nature of anti-trafficking efforts that seek increased powers for the state and greater legal authority to intervene in the lives of Indigenous persons. Although Canada "*says* it is an anti-trafficker by adding a sense of urgency to a long-standing anti-trafficking discourse" (Roots & De Shalit, 2015, p. 68; emphasis in original), the nation-building project of settler-colonial Canada was and remains premised on the activities underpinning human trafficking — force, fraud, manipulations, and coercion (Bourgeois, 2015; Deer, 2011; Hunt, 2008, 2015; Kaye, 2017). Sarah Hunt (2015) further highlights that "the trafficking framework reinforces power relations that represent Indigenous women as dependent on the colonial government and law to be 'saved' and 'protected' from physical and sexual violence" (p. 26). In turn, dependency on colonial rescue reinforces settler-colonial oppression and the reproduction of violence in the lives of Indigenous WG2S+.

Theories of settler colonialism and decolonial thought alongside Indigenous refusal of settler-colonial forms of rescue and dependency (Flowers, 2015; Simpson, 2016) unsettle efforts to make Indigenous lives matter to settler-colonial systems. Such theorizing identifies that recognition efforts, often enacted through discourses of protection, benevolence, and rescue, reinforce systemic forms of dehumanization and reproduce state-based criminalization of Indigenous and racialized bodies. As Hope Restored Canada (2022) underscores, anti-trafficking legislation

> is based on a sensationalized moral panic that has not improved the safety of sex workers but rather made it more precarious. The moral panic has allowed for the channeling of government funds into policing and incarceration as well as to support programs based on awareness and education.... In short, the current human trafficking framework is an approach that has a high cost, not only, for the individuals involved within it, but for all systems. (p. 36)

Examinations of anti-trafficking make evident the pervasiveness of settler-colonial enforcement-based and carceral interventions, which are particularly upheld in Canadian prairie contexts in spite of the ongoing refusal and advocacy of individuals living and surviving in the face of colonial violence.

Anti-Trafficking in the Settler-Colonial Prairies: Unfolding Approaches in Manitoba

Anti-trafficking policies and practices in Canada have advanced a framework that renders all people who trade or sell sex as victims of sexual exploitation and specifically targets Indigenous WG2S+ who trade and sell sex as populations at risk of human trafficking (Public Safety Canada, 2012). In this context, Indigenous women and youth become the specific focus of anti-trafficking efforts that remain predominantly grounded in enforcement-based interventions, as well as the claims used to acquire additional resourcing for law enforcement (Kaye, 2017; Maynard, 2015).

This targeted approach has specific implications in settler-colonial prairie contexts, where Indigenous women are heavily overrepresented in survival and street-based sex trades (Amnesty International, 2004; Monture, 2007; Seshia, 2010). In Winnipeg, Manitoba, for example, it is estimated that "70 percent of individuals in the street sex trade are of Indigenous ancestry," emphasizing how the "street sex trade cannot be divorced from colonization and the construction of a white settler nation" (Seshia, 2010, p. 4). With the overarching aim of criminalizing and eliminating all forms of prostitution, the state uses the terms "sexual exploitation" and "domestic trafficking" in largely synonymous ways when referring to Indigenous women and youth involved in a range of activities related to trading or selling sex (Hope Restored Canada, 2022; Hunt, 2015; Kaye, 2017). Anti-trafficking initiatives are legitimized as community groups, activists, and academics take up this framework in efforts to make the varying forms of violence faced by Indigenous women and girls matter to the state and Canadians. As Hunt (2015) details, anti-trafficking becomes "one of many efforts to recategorize violence against Indigenous women as worthy of legal response" (p. 25). However, enforcement-based responses remain the dominant focus of anti-trafficking interventions in Canada; meanwhile, Indigenous and racialized women facing violence, including sexual exploitation or assault, describe negative experiences after reporting to the police, including accounts of encountering criminalization and disbelief, as well as harassment and physical and sexual abuse, from officers (Human Rights Watch, 2017; Raguparan, 2023; Roots, 2022). Efforts to make the lives of Indigenous women and girls matter to the Canadian state can thus conceal the role of the state in its enactment of ongoing colonial gendered violence, including the violence of human trafficking.

In Manitoba, human trafficking is unapologetically equated with the sexual exploitation of predominantly Indigenous children and youth, providing an additional tool of intervention to law enforcement and child welfare officials (Kaye, 2017). Recognizing racialized stereotypes of Indigenous women, anti-trafficking advocates "perceived that an emphasis on children would invoke responses and interventions that are not afforded to Indigenous women" (Kaye, 2017, pp. 95–96). As one such advocate put it, "The general public is a lot more sensitive to children, more sympathetic to children" (Kaye, 2017, p. 96). In this way, anti-trafficking interventions designed for sexually exploited children and youth in Manitoba extended to encompass Indigenous women, who are thereby infantilized within the rescue-oriented strategies.

From this starting point, anti-trafficking in Manitoba emphasizes Indigenous children and youth as "at-risk" (and "risky") subjects in need of paternalistic state intervention and surveillance (Hunt, 2015; Kaye, 2017; Maynard, 2015). According to Shawna Ferris (2015):

> Moral panic about sexually exploited youth in Canada too often neglects the involvement of a high percentage of these at-risk youth in the survival sex trade. Such an oversight facilitates the blaming of the sex industry for problems inherent in child welfare and family services that increase the numbers of homeless youth who, in the absence of family or state support, exchange sex for money, drugs, food, a clean or safe place to sleep, etc. (p. 45)

Rescue-driven interventions in the lives of Indigenous WG2S+ involved in trading and selling sex are reinforced, as are settler-colonial relations of power that position Indigenous bodies as objects of intervention and white saviours as necessary interveners (De Shalit et al., 2014). Meanwhile, the conditions of violence and deprivation endemic to government services escape systemic transformation.

In this way, anti-trafficking efforts have what Nicole D. McFadyen (2022) describes as a "distinct colonial flavour" (p. 7), wherein conceptions of Indigenous "risks" and "vulnerabilities" are recognized as stemming from ongoing racism, inequality, and poverty, yet the role of colonial governments and police agencies in creating, sustaining, and reinforcing conditions of inequality remains hidden and unaddressed. Structures of inequality remain unexamined as anti-trafficking conceals ongoing colonial policies and interventions that create the conditions of vulnerability in the first place. As Hope Restored Canada (2022) succinctly concludes, "In Manitoba, human trafficking legislation is informed entirely on a tragic and sensationalized narrative rather than evidence" (p. 26).

Tracing the development of Manitoba's sexual exploitation strategy clearly reveals how anti-trafficking reproduces, rather than unsettles, existing structures of inequality and violence. Enacted in 2002, the first phase of the strategy focused exclusively on children and youth and was aimed at combating child prostitution and sexual exploitation and abuse in the sex trade. In 2008, the second phase of Manitoba's strategy was launched. It emphasized interventions in the sex trade for the purposes of stopping sexual exploitation for people of all ages, including children, youth, and adults (Government of Manitoba, 2019). This strategy was named Tracia's Trust after Tracia Owen, an Indigenous girl who had been apprehended from her parents when she was two months old and moved more than sixty times to different foster families, group homes, and drug treatment facilities over the subsequent years. She reportedly experienced sexual violence and abuse, and tragically took her own life after running away from provincial Child and Family Services guardianship at the age of fourteen (Government of Manitoba, 2019; Guy, 2008). By 2011, the Tracia's Trust strategy had expanded into a third phase "to include services for adults and a focus on human trafficking" (Government of Manitoba, 2019, p. 18).

This extension into adult sex trafficking in Manitoba came on the heels of contested claims about the early and forced entry into the sex trade of now-adult sex workers (Manitoba Family Services and Housing, n.d.), actively conflating children's experiences of sexual exploitation with the experiences of adults working in the sex trade (Kaye, 2017). Evaluating provincial responses to human trafficking in the prairies, Hope Restored Canada (2022) highlights how Manitoba's "Tracia's Trust programs conceptualize human trafficking as sexual exploitation and under that banner, link legislation pertaining to child exploitation and adult prostitution together" (p. 26). Such a conflation is central to solidifying anti-trafficking ideologies in Manitoba and throughout the prairies more broadly. With long-standing roots in "unaddressed colonial biases about sexuality" (Hope Restored Canada, 2022, p. 23), it reinforces the centuries-long paternalistic and infantilizing treatment of Indigenous WG2S+ by the colonial nation-state. By equating human trafficking with sexual exploitation, sex trafficking, and sex work, anti-trafficking policies and approaches denigrate Indigenous women's involvement in the sex trade and legitimize continued state-sanctioned rescue-driven missions.

As both Hunt (2013b, 2015) and Maynard (2015) illuminate, intentionally coupling Indigenous women and children in anti-trafficking and sexual exploitation contexts undermines the autonomy and agency of Indigenous women. It "echoes colonial views of Indigenous people as children in need of paternalistic surveillance and control" (Hunt, 2013b, p. 90), and actively erases personhood and agency from Indigenous women involved in trading and selling sexual services, resulting in minimization and disbelief in instances of violence, which restricts their access to legal protections. False dichotomies in which "women who are victimized in the context of sex work, cannot claim victimhood and agency at the same time" (Hope Restored Canada, 2022, p. 23) have real and deadly consequence in their denial of legal personhood for Indigenous women who have experienced violence.

Through Tracia's Trust, Manitoba's Sexual Exploitation Unit, which is embedded within Child and Family Services, works with other government, nonprofit, and community agencies (Government of Manitoba, 2019). Although the provincial strategy recognizes that "cases of forced labour (e.g., agriculture, construction and domestic servitude)" follow "trafficking for the purpose of commercial sexual exploitation" as the most common forms of human trafficking in the province (Government of Manitoba, 2019, p. 21), the anti-trafficking movement in Manitoba remains almost exclusively focused on sex trafficking and sexual exploitation. Discussions on how to address forms of human trafficking besides sex trafficking are not afforded similar media, government, and police attention.

Hegemonic notions of sex trafficking that underpin these provincial anti-trafficking approaches and mechanisms are maintained further at municipal levels within Manitoba. The Winnipeg Police Service (n.d.) operates a Counter Exploitation Unit that is responsible for investigations involving human trafficking, street prostitution, and escorts and massage parlours, claiming that "the safety and wellbeing of those involved in the sex trade" (n.p.) is central to the unit's operation. The unit has adopted the anti-trafficking framework of the province and conflates sexual exploitation and trafficking with sex work and prostitution, as evidenced through its labelling of all clients of the sex trade as "exploiters" and making clear its commitment to enforcement against all those "who seek out and purchase sex" (Winnipeg Police Service, n.d., n.p.). Upholding the narrative that sex workers' clients are exploiters further positions those who sell or trade sex as agency-less victims deprived of their personhood, and provides justification for police-led rescue-oriented interventions in the lives of sex workers. In settler-colonial contexts of overpolicing and underprotection, rescue-oriented anti-trafficking investigations have been denounced as a form of violence "with the impact of intimidating sex workers, violating their right to privacy and putting their confidentiality and safety at risk" (Canadian Alliance for Sex Work Law Reform, 2017, n.p.).

Though the Winnipeg Police Service (n.d.) states that the Counter Exploitation Unit collaborates with "sex trade workers themselves" for investigations into "street prostitution" (n.p.), sex worker rights activists in Winnipeg have challenged its actions as harmful to individuals, including street-engaged persons, who trade and sell sexual services. The Sex Workers of Winnipeg Action Coalition (2022) has publicly expressed that it "does not partner with the Winnipeg Police Service and is not included in the … Counter Exploitation Unit claims that they partner with 'sex trade workers themselves' to fight street prostitution" (p. 115). Despite clear messaging from sex workers delineating consensual sex work and sex trafficking and exploitation, the Winnipeg Police Service continues to act as an appendage of the settler-colonial state by welcoming and enforcing its anti-trafficking legislation, once again reifying the colonial state as the saviour and sole mechanism through which to end sexual violence and exploitation. Meanwhile, systemic inequalities and the conditions underpinning colonial gendered violence remain intact and uninterrogated by the state.

The Hospitality Sector Customer Registry Act: A "Benevolent'" Policing Intervention

Another iteration of anti-trafficking campaigns in Manitoba has recently emerged with the *Hospitality Sector Customer Registry Act*, introduced by the Manitoba Progressive Conservative government. Given royal assent on November 3, 2022, the Act requires "hotels, online accommodation platforms and other persons prescribed by regulation to record information about their customers, including a customer's name and primary residence" (n.p.). It provides police services in Manitoba with the power to obtain this information as part of human trafficking investigations by "obtaining a court order or by issuing an urgent demand" (n.p.), raising significant concerns about police possessing unfettered access to personal information. The Act was introduced alongside an amendment to the *Child Sexual Exploitation and Human Trafficking Act* that similarly requires "hotels, online accommodation platforms, drivers of vehicles for hire and other persons to report human trafficking to a police service if they reasonably believe another person is subject to human trafficking" (n.p.).

The Manitoba provincial government insisted the new legislation would focus on police interventions for the purposes of protecting potentially exploited persons (Stelter, 2022). This notion of "potentially exploited" hinges on the erasure of agency and autonomy by presupposing that individuals trading or selling sexual services are inherently "at-risk," and on the idea that a potential to experience sexual exploitation can be identified through increased policing. The tools and technologies of surveillance that are applied become constant, sustained even by public civilians when police are not directly doing the work. Though the legislation may appear to serve as a preventive action or measure to protect exploited persons, its enforcement by police will undoubtedly be felt by sex workers, who have identified that increased surveillance and assumptions of victimhood decrease their safety and are part of the conditions of violence that create risk for them (Ferris, 2015; Maynard, 2015).

Minister of Families Rochelle Squires detailed how the *Hospitality Sector Customer Registry Act* broadens the scope of police intervention and surveillance into spaces that were previously inaccessible, stating that "much of human trafficking happens out of sight in hotel rooms, taxi cabs and in temporary accommodations" (*CBC News*, 2022, n.p.).

She added, "This bill creates a duty to report by those who often have a line of sight into exploitation and will make Manitoba a leader with some of the strongest laws in the nation on combating sexual exploitation and human trafficking" (Baxter, 2022, n.p.).[1] Yet, by legislating a duty to report suspicions to police, the provincial government has legitimized a culture of surveillance and profiling to be carried out by well-meaning civilians, including hotel and accommodation staff and taxi drivers — the majority of whom are undertrained or not trained at all in distinguishing exploitation beyond what the government has suggested as potential signs of exploitation.

Sex workers have expressed how the duty to report and surveil solidifies anti-trafficking assumptions that anyone involved in the sex trade is a victim of trafficking or exploitation, further propping up the alleged need for rescue-driven interventions by police. As one Winnipeg sex worker expressed, "When you're bringing people in that are not trained and have really no idea about sex work, I think you're going to run into a lot of problems" (Froese, 2022, n.p.). Elene Lam and Chanelle Gallant (2022) further identify that such anti-trafficking interventions directly contribute to increases in law enforcement harassment and abuse toward sex workers. Tasking organizations and individuals with the duty to report what they perceive as trafficking and exploitation, especially when these perceptions are rooted in prominent anti-trafficking messaging and ideology, turns them into "the 'eyes and ears' of police, collecting information on sex workers and providing it to police, often covertly and without consent" (p. 123) of those they are surveilling. This information then "provides moral justification for police" (p. 123) intervention in the lives of those working in the sex trade.

Anti-trafficking legislation such as Manitoba's *Hospitality Sector Customer Registry Act* not only subjects sex workers to increased surveillance and profiling from police and the public, it also restricts the safety strategies that sex workers can employ in their work. When the Act was initially tabled, sex workers in Winnipeg quickly responded with explanations of how this legislation would create harm for them and their communities. Kate Sinclaire, an adult filmmaker, highlighted how police have embraced anti-trafficking messaging that links sex work with exploitation, stressing that the legislation would empower police officers, who already "consider our work to be inherently trafficking or exploitative," to "go and get information, tracking our whereabouts, even on personal time" (Froese, 2022, n.p.). The increased likelihood of having their personal information recorded and passed to police without their knowledge or consent presents implications for sex workers. As presumed victims of trafficking and exploitation, they may face more unsolicited visits or "wellness" checks from police under the guise of protectionism. Further, the threat of increased police surveillance is known to push sex workers out of spaces they utilize as part of safety measures, such as hotels and cabs, which could lead them to use their homes for work or accept private rides, possibly exposing them to danger. Sinclaire pointed out that the Act could also drive purchasers of sexual services away from using hotels and cabs: "As soon as traffickers and people who actually are doing harm know that these laws are coming in, they're going to use [those areas] less, which means there are actually fewer ways to find these people" (Froese, 2022, n.p.).

In spite of harms identified by sex workers, the Winnipeg Police Service defends "the use of wellness checks with sex workers," saying they are conducted "due to the inherent risk of sex work" and to "ensure individuals are aware of resources available to them" (Froese, 2022, n.p.). Positioning sex work as inherently risky obscures decades of activism and research by and with sex workers that outlines how structural conditions of oppression and disempowerment permeate and shape their social realities, and how these broader structural conditions require sustained attention and transformative change (De Shalit & van der Meulen, 2015; Durisin, 2010; Hope Restored Canada, 2022; Hunt, 2013b; Kaye, 2017). Alongside conditions of poverty, inadequate housing, and food insecurity, threats of violence include unwanted police presence, surveillance, and intercession in the lives of racialized and Indigenous sex workers (Lam & Gallant, 2022). Instead of addressing structures and systems that actively manifest violence in the lives and work of those engaged in the sex trade — including policing itself — anti-trafficking legislation such as the *Hospitality Sector Customer Registry Act* creates and perpetuates the dangers associated with increased benevolent police interventions on sex workers.

The *Hospitality Sector Customer Registry Act* therefore operates as another tool for police intervention in the lives of sex workers and, in the context of Manitoba, predominantly targets Indigenous women involved in trading and selling sexual services. Winnipeg police chief Danny Smyth endorsed the legislative changes, claiming they "enhance the ability to safeguard our most vulnerable populations" from the harms of trafficking and sexual exploitation (CBC News, 2022, n.p.; see also Stelter, 2022). However, Cindy Woodhouse, the Assembly of First Nations regional chief for Manitoba, raised concerns that the new legislation could lead to more Indigenous people being targeted by police: "We hope that with such legislation, it does not become an excuse to increase policing of First Nations children and youth, and that the focus lies on the individuals and systems that create these violent conditions that harm our families" (Assembly of Manitoba Chiefs, 2022, n.p.).

Instead of interrogating structural conditions in need of address, the state turns to policing the lives of Indigenous women and youth "based on moral panic, fueled by a rush to rescue and save" (Hope Restored Canada, 2022, p. 22). The state's refusal to take up an anticolonial framework in the context of trafficking "leaves the structures of inequity untouched" (Maynard, 2015, p. 44), which only serves to perpetuate these structures. While it claims to rescue and save with one arm, the state continues to criminalize Indigenous, migrant, and racialized sex workers with the other. As Lam and Gallant (2022) surmise, "Anti-trafficking investigations are sex work criminalization. Anti-trafficking laws assume that sex work is trafficking.... [A]ll anti-trafficking laws contain measures that criminalize sex work. Anti-trafficking 'investigations' are not rescues" (p. 121). Examining Manitoba's legislation through a critical anti-trafficking lens makes clear how anti-trafficking legislation functions as a site of police power and how "harmful laws that criminalize sex work in Canada only justify a further expansion of carceral systems and policing technologies" (Ade Kur & Duffy, 2022, p. 101). The tactics "used to police sex workers are often characterized as a form of 'rescue' and 'saviourship'" (Ade Kur & Duffy, 2022, p. 101) but hinge on deeply rooted discourses that frame those engaged in the sex trade as in need of saving.

In a context of colonial gendered violence, such interventions elucidate the moralistic and paternalistic attitudes of the state in how it positions Indigenous WG2S+ as "at-risk" subjects in need of benevolent interventions. Anti-trafficking policies rely on the enactment of gendered and racial stereotypes, biases, and assumptions of perceived risk and vulnerability that, in effect, are reproduced through heightened surveillance. Through a reliance on veiled and even overt racism, they target Indigenous women and youth as "individuals making bad choices, in need of saving, and educating" (Hope Restored Canada, 2022, p. 33), rather than as persons with agency and capacity for making decisions within the constraints imposed by settler colonialism.

Conclusion

Detailing the unfolding of anti-trafficking interventions in Manitoba exemplifies how notions of benevolence in relation to anti-trafficking policing continue to produce insecurity for individuals targeted as "at-risk," particularly Indigenous WG2S+. At the same time, such approaches effectively invisibilize the ongoing violence of the settler-colonial state and systems of oppression that produce vulnerabilities to violence. As analysis of the countereffects of the *Hospitality Sector Customer Registry Act* underscores, Indigenous youth are not inherently vulnerable; they are targeted in a context of ongoing colonial violence. Acting Grand Chief Cornell McLean of the Assembly of Manitoba Chiefs made visible what such legislation renders invisible when he stated, "Institutionalization via the child and family services system and justice system, combined with constant removal and re-placement creates incredible chaos in the lives of First Nations youth" (Assembly of Manitoba Chiefs, 2022, n.p.). Through anti-trafficking interventions, such institutional structures remain firmly intact and are often reinforced, while systemic racism and sexism continue to manifest the chaos experienced by Indigenous youth and reproduce their overrepresentation in systems of criminalization.

Anti-trafficking interventions also infantilize Indigenous women by conflating the experiences of adult women involved in the sex trade with youth and children experiencing sexual exploitation. This infantilization upholds systems of colonial oppression and the coercive power they enact against Indigenous women. As Ferris (2015) highlights, far from addressing the role of "state-sanctioned racism and colonial violence in populating the survival sex industry" (p. 136), police interventions in settler-colonial prairie contexts repeatedly reinforce notions of Indigenous WG2S+ as dependent on the rescue of police in ways that increase, rather than address, insecurities and violence.

Critical examinations of anti-trafficking call for strategies that address oppressive systems and structures while decreasing the harms associated with living and surviving in contexts of ongoing settler-colonial gendered violence. Those harms include ones associated with anti-trafficking interventions. As Maynard (2015) identifies, "While it is important to consider the victims of trafficking as well as when and where trafficking takes place, it is equally important to consider those who are victimized by the anti-trafficking efforts that claim to help them" (p. 49). At present, government anti-trafficking efforts perpetuate the ongoing conditions of settler-colonial gendered violence that create vulnerabilities in the lives of Indigenous WG2S+, regardless of whether they are involved in trading or selling sexual services. Moving beyond notions of rescue, Maynard (2015) suggests, "Any effective anti-trafficking effort must place at the forefront Indigenous, migrant, sex working, and racialized women's voices. It must challenge systemic violence and disenfranchisement in all of its forms in order to achieve reproductive, sexual, and bodily autonomy as well as freedom from state or state-endorsed violence and discrimination" (p. 52).

In the context of anti-trafficking in the settler-colonial prairies of Canada, significant work remains to foreground the voices of Indigenous and racialized women. Moreover, complete disregard for the personhood of individuals who trade and sell sexual services perpetuates notions of voicelessness that dominant colonial gendered structures are eager to fill. Continued critical examinations of anti-trafficking remain necessary to unsettle the perpetuation of systemic violence imposed in settler-colonial contexts.

Note

1. Such legislative changes are not limited to Manitoba — a similar law, the *Combating Human Trafficking Act*, 2021, was passed in Ontario.

References

Ade Kur, E., & Duffy, J. (2022). Sex worker justice — by us, for us: Toronto sex workers resisting carceral violence. In S. Pasternak, K. Walby, & A. Stadnyk (eds.), *Disarm, defund, dismantle: Police abolition in Canada* (pp. 98–112). Between the Lines.

Amnesty International. (2004). *Stolen sisters: A human rights response to discrimination and violence against Indigenous women in Canada*. http://www.amnesty.ca/campaigns/resources/amr2000304.pdf

Arvin, M., Tuck, E., & Morrill, A. (2013). Decolonizing feminism: Challenging connection between settler colonialism and heteropatriarchy. *Feminist Formations*, 25, 1: 8–34.

Assembly of Manitoba Chiefs. (2022, May 13). *The Assembly of Manitoba Chiefs responds to Manitoba's proposed legislation to reduce human trafficking and sexual exploitation of Youth* [News release]. https://manitobachiefs.com/amc-responds-to-mb-legislation/

Baxter, D. (2022, May 16). Advocate hopes human trafficking legislation is "wake-up call." *Winnipeg Sun.* https://winnipegsun.com/news/news-news/advocate-hopes-human-trafficking-legislation-is-wake-up-call

Bird, D., & Kaye, J. (2020). Social control, settler colonialism, and representations of violence against Indigenous women. In M.D. Daschuk, C. Brooks, & J.F. Popham (eds.), *Critical perspectives on social control and social regulation in Canada* (pp. 318–351). Fernwood Publishing.

Bourgeois, R. (2015). Colonial exploitation: The Canadian state and the trafficking of Indigenous women and girls in Canada. *UCLA Law Review,* 62: 1462–1463.

Canadian Alliance for Sex Work Law Reform. (2017, June 19). *Turn off the spotlight: Sex workers and allies urge an end to Operation Northern Spotlight.* https://sjwomenscentre.ca/2017/10/20/immediate-release-turn-off-spotlight-sex-workers-allies-urge-end-operation-northern-spotlight/

CBC News. (2022, May 12). *Manitoba human trafficking legislation would require hotel, Airbnb owners to give police client info on demand.* https://www.cbc.ca/news/canada/manitoba/manitoba-human-trafficking-law-bill-change-1.6451706

Comack, E. (2018). *Coming back to jail: Women, trauma, and criminalization.* Fernwood Publishing.

Comack, E., Deane, L., Morrissette, L., & Silver, J. (2013). *"Indians wear red:" Colonialism, resistance, and Aboriginal street gangs.* Fernwood Publishing.

Coulthard, G. (2014). *Red skin, white masks: Rejecting the colonial politics of recognition.* University of Minnesota Press.

Dean, A. (2015). *Remembering Vancouver's disappeared women: Settler colonialism and the difficulty of inheritance.* University of Toronto Press.

De Shalit, A., Heynen, R., & van der Meulen, E. (2014). Human trafficking and media myths: Federal funding, communication strategies, and Canadian anti-trafficking programs. *Canadian Journal of Communication,* 39: 385–412.

De Shalit, A., & van der Meulen, E. (2015). Critical perspectives on Canadian anti-trafficking discourse and policy. *Atlantis: Critical Studies in Gender, Culture & Social Justice,* 37.2, 1: 2–7.

Deer, S. (2011). Relocation revisited: Sex trafficking and native women in the United States. *William Mitchel Law Review,* 36, 2: 62–83.

Dhillon, J. (2017). *Prairie rising: Indigenous youth, decolonization, and the politics of intervention.* University of Toronto Press.

Doenmez, C.F.T. (2016). The unmournable body of Cindy Gladue: On corporeal integrity and grievability. In D.M. Lavell-Harvard & J. Brant (eds.), *Forever loved: Exposing the hidden crisis of missing and murdered Indigenous women and girls in Canada* (pp. 111–127). Demeter Press.

Durisin, E.M. (2010). Perspectives on rape in the Canadian sex industry: Navigating the terrain between sex work as labour and sex work as violence paradigms. *Canadian Woman Studies,* 28, 1: 128–135.

Ferris, S. (2015). *Street sex work and Canadian cities: Resisting a dangerous order.* University of Alberta Press.

Flowers, R. (2015). Refusal to forgive: Indigenous women's love and rage. *Decolonization: Indigeneity, Education and Society,* 4, 2: 32–49.

Fontaine, N. (2014). Surviving colonization: Anishinaabe Ikwe street gang participation. In G. Balfour & E. Comack (eds.), *Criminalizing women: Gender and (in)justice in neo-liberal times* (2nd ed.; pp. 113–129). Fernwood Publishing.

Froese, I. (2022, June 16). Sex workers say they're caught in the middle by Manitoba bill meant to target traffickers, not them. *CBC News*. https://www.cbc.ca/news/canada/manitoba/sex-workers-manitoba-legislation-trafficking-exploitation-1.6489552

Gebhard, A., McLean, S., & St. Denis, V. (eds.). (2022). *White benevolence: Racism and colonial violence in the helping professions*. Fernwood Publishing.

Global Slavery Index. (2018). *The global slavery index 2018*. https://www.globalslaveryindex.org/resources/downloads/

Government of Manitoba. (2019). *Collaboration and best practices to end sexual exploitation and sex trafficking in Manitoba*. https://www.manitoba.ca/fs/traciastrust/pubs/tracias_trust_report_2019.pdf

Guy, J. (2008). *The Fatality Inquiries Act: Report by provincial judge on inquest respecting the death of Tracia Owen*. https://www.manitobacourts.mb.ca/pdf/tracia_owen.pdf

Hope Restored Canada. (2022). *Human trafficking in the prairie provinces: System responses to domestic human trafficking of young girls and women within and across Alberta, Saskatchewan, and Manitoba*. https://www.mbcradio.com/wp-content/uploads/2023/01/HRC-Final-Human_Trafficking_Report-4.pdf

Human Rights Watch. (2017). *Submission to the Government of Canada on police abuse of Indigenous women in Saskatchewan and failures to protect Indigenous women from violence*. https://www.hrw.org/sites/default/files/supporting_resources/canada_saskatchewan_submission_june_2017.pdf

Hunt, S. (2008, June 27). *Trafficking of Aboriginal girls and youth: Risk factors and historical context*. http://www.interfaithjustpeace.org/pdf/sara_hunt-human_trafficking/sara_hunthuman_trafficking.pdf

___ [thesarahhunt]. (2013a, June 12). *Sex work and self-determination: In solidarity with the Bedford Case*. https://becomingcollective.wordpress.com/2013/06/12/sex-work-and-self-determination-in-solidarity-with-the-bedford-case/

___. (2013b). Decolonizing sex work: Developing an intersectional Indigenous approach. In E. van der Meulen, E.M. Durisin, & V. Love (eds.), *Selling sex: Experience, advocacy, and research on sex work in Canada* (pp. 82–100). UBC Press.

___. (2015). Representing colonial violence: Trafficking, sex work, and the violence of law. *Atlantis: Critical Studies in Gender, Culture & Social Justice*, 37.2, 1: 25–39.

Kaye, J. (2016). Reconciliation in the context of settler-colonial gender violence: "How do we reconcile with an abuser?" *The Canadian Review of Sociology*, 53, 4: 461–467.

___. (2017). *Responding to human trafficking: Dispossession, colonial violence, and resistance among Indigenous and racialized women*. University of Toronto Press.

___. (2022). Anti-trafficking and settler-colonial discourses of protection: The coloniality of racialized interventions. In K. Kempadoo & E. Shih (eds.), *White supremacy, racism and the coloniality of anti-trafficking*. Routledge.

Lam, E., & Gallant, C. (2022). Rights not rescue: Defending migrant sex workers from policing. In S. Pasternak, K. Walby, & A. Stadnyk (eds.), *Disarm, defund, dismantle: Police abolition in Canada* (pp. 118–130). Between the Lines.

Manitoba Family Services and Housing. (n.d.). *Responding to sexual exploitation: Tracia's Trust*. https://www.gov.mb.ca/fs/traciastrust/history.html

Maynard, R. (2015). Fighting wrongs with wrongs? How Canadian anti-trafficking crusades have failed sex workers, migrants, and Indigenous communities. *Atlantis Critical Studies in Gender, Culture & Social Justice*, 37.2, 1: 40–56.

McFadyen, N.D. (2022). Maintaining the carceral echo chamber: Tensions within the anti-trafficking movement in Canada. *Anthropologica*, 64, 1: 1–26.

Millar, H., & O'Doherty, T. (2020). Racialized, gendered, and sensationalized: An examination of Canadian anti-trafficking laws, their enforcement and their (re)presentation. *Canadian Journal of Law and Society*, 35, 1: 23–44.

Monture, P. (2006). Confronting power: Aboriginal women and justice reform. *Canadian Woman Studies*, 25, 3: 25–33.

___. (2007). Racing and erasing: Law and gender in white settler societies. In B.S. Bolora & S.P. Hier (eds.), *Race and racism in 21st century Canada: Continuity, complexity, and change* (pp. 197–216). Broadview Press.

Pollack, S. (2009). "You can't have it both ways": Punishment and treatment of imprisoned women. *Journal of Progressive Human Services*, 20, 2: 112–128.

Public Safety Canada. (2012). *National action plan to combat human trafficking*. https://www.publicsafety.gc.ca/cnt/rsrcs/pblctns/ntnl-ctn-pln-cmbt/index-eng.aspx

Raguparan, M. (2023). "Is it because I'm not young and white with blue eyes?": Canadian police response to sex workers of colour's experiences of exploitation and trafficking. In K. Kempadoo & E. Shih (eds.), *White supremacy, racism, and the coloniality of anti-trafficking* (pp. 170–186). Routledge.

Roots, K. (2022). *The domestication of human trafficking: Law, policing, and prosecution in Canada*. University of Toronto Press.

Roots, K., & De Shalit, A. (2015). Evidence that evidence doesn't matter: Human trafficking cases in Canada. *Atlantis: Critical Studies in Gender, Culture & Social Justice*, 37.2, 1: 65–80.

Seshia, M. (2010). Naming systemic violence in Winnipeg's street sex trade. *Canadian Journal of Urban Research*, 19, 1: 1–17.

Simpson, A. (2014). R.A.C.E. 2014: Keynote 1: "The chiefs two bodies: Theresa Spence & the gender of settler sovereignty: Unsettling conversations" [video]. https://vimeo.com/110948627

___. (2016). The state is a man: Theresa Spence, Loretta Saunders and the gender of settler sovereignty. *Theory & Event*, 19, 4: 1–30.

Sex Workers of Winnipeg Action Coalition. (2022). DIY defunding the police: How Winnipeg sex workers stopped the police from taking driver's money. In S. Pasternak, K. Walby, & A. Stadnyk (eds.), *Disarm, defund, dismantle: Police abolition in Canada* (pp. 113–117). Between the Lines.

Stelter, R. (2022, May 12). New legislation aims to crack down on human trafficking. *Winnipeg Sun*. https://winnipegsun.com/news/news-news/new-legislation-aims-to-crack-down-on-human-trafficking

Thobani S. (2012). *Exalted subjects: Studies in the making of race and nation in Canada*. University of Toronto Press.

Winnipeg Police Service. (n.d.). *Counter exploitation unit*. https://legacy.winnipeg.ca/police/ceu/

Wolfe, P. (1999). *Settler colonialism and the transforming of anthropology: The politics and poetics of an ethnographic event*. Cassell.

Legislation

Combating Human Trafficking Act, 2021, SO 2021, c. 21 (Ontario).

The Hospitality Sector Customer Registry Act and Amendments to The Child and Family Services Act and The Child Sexual Exploitation and Human Trafficking Act, SM 2022, c. 43 (Manitoba).

13

A Narrative on Being an Indigenous and Trans Sex Worker in Winnipeg

Victoria Erin Flett

My name is Victoria Flett and I live in Winnipeg, Manitoba. I am originally from Peguis First Nation, about two hours north of the city. I am a Sixties Scoop survivor and have never lived on my reserve. I was stolen from my family twice: the first time at birth and the second time at ten years old when I was taken from my grandmother. By age eleven, I was introduced to the sex trade, and by fourteen, I was using drugs. I did both outdoor and indoor sex work for the better part of twenty-three years. There's been a lot of emphasis in recent years on the trafficking of Indigenous women and girls in the sex trade, with clients and those who work with or for sex workers receiving a lot of the blame. But in my opinion, that focus minimizes the long-term harmful impacts of colonialism, such as anti-Indigenous racism and the removal of Indigenous children from their families, and ignores the regular harassment we experience from police.

Clients

There's a big difference between indoor and outdoor clients in Winnipeg. I was introduced to online sex work around 2010, which helped me transition from street-based work to indoors, where I found the clients to be more upscale and gentlemanly. My experience with outdoor clientele was generally more negative, as they tended to be rougher and more rugged. Because clients can be charged under the sex work laws for "purchasing sexual services," workers are more likely to experience safety issues. This is especially true with outdoor sex work, where we cannot collect phone numbers and names, and clients are often in a rush to avoid being seen by the police when they are talking to us. We do not have a lot of time to screen them before getting into their car. I have found indoor sex work to be safer because I can ask for phone numbers and names and so on before meeting someone. Even though the new sex work laws that came in 2014 were supposed to make life easier for us, since the police were not supposed to target sex workers in the same way anymore, we still have to be really careful because the people whom we work with or for can be charged.

Experiences with Police

When I have come into contact with the police, the experience has been negative and often terrible for me, not only as an Indigenous sex worker but as a transgender person as well. Police officers are not too fond of trans people. They really look down on us. Just before I got sober in 2021, I tried to take my own life. The police officer who arrived at the scene was very nasty toward me. I was in my room and could hear him talking outside the door about my gender and my involvement in sex work, saying that it was just another day at Club 200, a gay bar in Winnipeg. I never went to Club 200. I do not know why he would make that reference.

I had a number of negative and transphobic experiences on the street too. The police would come to the track and go on their speaker system, yelling: "They're all guys around here.… This whole block, they're all guys!" They would constantly out us. They would also confiscate our alcohol, put it in their trunk, and take it away with them. One time the police came to arrest a friend of mine, but the cop said he would not arrest her if we took part in a video for his captain. He videotaped us saying things that he wanted us to say. It was the captain's birthday, so we had to dance around and be sexy for him. It was a joke because he knew that we were trans women and they would get a laugh out of it back at the station. The only time that the police treated me nicely, or as a human being, was when they came to my house to arrest me once. I do not remember what it was for but the officers that charged me ended up cooking breakfast for my grandmother while I had a shower and got ready to go to the station.

After moving to indoor work, I had very little contact with the police. On the street, it was constant, every day, all day, all night. They harassed us and were very brutal. Most often it was the police being nasty to us rather than the clients. Everyone is concerned about Indigenous women being trafficked into sex work, but it is the police we need to watch out for. We cannot even rely on them if we need their help. For example, I had a bad date on May 17, 2021, just before I quit working and using drugs. The next day, May 18, was my birthday — that is when I decided to get sober. I was like, okay, I am done. It was a really bad date. I thought I was going to lose my life that night. He strangled me to the point where I could not breathe. I smashed my phone on his head and was able to get away from him. I called 911 while I was standing outside the guy's house. The police did not respond to the call. They totally blew it off. They didn't want to hear my side of the story. They didn't want to hear anything. They just said, "Well, you're in that profession," which they knew because I had a criminal record and was identified as a "known sex worker." They told me I deserved the violent attack. The way they treated me was completely contradictory to government and police messaging that the police approach to sex workers has changed in recent years and that they are now helping us instead of considering us criminals.

While the police now do come and check up on the street-based girls more, I do not feel that they are 100 percent genuine in their supposed acts of kindness. When they are driving along the track, they ask the workers how they are doing and if they need anything, but I think it is just to maintain a reputation, to make themselves look better than they actually are, to make it seem like they care about us because they are public figures. Now that everyone has a cell phone with a video camera, the police have to be more careful about how they treat and interact with members of the public. Everyone is watching. When I first came into the trade there were no cell phones, so police violence was not recorded and documented like it is now.

Community Support and Social Services

When I was still working on the street, I would stay as far away as possible from the police because they kill our business. If people see you talking to a cop, they think that you may be a police officer yourself or that you are working with them in some way. Unless the girls ask for and need police help with something, the presence of police is not wanted. Instead, sisters who used to work on the street like me can step in when needed. We are members of the same community and so we are able to help and support those girls in whatever way necessary. The police have not been there to help us for many years, and they continue to carry too many negative racist and transphobic stereotypes about us. The police have abused and hurt us too many times.

Instead, a lot of street-based sex workers, me included, found support through the Sage House program at Mount Carmel Clinic in Winnipeg. The whole program is designed for sex workers, street-involved women, and trans folks. I really feel that without Sage House, I would not be sitting here today. The program helped me through a lot of things in my life and got me access to food, laundry facilities, and even some place to go since I was homeless for a long time. However, in recent years a lot of the funding to community organizations that support sex workers has been coming from anti-trafficking grants. The problem is that organizations that accept this kind of money have to abide by certain restrictions and rules, which sometimes means being able to support only those sex workers who are willing to exit the trade, which obviously prevents a lot of workers from accessing services. Those who choose to stay working are unlikely to get the support they need. My message to the community is to stay strong! Help is there if you need it, especially from your peers.

Section Four

TRAFFICKING AND MIGRANT LABOUR EXPLOITATION

14

Discretionary Decisions in Immigration

Accessing a Temporary Resident Permit as a Victim of Trafficking

Jessica Templeman

York Regional Police executed search warrants at properties across four cities in the Greater Toronto Area in February 2023. The searches resulted in the "rescue" of sixty-four migrants who the police service alleged were victims of labour trafficking subjected to abuse and exploitation. These migrants were reportedly forced to work long hours and made to reside in squalid living conditions. When later asked what happened to the migrants after their rescue, the Canada Border Services Agency (CBSA) stated that "a victim-centric approach" (Rodrigues, 2023, n.p.) was taken, elaborating that migrants who experience trafficking are typically referred to Immigration, Refugees and Citizenship Canada (IRCC) for interviews. Based on these interviews, they may be issued a temporary resident permit (TRP) for victims of trafficking in persons (VTIP), allowing them to temporarily remain in Canada (Rodrigues, 2023). The CBSA did not confirm whether the migrants picked up by the York Regional Police were offered VTIP TRPs.

The Canadian government promotes the VTIP TRP as one tool contributing to its efforts to combat human trafficking. This permit forms part of a broader package of strategies introduced by the government since its 2002 ratification of the 2000 *United Nations Convention against Transnational Organized Crime*, which includes the *Trafficking Protocol* (Public Safety Canada, 2019). To date, limited scholarship has explored how VTIP TRP applications are processed in practice (e.g., see Wallace, 2014). This chapter begins to address the gap in research. I focus specifically on the discourses that have served to rationalize the VTIP TRPs and that inform the assessment of VTIP TRP applications in practice (Murdocca, 2014, p. 9). Discourse is understood herein as a way of using language to represent knowledge held on "a particular topic at a particular historical moment" (Hall, 1992, as cited in Murdocca, 2014, p. 11). I use this analysis to uncover the targets of the federal government (the "who or what" to be governed) and how knowledge of these targets is transformed into regulatory policy or practice (the "how" of governance) (Hunt, 1993; Rose & Miller, 1992; Rose et al., 2006). I specifically consider how migrants who have experienced trafficking or trafficking-like conditions are discussed as targets for government intervention, how the VTIP TRP has been imagined as a response to victimization, and how this permit is issued in practice.

The discourse analysis is supported by a review of documentary materials. I examine key parliamentary debates, instructions, and assessments of the VTIP TRP program from its inception in 2006 through to 2018. I rely on publicly available documentation, including ministerial instructions, transcripts of parliamentary debates and meetings of committees in the House of Commons, evidence submitted to committees by community stakeholders, and committee reports. Through an analysis of three federal court decisions, I then consider if and how discourses identified through this documentary review are deployed in practice by decision-makers examining VTIP TRP applications.

The key sources of data reveal the persistence of two dominant narratives: (a) fraud and illegality, and (b) foreignness and temporariness. Reliance on these narratives is largely confirmed through the requirement that migrants "credibly" demonstrate their experiences of victimization in order to access a VTIP TRP. What renders a claim "credible" is undefined, which enables immigration officers to enjoy wide discretionary authority in assessing (and refusing) trafficking claims.

Following a brief overview of the VTIP TRP program, this chapter moves to trace how the narratives of fraud and illegality, and of foreignness and temporariness, are operationalized within parliamentary debates of the legislation and in assessment of VTIP TRP applications. I illustrate that the deployment of the noted narratives functions to reaffirm sovereign authority over the border. I argue that the legislative and practical prohibitions on victims' ongoing presence in Canada via discretionary decisions on VTIP TRP applications ultimately serve to reaffirm sovereign authority through exclusion. More specifically, by stating that migrants have entered the nation "fraudulently and illegally" and thus challenged Canada's sovereign power to decide who may enter and remain, and by positioning these persons as continuously "foreign and temporary" despite any desire on their part to remain, the state contends that it is justified in refusing VTIP TRPs.

A final note before turning to the substantive material: The examination herein critiques decision-making on VTIP TRP applications, noting the lack of access to protection for migrants in Canada. In raising these critiques, my intent is not to advocate for the expansion of the human trafficking framework, which has proven to have inequitable and damaging outcomes. The goal of this analysis is rather to trace the discourses that undergird the processes leading to refusal of these applications. By focusing on the "how" of migration practice, I hope to inspire opportunities to resist government practices of removal.

Temporary Resident Permits for Victims of Trafficking in Persons

The VTIP TRP program was introduced by IRCC in May 2006 (at the time, the federal agency was called Citizenship and Immigration Canada; its name changed in 2015). Alongside the announcement of the program, Monte Solberg, then the minister of citizenship and immigration, released ministerial instructions directing immigration officers to grant TRPs to trafficking victims for a period of 120 days, pursuant to section 24(3) of the *Immigration and Refugee Protection Act* (IRPA) (Standing Committee on the Status of Women, 2007). The time limit for short-term TRPs was increased to 180 days upon the release of subsequent ministerial instructions on June 12, 2007 (IRCC, 2007). These secondary instructions provided guidance on the assessment process for VTIP TRP applications, which IRCC continues to rely on. Some additional clarification on processing has been provided by IRCC in online descriptions of the program. For example, materials state that migrants who receive an initial VTIP TRP may apply for a subsequent TRP following the expiration of their first permit (IRCC, 2016b). The second VTIP TRP may be issued for up to three years, pursuant to section 63 of the *Immigration and Refugee Protection Regulations*.

The 2007 instructions directed that the assessment of VTIP TRP applications should proceed in two stages. Immigration officers must first determine if a "foreign national" is a victim of trafficking, with the onus for demonstrating the experience of trafficking placed on the migrant. Officers are here required to engage in a credibility assessment; they must specifically determine if there are reasonable grounds to believe that the migrant is or was a victim of trafficking based on the circumstances presented (IRCC, 2016b). Critically, though, no evidentiary requirements for VTIP TRP applications are specified in the instructions, nor in subsequent guidance provided by IRCC. The instructions, for example, do not detail what information may be referenced by migrants to demonstrate the occurrence of trafficking.

The guidelines do identify three "key elements" to be considered in assessing VTIP TRPs:

1. a physical act: for example, recruitment, transportation or harbouring of a person;
2. accomplished through means: for example, threats, force, coercion or deception;
3. for a specified purpose: exploitation of victims. (*Shala v. Canada*, 2021, para. 30)

These elements derive from the United Nations definition of trafficking. IRCC (2016b) also identifies indicators of human trafficking, any of which may be sufficient to demonstrate the occurrence of tracking: (a) "the recruitment of the individual was fraudulent or coerced, for the purposes (actual or intended) of exploitation" (consistent with the "physical act" and "means" elements noted above); (b) "the individual was coerced into employment or other activity" (again consistent with the "means" element); (c) "the conditions of employment or any other activity were exploitive" (consistent with the "purpose" element); and (d) "the individual's freedom was restricted" (see also IRCC, 2007).

It remains unclear from the initial and subsequent instructions, however, how these elements and indicators of trafficking are assessed in practice, including what evidence supports establishment of the means and purpose. Also unclarified is how these elements and indicators relate to determinations of credibility. This is particularly concerning given that migrants are not automatically granted an interview with officers during which any credibility concerns can be canvassed (IRCC, 2016b). Given the limits of these instructions, immigration officers appear to have significant freedom in assessing and rendering decisions on the credibility of migrant claims of trafficking based on their review of any documentary evidence submitted by the applicant.

If, following this first-stage credibility assessment, the officer determines that there are reasonable grounds to believe that the migrant has been trafficked, the application then moves to the second stage of processing. IRCC (2016b) instructions state that during the secondary stage officers must determine if a VTIP TRP is in fact "warranted given the circumstances" (n.p.). A short-term VTIP TRP may be issued to victims of trafficking to "provide a period of reflection," "to consider their options for returning home," or to facilitate participation in a criminal investigation (IRCC, 2016b, n.p.). Officers must additionally consider the length of time required for the migrant to remain in Canada depending on the purpose of their stay. There is no concomitant requirement that officers assess the availability of permanent resident status for applicants.

Notions of Fraud and Illegality

In debates of the policy before the Standing Committee on Citizenship and Immigration in 2006, as well as in subsequent reviews conducted by the Standing Committee on the Status of Women (2007) and the Standing Committee on Justice and Human Rights (2018), government officials primarily positioned VTIP TRP applicants as having entered Canada without authorization. They contended that "illegal" migrants seek access to the VTIP TRPs despite not having experienced trafficking. Migrants are understood through these narratives as liars who submit fraudulent claims in order to regularize their status. This narrative of fraud and illegality has the powerful effect of framing migrants as a threat to state sovereignty (Razack, 2000). Sovereign authority is at risk with the entrance of migrants without state authorization. Sovereignty can only be restored through removal of so-called fraudulent and illegal migrants.

Reference to migrant fraud and illegality can be traced back to the introduction of the VTIP TRP policy itself. Consider, for example, Minister Solberg's May 2006 speech introducing the program. Solberg used the policy announcement to assure the Canadian public that "the new measures have been carefully designed so that only bona fide victims of human trafficking will benefit from them" (Wallace, 2014, pp. 11–12). This statement suggests a belief that migrants applying for the program may misrepresent their experience and thus try to remain in Canada through fraud. The reliance on rationales of migrant illegality to direct this program is further evidenced in considering the primary purpose of TRPs. As per section 24(1) of the IRPA, TRPs are issued to allow migrants who are otherwise inadmissible or who do not meet the requirements of the Act to enter or remain in Canada. Grounds for inadmissibility are statutorily defined at sections 34–42 of the IRPA and include criminality, involvement in organized crime, and misrepresentation. Migrants found to be inadmissible are not permitted to enter Canada, as per section 45 of the IRPA. A TRP allows a migrant to overcome the legislative bars to their entrance or presence in the country. The extension of TRPs to victims of trafficking thus implies that migrants who have been trafficked are similarly inadmissible and thus "illegal."

Following the introduction of VTIP TRPs in 2006, critics noted the practical effects of conceptualizations related to fraud and illegality in the processing of applications. For example, concerns with assessments of migrant credibility were raised to the Standing Committee on the Status of Women in 2007 during a program review. The committee relayed stakeholder testimony on the experiences of applicants in its final report: "Women who have made applications 'were scrutinized and interrogated for hours … in the same way that victims of domestic violence used to be asked, if you knew something was wrong, why did you not leave?'" (Standing Committee on the Status of Women, 2007, p. 38). Questions about migrants' ability to leave demonstrate immigration officers' reliance on ideas of fraud and illegality; the underlying assumption is that migrants are lying about their victimization, having made the "choice" to stay in their abusive circumstances. Such credibility concerns in turn confirm for the officers that the freedom of the migrants was not "restricted," and thus they determine that the migrants do not meet the required criteria for exploitation (per the ministerial instructions noted above).

Similar critiques were raised a decade later in 2018 during a secondary parliamentary study of VTIP TRPs conducted by the Standing Committee on Justice and Human Rights. Briefs submitted by stakeholders highlighted the lack of clear instructions or standards for consideration of migrant claims. They argued that, as a result, discrepancies emerged in decisions across different regions in Canada (Canadian Council for Refugees [CCR], 2018; FCJ Refugee Centre, 2018). Stakeholders further claimed that officers were not consistently following the limited instructions provided to them, and underlined that, although ministerial instructions did not require victims to assist law enforcement in order to receive a TRP, in practice, permits were not issued *unless* a migrant cooperated with the police (CCR, 2018; FCJ Refugee Centre, 2018).[1] Finally, while assessment guidelines do not specify a time limit for submitting a VTIP TRP request, stakeholders were aware of cases that were denied as a result of officers deeming it "'too late' to consider issuing a TRP" (CCR, 2013, p. 2). On the basis of these statements from stakeholders, it appears that in practice officers operationalize the narrative of fraud and illegality that has infused the VTIP TRP program from its inception, which then supports the disavowal of victimization claims. It additionally appears, however, that decisions on credibility are not consistent. Officers vary in the use of their significant discretion across IRCC offices in Canada.

Interestingly, in providing evidence before the Standing Committee on Justice and Human Rights in 2018, the director general of the Immigration Branch, Natasha Kim, held that the approval rate for VTIP TRP applications was 92 percent, having fallen from the previous 100 percent approval rating in 2016 due to the rejection of two applications. Yet stakeholders argued that applications from migrants who experienced trafficking were consistently and regularly refused (CCR, 2018; Embarkation Law Corporation, 2018). Even further, a report from IRCC (2016b) on the TRP program acknowledged that reporting on the issuance of VTIP TRPs was unclear and inconsistent, in particular regarding the issuance of secondary permits,[2] raising significant questions with respect to the records that are kept and reported on by IRCC. Given the disparity between the positions of IRCC and stakeholders on VTIP TRP outcomes, these statements also signal a clear need to better understand *how* decisions are actually rendered on these applications.

To further substantiate this analysis of government documentation, and to better understand how officers deploy the narrative of fraud and illegality in practice, I sourced the following three cases from the Federal Court of Canada wherein decisions on VTIP TRPs were subject to judicial review: *Shala v. Canada (Citizenship and Immigration)* (2021); *De Guzman v. Canada (Citizenship and Immigration)* (2020); and *Lorenzo v. Canada (Citizenship and Immigration)* (2016). Accessed through a review of legal databases, namely CanLII and Westlaw, these were the only publicly available cases that provided a review of VTIP TRP decisions at the time of writing. Analysis of even this limited material confirms reliance on the noted narrative in assessments of VTIP TRP applications.

A close review of the decision in *Shala v. Canada* provides a helpful illustration, as it demonstrates the endemic assumption of migrant fraud and illegality and reveals how this assumption can lead to the disavowal of migrant claims of victimization. The finding in this case followed the judicial review of the refusal of a VTIP TRP application submitted by Xhevdet Shala, Ajshe Shala, and their four children. The Shala family's migration process was facilitated by the payment of a recruitment fee of €30,000 to the Azemaj family, which the Shalas arranged through multiple unsanctioned loans. Mr. Shala was promised an open work permit in Canada, a furnished apartment, registration in schools for his children, and a salary that would allow him to repay the recruitment fee within a year. These promises were not met. Instead, when the family arrived in Canada in September 2013, they were placed in an unsanitary apartment filled with garbage and mould. The children were not registered in school and Mr. Shala was given an employer-specific work permit that allowed him to work in Canada but only for Selman Azemaj.

The Federal Court found that once he commenced his employment, Mr. Shala was exploited by Mr. Azemaj. He was required to work long hours without breaks and under strenuous and abusive conditions, including being subject to verbal abuse. He was often not compensated for the hours worked and improper deductions of his pay were made regularly. Complaints from Mr. Shala were met with threats of deportation and reminders that he would never be able to repay loans for the recruitment fees if he returned to his country of origin. He was eventually fired from his position in October 2015 for refusing to pay an additional $7,000 in "union fees" to Mr. Azemaj.

Mr. Shala thereafter applied for a VTIP TRP. The court decision relays that the immigration officer was provided with evidence and legal submissions in support of this application. An interview with Mr. Shala was also convened. The application was refused in September 2019. The decision demonstrates that the officer considered whether Mr. Shala's claims contained the three constitutive elements of trafficking identified by the United Nations and repeated in the 2007 ministerial instructions — namely, the act, means, and purpose. The officer determined that although Mr. Shala experienced labour exploitation after arrival, the means element was not credibly established in his application. According to the court, the means element required that trafficking be accomplished through threats, force, coercion, or deception (IRCC, 2016). The officer found that Mr. Shala was not a victim of labour trafficking because he was not "forced" or "compelled" to "undertake a job" against his will (*Shala v. Canada*, 2021, paras. 35–36). According to the court, the officer concluded that there was a distinction between persons who are "under some form of economic compulsion to accept sub-standard working conditions because they simply have no alternative (exploitation or abuse of vulnerability, but not necessarily forced labour) and those against whom actual coercion is exercised by a third party to force them to undertake a job against their will" (*Shala v. Canada*, 2021, para. 35). The Federal Court determined that this assessment was reasonable and thus refused to intervene. The underlying assumption appears to be that Mr. Shala, although exploited based on his experiences of poverty, was not actually trafficked. His application for authorization to remain was therefore assumed to be based on a misrepresentation of his working experiences as trafficking. Therein lies the impact of positioning migrants as frauds and illegals; Mr. Shala's claims of victimization, although accepted, are easily repositioned as distinct from trafficking and thus fraudulent. The credibility of these claims is then impugned, in turn justifying the refusal of his application for a VTIP TRP.

It is of note that the immigration officer appears to not have followed the limited guidelines available for processing VTIP TRPs in rendering their decision. The officer's assessment of means specifically referenced Mr. Shala's ability to physically leave his employment. It then highlighted that Mr. Shala did not alert the police to his experiences. The court writes that these very brief reasons support the negative decision rendered. Thus, the officer seems to have relied on the lack of participation in a police investigation to refuse Mr. Shala's application, which undermines instructions prohibiting refusal based on lack of engagement with police. It also confirms the arguments of community stakeholders (see CCR, 2018; FCJ Refugee Centre, 2018) who point out that credibility assessments are often tied to evidence of cooperation with law enforcement. Finally, it demonstrates the adoption of the narrative of fraud and illegality that imagines migrants as misrepresenting their experiences. The credibility of Mr. Shala's claim relies on his engagement with Canadian police services. It did not matter that Mr. Shala feared deportation if he alerted the police to his circumstances. Instead, his failure to contact police is taken as confirmation that he lied about his experiences.

Even further, the officer's decision lacked substantive consideration of the structurally determined coercion experienced by migrant workers in Canada. According to the officer, confirmation of labour trafficking requires *tangible* evidence of constraints on a migrant's ability to exit their employment. Such evidence includes material to demonstrate that the migrant was confined or restricted from seeking assistance, such as through removal of their passport. Again, this requirement suggests that migrants lie and thus extension of authorization to remain may be based only on clear and substantive proof of their experiences of trafficking. Yet such a position critically ignores the structural constraints imposed on migrants by their temporary immigration status, which prevents them from leaving or changing their employer and from accessing alternative economic and social supports.

Mr. Shala's experience offers an example to further support these claims. The applicant was unable to leave his place of employment due to his low income and precarious status in Canada. He was lured into taking a debt that he could not repay, on the basis of a promise of work that was not met, following which he was forced into a working relationship defined by exploitation. He did not alert the police because he feared deportation. While he may not have been physically coerced to work against his will, these circumstances created a level of psychological and economic control that forced him to remain in the situation of exploitation. The assumption that migrants lie and abuse the system, and thus tangible evidence of coercion is required, justified the negation of these situational forms of force in the decision-making process.

It should be noted here that the officer *did* acknowledge that poverty shaped Mr. Shala's experience. However, by distinguishing between the impacts of poverty and coercion, the officer was able to again deny the equation of Mr. Shala's experiences with trafficking. The officer reasoned that Mr. Shala did not work against his will because he was "coerced" but rather that he was exploited because he was poor. Coercion was thus not considered to be a contributing factor to Mr. Shala's exploitation; poverty was. This negotiating of language in turn confirmed that the applicant's claims lacked credibility, misrepresenting experiences of "exploitation due to poverty" as trafficking. Altogether, the operation of notions of fraud and illegality upheld the exclusion of Mr. Shala via disavowal of his claim of trafficking, affirming the state's sovereign authority over the border.

Critically, speculation of fraud and illegality within the promotion and assessment of VTIP TRPs is consistent with discussions of immigration programs targeting trafficking more broadly. For example, the IRPA, enacted in June 2002, includes section 118(1), which criminalizes any persons who "knowingly organize the coming into Canada of one or more persons by means of abduction, fraud, deception or use or threat of force or coercion." No measures were introduced at the time to assist victims of trafficking (Jeffrey, 2004). The focus of the legislation was squarely on the potential criminality of migrants. With the concurrent expansion of enforcement authority and tools of detention and deportation, trafficking victims were at a *greater risk* of being arrested and placed in detention following the adoption of section 118(1) of the IRPA.

The risk of victim criminalization and deportation was confirmed in 2003 with the publication of the annual Trafficking in Persons Report by the United States government (Soderlund, 2005), which includes a three-tiered ranking system for cataloguing foreign governments based on their compliance with US-defined standards for combating trafficking. Nations that fall within the second or third tier are at risk of losing nonhumanitarian aid from the United States. In 2003, Canada was dropped in the ranking system to a Tier 2. Justification for this assessment pointed in part to Canada's deportation of several purported victims of trafficking, as well as to its failure to identify and prosecute trafficking cases (CCR, 2003). That same year, the United Nations Committee on the Elimination of Discrimination against Women criticized the Canadian government for its lack of programs to identify and assist trafficking victims (Future Group, 2006). Rather than addressing these concerns, the federal government introduced further legislative provisions criminalizing trafficking through the addition of subsections 279.01 to 279.04 to the *Criminal Code* in 2005 (for a fulsome analysis of the operation and effects of this legislation, see Roots, 2022).

Of course, the addition of the VTIP TRP in May 2006 may be framed as a response to these critiques. This positioning was indeed reflected in Minister Solberg's statements to the Standing Committee on Citizenship and Immigration in June 2006:

We've been one of the countries that has signed ... [and] we were a lead negotiator in the protocol on human trafficking in 2000, but we really didn't take steps to deal with the issue. The steps we took were in many respects modest, but so important to the victims of human trafficking. We will issue a temporary residency permit of 120 days for someone who the RCMP and CBSA determine to be a victim of human trafficking. They will immediately get health benefits and counselling. And if they are in a position to do it, obviously we'd love to have their help to identify who the traffickers are so other people aren't victimized. (Standing Committee on Citizenship and Immigration, 2006)

Yet the noted repetition of the narrative of fraud and illegality within subsequent government discussions of the VTIP TRP program and in decision-making on applications confirms the ongoing primary focus on exclusion. While bona fide victims may be able to access VTIP TRPs, government officials have continued to reiterate that migrants who abuse the Canadian state by entering the nation without authorization, and who thereafter fraudulently request temporary residence, will not be able to regularize their status. Despite a purported focus on victims, the program is consistent with the broader attempts to criminalize and remove migrants through trafficking provisions under the IRPA.

Notions of Foreignness and Temporariness

The preeminence of expulsion is particularly apparent in ministerial instructions at the second stage of VTIP TRP processing, mentioned above. The instructions state that a positive assessment of victimization may lead to the issuance of a VTIP TRP if the officer determines that it is necessary based on a list of possible purposes. This list includes, for example, allowing a victim time to access a passport in order to facilitate their travel back to their country of origin.

They may also be required to remain in Canada in order to assist in any ongoing criminal investigations (IRCC, 2016). Each factor necessitates a review of the length of time required in Canada. There is no concomitant requirement that officers assess the availability of permanent resident status for applicants. The assumption is that migrants will eventually return to their country of origin and thus their residence in Canada is time limited. This assumption is particularly clear in instructions for longer term or subsequent TRPs, which require that officers assess whether it is safe and possible for the applicant to return. The underlying knowledge appears to be that the purpose of these VTIP TRPs is to allow "foreigners" who have experienced trafficking a temporary period of stay in Canada, following which they will be removed. The ultimate removal of the migrant again serves sovereign authority; even after a temporary allowance of stay, the sovereign reaffirms power and control over the border via the expulsion of the victim of trafficking from the nation.

Statements from government officials (including Brian Grant, director general of international and intergovernmental relations for IRCC, and Kimber Johnston, director general of the Policy and Program Development Directorate for the CBSA) made during a review of the VTIP TRP by the Standing Committee on the Status of Women in 2007 further confirm the state's reliance on the narrative of foreignness and temporariness. Stakeholders appearing before the committee on behalf of victims of trafficking noted that while the program (at the time) allowed migrants to remain in the country for 120 days, with the possibility of short-term extension, it did not ensure access to permanent resident status. The probability of migrant removal thus ultimately remained high. The focus on removal was indeed confirmed by government officials. In testimony given to the committee, one stakeholder advanced narratives of fraud and of foreignness to caution against the provision of permanent status, including to "credible" or "legitimate" victims of trafficking, stating:

> A mechanism has to be found to enable us to know whether such people are actually victims or not. *If we open the doors wide and say that anyone who declares herself a victim is welcome in Canada, there will be a flood of people wanting to immigrate illegally to Canada who will declare themselves victims.* We have to be careful because it could actually work against victims. (Standing Committee on the Status of Women, 2007, p. 40, emphasis added)

Ideas about migrant foreignness and temporariness, driven by notions of fraud and illegality, thus infused the early rationalizations for the VTIP TRPs.

The same focus on fraud, illegality, and expulsion can be found in *Lorenzo v. Canada* (2016). Mr. Lorenzo claimed to have experienced labour trafficking while working as a waiter from June 2012 to June 2013. Like Mr. Shala, Mr. Lorenzo confirmed that he was forced to live in squalor, as he was housed by his employer in a five-bedroom, two-bath home with twenty-six other employees. He was also required to work long hours and not compensated for overtime. Mr. Lorenzo's complaints regarding the conditions were met with threats of deportation. Still, and unlike Mr. Shala, Mr. Lorenzo did advise both the Newfoundland and Labrador Labour Standards Division and Citizenship and Immigration Canada of his living and employment conditions.

Mr. Lorenzo applied for a VTIP TRP in April 2015, and was interviewed by an immigration officer a month later in May. The application was refused in June 2015. Mr. Lorenzo's application for judicial review of the decision was also dismissed. In the initial reasons for the decision, the officer referenced the passage of time between Mr. Lorenzo's end of employment and the submission of his VTIP TRP application. The officer confirmed that Mr. Lorenzo had successfully maintained his status as a temporary worker in Canada during that time and held a permit issued under the Provincial Nominee Program that was valid until October 2015. The officer additionally noted that Mr. Lorenzo had limited ties to Canada, stating that he had "no family members in Canada and … no extenuating circumstances that required him to continue to remain" (*Lorenzo v. Canada*, 2016, para. 15). The officer determined that Mr. Lorenzo did, however, have family in his country of origin. The officer further found that there was no pending criminal investigation of Mr. Lorenzo's former employer. Finally, in assessing claims of Mr. Lorenzo's limited ability to re-establish himself in his country of origin, the officer advanced the notion that all applicants will eventually be required to leave Canada. Altogether, these considerations were held to justify the refusal of the application.

The officer in *Lorenzo* clearly deployed the narrative of foreignness and temporariness to justify refusal of the application. The decision provided minimal assessment of grounds for refuting Mr. Lorenzo's claims of having been a victim of human trafficking. Instead, the primary focus of the decision rested on Mr. Lorenzo's ability to depart from Canada, given his ties to his country of origin and his lack of need to remain. The logic was simple — Mr. Lorenzo was a "foreigner" in this country whose temporary stay was justifiably at an end and who should leave Canada to return to his family.

Similar reasoning can be traced in *De Guzman v. Canada* (2020). Ms. De Guzman was determined by an immigration officer to be a victim of trafficking and received a VTIP TRP for 180 days in 2018. During that period, the British Columbia Employment Standards Branch was considering the complaint she had filed against her former employers, with whom she travelled to Canada as a domestic worker without status. At the time of her application for a subsequent VTIP TRP, the complaint against her employers had been resolved and Ms. De Guzman was awarded $16,500 in compensation. In refusing the application for a second VTIP TRP, the officer referenced Ms. De Guzman's "need" to remain in Canada. Perpetuating the idea that a migrant's purpose for remaining after experiences of trafficking must be temporary, the officer stated that Ms. De Guzman could return to her country of origin given that she had family there, was previously employed in that country, and her complaint in Canada against her employer was finalized. Ms. De Guzman thus no longer had a purpose for remaining and the second VTIP TRP was refused.

Interestingly, it is noted in the court decision that the immigration officer discussed Ms. De Guzman's access to support from Canadian organizations and the compensation she received as a result of the complaint. No further statement on the officer's consideration of the compensation received was provided by the court. The purpose of including this statement in the decision remains unclear. The court may be suggesting that the officer's refusal was based on the position that Ms. De Guzman's temporary need to remain in Canada had expired given the closure of her complaint, her ongoing connections to her country of origin, *and* the provision of compensation for her experience of trafficking.

The refusal decision was notably overturned by the Federal Court of Canada, which determined that the assessing officer failed to consider a number of factors relevant to Ms. De Guzman's ongoing need to remain, including her need to access counselling for symptoms of post-traumatic stress disorder following her experiences of trafficking. The court additionally determined that the officer did not consider Ms. De Guzman's claims that she had a secondary experience of trafficking while working at a restaurant in Canada. It was based on this experience that she had applied for the subsequent VTIP TRP. In enacting their broad discretionary authority, the officer thus overlooked important evidence provided by Ms. De Guzman with respect to her new claims of exploitation.

While the initial deciding officer clearly relied on the narrative of foreignness and temporariness in refusing Ms. De Guzman's application, space for challenge to removal remained at the court. Why the court accepted Ms. De Guzman's claims versus those made by Mr. Shala and Mr. Lorenzo is unclear. Consider, for example, that Mr. Lorenzo similarly claimed a need to access mental health treatment in his application for a VTIP TRP. The deciding officer, however, disagreed, stating that Mr. Lorenzo had significant opportunity to seek treatment during the two years he had remained in Canada after leaving the impugned employer. Further, Ms. De Guzman is the only claimant before the court whose initial application for a VTIP TRP was accepted. Although speculative, it might be that gender (as one of the only significant differences between the claimants) shaped these decisions. Future research should consider how ideas of gender shape VTIP TRP decisions.

Conclusion

The preceding analysis demonstrates that, despite the proclamation of protection for victims, the VTIP TRP program is directed, in part, by notions of fraud and illegality that suggest applicants enter Canada without authorization and thereafter submit false claims of trafficking. This finding was confirmed through a review of the initial ministerial instructions introducing the VTIP TRP and traced within subsequent committee considerations of the permits. The requirement that victims must prove their experiences of trafficking is particularly telling and is motivated by an understanding of migrants as unscrupulous criminals who abuse the immigration system and should thus be deported. The review of the decision in *Shala v. Canada* (2021) illustrated the practical deployment of the discourse to refuse applications for VTIP TRPs.

Even when migrants are able to credibly establish their experiences of trafficking, ideas related to foreignness and temporariness position them as always removable. Any purpose "victims" may have for remaining was described in government statements as temporary, the underlying assumption being that migrants will eventually return to their country of origin. The refusal of applications for VTIP TRPs described in decisions on *Lorenzo v. Canada* (2016) and *De Guzman v. Canada* (2020) demonstrated the reliance on this narrative in practice. Together with the IRPA provisions criminalizing migrants, notions of fraud and illegality, and foreignness and temporariness, operate to confirm sovereign authority over the border by justifying migrant expulsion.

The analysis presented here is limited to a review of the minimal publicly available material on VTIP TRPs. Additional research is needed to provide a more detailed analysis of both instructions and decisions on these applications, as evidenced by the ongoing points of contention between stakeholders and the government on outcomes of the VTIP TRP policy. Future research should also consider the racialized and gendered outcomes of VTIP TRP decisions, in particular given testimony from stakeholders that marginalized communities are more vulnerable to both trafficking or trafficking-like conditions *and* removal (Butterfly, 2018). Relatedly, this chapter has highlighted definitional issues with respect to concepts such as exploitation, level of force, and coercion. Scholarly work on trafficking is beginning to explore how these terms are institutionally defined and practically applied, including across systems in Canada, such as the criminal punishment system (e.g., see Roots, 2022; Sibley & van der Meulen, 2022). Differential application of these concepts could further support arguments rendered in this chapter on the primary promotion of state interests where it is determined that different definitions are utilized depending on preferred government outcomes.

Notes

1. Stakeholders also highlighted the cooptation of the trafficking program by enforcement officials. They held that immigration officers used the trafficking program to justify investigations of predominantly racialized businesses. As stated by Butterfly (2018), immigration officers "assume that people who are not Canadian born, do not speak English, do not have identification, and/or receive assistance from a third party are trafficked victims. These ideas are based on a racist image of im/migrant and racialized people" (p. 5). Stakeholders held that racialized migrants are thus distrustful of the police, thereby creating barriers to their cooperation with law enforcement. Reluctance to report is compounded when migrants are without status and fear deportation (CCR, 2018). This in turn impacts access to VTIP TRPs given the recognized requirement that migrants assist with police investigations. Future research should consider the racialized outcomes of VTIP TRP decisions.
2. I was able to access statistical information on the issuance of TRPs via access to information requests. The released data shows that from 2016 to 2018, IRCC received 195 applications for VTIP TRPs (Release #2A-2020-20075). According to reports issued by IRCC (Release #2A-2020-14986) and statements by Public Safety Canada (2019), 146 applications were approved during this period. These numbers suggest that the approval rating is much lower than 92 percent (and closer to 75 percent). The data do not make clear, however, whether the issued permits were initial TRPs or based on subsequent applications. As a result, estimates of the approval rating are limited

and unreliable. Further, the availability of the three refused TRP decisions reviewed in this chapter demonstrates the inaccuracy of statements suggesting a 100 percent approval rate for applications. While this may have been true before 2016 (data to test this statement are not publicly available), it is certainly clear that refusals on these applications are being rendered post-2016.

References

Butterfly (Asian and Migrant Sex Workers Support Network). (2018). *Brief to the House of Commons Standing Committee on Justice and Human Rights on Human Trafficking in Canada: How migrant sex workers are harmed by anti-trafficking initiatives and policies.* https://www.ourcommons.ca/Content/Committee/421/JUST/Brief/BR10005482/br-external/ButterflyAsianAndMigrantSexWorkersSupportNetwork-e.pdf

Canadian Council for Refugees. (2003). *Trafficking in women and girls: Report of meetings.* https://ccrweb.ca/files/ccrtrafficking.pdf

___. (2013). *Temporary resident permits: Limits to protection for trafficked persons.* https://ccrweb.ca/sites/ccrweb.ca/files/temporary-resident-permit-report.pdf

___. (2018). *CCR concerns: Human trafficking in Canada. A submission to the House of Commons Standing Committee on Justice and Human Rights for their study on human trafficking in Canada.* https://www.ourcommons.ca/Content/Committee/421/JUST/Brief/BR9826273/br-external/CanadianCouncilForRefugees-e.pdf

Embarkation Law Corporation. (2018). *Brief to the Standing Committee on Justice and Human Rights study of human trafficking.* https://www.ourcommons.ca/Content/Committee/421/JUST/Brief/BR10006316/br-external/EmbarkationLawCorporation-e.pdf

FCJ Refugee Centre. (2018). [Submission regarding exploitation and human trafficking]. https://www.ourcommons.ca/Content/Committee/421/JUST/Brief/BR9761473/br-external/FCJRefugeeCentre-e.pdf

Future Group. (2006). *Falling short of the mark: An international study on the treatment of victims of human trafficking.* https://commons.allard.ubc.ca/cgi/viewcontent.cgi?article=1254&context=fac_pubs

Hunt, A. (1993). *Explorations in law and society: Towards a constitutive theory of law.* Routledge.

Immigration, Refugees and Citizenship Canada. (2007, June 12). *Ministerial instructions regarding the issuance of temporary resident permits to victims of human trafficking.* https://www.canada.ca/en/immigration-refugees-citizenship/corporate/mandate/policies-operational-instructions-agreements/ministerial-instructions/other-goals/mi-htv.html

___. (2016a). *Evaluation of temporary resident permits.* https://www.canada.ca/content/dam/ircc/migration/ircc/english/resources/evaluation/pdf/temporary-resident-permits.pdf

___. (2016b, May 5). *Temporary resident permits (TRPs): Considerations specific to victims of trafficking in persons.* https://www.canada.ca/en/immigration-refugees-citizenship/corporate/publications-manuals/operational-bulletins-manuals/temporary-residents/permits/considerations-specific-victims-human-trafficking.html

Jeffrey, L.A. (2004). Canada and migrant sex work: Challenging the "foreign" in foreign policy. *Canadian Foreign Policy*, 12, 1: 33–48.

Murdocca, C. (2014). Michel Foucault: Theories and "method." In D. Brock, A. Glasbeek, & C. Murdocca (eds.), *Criminalization, representation, regulation: Thinking differently about crime* (pp. 5–28). University of Toronto Press.

Public Safety Canada. (2019). *National strategy to combat human trafficking 2019–2024.* https://www.publicsafety.gc.ca/cnt/rsrcs/pblctns/2019-ntnl-strtgy-hmnn-trffc/2019-ntnl-strtgy-hmnn-trffc-en.pdf

Razack, S.H. (2000). "Simple logic": Race, the identity documents rule and the story of a nation besieged and betrayed. *Journal of Law and Social Policy*, 15: 181–209.

Rodrigues, G. (2023, 3 March). "Deplorable living conditions": 64 Mexicans rescued from Ontario human trafficking ring. *Global News.* https://globalnews.ca/news/9525649/mexican-nationals-rescued-ontario-human-trafficking-ring/

Roots, K. (2022). *Domestication of human trafficking: Law, policing and prosecution in Canada.* University of Toronto Press.

Rose, N., & Miller, P. (1992). Political power beyond the State: Problematics of government. *British Journal of Sociology*, 43, 2: 173–205.

Rose, N., O'Malley, P., & Valverde, M. (2006). Governmentality. *Annual Review of Law and Social Science*, 2, 1: 83–104.

Sibley, M., & van der Meulen, E. (2022). Courting victims: Exploring the legal framing of exploitation in human trafficking cases. *Canadian Journal of Law and Society*, 37, 3: 409–429.

Soderlund, G. (2005). Running from the rescuers: New U.S. crusades against sex trafficking and the rhetoric of abolition. *NWSA Journal*, 17, 3: 64–87.

Standing Committee on Citizenship and Immigration. (2006, June 7). *Evidence.* https://www.ourcommons.ca/DocumentViewer/en/39-1/CIMM/meeting-11/evidence

Standing Committee on Justice and Human Rights. (2018, February 27). *Evidence.* https://www.ourcommons.ca/DocumentViewer/en/42-1/JUST/meeting-88/evidence

Standing Committee on the Status of Women. (2007). *Turning outrage into action to address trafficking for the purpose of sexual exploitation in Canada.* https://www.ourcommons.ca/Content/Committee/391/FEWO/Reports/RP2738918/feworp12/feworp12-e.pdf

Wallace, F. (2014). *A fragile promise — The inadequacy of assistance measures for victims of human trafficking in Canada.* Faculty of Law, University of Alberta.

Cases

De Guzman v. Canada (Citizenship and Immigration), 2020, FC 13.
Lorenzo v. Canada (Citizenship and Immigration), 2016, FC 37.
Shala v. Canada (Citizenship and Immigration), 2021, FC 326.

Legislation

Criminal Code, RSC 1985, c. C-46.
Immigration and Refugee Protection Act, SC 2001, c. 27.
Immigration and Refugee Protection Regulations, SOR/2002-227.
United Nations Convention against Transnational Organized Crime and the Protocols Thereto, November 15, 2000, https://www.unodc.org/unodc/en/organized-crime/intro/UNTOC.html

Access to Information Requests

Immigration, Refugees and Citizenship Canada, Access to Information Request, Release #2A-2020-20075.

Immigration, Refugees and Citizenship Canada, Access to Information Request, Release # 2A-2020-14986.

15

Redefining "Exploitation"

Reconciling Human Trafficking Provisions with Canada's Migrant Farm Work Program

Shane Martínez

The Seasonal Agricultural Worker Program (SAWP) is administered by the Canadian government to provide farms, greenhouses, and similar operations with labourers recruited from Mexico and the Eastern Caribbean. Established in 1966, it brings approximately 25,000 racialized workers to Canada to live on-site at farms for up to eight months out of the year and engage in difficult and dangerous work that Canadians refuse to do. Their labour helps sustain important parts of the country's multi-billion-dollar agriculture industry, yet many of these workers are subjected to discriminatory and abusive treatment that has generated international criticism (Binford, 2013; Hennebry & Preibisch, 2012; Smith, 2015).

Over the last two decades, the plight of migrant farm workers has attracted increased attention from courts and administrative tribunals alike. The Supreme Court of Canada has commented on the exceptional vulnerability of farm workers, noting the "political impotence" that results from poor pay, difficult working conditions, and limited employment mobility (*Dunmore v. Ontario (Attorney General)*, 2001, para. 41). The Federal Court of Appeal has recognized the "unique disadvantages in the Canadian labour market of agricultural workers as a whole, and migrant workers in particular," including but not limited to "exclusion from many statutory protections of workers (including representation by a union) ... long and arduous working schedules with little free time; and fear of employer reprisal and deportation" (*De Jesus v. Canada (Attorney General)*, 2013, para. 13). Similarly, Ontario's Divisional Court acknowledged that migrant farm workers "are exceptionally vulnerable because of their immigration status, race and the precarious employment relationships imposed by the structure of the programs under which they are employed" (*Schuyler Farms Limited v. Dr. Nesathurai*, 2020, para. 86). Further, the Human Rights Tribunal of Ontario has repeatedly addressed the vulnerability of SAWP participants, most recently finding that "the SAWP is rooted in structural racism both historically and in the present day and creates vulnerabilities that impact migrant workers' ability to assert their rights" (*Logan v. Ontario (Solicitor General)*, 2022, para. 93).

During the same period in which these decisions have emerged, an extensive legal framework aimed at human trafficking has developed.[1] The first provisions directly addressing trafficking added a series of offences to the *Criminal Code* in 2005, including trafficking in persons (section 279.01), receiving a material benefit from trafficking in persons (section 279.02), and withholding or destroying documents to facilitate trafficking in persons (section 279.03). Since then, a number of further amendments to the *Criminal Code* have been made to include additional related offences. These legislative measures have been intended to give effect to Canada's ratification of the United Nations *Trafficking Protocol* in 2002, and include carceral consequences as high as life imprisonment for those convicted of trafficking. Canada claims that these measures are aimed at preventing human trafficking, protecting victims (especially vulnerable women and children), and holding traffickers accountable for their profitable exploitation of these individuals (*R. v. D'Souza*, 2016, para. 164).

The federal government has trumpeted its criminalization of human trafficking, in particular as it relates to the sex trade. However, an internal contradiction arises when anti-trafficking laws are juxtaposed with the systemic oppression and exploitation that has historically characterized the SAWP. Participants in the SAWP contend with conditions that, in many ways, mirror trafficking or trafficking-like conditions —they lack labour mobility, experience isolation from society, and fall among the "most economically exploited and politically neutralized individuals in our society" (*Hosein v. Ontario (Community Safety and Correctional Services)*, 2018, paras. 25 and 267; see also *Ontario (Attorney General) v. Fraser*, 2011, para. 348). Canada has also refused to sign or accede to the United Nations *International Convention on the Protection of the Rights of All Migrant Workers and Members of Their Families* (1990). These factors necessitate a closer examination of how Canada determines which activity is criminalized as human trafficking and which is not — a determination that turns on how it has redefined "exploitation" within the *Criminal Code*. Such an examination helps us to better ascertain the political and economic interests at play.

Defining and Redefining "Exploitation"

Section 279.01 of the *Criminal Code* frames "human trafficking" as follows: "Every person who recruits, transports, receives, holds, conceals or harbours a person, or exercises control, direction or influence over the movements of a person, for the purpose of exploiting them or facilitating their exploitation is guilty of an indictable offence." For the purpose of analyzing whether the SAWP could fall within the scope of this offence, we can distill the section into the two principal parts of any crime. First there is the criminal act, which in the context of human trafficking consists of recruiting, transporting, receiving, holding, concealing, or harbouring a person. Alternatively, this act could consist of exercising control, direction, or influence over the movements of a person. And second, there is the criminal intent to engage in human trafficking, which consists of intentionally carrying out one of the aforementioned acts for the purpose of exploiting a person or facilitating their exploitation.

As for the first part of this analysis, it is uncontroversial to point out that employers in the agriculture industry — in consultation with Employment and Service Development Canada — routinely *recruit* people from abroad to work in Canada under the SAWP. These employers then engage the services of third parties to *transport* workers to Canada. Employers or their representatives *receive* the workers at the airport, and then *transport* them again directly to the rural farms where they will work and reside during their time in Canada (for further discussion, see Moore-Kloss & Roots, 2022). Once SAWP participants are in Canada, their employers exercise significant *influence* over their movements. While some migrant farm workers may have bicycles to travel short distances, many rely on their employers to provide them with rides to nearby towns in order to buy food or send money to loved ones back home. These workers are constantly aware that their movement and engagement with Canadian society must not be such that it upsets their employers.

Control of movement is also accomplished through contracts that significantly favour employers and provide few protections to workers. Nearly all SAWP participants are *directed* to live in bunkhouses or similar dwellings on the isolated farms where they work (Smith, 2015). They lack labour mobility as a result of being contractually tied to a single employer in Canada, a practice rooted in racist policy objectives (Mooten, 2021). Employers are further able to exercise *control* over workers' movements — and over every other facet of their lives in Canada — through a repatriation clause in SAWP contracts that allows employers to immediately have workers sent home for any reason (Hjalmarson, 2022).[2]

If the SAWP appears to resemble some or all the ways in which human trafficking can occur, that is because it does. On the face of it, this resemblance can raise questions about how such a state-sanctioned arrangement can be reconciled with anti-trafficking legislation. Marcus Sibley and Emily van der Meulen (2022) point out:

> If the trafficking in persons provision is activated by the exercise of influence over a person's movements with the intent to exploit, then instances captured under this offence could be so broad that many forms of labour, including those considered normal or commonplace in late capitalist economies, may also trigger the offence. (p. 417)

To address this apparent contradiction — that the state is engaging in conduct that bears the trappings of what it frames as "human trafficking" — we must turn to the second part of the analysis and look at what is the intent or purpose of the SAWP. This requires us to look at whether its purpose is to exploit migrant farm workers or facilitate their exploitation. The *Oxford Advanced Learner's Dictionary of Current English* defines exploitation as "the action or fact of treating someone unfairly in order to benefit from their work" (Hornby & Crowther, 1995). *Black's Law Dictionary* defines exploitation as "the act of taking advantage of something; especially the act of taking unjust advantage of another for one's own benefit" (Garner & Black, 2004, p. 619). These dictionary meanings of "exploitation" represent the ordinary or literal definitions of the word (Sullivan, 2014). Indeed, the Ontario Court of Appeal in *R. v. A.A.* (2015) observed that a plain reading "without any interpretive assistance would support the conclusion that the terms 'exploiting' and 'exploitation' would bear their normal, natural every day meaning of taking advantage of or using another person for one's own ends" (para. 83).

With this definition of "exploitation," the SAWP could be construed as meeting the legal threshold for human trafficking. However, as is noted in *A.A.*, section 279.04(1) of the *Criminal Code* defines "exploitation" differently from how the word is widely understood. The section reads:

> For the purposes of sections 279.01 to 279.03, a person exploits another person if they cause them to provide, or offer to provide, labour or a service by engaging in conduct that, in all the circumstances, could reasonably be expected to cause the other person to believe that their safety or the safety of a person known to them would be threatened if they failed to provide, or offer to provide, the labour or service.

In determining whether an accused exploits another person, section 279.04(2) states that the court may consider, among other factors, whether the accused (a) used or threatened to use force or another form of coercion; (b) used deception; or (c) abused a position of trust, power, or authority. This redefinition makes a finding of "exploitation" contingent on the contextual presence of factors such as threats, use of force, fear, or coercion. The SAWP and the farming corporations that rely on it are accordingly distinguished in law from traffickers, while migrant farm workers who toil under the SAWP are distinguished from victims.

It should also be noted that at the time of writing, Bill S-224, *An Act to amend the Criminal Code (trafficking in persons)*, is before the House of Commons. Bill S-224 proposes amending the definition of "exploitation" under section 279.04(1) to apply to conduct that "(a) causes the other person to provide or offer to provide labour or a service; and (b) involves, in relation to any person, the use or threatened use of force or another form of coercion, the use of deception or fraud, the abuse of a position of trust, power or authority, or any other similar act." This amendment simplifies the offence and removes the Crown's burden of having to prove that the complainant believed "that their safety or the safety of a person known to them would be threatened if they failed to provide, or offer to provide, the labour or service."[3] What the existing and proposed *Criminal Code* definitions of "exploitation" have in common though is that they both legally redefine the word by divorcing it from its "normal, natural every day meaning" (*A.A.*, para. 83). So why does the lawmaking intelligentsia reinvent what we understand the word to mean? A textual analysis reveals that this redefinition is very much the intended product of careful drafting by lawmakers.

Insulation through Redefinition

Before exploring the central question of who benefits (*cui bono*) from redefining "exploitation," it is worth examining the intentionality with which the law is written. Ruth Sullivan (2014) suggests that "the executive branch generally expends considerable resources mastering what it needs to know to construct an effective and efficient legislative scheme" (p. 206). The view that "the legislature is presumed to know all that is necessary to produce rational and effective legislation," including "whatever facts are relevant to the conception and operation of its legislation," has been quoted approvingly by the Supreme Court of Canada (Sullivan, 2014, p. 205; see also *2747–3174 Québec Inc. v. Quebec (Régie des permis d'alcool)*, 1996, para. 237). Therefore, the courts generally accept that "legislatures say what they mean and mean what they say" (Sullivan, 2014, p. 206).

The political economy of lawmaking and legal systems reveals the law to be, for the most part, an ideological superstructure that often emerges from and advances the interests of the state and the mode of production it facilitates. Karl Marx (1887) addressed this base-superstructure relationship in observing that "the economic structure of society, is the real basis on which the juridical and political superstructure is raised and to which definite social forms of thought correspond" (p. 58). In other words, the state's mode of production — which consists of productive forces (labour and the means of production) and the relations of production (class and social relations) — frequently determines the character of the law.

Care should be taken to not misunderstand this analysis as suggesting that the law is solely determined by economic interests. Such an absolutist approach is erroneous in its oversimplification of a complex issue that was never fully explored by Marx (Stone, 1985). It particularly disregards how issues of race, gender, nationality, and class struggle influence the development of the law (and sometimes even the mode of production itself). However, while the character of the law is not exclusively informed by the state's mode of production, and while the law does not function solely to advance state interests, the role of the law in fundamentally preserving exploitative class relations under capitalism is an incontrovertible takeaway from Marx's analysis. This role is evidenced by how the state's redefinition of "exploitation" in the human trafficking context can effectively criminalize some forms of exploitation, including circumstances that are deemed inherently exploitative, such as selling or exchanging sex, and those involving individual "bad" recruiters or employers, while contemporaneously insulating the much broader dependence of capitalist agribusiness on the (ordinarily defined) exploitation of migrant farm workers. The proposed amendment to trafficking legislation via Bill S-224 will similarly fail to capture this context of exploitation — a problem not of inadequate law enforcement or moral order but of socioeconomic relations requiring broader systemic change.

In the Ontario Court of Appeal decision of *F. (M.) v. Dr. Sutherland* (2000), the court stated that "the ordinary meaning [of a word] is presumed to be the intended or most appropriate meaning unless the context, or the purpose and scheme of the legislation, or the consequences of adopting the ordinary meaning suggest otherwise" (para. 28). When the human trafficking provisions of the *Criminal Code* were drafted, the existence of programs such as the SAWP ostensibly required lawmakers to reconceptualize and redefine what is meant by the word "exploitation." This was because exploitation — as it is plainly and ordinarily understood — is reflected in every aspect of the SAWP and is at the core of the relationships between migrant farm workers, their employers, and the Canadian government.

Employers recruit, transport, receive, and control migrant farm workers for a basic purpose: to generate profit by extracting the maximum amount of labour from them at a minimal cost. This is accomplished in part by employers taking advantage of the pre-existing economic desperation that compels individuals overseas to seek work on Canadian farms. Michael Parenti (2009) has described the opportunity that economic disparity abroad presents for capitalism at home, noting that "the poorer you are, the harder you will work — for less. The poorer you are, the less equipped you are to defend yourself against the abuses of wealth" (n.p.). Canadian farm owners make the most of this situation by having migrant workers endure conditions that most Canadians are not desperate enough to accept. These conditions include working six days a week for sixty to seventy hours and making minimum wage regardless of years of service (Martin, 2016). Employers can also save money by providing workers with substandard accommodations, typically in overcrowded bunkhouses, which in Ontario are exempt from the protections provided by the *Residential Tenancies Act, 2006*. Migrant farm workers often receive inadequate safety training and personal protective equipment, and some employers expeditiously repatriate workers who fall sick or injured on the job — thereby avoiding potential costs associated with workers' compensation claims (Depatie-Pelletier, 2016; McLaughlin et al., 2014).

The federal government, as the architect and overseer of the SAWP, facilitates this exploitative relationship to its own benefit as well. Employment and Social Development Canada, in collaboration with representatives from the Canadian agriculture industry, negotiates annual contracts with the governments of Mexico, Jamaica, and Eastern Caribbean countries. These negotiations are orchestrated in such a way that migrant farm workers have no participation or voice whatsoever, with the sole focus being on satisfying the interests and objectives of governments and farming corporations (Basok et al., 2023).[4] A reliable supply of contractually disempowered workers kept on the margins of society enables Canada to sustain its agriculture industry in the face of an otherwise insurmountable domestic shortage of farm labour. In this way Canada's exploitation of migrant farm workers is tacitly endorsed not only by the redefinition of "exploitation" but also by domestic policy and the state's long-standing pursuit of "financial imperialism and structural adjustment" (John, 2021, n.p.).

Exclusionary practices also allow the federal government to capitalize off migrant farm workers in the Employment Insurance (EI) system. Even though these workers are required to contribute to EI in the same manner that Canadian workers do, the government structures the SAWP in such a way that migrant farm workers are denied any opportunity to collect regular benefits. Section 18(1) of the *Employment Insurance Act* requires that a person be "capable of and available for work" in order to collect EI. The state collects EI premiums from SAWP participants, even though those workers are permitted to work and be present in Canada only while they are actively working with a single employer. When their work ends, they are required to leave the country and thus cannot satisfy the requirement of being "available for work." This situation has resulted in the government reaping hundreds of millions of dollars in contributions from SAWP participants without any risk of having to pay them regular benefits in the off-season (United Food and Commercial Workers Canada, 2014).

All of this occurs within the context of the federal government taking advantage of migrant workers' economic desperation, knowing that

SAWP participants will come to work in Canada even though they are denied the opportunity to have their families join them. Any prospect of starting a life in Canada is also quashed by the federal government, which treats seasonal migrant farm workers as good enough to work but not good enough to stay. SAWP participants are denied a pathway to become permanent residents, even if they have contributed years or decades of their lives to sustaining Canada's agriculture industry (Landry et al., 2021).

While enforcement action has occasionally led to some migrant farm workers (typically those who are undocumented) being relieved from indentured circumstances, it has done nothing to disrupt the root causes of exploitation and has instead invited greater surveillance and policing into their lives. Raids by immigration authorities purportedly to preserve the integrity of the SAWP and similar programs come across as little more than efforts to consolidate market control of an exploitative system for the benefit of the state and farming corporations. The widely documented systemic exploitation that is entrenched in the SAWP attracts little, if any, regulatory attention (Narushima & Sanchez, 2014). This reaffirms findings from Jenna L. Hennebry and Gabriel Williams (2015) that the health, safety, and general well-being of migrant farm workers is, at best, a secondary concern for the Canadian state. Enforcement and regulatory action in the agriculture industry instead reflects a preoccupation with ensuring that the government and its corporate partners maintain order and exclusive benefit of the racialized foreign labour that is used to generate billions of dollars in revenue every year. The purposeful redefinition of "exploitation" from its everyday use has also meant that enforcement of trafficking laws can primarily concentrate on activities that the state has historically sought to legislate and control, such as sexual labour. This approach will likely persist if Bill S-244 is passed, as the legislative amendment will not materially disrupt — and might even reinforce — the exploitative conditions that Canadian anti-trafficking legislation supposedly targets.

Conclusion

The SAWP continues to operate very much as it did when it was founded over fifty years ago, with the Canadian government and the farming industry working together to import racialized and economically oppressed migrant farm workers for the purpose of exploiting their labour (Mooten, 2021). The redefinition of "exploitation" from its ordinary meaning to that which is used under section 279.04(1) of the *Criminal Code* raises important questions about how and why the state arranges its anti-trafficking apparatus in the manner that it does.

An honest approach to answering those questions shows us that legal structures for exploitation (such as the SAWP) can and do operate in ways and for purposes similar to those that could meet the criminal definition of human trafficking. The state and the agriculture industry, like those individuals who contribute to the trafficking or trafficking-like conditions of undocumented workers, identify a need within the Canadian labour market. All three target and recruit the most vulnerable workers available — workers who are often racialized, impoverished, and from the Global South. Then they proceed to have migrants work in conditions that most Canadians have rejected while taking advantage of legal exclusions that reinforce vulnerability (such as no access to regular EI benefits, no ability to unionize, and precarious immigration status). All three also isolate workers in a way that effectively keeps them invisible, ensuring that they are denied a voice or participation in civil society. At all times, the state, the agriculture industry, and those who might meet the criminal definition of traffickers are motivated by the same overriding goal: the accumulation of profit. Through purposeful denial of protections for migrant farm workers, and short-sighted proposals to address the valid concerns of this exploited group, the anti-trafficking framework in Canada has served only to endorse that goal.

Notes

1. "Human trafficking" is considered to be a problematic term within some circles focused on migrant rights, as it is seen as perpetuating victimhood and a lack of autonomy while reinforcing dominant state narratives around undocumented persons. However, it is a term that necessarily must be used (and deconstructed) in this legal analysis, as it is the reflected in the legislation at issue.
2. In 2019, following years of campaigning by grassroots activist groups such as Justicia for Migrant Workers, the federal government introduced the possibility of open work permits for vulnerable workers who are experiencing or are at a risk of abuse in the context of their employment (per section 207.1 of the *Immigration and Refugee Protection Regulations*). Although this measure represents a modest improvement, critics have described it as woefully inadequate (see Depatie-Pelletier et al., 2022).
3. In the civil context, Ontario has recognized the tort of human trafficking. This was established by the *Prevention of and Remedies for Human Trafficking Act* (2017) In *Osmani v. Universal Structural Restorations Ltd.*, 2022, the court noted at para. 357

that "while section 279.04 of the *Criminal Code* is not explicitly included in the definition of human trafficking found in the PRHTA, in my view it must be considered nonetheless as it is a section intended to assist in interpreting the exploitation component in the offence provisions of sections 279.01, 279.011, 279.02 and 279.03." For a discussion on the challenges experienced by migrant workers in enforcing their rights under the law, see Hastie (2018).
4. This exclusionary framework is made worse by the fact that farm workers in Ontario are denied the right to unionize. See *Labour Relations Act, 1995*, s. 3(b.1) and (c).

References

Basok, T., Tucker, E.M., Vosko, L.F., Caxaj, C.S., Hennebry, J.L., Mayell, S., McLaughlin, J., & Weiler, A.M. (2023). The "contract" and its discontents: Can it address protection gaps for migrant agricultural workers in Canada? *International Migration*. https://doi.org/10.1111/imig.13121

Binford, L. (2013). *Tomorrow we're all going to the harvest: Temporary Foreign Worker Programs and neoliberal political economy*. University of Texas Press.

Depatie-Pelletier, E. (2016). Judicial review and temporary labour migration as "modern form of slavery": State deprivation of (im/migrant) workers' right to liberty and security (right not to be held under slavery or servitude) resulting from employer-tying policies [unpublished doctoral dissertation]. University of Montreal.

Depatie-Pelletier, E., Deegan, H., & Berze, K. (2022). Band-aid on a bullet wound — Canada's open work permit for vulnerable workers policy. *Laws*, 11, 3: Article 36.

Garner, B.A., & Black, H.C. (2004). *Black's law dictionary* (8th ed.). Thomson/West.

Hastie, B. (2018). The inaccessibility of justice for migrant workers: A capabilities-based perspective. *Windsor Yearbook of Access to Justice*, 34, 2: 20–39.

Hennebry, J.L., & Preibisch, K. (2012). A model for managed migration? Re-examining best practices in Canada's Seasonal Agricultural Worker Program. *International Migration*, 50, s1: e20–e40.

Hennebry, J.L., & Williams, G. (2015). Making vulnerability visible: Medical repatriation and Canada's migrant agricultural workers. CMAJ: *Canadian Medical Association*, 187, 6: 391–392.

Hjalmarson, E. (2022). Sentenced for the season: Jamaican migrant farmworkers on Okanagan orchards. *Race & Class*, 63, 4:L 81–100.

Hornby, A.S., & Crowther, J. (1995). *Oxford advanced learner's dictionary of current English*. Oxford University Press.

John, T.J. (2021). Canadian financial imperialism and structural adjustment in the Caribbean. *Class, Race and Corporate Power*, 9, 2: Article 1.

Landry, V., Semsar-Kazerooni, K., Tjong, J., Alj, A., Darnley, A., Lipp, R., & Guberman, G.I. (2021). The systemized exploitation of temporary migrant agricultural workers in Canada: Exacerbation of health vulnerabilities during the COVID-19 pandemic and recommendations for the future. *Journal of Migration and Health*, 3: Article 100035.

Martin, P.L. (2016). *Migrant workers in commercial agriculture*. International Labour Organization. https://www.ilo.org/wcmsp5/groups/public/---ed_protect/---protrav/---migrant/documents/publication/wcms_538710.pdf

Marx, K. (1887). *Capital: A critique of political economy. Vol. 1, Book 1: The process of production of capital*. https://www.marxists.org/archive/marx/works/download/

pdf/Capital-Volume-I.pdf
McLaughlin, J., Hennebry, J., & Haines, T. (2014). Paper versus practice: Occupational health and safety protections and realities for temporary foreign agricultural workers in Ontario. *PISTES*, 16, 16-2. https://doi.org/10.4000/pistes.3844
Moore-Kloss, A. (Host), & Roots, K. (Executive Producer). (2022). "Human trafficking: Questioning Canada's anti-trafficking framework" [Audio podcast episode]. CRSP Talk. Wilfrid Laurier University Centre for Research on Security Practices and Folktale Studio. https://crsp-talk.simplecast.com/
Mooten, N. (2021). *Racism, discrimination and migrant workers in Canada: Evidence from the literature*. Immigration, Refugees and Citizenship Canada. https://www.canada.ca/content/dam/ircc/documents/pdf/english/corporate/reports-statistics/research/racism/r8-2020-racism-eng.pdf
Narushima, M., & Sanchez, A.L. (2014). Employers' paradoxical views about temporary foreign migrant workers' health: A qualitative study in rural farms in Southern Ontario. *International Journal for Equity in Health*, 13: Article 65.
Parenti, M. (2009, January 23). Capitalism's self-inflicted apocalypse. *Countercurrents*. https://www.countercurrents.org/parenti230109.htm
Sibley, M., & van der Meulen, E. (2022). Courting victims: Exploring the legal framing of exploitation in human trafficking cases. *Canadian Journal of Law and Society*, 37, 3: 409–429.
Smith, A.A. (2015). The bunk house rules: Housing migrant labour in Ontario. *Osgoode Legal Studies Research Paper Series*, 98. https://digitalcommons.osgoode.yorku.ca/olsrps/98
Stone, A. (1985). The place of law in the Marxian structure-superstructure archetype. *Law & Society Review*, 19, 1: 39–68.
Sullivan, R. (2014). *The construction of statute* (6th ed.). LexisNexis Canada.
United Food and Commercial Workers Canada. (2014). *The great Canadian rip-off! An economic case for restoring full EI special benefits access to SAWP workers*. UFCW Canada and the Agriculture Workers Alliance. https://www.ufcw.ca/templates/ufcwcanada/images/directions14/march/1420/The-Great-Canadian-Rip-Off-An-Economic-Case-for-Restoring-Full-EI-Special-Benefits-Access-to-SAWP-Workers.pdf

Cases

2747-3174 Québec Inc. v. Quebec (Régie des permis d'alcool), 1996 CanLII 153 (SCC).
De Jesus v. Canada (Attorney General), 2013 FCA 264.
Dunmore v. Ontario (Attorney General), 2001 SCC 94.
F. (M.) v. Dr. Sutherland, 2000 CanLII 5761 (ON CA).
Hosein v. Ontario (Community Safety and Correctional Services), 2018 HRTO 298.
Logan v. Ontario (Solicitor General), 2022 HRTO 1004.
Ontario (Attorney General) v. Fraser, 2011 SCC 20.
Osmani v. Universal Structural Restorations Ltd., 2022 ONSC 6979.
R. v. A.A., 2015 ONCA 558.
R. v. D'Souza, 2016 ONSC 2749.
Schuyler Farms Limited v. Dr. Nesathurai, 2020 ONSC 4711.

Legislation

Bill S-224, *An Act to amend the Criminal Code (trafficking in persons)*, 44th Parliament, 1st Session, 2021 (second reading in the House of Commons on March 22, 2023).
Criminal Code, RSC 1985, c. C-46.

Employment Insurance Act, SC 1996, c. 23.

Immigration and Refugee Protection Regulations, SOR/2002-227.

International Convention on the Protection of the Rights of All Migrant Workers and Members of Their Families, December 18, 1990, https://www.ohchr.org/en/instruments-mechanisms/instruments/international-convention-protection-rights-all-migrant-workers

Labour Relations Act, 1995, S.O. 1995, c. 1, Sched. A (Ontario).

Prevention of and Remedies for Human Trafficking Act, 2017, S.O. 2017, c.12 (Ontario).

Protocol to Prevent, Suppress and Punish Trafficking in Persons, Especially Women and Children, supplementing the United Nations Convention against Transnational Organized Crime, November 15, 2000, https://www.unodc.org/res/human-trafficking/2021the-protocol-tip_html/TIP.pdf

Residential Tenancies Act, 2006, SO 2006, c. 17 (Ontario).

16

A Narrative on Organizing for Migrant Farm Worker Justice

Chris Ramsaroop

I have worked with farm and agricultural workers for over twenty-two years, predominantly in Ontario but at times across Canada as well as internationally. For the past twenty of those years, I have been an organizer with Justicia for Migrant Workers, also known as J4MW, an all-volunteer activist collective. Many of us started in the mainstream labour movement and then left to establish J4MW. We wanted to undertake a different way of organizing so that we could be reactive — dealing with crises, the media, terminations, and so on — but also proactive. As an organization, we do outreach and workshops on how to think about the law outside of mainstream normative ways. We also connect migrant workers with legal, health care, housing, food, and other social supports. Rather than charity, paternalism, and carcerality, our work is grounded in challenging the larger power dynamics that lead people, particularly those who help put food on our tables, to experiencing hunger and houselessness, and to being abused and exploited in their workplaces.

Every few months, mainstream media report on the success of police forces in stopping what they deem a human trafficking ring, typically focused on workers being employed under exploitative working conditions, particularly on farms, or sex workers being arrested at their places of work or residences. And yet these responses rarely generate long-term supports for workers and can leave people in worse situations. At a recent meeting of a student union I belonged to when I was an undergraduate student at the University of Toronto, several people approached me with news of successful police actions. It was a long night of uncomfortable conversations regarding the role of policing and how immigration policies actually perpetuate exploitation and abuse for people with precarious immigration status.

Defining and Mobilizing "Human Trafficking"

The mainstream definition of "human trafficking" raises many red flags. Although the term can be used to describe exploitation faced by workers, it can only do so on an individual basis, capturing at most a small group of people. A major issue with the normative understanding of trafficking is its reliance on a hierarchy of what is defined as abuse and what is not. For instance, at J4MW, we supported a group of labourers in Windsor, Ontario, who faced sexual harassment in the workplace. They were treated as victims of trafficking by police authorities, immigration officials, local media, and regional nonprofit organizations. As a result, some of them received social supports, and several are now permanent residents. In contrast, another group in the same community that was facing the same problematic conditions was not labelled as trafficked. This demonstrates that some people get overlooked because they do not meet a specific threshold of trafficking set out by state and legal practices.

We also supported a group of workers that was used by the state for a media campaign to show off its role in cracking down on human trafficking. The workers were employed in construction and sought help from an anti-trafficking organization that connected them to resources and social services. As a result of this intervention, the Royal Canadian Mounted Police (RCMP) and Hamilton Police Services arrested the employers, the workers received temporary resident permits, and the RCMP held a massive press conference discussing its success. When the media cameras were gone, however, the support from the government was also gone — the workers did not receive supports related to mental health, social services, income, and so on. It was just a dog and pony show.

To add to the contradictions of state anti-trafficking interventions, I can recall multiple times when actions undertaken by migrant justice activists could have been defined by the state as trafficking — whether going to the airport to support injured and sick workers whose employment had been terminated to remain in Canada and receive treatment rather than face repatriation and disbarment, or supporting migrant workers to leave exploitative and discriminatory workplaces and connecting workers with community supports, such as housing. Because movement of exploited people without status or permanent residency is involved, these acts of resistance can be interpreted as trafficking.

The trafficking label has additionally been mobilized to reinforce tropes about racialized communities as involved in and enacting human trafficking, rather than to look at the failures of state policies and the vulnerability of racialized migrants to labour exploitation. And while some individuals, for instance employers or contractors, may be perpetuating abusive employment practices and doing other unacceptable things, the problem stretches far beyond them. Indeed, the problem lies largely in the systemic barriers that create precarious immigration status and workplace exploitation to begin with, including immigration and labour policies. The Seasonal Agricultural Worker Program (SAWP) is a key example. It facilitates state-accepted indentured labour — a system where people are tied to a single employer — and yet in no way is SAWP seen by the government or the general public as a form of exploitation.

The SAWP employs approximately sixty thousand migrant farm workers annually, predominantly in export-oriented agriculture. As a temporary migration stream, the program is employer-driven, workers are tied to an employer, and once their contract is over, they lose their immigration status and accompanying entitlements, such as health care and access to Employment Insurance. For SAWP workers specifically, they are under constant threat of repatriation and disbarment from the program if their employer deems them no longer of use, for example, in the event they sustain an injury. Workers can also be terminated for exercising or demanding their labour rights. The program and its practices are accepted by the state and the general public because it maximizes profits for the agricultural industrial complex and is therefore justified in continuing the subordination and subjugation of racialized populations from the Global South who are working in Canada. In the current human trafficking framework, the undertones of unfree labour and a history of racialized labour based on precarious immigration status are not being addressed. Immigration scholar and activist Vasanthi Venkatesh (2023) describes the implications of anti-trafficking regimes on migrants but also on society as a whole:

> Migrant workers are canaries in the racial capitalist coal mine. If we see incidents of extreme exploitation and dehumanization, understand that there is a serious problem in that labour sector.

> And hint: the problem is not "trafficking" of "foreign people." There are deep underlying issues that have legitimated extreme forms of capital and employer power. You can see that in legal exceptionalism, from workers' rights in that sector, anti-union and organizing policies implemented in that sector. These are concerns for everyone. So mere incarceration of the "bad apple" traffickers is a distraction. (n.p.)

Anti-trafficking reinforces racial hierarchies between Canadian (white) society and migrant foreign Others whereby the state deems it necessary to engage in heightened forms of surveillance and securitization. Venkatesh (2023) continues:

> If migrant workers or the foreign population is put under increased surveillance to find the undocumented, the traffickers, and so on, the repression and surveillance is soon going to be deployed on everyone, especially racialized people, even Canadians. And all such securitization is most often privatized, and it is going to only further empower employers and the bosses to then surveil all workers and create fear and mistrust. (n.p.)

The Anti-Trafficking Capitalist Response

Responses to human trafficking are also problematic in a number of other ways. First is the harmful use of law enforcement. When police engage in raids on businesses that are seen as illegitimate or functioning in clandestine ways, and uncover undocumented workers, these workers are sometimes deemed trafficked and thus provided with various social and other supports. When that is the case, the police will promote the raid as a "success" and use it to bolster their public image as "rescuers." And yet there are numerous other examples in a range of industries where police raids ultimately lead to the detention and deportation of undocumented migrants, even if they were working in exploitative and abusive conditions. Instead of receiving necessary supports, they are penalized and treated as undesirable. In my experience, law enforcement does not usually protect undocumented and migrant workers from harm but rather is the cause of harm to these communities.

The hypocrisy of law enforcement, then, is that on the one hand, border officials and police say that they are "saving" victims of exploitation, and on the other hand, they are racially profiling and arbitrarily detaining or deporting migrant workers. This raises an important discussion about defunding law enforcement and border control. Is it really a cost-effective and worthwhile use of resources for police and border services to be arresting undocumented people who have families to feed? Or is it more pressing to build community centres, enhance local resources, supply decent and affordable housing, and ensure that rural communities have access to the internet?

Equally concerning is that police continue to be heavily involved in civil infractions, arresting workers who are undocumented, intervening in workplace violations such as wage theft or illegal deductions, and policing deplorable housing. Rather than have access to necessary civil tools, workers with precarious immigration status must vie for restrictive work permits such as temporary resident permits, which have very specific criteria. It goes back to the fact that industry and capitalism grow without being held responsible for their role in the abuse and exploitation of workers. There must be an understanding that Canada's migrant worker programs, such as the SAWP, promote capitalism by ensuring that employers have full control in the workplace. They perpetuate an asymmetrical balance of power by denying workers access to benefits like health care and Employment Insurance, and by deporting them if they lose their jobs. Migrant workers employed under the Temporary Foreign Worker Program (TFWP), which houses the SAWP, may be terminated for sustaining a workplace injury, becoming sick, exercising their rights, missing a day of work, or working too slowly in the eyes of employers or supervisors. Anecdotally, at J4MW we have come into contact with groups of women who were terminated for the actions of one or two workers who were in conflict with another.

The police are there to reinforce and buttress this capitalist dynamic, to protect private property, and to defend big business. That is also their role in human trafficking cases: targeting a few individual situations while letting rampant unsafe and problematic work environments remain the same or allowing them to grow and fester. For this and many other reasons, J4MW does not get involved with the police. Too often, they support only the employer. For instance, if we were protesting outside of a farm against wage theft, the police would take the side of the employer. And if an employer or a contractor were held responsible, they would most likely receive a slap on the wrist.

Another egregious issue is the direct threat to our work from state-funded anti-trafficking organizations that often collaborate with police. The funding of community organizations that advance the human trafficking framework shuts out any critique of human trafficking and the role of the state as the perpetrator of abuse and exploitation. Therefore, organizations like ours that do not use the human trafficking discourse are frequently perceived as troublemakers or as people who do not play by the rules. Social service organizations need to have tough conversations about jettisoning the normative idea of human trafficking. They need to recommit to supporting worker communities in organizing and fighting back not only against workplace injustices but also against immigration laws, and not arbitrarily pick those who are "deserving" of a response. Many heavily resourced anti-trafficking organizations, operating both nationally and internationally, should instead look at practices of white supremacy and colonialism, and address those systems that create and perpetuate capitalist dynamics between the Global South and North.

Anti-trafficking efforts also contribute to the displacement of worker resistance and organizing. For example, Presteve Foods, a fish processing plant in Wheatley, Ontario, employed Canadian women and Thai and Mexican migrant women, among others. A few years ago, the workers organized to fight against workplace injustices, including sexual harassment. The workplace was already unionized (and remains so today) and the employer tried to pit workers against each other. I believe the employer intended to use the migrant workers as scabs to break the union. J4MW showed up to support ongoing solidarity with the workers and to counter anti-union narratives and myths. But it was this unified group of Mexican and Thai migrant women, along with support from local Mennonite farm workers, who saved the union in that workplace. At around the same time that the migrant women were employed, a union decertification vote was brought forth. Workplace solidarity meant that Mennonite and other Canadian women worked with Thai and Mexican workers to save the union and to ensure that Presteve Foods remained an organized facility. They were fierce resistance fighters standing up for their labour rights well before J4MW got involved, and afterward. Because of the conditions the migrant women were facing at their workplace, they were ultimately framed by media and the police as human trafficking victims rather than as workers organizing, resisting, and fighting for change. And while the trafficking framing led to a critically important human rights case, the question is at what cost.

Beyond the Trafficking Framework

The right and ability of people to engage in labour organizing must be protected and amplified. Instead, the federal government of Canada produces short-term solutions, like the recently enacted open work permits for vulnerable workers. A worker with a tied work permit who is facing abuse in the workplace can apply and, if approved, receive an open work permit for up to one year. Although in some instances the open work permit can help workers gain mobility, the program remains incredibly flawed, as it does not address demands for permanent status on arrival. After their open work permit expires, it is incumbent on the worker to find another tied work permit under the "low-skill" stream of the TFWP or the SAWP. At the time of writing in 2023, J4MW has been in contact with dozens of workers who, once their open work permits expire, will become undocumented and subject to removal by the Canadian Border Services Agency. There is no outcry from government agencies or law enforcement regarding the perpetual precariousness and vicious cycle that the temporary open work permits create for workers.

The fight is not simply about immigration changes at the federal level: It is about a new way of understanding emancipation and freedom. It is about people not being tied to a single workplace or employer. It is about ensuring that people have full protections from the state, including access to social benefits, welfare, education, the right to form unions and worker associations, the right to address labour injustices by changing the laws, and the freedom to stay and to move. People should not be subjected to control of their bodies through an unjust immigration system. Instead of trying to cherry-pick who is worthy of protections and who is not, who is vulnerable and who is not, Canada must get rid of the restrictions being imposed on people by short-sighted and restrictive labour and immigration processes.

Let's put narratives around human trafficking to the side for a moment and just deal with the fact that many people are unfree. Migrant workers are tied to a work permit and, through no fault of their own, they are fired or their work permits end. They may also have debts to pay off back home. People end up without status because of the immigration process and are subjected to full enforcement of border control. Those who are trying to address this power imbalance are being stopped, detained, and deported. That is the fundamental failure of this entire system — a failure for the workers, not the system itself. The system works properly in the interest of the state, exactly as it was designed.

It also does not escape me that the anti-trafficking narrative is concerned with individuals undertaking large debts to come to Canada. This idea of debt bondage rarely if ever extends to global economics and the fact that many "sending" states in the Global South are themselves debt-bonded to the Global North. With their economies dependent on other states and on transnational corporations, Global South states are turned into export-processing zones and become indentured societies. Within the discourse on debt bondage, we do not talk about how the Global North is pushing and creating conditions of debt bondage across nations. We do not talk about ongoing legacies of colonialism in creating indentureship. We frame debt bondage as an individual-level problem rather than a Global North–Global South dynamic.

As a colonial nation-state, the Canadian government has largely considered low-income and racialized communities from the Global South as undesirable immigrants, not as valuable members of our society. Migration scholar Nandita Sharma aptly argued many years ago that Canada has developed immigration programs that preclude people from engaging in civic participation. This remains the case today. The migrant communities that we work with at J4MW cannot change their working conditions or societal conditions and thus become indentured. It is not just about granting workers opportunities to live here as equals but also about understanding the role of the state in creating programs where people are unfree. The fact is that hundreds of thousands of people come to Canada as unfree labourers, and Canadians prosper from their sacrifices and their blood, sweat, and tears.

As labour rights and migrant justice organizers, we are not saviours. Organizers and activists involved with immigration and worker justice movements must not fall into the trap posed by anti-trafficking narratives. This means being direct, intentional, and overt with our opposition to these frameworks. In addition, we must name the harms created by the anti–human trafficking discourse in perpetuating divisions among NGOs and activists, as well as the threat that such a framing will lead only to heightened criminalization and surveillance of groups who organize to address the root causes of exploitation in our society: colonialism, white supremacy, capitalism, patriarchy, and racism. Collectives such as J4MW work with and alongside communities that are fighting for their rights. And in so doing, we aim to facilitate forms of freedom and to rupture harmful state practices and policies.

References

Venkatesh, V. (2023, March 9). *Ending exploitation: Migrant workers and collective justice* [conference presentation]. Progress Summit 2023, Ottawa, Canada. https://www.broadbentinstitute.ca/summit2023

Index

2SLGBTQI+ people, 34, 161, 168, 172

abolition,
  backyard, 18
  carceral, 35, 38–9, 42
  democracy, 36
  feminism and, 38–40
  modern-day, 34–6, 42, 48
  movements, 48–9, 114
  new, 4–5, 44
  prison, 36–40, 45, 114
  varied meanings of, 34–6, 38–9, 49
abuse,
  child, 2, 44, 58, 70n5, 202
  emotional/psychological, 12, 21, 168
  employer/labour, 21, 62, 113, 227–8, 243–5, 248n2
  intimate partner, 18
  perceived sex worker vulnerability to, 10–11, 57–9, 220
  by police, 107–10, 123, 132–3, 161, 201, 217
  of power, 93, 95–6, 123
  racist, 109, 122–3, 194
  sexual, 201–2
  state fostering of sex worker, 3, 13, 21, 112, 161, 206, 257–8
  steps to mitigate, 22–4, 113, 127, 183, 252–3, 256
  substance, 44
Alberta, 59, 90, 114n1, 154–5
anti-Asian racism, 109–10, 125, 132
antiblackness,
  of anti-trafficking apparatus, 5, 37, 45, 48–50
  anti-Black racism versus, 35–6, 49–50
anti-Black racism, 107
  antiblackness versus, 35–6, 49–50
  of anti-trafficking apparatus, 112–13

Anti-Human Trafficking Strategy Act (2021),
  harmful provisions of, 105–7, 112–13, 114n2
  passage of, 13, 104
anti-prostitution assumptions, *see* anti–sex work sentiments
anti-racism movements, 5, 23
anti–sex work sentiments, 1–3
  anti-trafficking organizations, 38, 64, 68, 155–60, 169–72
  Criminal Code, 56
  immigration regulations, 104, 113
  massage workers facing, 120, 135–6
  in legislation, 9–10, 87, 103, 177, 214–15
  in policing, 66, 79, 162
anti-trafficking apparatus, 24, 93
  NGO involvement in, 16, 41–2, 46, 155–7, 167, 172
  policing-centred narratives of, 13, 21–2, 41–4, 167, 172, 248
  racism of, 5, 35, 42–5, 48
  technologies of, 88, 157, 163–7, 171, 205, 208
  whole-of-society approaches by, *see* whole-of-society approaches, anti-trafficking
anti-trafficking efforts, 1
  international, *see* international anti-trafficking efforts
  policies, *see* anti-trafficking policies
  scholarship, *see* critical anti-trafficking studies
  whole-of-society approaches by, *see* whole-of-society approaches, anti-trafficking
anti-trafficking organizations, 253
  anti–sex work, 38, 64, 68, 155–60, 169–72

anti-trafficking apparatus, 155–7, 167, 257
  focus on violence against women, 8, 120, 123
  racial justice narratives of, 35–6, 39–44, 46–50, 120
  racism of, 35, 41–5, 48–50, 120, 257
anti-trafficking policies,
  anti-trafficking apparatus, 45–7, 106–7, 135, 136n2, 170
  borders, focus on, *see* borders
  definition of trafficking and, 2, 200, 203
  harm from, 9–11, 39, 156, 162, 192
  immigration policy and, 2, 87, 221, 224, 232, 236
  policing in, 41, 45, 179–80, 208–9
  seasonal workers and, 242, 246
  steps to mitigate harm, 113, 135, 179–80, 260
  US policing of other states', 42
  see also legislation, human trafficking
antiviolence organizing, 38, 112–14
  relationships with the state, 8, 198–9
  see also violence
Ariyo, Debbie, 44
Asian people,
  perceptions about, 49, 60, 120
  police targeting of, 41, 106–8, 110, 120
  racism facing, *see* anti-Asian racism
  women, *see* Asian women
Asian women,
  concerns over trafficking of, 7, 60, 121, 136
  migrants, 123–4, 178, 188
  organizational advocacy for, 177–8, 188
  perceptions of, 110, 120–4, 135–6, 180
  police targeting of, 108, 120–3, 131–2, 135
  research with, 123–4, 136n2
  sex workers, 13–14, 60, 106, 136n2, 144, 177–80
  targeting of massage parlours/spas, 14, 41–3, 122–5, 131, 135
  violence against, 120, 177–80, 188
assault,
  defence lawyers for, 139–41
  physical, 111, 119, 129
  by police, 79, 97n9, 108, 111, 171
  reporting (lack of), 78, 95, 179–84, 201, 206, 236n1
  sexual, 2, 67, 79, 122, 127–8

Ba, Madani, 142–4
bawdy-houses, repealing criminalization of, 9–10, 103
Bernstein, Elizabeth, 8, 39, 156
Black Lives Matter, 34–5, 42–5, 156, 158
Black men, 143, 148
  criminalization of, 18, 67, 91, 146
  as predatory pimps, 7, 54–6, 67, 112
  racial profiling of, 111–12, 146
Black people,
  activism and mobilizing, 36, 39, 45
  anti-trafficking apparatus versus, 5, 42–5
  supposed criminality of, 5, 70n4, 90, 112, 167
  systemic racism facing, 106–7, 161, 171–2
  white narratives about, 47–9, 87
  women, *see* Black women
Black women, 50n1
  association with prostitution, 109
  criminalization of, 39, 107–9
  harm facing, 109, 112
  policing of, 41, 107–9
  sex workers, 41, 104, 107, 112
Blue Door (St. John's), 76–7, 79
borders,
  anti-trafficking prosecution and, 85, 87–8
  capital movement across, 19
  controlling, 7, 20, 34, 155, 255–9
  as dimension of trafficking, 2, 22, 63
  legal regulation of, 9, 258–9
  perceived threats to, 2–3
  portrayals of trafficking and, 1, 45, 255–6
  sovereign state authority over, 221, 229–30, 232, 236
  see also Canada Border Services Agency (CBSA); international human trafficking
British Columbia, 170, 234
  anti-trafficking strategies in, 13, 159, 189n2

policing of (im)migrant sex workers, 178–9, 182, 185–6
Butterfly, 104, 109–10, 113, 236n1
bylaws, 6
    enforcement of, 13, 104–5, 108–10, 129–35
    massage parlour and holistic centre licensing, 119–23, 125–9
    targeting sex work, 13–14, 75, 87

campaigns, 178, 253
    anti-trafficking, 34, 42, 70n3, 120–2, 160–1, 205
    law enforcement, 88, 104
    public awareness, 17, 155
    racial justice, 35
    status for all, 23, 248n2
Canada, 121, 172, 222
    anti-prostitution law in, 84, 87–8, 94–5, 111, 179
    anti-trafficking apparatus in, 82–6, 89–93, 157–9, 165, 230
    criminal legal system, 22, 70n7, 132, 139, 154
    domestic trafficking focus, 3, 192–3
    narratives on human trafficking, 61–4, 83, 90, 107, 112
    racism in, 54, 96, 108–12, 187–8
    settler colonial dynamics in, 192, 194–7, 200–1, 208
    temporary foreign/migrant worker exploitation, 19–22, 240–2, 246–7, 254–6
    temporary resident permits, *see* victims of trafficking in persons (VTIP)
    UN *Trafficking Protocol* ratification, 2, 6, 9, 21, 220, 240
Canada v. Bedford, 9–10, 84, 88, 103
Canada Border Services Agency (CBSA), 256
    anti-trafficking apparatus, 15, 20, 105, 154, 232
    immigration enforcement, 119, 132, 182–5, 258
    temporary resident permits from, 220, 231
Canadian Alliance for Sex Work Law Reform, 16

Canadian Centre to End Human Trafficking, 163
    anti-trafficking hotline, 120–1, 154, 157, 165–6, 169
    indicator list, 169–70
    support for policing, 160–2, 167, 171–2
capitalism, 44
    abolition feminist critiques, 37–8
    anti-trafficking discourse, 47–8, 257
    constraints on workers, 3, 69
    exploitative business model of, 19–23, 162, 244–5, 156, 260
    racial, 38, 46, 254
carceral habitus, 39
carceral humanitarianism, 35
    in anti-trafficking discourse, 41–2, 48
    carceral humanism versus, 40
    moving beyond, 45–6, 48
carceral protectionism, 88, 207
    concept of, 16, 156
    reliance on, 162, 168, 172, 198
carceral system, 1, 139
    abolition of, 40, 104, 114
    anti-trafficking movement support for, 39–40, 96, 154, 162, 208
    women's experiences with, 75, 172, 182–3
charges, 189n1
    acquitted, stayed, or withdrawn, 12, 18, 41, 97n8, 143–5, 160, 180
    analysis of criminal, 83–5, 88–94, 96n1, 112, 147n1
    bylaw infraction, 104, 126–35
    co-charging with, 84–5, 93, 140–1, 168
    defence counsel for trafficking, 139–45, 150–1
    harm from media coverage of, 152, 159
    organization facing, 185–9
    overzealous police use of, 12, 18, 85, 93–4, 121, 140–1
    racialized people and, 18, 41, 54–6, 104–9, 111, 121–3
    sex work cases, 9, 12, 56, 85, 106–9, 111, 149, 214–15
    for trafficking, 18, 54, 68, 70n7, 90, 112, 146–51
    unwarranted, 14, 61, 109, 141–4, 152

Charter of Rights and Freedoms, 9, 91, 93, 97n3, 146
children, 85, 104, 129, 227
 abuse of, 2, 44, 57–8, 94
 apprehension of, 106, 197, 202
 girl, *see* girls
 Indigenous, 111, 192, 195–7, 201–3, 208–9, 214
 narratives of rescuing, 13, 41–4, 59–60, 70n5, 196, 240
 panics over sex trafficking of, 59–62, 66, 192, 201–3
 see also youth
child welfare system, 44, 57–8, 69, 192, 196, 201
Chinese people,
 racism facing, 60, 109–10, 144
 women massage parlour workers, 123–4, 128–30, 132
civil rights, 112
 movement, 47–8
civil society organizations, 2, 47, 90, 163, 248
class, 125
 dimension of trafficking, 2, 17, 67
 law enforcement and, 158, 244
 notion of pimp and, 7, 55–6, 59
 trafficking as threat to middle, 59, 69, 122
Cohen, Stanley, 54, 68
colonialism, *see* settler colonialism
Combating Human Trafficking Act (2021), 13, 105, 210n1
consent, 105
 express versus implied, 95
 lack of, 159, 206–7
 legal age of, 59, 70n6
 minors and, 86
 misperceptions about, 3–4, 76, 91, 204
 sex work and, 4, 62, 65, 76–7, 179
Conservative governments,
 anti–sex work legislation, 10, 84, 103
 strengthening anti-trafficking law, 84, 205
construction industry, 22, 203, 253
Cook, Sophia, 108
corporations,
 anti-trafficking apparatus, 40–1, 46, 50, 155–7, 171
 humanitarianism and, 40, 47
 exploitive practices of, 19–20, 105, 243, 246–7, 259
 prison work and, 37
courts, 85, 131, 244
 anti-trafficking narratives in, 91, 95, 97n5
 case acquittals, 12, 18, 140, 143–4
 determinations of trafficking, 2, 227–8, 234–5, 243–5, 248n3
 migrant farm worker cases in, 239
 transnational trafficking cases in, 12, 22
 see also Supreme Court of Canada
Criminal Code, 22, 93
 amendments to, 230, 240, 243
 exploitation, definition of, 195, 241–3, 245, 248
 human trafficking definition, 241, 248n3
 legal challenges to, 9–10, 195
 organization charges through, 185–6
 regulation of human trafficking, 9, 11, 63–4, 103, 161, 169
 sex work laws in, 11, 56, 94, 127, 168
criminalization,
 anti-trafficking apparatus and, 16, 92–3, 156–7, 189, 208, 240–4
 asymmetrical, 9–10, 41, 93–5
 of community organizations, 177–8, 188–9
 Indigenous, 194, 196–200, 208–9
 migrant, 230–1, 235–6, 240
 policies of, 3, 82–7, 106–9, 112–13, 179, 259–60
 of poverty, 18, 112–14, 156
 racialized groups and, 18, 90–1, 96, 109, 172, 198
 of sex work, 18–19, 39–43, 64, 103–4, 171, 181, 208
 transnational trafficking and, 2
critical anti-trafficking studies, 35, 38–40, 45, 136, 199, 208
critical prison studies, 35, 37, 40
critical sociolegal scholarship, 82–3, 86–7, 167, 177
Davis, Angela Y., 34, 36
decolonial thought, 193, 199–200

decriminalization,
    anti-trafficking narratives of, 46
    disregarding evidence for, 103–4
    sex worker fight for, 41–2, 69, 113–14
De Guzman v. Canada (2020), 226, 234–5
deportation, 131
    anti-trafficking policing, 19, 41, 108, 129, 233–5, 255–6
    cases involving, 22, 61, 105, 110, 119–22, 259
    threats of, 21, 170–1, 181–2, 227–30, 239
De Shalit, Ann, 17
discourses, (anti-)trafficking,
    assumptions in, 11, 45–6, 221, 259
    contradictions in, 34, 39–41, 44–6, 257
    domestic focus, 6–7, 16, 59, 61–8
    Enlightenment thought, 36, 41–2, 49
    government intervention, 4–6, 156, 195, 199, 220–1, 235
    infantilizing, 59, 63, 136, 195, 208
    on pimps, 54–9, 68–9, 70n2
    police-directed, 13, 21–2, 41–4, 78–80, 167, 248
    racism/antiblackness in, 4–5, 34–5, 47–50
    sex industry, 76–7, 80, 156
    slavery aesthetics, 35–6, 47–9
    on traffickers, 7, 59–62
    white indemnity in, 47–8
Doezema, Jo, 4
domestic trafficking,
    discourse about, 6–7, 16, 59, 61–8
    law, 9–12, 22, 85–90, 105
    media coverage, 61–8
    for sex, 3, 43–4, 85–6, 105–7, 200, 202–3
    victims, representations of, 6, 156, 167, 193, 203
Douglass, Frederick, 34
drugs, 202
    decriminalizing, 114
    dependency on, 85, 142
    narratives of pimps and, 54, 58, 64–6
    trafficking, 78, 85, 142, 158
    use of, 149, 159, 201, 214–16
Drydyk, Julie, 161
Du Bois, W.E.B., 36
Durisin, Elya M., 6, 159, 167

Eastern Europe, 69
    women from, 5, 7, 60–1, 64
employers, 156
    abuse by, 20–2, 227–30, 233–5, 254, 257
    requirements of, 20, 105
    of sex workers, 148–50
employment,
    exploitative systems of, 227–30, 233, 239–46, 252–6
    global lack of, 6, 125, 241
    massage parlour, *see* massage parlours
    precarious, 39, 82, 89, 156–8, 199, 239–41
    racism in, 106–7, 125, 161, 171–2
    regulations, 3, 156, 223, 234, 239–43, 245
    worker organizing for fairer, 22, 253, 257–8
Employment Insurance (EI), 246, 254, 256
Employment and Social Development Canada (ESDC), 20, 246
Enlightenment discourse, 36, 41–2, 49
enslavement, narratives of African/transatlantic, 36–8, 41–2, 44, 48–9; *see also* slavery
exploitation,
    anti-trafficking apparatus and, 1, 34, 43, 104, 120, 132, 162, 200–2, 252–3
    assumptions about sex work, 3, 7–10, 59–63, 94–6, 107, 141–2, 206–7
    child and youth, 59, 74, 85–7, 111, 201, 209
    Criminal Code on, 195, 241–3, 245, 248
    debates about extreme, 23, 62, 254–5
    definitions of, 223, 241–5, 247–8
    discourse on, 59–62, 77–82, 92–5, 205–6
    labour, 20–3, 82, 104, 110–13, 223, 227–30, 246–8, 254–7
    legislation on, *see Protection of Communities and Exploited Persons Act* (PCEPA)
    pimp depictions of, 8, 54, 58, 63–8, 87
    police responses to, 141–2, 146, 156, 169, 179–84, 203–4

sexual, 4, 6, 11–12, 44, 65, 165, 200–7
  see also Anti-Human Trafficking Strategy Act

farms, 254, 258
  cacao, 41–2
  industry prioritization on, 243, 246–8, 256
  worker vulnerability on, 239–42, 245–8, 252
  see also Seasonal Agricultural Worker Program (SAWP)
Federal Court of Canada,
  victims of trafficking in persons (VTIP) cases, 221, 226–30, 234
federal government, 9, 17–18
  anti-trafficking apparatus, 22, 76, 155, 160, 163, 240
  Conservative, *see* Conservative governments
  exploitation through work permits, 21–2, 248n2, 258
  legislation, *see* legislation, human trafficking
  policing investment, 15, 79, 135, 154–6
  SAWP oversight, 246–7
feminists,
  abolition versus abolitionist, 38–40
  anticarceral, 38–9
  Black, 39, 45, 108
  carceral, 8, 38–40, 156
  decolonial, 193
  Indigenous, 45, 198
  mobilizing, 76, 108
  organizations, 74–5
Ferris, Shawna, 201, 209
Financial Transactions and Reports Analysis Centre of Canada (FINTRAC), 154, 160, 165, 168
F. (M.) v. Dr. Sutherland (2000), 245
folk devils, pimps/traffickers as super, 54–5, 68–9
forced labour,
  case analysis of, 228–30, 232–3
  migrant, 113, 220
  perceptions of, 3, 60, 70n5, 141, 184
  sexual, 60–4, 203
forced marriage, 36, 86, 89

Fukushima, Annie, 39
fusion centres, 158, 160, 166

gender, 79, 114, 244
  criminalization and, 82–3, 86–7, 96
  dimension of trafficking, 2, 88–91, 95, 158, 235–6
  pimp trope and, 7, 55, 67
  sex work and, 121, 123–4, 155, 181, 204, 215
  violence and, 38–40, 104, 108–14, 192–201, 208–10
Ghana, 41–2, 48
girls,
  Black, 106, 108
  trafficking discourse about, 4–7, 57–68, 84, 168
  Indigenous, 2, 106, 111, 172, 193–6, 200–2, 214
  white, 70n5, 87–90, 108
Global Alliance Against Traffic in Women, 45, 62
Global South, 16, 36
  corporation movement to, 19–20
  workers from, 248, 254, 257–9
Gosse, Barbara, 121

Haiti, 41, 48, 70n4
Hamilton, Ontario, 22, 122, 180, 253
Hamilton Spectator, trafficking coverage, 57, 60–1
harm reduction work, 75–9
health care, 104
  lack of, 21, 113–14, 185
  migrant workers and, 252, 254, 256
  sex worker access to, 74–5, 181
  surveillance for trafficking in, 17, 87–8, 159
hotline, human trafficking, 17–18, 43, 154
  police involvement, 43, 120–1, 157, 161, 165–9
housing, 142
  lack of adequate, 21, 162, 207, 256
  mobilizing for affordable, 114, 196, 252–4
  structural barriers to, 18, 112–13, 172, 196–8
humanitarianism, 40
  carceral, *see* carceral humanitarianism

white/settler-colonial, 16, 47, 193, 197–8
human rights, 258
    government undermining of, 20, 224–6, 240
    intrawhite agreement on, 40
    organizational focus on sex worker, 74–5, 77–80, 83
    paradoxical messaging on, 43, 49, 106, 161
    violations, 3, 89, 108–12, 132, 135
human traffickers, portrayals of, 54–5, 59–68, 143
human trafficking,
    definitions of, 2, 96n1, 106–7, 253
    oversimplified solutions, 20, 243–4
Hunt, Sarah, 199, 200, 203

Immigration and Refugee Protection Act (IRPA), 9, 22, 63, 222, 225, 230–1, 235
immigrants,
    loss of status, 106, 110, 131–2, 143
    precarious status of, 11–14, 113, 124, 179–80, 248, 252–6
    as trafficking victims, 44, 168, 170, 232, 235
immigration, 221
    (ir)regularized status, 18, 23, 113, 239, 252–4
    offences/charges, 61, 84, 104, 108, 226–31
    officer conduct, 119, 221–8, 233–4, 236n1, 247
    policies to address sex work, 10, 87, 103–4, 121–2
    rights, struggles for, 22, 34, 112, 257–9
    stricter policies/enforcement, 2, 6, 110, 119, 156, 182–3
    system inadequacies, 20–1, 83, 126, 229–30, 252–4, 259
    see also Standing Committee on Citizenship and Immigration
Immigration, Refugees and Citizenship Canada (IRCC), 220, 222–6, 232, 236n2
immorality,
    massage parlours and, 120–2, 136
    racist assumptions about, 5–6, 54, 57

Incarcerated Workers Organizing Committee, 37
incarceration, 34, 37–8
    anti-trafficking advocate reliance on, 37, 199, 255
    racialized communities and, 109, 111, 197
India, 41, 49, 124
indicator lists, anti-trafficking, 17, 157, 164–71, 223
Indigenous people, 194
    anti-trafficking responses and, 192–6, 200–2, 207–10
    police, relations with, 90, 106, 113–14, 158–61, 167, 215–16
    racial profiling of, 106–7, 111, 193, 206
    settler colonial/systemic racism, 161, 171–2, 194, 197–202, 214
    women, *see* Indigenous women
Indigenous women, 95, 168
    gendered violence facing, 192–201, 208–10
    missing and murdered, 2, 7, 111
    sex worker criminalization and harms, 18–19, 90–1, 104–12, 200–3, 207–10
    victimizing narratives about, 6–7, 106, 155–6, 193–6, 200–2, 209–10
Integrated Security Units, 158–9
intelligence-led policing (ILP), 13, 157–63, 165–7, 171–2
international anti-trafficking efforts, 15
    laws on, 11, 85
    police in, 41–2, 180, 183–4
international human trafficking, 69
    discourse on, 4, 59–61, 64, 257
    prosecuted cases, 85–6, 89
    see also transnational trafficking
intimate relationships,
    partner violence, 2, 18, 106, 181
    trafficking through, 5–6, 12, 17–18, 85
It's a Penalty, 43
Ivory Coast, 41–2

Jeffrey, Leslie Ann, 54, 70n5
Justicia for Migrant Workers (J4MW), 248n2, 252–3, 256–60

Kaba, Mariame, 37, 40
Kaye, Julie, 154, 194
Kilgore, James, 40

labour,
    discourse of prison slave, 37–8
    low-wage, 20–1, 38
    migrant, *see* migrant labour
    precarious, 39, 82, 89, 158, 162, 258
    rights, 3, 9, 74–6, 83, 161, 185–9, 254, 257–9
    sexual, 3, 5, 247
    trafficking, 12, 85–6, 165, 220, 228–9
    transnational, 2, 12, 155
    unfree, 5, 37–8, 48–9, 62, 85, 254, 258–9
    unpaid overtime in, 21, 233
Lam, Elene, 13–14, 206, 208
Latin American women, 5–7
law, anti-trafficking, 64, 257–8
    analysis of, 82–9, 93
    Canadian development of, 9, 70n7
    Criminal Code, see Criminal Code
    expansion of, 6, 83, 87–9, 105, 206–7
    inequitable enforcement of, 21, 89, 94, 240, 247
    infringing on rule of law, 82, 91, 93–4
    sex work conflation with trafficking, 8–13, 64, 93, 106–7, 208
law enforcement, 23, 256
    anti–sex work sentiments, 38, 64–6, 79, 144, 166, 181, 206
    anti-trafficking apparatus, 1, 17–18, 89–90, 177, 192
    coordination across, 1, 15, 158–61, 164
    distrust of, 90, 170, 184, 188–9, 236n1
    funding, 90, 94, 155, 196, 200–1
    racism in, 14, 108–13, 129–35, 226–8
    raids, *see* raids, workplace
    social service agencies and, 8, 16, 77, 88, 157, 177, 253
    as source of repression, 108–10, 187, 245, 258
    targeting racialized people, 91, 94, 103–4, 112, 120–3
    see also bylaws
legislation, human trafficking,
    anti–sex work sentiments, 9–10, 87, 103, 177, 214–15
    harm from, 9–11, 39, 156, 162, 192
    ideological goals in, 87, 199, 202
    inconsistent objectives of, 11–12, 93–4, 114
    policing in, 41, 45, 179–80, 206–9
liberalism, 37, 197
    Enlightenment thought, 36, 41–2
    antiblackness and racial, 40–2, 46, 48, 50
licensing,
    anti-trafficking pretenses for, 13, 41, 123, 135
    challenging process of, 125–9, 131–5
    massage parlours, 13, 41, 122–6, 129, 133–5, 136n1, 179
    penalties for lack of, 119, 131–2
Lorenzo v. Canada (2016), 226, 232–3, 235

MacDonald, Gayle, 54, 70n4
Maggie's (Toronto), 74, 166
mandatory minimum sentences, 12, 91, 140, 147n2, 151
Manitoba,
    anti-trafficking strategies in, 13, 90, 192, 201–9
    human trafficking legislation, 114n1, 193, 202, 205–8
    Indigenous sex workers in, 200, 202–3, 206–8, 214
    Tracia's Trust, 202–3
    trafficking as child exploitation in, 192, 201–8
marginalized people, 236
    anti-trafficking law impacts, 82, 104, 170, 177, 192
    overpolicing of, 159, 168, 198
Marcus, Anthony, 7, 112
Marx, Karl, 244
massage parlours, 136n1
    anti-trafficking policies and, 13, 41, 62, 70n7, 123, 135
    licensing, 13, 122–6, 129, 133–5, 136n1, 179
    narratives about, 62, 66, 120–3, 130–6
    policing/ticketing of, 120–2, 129–35, 159, 178, 204
    working in, 119, 123–6, 128–34

INDEX 269

Massé, Philippe, 20–1
Maynard, Robyn, 5, 39, 109, 195, 203, 210
McQuade, Brendan, 158, 166
media,
    anti-Black racism, 54–6, 70nn4,5, 111–12
    anti-trafficking discourse in, 35–7, 44–9, 203–4
    domestic trafficker trope in, 61–8, 143
    Indigenous women and girls, 111, 193–6, 200–2, 209–10
    international trafficker trope in, 59–62
    pimp trope in, 54–9, 66, 68–9, 70n2, 112
    on policing, 16, 59–61, 66, 78–9, 252
    qualitative analysis of, 44–9, 55–56, 70n3, 83
    representations of sex work, 57, 61–2, 67–70, 76, 152, 159
    representations of trafficking victims, 6, 56–60, 62–9, 90, 253
    sex worker organization, 77–8
    worker organizing, 253, 257
men, 108, 181
    anti-trafficking discourse on, 22
    assumptions about racialized, 4, 8, 56, 68, 91
    Black, *see* Black men
    as parasitic, 97n5
    perceptions about trafficked, 2, 22
    as pimps, *see* pimps
    as traffickers, 6–7, 54, 60
Mendicino, Marco, 163
Mexico, migrant workers from, 239, 246, 257
migrant labour, 21, 222, 226–7, 230, 239, 256
    legislation governing, 9, 88–9, 103–4, 112–13, 156
Migrant Rights Network, 23
migrant workers, 135
    anti-trafficking strategies and, 13, 23, 112, 162, 177–80, 236n1
    assumptions about, 20, 107, 221–2, 225–9, 232–5, 252
    criminalization of, 14, 22, 121–3, 170–1, 181
    deportation of, 19, 61, 110, 119–22, 237, 256
    discourse about, 47, 123–4, 178, 188, 224–5, 257–60
    exploitation of, 11–12, 21–2, 82, 223, 119, 242–8
    immigration status of, 103–4, 113, 171, 180–2, 231
    organizing for justice, 22, 210, 253–60
    policing of, 104–10, 112, 157, 185–9, 220, 247, 255
    research with, 123–4, 136n2
    rights of, 3, 21, 240, 248n1
    in sex work, 14, 19–20, 61–3, 103–12, 135–6, 170–1, 177
    temporary resident permits (TRPs) for, 220–5
    trafficking experiences, 9, 168, 221–6
    violence targeting, 120, 177–83, 188
    work permits, 21–3, 63, 248n2, 256–9
Migrant Workers Alliance for Change, 23
migration,
    dimension of trafficking, 1–2, 19–20, 45, 155
    policy, 21, 155
    process of, 227, 254
    risks with, 3, 90, 171, 254
    for sex work, 5–6, 67, 171
    waves of, 2, 5
Minna, Maria, 64–5
modern-day slavery, 2, 44
    equation with trafficking, 5, 34–6, 41–2, 45, 48–9
    multiple definitions of, 37, 39
modernity, liberal, 36, 48, 50
Montreal Gazette, trafficking coverage, 63
Moon (personal narrative), 119
municipalities,
    anti-trafficking strategies, 2, 70n3, 135, 159–60, 203–4
    bylaw enforcement, *see* bylaws
    human trafficking in, 7
    policing in, 13, 104, 154, 179–80, 196
    sex work regulation, 13, 121–2, 136n1, 180
Musto, Jennifer, 16, 41, 156

National Action Plan to Combat Human Trafficking, 15, 154, 196

National Strategy to Combat Human Trafficking, 15, 154, 163, 165
nation-states, 156
　settler colonialism in, 193, 203, 259
　transnational migration and, 2, 5
neoliberalism, 1, 37, 40, 69, 198
　individualization of trafficking, 6–8, 17–18, 22, 172, 192–3, 259
New Brunswick, 61
Newfoundland, 76, 233
　policing in, 78–80
　sex worker rights movement, 74
　see also Blue Door (St. John's); Safe Harbour Outreach Project (SHOP)
nongovernmental organizations (NGOs), 1, 167–8
　anti-trafficking strategies, 16–17, 41–3, 154, 157–64, 171
　discourse of, 6, 8–9, 49, 259
Nova Scotia, 90, 108–9
　anti-Black racism, 54, 70n4

O'Connell Davidson, Julia, 5
Ontario,
　anti-trafficking strategies in, 13, 16–17, 104–6, 155, 168–70, 172
　conflation of sex work and trafficking, 106–7
　legislation in, 13, 104–7, 112–14, 145, 210n1, 248n3
　migrant farm workers in, 239–45, 249n4, 253–7
　policing in, 61, 65, 109, 121, 158–61, 178
　#ProjectONroute, 161, 166
　trafficking cases in, 12, 22, 70n3, 88–90, 143
　sex work in, 107, 112–14, 119
Operation Northern Spotlight, 16, 178–9
　Newfoundland, 78–80
　Ontario, 104–5
organized crime, 78, 225
　anti-trafficking apparatus, 15, 96, 220
　lack of Canadian cases involving, 85, 89
　notions of trafficking and, 2, 7, 55, 60, 63, 69
Othering, racialized, 3, 6, 16, 208
Ottawa, 139

policing in, 119, 122, 140–1, 143, 160, 164–5

panics, 54
　moral, 69, 105, 120–2, 196, 199, 201
　white slavery, 4–5
passports, 231
　confiscation of, 21, 151, 229
paternalism, 18, 38, 193, 201–3, 208, 252
patriarchy, 38, 69, 260
permits,
　closed federal work, 21–2, 258
　exemptions on, 62–3
　lack of, 126, 131–2
　temporary residence, 220–2, 226–7, 231–5, 236n2, 253, 256
　vulnerable worker open work, 22–3, 227, 248n2, 258
Perrin, Benjamin, 65
Pickton, Robert, 179, 182, 189n1
pimps,
　anti-trafficking discourses on, 54–9, 68–9, 70n2
　badder, 57–8, 65
　Black men as, 7, 54–6, 67, 112
　classed notion of, 7, 55–6, 59
　drug use narratives and, 54, 58, 64–6
　as exploitative, 8, 54, 58, 63–8, 87
　folk devils, super, 54–5, 68–9
　gendered notion of, 7, 55, 67
　gorilla, 67
　media tropes of, 54–9, 66, 68–9, 70n2, 111–12
　"plus," 85, 91
　as predatory, 54, 57–9, 65–9
　Romeo, 67
　sex worker ascribed agency versus, 56–9, 68–9
　as super folk devils, 54–5, 68–9
police,
　assaults by, 79, 97n9, 108, 111, 171
　defunding, 34, 46, 48, 256
　distrust of, 16, 78, 80, 90, 170–1, 188, 236n1
　excessive use of charging, 12, 18, 85, 93–4, 121, 140–1
　exploitation, responses to, 141–2, 146, 156, 169, 179–84, 203–4

harassment, 107–10, 123, 132–3, 161, 201, 217
hotline, human trafficking, 43, 120–1, 157, 161, 165–9
Indigenous relations, 90, 106, 113–14, 158–61, 167, 215–16
media representations of, 16, 59–61, 66, 78–9, 252
organization relationships with, 78–80, 160–2, 167, 171–2
Royal Canadian Mounted, *see* RCMP
policing, 1
    anti-Asian, 41, 106–10, 120–3, 131–2, 135
    anti-Black, 18, 41, 67, 91, 107–9, 146
    anti-sex work, 66, 79, 162
    anti-trafficking apparatus, 13, 21–2, 41–4, 167, 172, 248
    discourse, 13, 21–2, 41–4, 78–80, 167, 248
    federal investment in, 15, 79, 90, 135, 154–6
    international anti-trafficking efforts, 41–2, 180, 183–4
    massage parlours and, 119–22, 129–35, 159, 178, 204
    migrant sex workers, 178–9, 182, 185–6
    migrant workers, 104–10, 112, 157, 185–9, 220, 247, 255
    municipal, 13, 104, 154, 179–80, 196
    settler colonialism and, 192, 198–9, 204–5, 214
policymaking, 179
    anti-trafficking, *see* anti-trafficking policies
    criminalization through, 3, 82–7, 106–9, 112–13, 259–60
    harm through, 103–4, 111–12
    immigration, 2, 6, 110, 119, 156, 182–3
    massage parlour, 13, 41, 62, 70n7, 123, 135
    migration, 21, 155
    police-centred, 41, 45, 179–80, 208–9
    on sex work, 10, 87, 103–4, 121–2
political economy, 37–8, 244
poverty, 12, 34, 248

criminalization of, 18–19, 156–7, 167, 202
exploitation due to, 60, 161, 168, 228–9, 239, 245
migration due to, 61–2 , 245
racialization of, 18, 112, 207
structural, 6, 45, 113–14, 161
prisons,
    abolishing, 34–40, 45
    anti-trafficking apparatus reliance on, 8, 34, 45, 194
    carceral feminism and, 8, 40, 156
    sentences in, 22, 45, 92, 152, 189n1, 240
    settler colonialism and, 194, 198
    slave labour in, 37–9, 41–2
    see also incarceration
prohibitionism, 3, 38
prosecutions, trafficking, 8, 63–4
    analysis of, 24, 82–4, 155
    international versus domestic cases, 9, 22, 85–89
    patterns in, 85–7, 89–91, 94–6, 230
    politicization of, 82–3, 90, 93–4, 129–30
    racial inequities in, 82–3, 87–91, 93–6, 111–12
    sentencing in, 91–2
    sex work cases and, 11, 14, 68, 121–3, 185
Protection of Communities and Exploited Persons Act (PCEPA), 64, 76, 84–92, 139
    introduction of, 10–11, 84
    new layers of criminalization in, 96, 103–4, 111, 177, 185, 188–9
provinces, 74, 87
    anti-trafficking strategies, 2, 79, 103–5, 135, 159–61, 192, 202–6
    human trafficking in, 7, 105–7, 151, 202–4
    law enforcement investment, 13, 70n3, 90, 105
    policing in, 15–16, 113, 154, 186, 203–4
punishments, human trafficking, 2, 236
    challenging, 91, 151
    harsher, 6, 8, 93, 136
    individualization of, 8, 105, 131

Quebec, 63, 70n3, 90, 244

racial capitalism, 38, 46, 254
racial chattel slavery, 37–8, 48, 50n1
racialization, 40, 236
    as dimension of trafficking, 2, 4, 7–8, 95, 167, 254
    of poverty, 112
racialized communities,
    anti-trafficking strategy impacts, 13, 42–5, 135, 161, 200–1, 236n1
    criminalizing, 18, 82–3, 87, 90–6, 198–200
    discourse, anti-trafficking, 16, 35, 37–40, 48–50, 195, 255
    exploited labour of, 239, 247–8, 254, 259
    legislation impacts on, 104–7, 112–13, 242
    policing of, 91, 125, 171, 193, 207–8
    stereotyping of, 55, 67–8, 82, 89–91, 95, 110, 217
    support for, 177, 188, 210
racial justice, 42–4, 46–7, 136
    movements, 34–5, 48, 112–14
racial profiling, 43, 106–11, 256
racism,
    anti-, *see* anti-racism movements
    anti-Asian, *see* anti-Asian racism
    anti-Black, *see* anti-Black racism
    anti-Indigenous, *see* Indigenous people
    anti-trafficking apparatus, 43–5, 48–50, 158, 164, 202
    discursive, 4, 35, 54, 186, 193
    historical reckoning with, 47–8, 110
    systemic, 17, 43–4, 91, 95, 107, 240
    violent, 120–1
raid-and-rescue operations, 6, 15–16, 79, 88, 159, 255
raids, workplace, 61, 122, 144, 178–80, 184–8, 247
    massage parlour, 41, 110, 113, 119–21, 178
R. v. Barton (2019), 95, 97n6
RCMP, 20, 65, 166–8, 182–3
    anti-trafficking effort expansion, 15–16, 104, 154, 196, 231, 253
R. v. Domotor (2011), 22, 86

religious organizations, 1, 6, 120, 123
responsibilization, 17–18, 68
rights, 9, 83, 161
    civil, *see* civil rights
    human, *see* human rights
    labour, 3, 74–6, 112, 185–9, 254, 257–9
    migrant worker, 3, 21, 240, 248n1
    sex worker, 111, 74–80, 83
    vacuum, 112
"risky" populations, 1–2, 10, 201, 207
Rodríguez, Dylan, 47
Royal Canadian Mounted Police, *see* RCMP

Safe Harbour Outreach Project (SHOP), 74–5
    funding for, 76–7
    police, relationships with, 78–80
Saskatchewan, 90, 114n1, 159
saviourism, 55, 76, 208, 259
settler state, 7, 22, 204
    white, 16, 44, 120, 193, 201
Schept, Judah, 39
Seasonal Agricultural Worker Program (SAWP), 21, 239–48, 254, 256–8
settler colonialism,
    anti-trafficking discourse and, 35, 95, 156, 192–6, 198–210, 257
    definition of, 198
    gendered violence of, 112, 172, 192–201, 204, 208–10
    Indigenous dispossession, 48, 156, 193–4, 197–8
    in Manitoba, 200–9
    narratives of modern-day slavery and, 35, 40, 43, 48
    oppressive systems of, 69, 111–12, 192–200, 208–9, 259–60
    policing and, 192, 198–9, 204–5, 214
    politics of recognition, 194–5
    sex work and, 95, 111, 195–6, 202–10, 214
    white saviourism and, 7, 16–17, 193, 195–9, 201, 204
sexual assault, *see* assault
sexualization, as dimension of trafficking, 2, 109, 159
sexualized nationalism, 159

INDEX 273

sex work,
    assumptions about, 3, 7–10, 59–63, 94–6, 107, 141–2, 206–7
    collective, 24, 87, 108, 111
    commercial, 82–7, 91, 95–6, 203
    consensual, 4, 62, 65, 76–7, 204
    criminalization of, 18–19, 38–43, 64, 103–4, 171, 181, 208
    decriminalization, 41–2, 46, 69, 103–4, 113–14
    laws, 11, 56, 94, 127, 168
    living on the avails of, 9, 68, 87, 97n5, 103, 139–40
    media representations of, 57, 61–2, 67–70, 76, 152, 159
    municipal regulation, 13, 121–2, 136n1, 180
    policymaking on, 10, 87, 103–4, 121–2
    portrayals of trafficking and, 1, 8–13, 38–9, 64, 93, 106–7, 208
sex workers,
    Asian, 13–14, 60, 106, 136n2, 144, 177–80
    advocacy for, 74–5, 178–81, 183–5, 188–9
    agency ascribed to, 56–8
    Black, 41, 104, 107, 112
    charges for, 9, 12, 56, 85, 106–9, 111, 149, 214–15
    Indigenous, 18–19, 90–1, 104–12, 200–3, 206–10
    law enforcement versus, 38, 64–6, 79, 144, 166, 181, 206
    migrant, 14, 19–20, 61–3, 103–12, 135–6, 170–1, 177
    perceived vulnerability to, 10–11, 57–9, 220
    policing of, 66, 79, 162, 178–9, 182, 185–6
    rights for, 74–80, 83, 111
    see also anti–sex work sentiments
Shala v. Canada (2021), 223, 226–30, 233, 235
Sharma, Nandita, 21, 155–6, 259
Shih, Elena, 18, 41, 43, 120
Shoppable Girls campaign, 17
Sibley, Marcus, 242
slavery,
    African, *see* enslavement
    chattel, 37, 43, 48, 50n1
    modern-day, *see* modern-day slavery
    narratives of prison, 35, 37–9, 41–2
    police-centred narratives of, 35–6, 41–2, 47–9
    settler colonialism and, 35, 40, 43, 48
    sexual, 4, 38, 60
    white, 4–5, 70n1
social service providers,
    in anti-trafficking apparatus, 16, 107, 155–9, 167, 257
    lack of community access, 113, 169, 172, 198
    law enforcement, relations with, 8, 40, 77, 88, 253
Solberg, Monte, 222, 224, 230
spas,
    police ticketing of, 14, 119, 130
    working in, 119–20, 124, 127–30, 132
Standing Committee on Citizenship and Immigration, 224, 230–1
Standing Committee on Justice and Human Rights, 20, 161, 167, 224–6
Standing Committee on Justice Policy, 107
Standing Committee on the Status of Women, 224–5, 232
    reports, 64
Status of Women Council (St. John's), 74–6, 78
Stella's Circle (St. John's), 75
stereotypes,
    Asian people, 49, 60, 110, 120–4, 135–6, 180
    Black people, 5, 47–9, 70n4, 87, 90, 112, 167
    on consent, 3–4, 76, 91, 204
    pimps, 54–9, 66, 68–9, 70n2, 111–12
    racialized communities, 55, 67–8, 82, 89–91, 95, 110, 217
strip clubs, 62–3, 121
    raids on, 61, 122–3
Suchland, Jennifer, 39, 45, 155, 162, 167
Supreme Court of Canada, 9–10, 84, 88, 95, 239, 244
surveillance, 1, 198
    anti-trafficking apparatus, 8, 15–16, 107, 122, 163–8, 255
    citizen, 17–18, 43, 161, 166

intelligence-led policing and, 157–60, 162–3
justifications for enhanced, 2, 13, 113, 127, 171, 193–4, 247
racialized communities, 18, 90, 96, 106, 168, 259
settler colonial, 201, 203, 206, 208
sex worker, 69, 85–8, 94, 105–10, 178–9, 206–8
technology, 41, 88, 163–7, 203–5
SWAN Vancouver Society, 83
  advocacy and support work of, 178–81, 183–5, 188–9
  police interactions, 177, 179–80, 182–7, 189
Sweden, 10, 41

Tech Against Trafficking coalition, 155
technologies, anti-trafficking, 88, 157, 163–7, 171, 205, 208
Temporary Foreign Worker Program (TFWP), 12, 21–2, 62–3, 172
  working conditions under, 256–7
temporary resident permits (TRPs), 231
  application and issuing process, 220–6, 228, 231–2
  court decisions on, 227–30, 232–5
  foreignness and temporariness, 231–6
  fraud and illegality in, 224–31, 235–6
  government discourse on, 220–5, 230–1, 232, 235–6
Thailand, 60–1, 257
Toronto, 74, 166, 180
  massage parlours in, 13–14, 110, 119–26, 135
  policing in, 17, 164, 168–70, 252–3
  trafficking in, 64, 66, 139, 220
Toronto Star, trafficking coverage, 57, 59–60, 70n3
transnational trafficking,
  cases of, 12, 22, 89
  perceptions of, 2, 6–7, 36, 167
  policymaking on, 9, 96, 220
  see also international human trafficking

United Kingdom, 4, 10
United Nations, 15, 38, 230
  Convention against Transnational Organized Crime and the Protocols Thereto, 96, 220
  definition/elements of trafficking, 223, 227
  International Convention on the Protection of the Rights of All Migrant Workers and Members of Their Families, 21, 240
  Protocol to Prevent, Suppress and Punish Trafficking in Persons, Especially Women and Children (Trafficking Protocol), 2, 4, 6, 9, 21, 220, 240
United States,
  anti-trafficking apparatus, 3, 8, 43, 112, 163–5
  fusion centres, 158
  modern-day slavery, notions in, 36–7, 41, 47–8
  police racism in, 18, 108–9
  stereotypical pimp dynamics in, 7
  Trafficking in Persons Reports, 42, 230

Vancouver Police Department (VPD),
  anti-trafficking focus, 180–5, 187–8
  Counter Exploitation Unit, 97n9, 180, 184
  raids by, 122, 178–80, 184–8
  robbery investigation, 180–5, 188
  Sex Work Enforcement Guidelines, 179–80, 187, 189
  threats to SWAN, 185–9
Vancouver Sex Workers Rights Collective, 111
Vancouver Winter Olympics, 158–9
van der Meulen, Emily, 6, 159, 167, 242
Van Doren, Marty, 54
Venkatesh, Vasanthi, 254–5
victims, sex trafficking,
  domestic, representations of, 6, 156, 167, 193, 203
  immigrants seen as, 44, 168, 170, 232, 235
  media representations of, 6, 56–60, 62–9, 90, 253
  narratives about Indigenous, 6–7, 106, 155–6, 193–6, 200–2, 209–10

portrayals of white, 5–6, 54–5, 87, 187
victims of trafficking in persons (VTIP), 96, 220
British Columbia office for, 159
Criminal Code provisions for, 161, 240, 242–3
Federal Court cases, 221, 226–31, 234, 236n1
temporary resident permit (TRP) program for, 222–6, 231–6
prosecution/penalties for, 83–4, 88, 91–3
violence,
Asian women facing, 120, 177–80, 188
gendered, 38–40, 104, 108–14, 192–201, 208–10
Indigenous women facing, 192–201, 208–10
intimate partner, 2, 18, 106, 181
settler colonial, 112, 172, 192–201, 204, 208–10
sexualized, 91, 94–5
targeting migrant workers, 120, 177–83, 188
see also antiviolence organizing

white supremacy, 1, 5–6, 37, 44, 47–50, 257, 260
whole-of-society approach, anti-trafficking, 154–5, 157, 166–7, 171–2
Winnipeg Police Service, 204, 207
women,
Black, *see* Black women
of colour, 37–8
government portrayals as rescuing, 2–3, 7, 22, 204
Indigenous, *see* Indigenous women
perceptions of trafficked, 2–3, 6, 56–60, 62–9, 90, 253
reproductive control, 4, 48, 50n1, 210
shelter for young, 75
trans, 75, 86, 109, 215
white, 4, 6–7, 87, 108–10, 188
workers,
exploitation, 19–22, 240–2, 246–7, 254–6
migrant, *see* migrant workers

organizing for fairer emp 253, 257–8
permits for, *see* permits
protections for, 3, 18, 20- 239–41, 248
rights, *see* rights
seasonal, 242, 246
sex, *see* sex workers

youth, 70n5, 74, 86, 167
anti-trafficking efforts f 167–8, 179, 192, 196
representations as traffi 4, 6–7, 16, 66, 163, 2